Caribbean Discourse in Inclusive Education: Historical and Contemporary Issues

A Volume in:
Caribbean Discourse in Inclusive Education

Series Editors
Stacey Blackman, University of the West Indies
Dennis Conrad, SUNY Potsdam.

Caribbean Discourse in Inclusive Education

Series Editors
Stacey Blackman
University of the West Indies.

Dennis Conrad,
SUNY Potsdam.

Caribbean Discourse in Inclusive Education: Historical and Contemporary Issues (2017)
Dennis Conrad and Stacey Blackman

Caribbean Discourse in Inclusive Education: Historical and Contemporary Issues

Edited by
Stacey Blackman and Dennis Conrad

INFORMATION AGE PUBLISHING, INC.
Charlotte, NC • www.infoagepub.com

Library of Congress Cataloging-in-Publication Data

The CIP data for this book can be found on the Library of Congress website (loc.gov).

Paperback: 978-1-68123-797-8
Hardcover: 978-1-68123-798-5
eBook: 978-1-68123-799-2

Copyright © 2017 Information Age Publishing Inc.

All rights reserved. No part of this publication may be reproduced, stored in a retrieval system, or transmitted, in any form or by any means, electronic, mechanical, photocopying, microfilming, recording or otherwise, without written permission from the publisher.

Printed in the United States of America

CONTENTS

Foreword: Caribbean Discourse in Inclusive Education:
Historical and Contemporary Issues ix
Jean B. Crockett

Preface xiii
Stacey Blackman

PART I
BUILDING THE STRUCTURE TO SUPPORT INCLUSIVE EDUCATION

1. From Charity Education Towards Inclusion: The Development of Special and Inclusive Education in Barbados 3
   Stacey Blackman

2. Special Education in Trinidad and Tobago: Does Educational Vision and Change Lead to Success? 21
   Joan Pedro

3. Towards Inclusive Education in Trinidad and Tobago: Policy Challenges and Implications 33
   Elna Carrington Blaides and Dennis Conrad

PART II
SHAPING THE LANDSCAPE OF INCLUSIVE EDUCATION

4. You Know Who Is Me? Culturally Inclusive Education 53
   Dyanis Popova

5. Inclusive Education Across the School Curriculum: Providing
   Greater Access Through Language 69
   Iris Hewitt-Bradshaw

6. Student Assessment Systems in the Caribbean as an Obstacle to
   Inclusive Education: The Case of Trinidad and Tobago 87
   Jerome De Lisle, Nadia Laptiste-Francis,
   Sabrina McMillan-Solomon, and Cheryl Bowrin-Williams

7. Historical Conundrums: Extending Inclusivity to Jamaica's
   Children in State Care Education in Jamaica:
   Inclusive of Whom? 107
   Sandra Richards Mayo

8. Inclusivity or Exclusivity: An Educational
   Leadership Perspective 123
   Ian Marshall

9. A Comparison of Barbadian and Grenadian Teachers' Beliefs
   About Creativity 139
   Grace-Anne Jackman and James E. J. Young

10. Exploring The Transition into Hybrid and Online College
    Teaching Through Collaborative Self-Study 159
    Dennis A. Conrad, Elna Carrington-Blaides, and Dyanis A. Popova

PART III
VOICES FROM THE TRENCHES

11. Voices From the Trenches: Teachers' Perspectives
    On Inclusion 187
    Kimberly Glasgow-Charles, Lisa Ibrahim-Joseph, and Laurette Bristol

12. The Invisible Student: Engaging in A Courageous Conversation
    About Homosexuality and Formal Schooling in Jamaica 209
    Andrew Campbell

13. Listening to The Voices of Children With Learning Disabilities
    (LD) and or Attention Deficit Hyperactivity Disorder (ADHD)
    on Their Experiences of Transitioning to High School 225
    Dawn-Marie Keaveny

14. Surviving the Serengeti: A Safe Corner Perspective 245
    *Kirk Felix, Margaret Bruce, Suzanne Charles,
    Nickisha Borris-Lezama, and Myrtle Blackman*

15. Mobilizing Critical Pedagogy to Teach Queerly 261
    Keitha-Gail Martin-Kerr

16. Barbadian Teachers' Perspectives of School Culture: Support
    and Inclusion of Students With Disabilities 277
    Stacey Blackman

    Biographies 297

FOREWORD

CARIBBEAN DISCOURSE IN INCLUSIVE EDUCATION

Historical and Contemporary Issues

Jean B. Crockett

In recent years, schools in many countries have become increasingly inclusive of children with a diversity of learning needs related to disability, poverty, foreign languages, and unusual cultural and social norms. The international movement toward inclusion stands for some of the best human values—a belief in equal opportunity, in education, in human dignity, and hope. The chapters comprising Volume I of the *Caribbean Discourse in Inclusive Education: Historical and Contemporary Issues* offer a powerful vision for social justice and equality in the education of students with disabilities and other traditionally marginalized youth in the nations of the Caribbean. This volume sets out the vision of inclusive education, and identifies historical and contemporary issues, challenges along the way, and what needs to happen to bring the vision to life.

Implementing inclusive education is highly complex and research reveals gaps between Utopian rhetoric and harsh realities with regard to appropriately educating students with diverse learning needs. Unfortunately it is not unusual to find students included for instruction, but underserved in general classes because their needs are not being met. Too often resources are in short supply, and teachers and

Caribbean Discourse in Inclusive Education:
Historical and Contemporary Issues, pages ix–xi.
Copyright © 2017 by Information Age Publishing
All rights of reproduction in any form reserved.

school principals are unprepared to meet their impressive learning needs. This is as true in well-developed countries, such as the United States and Australia, as it is for schools in developing countries. In this volume, Dr. Stacey Blackman and Professor Dennis Conrad examine these realities without flinching by bringing together contributing authors with a deep knowledge and understanding of the people, the politics, the policies, and the practices involved in the evolution of inclusive and special education in the Caribbean.

The rich history of educating marginalized youth in the Caribbean is used as a primary lens to examine both policies and practices over time. This lens allows contemporary readers to scrutinize current options, probe the presumptions of current claims, and scan the present context through an historical inventory of previous events and decisions. This approach also stimulates the imagination beyond the immediate and introduces readers to pioneering educational leaders who sought to build a common purpose in bringing children out of the shadows and into the schoolhouse.

Providing inclusive and special education to students with learning differences and difficulties can clash with the status quo and challenge long established values and practices. But along the path to change, members of any community must face daunting challenges and gauge the distance between where they are and where they want to be so they can select the strategies most likely to lead to success. In looking closely at a variety of challenges shaping the educational landscape, chapters in this volume help readers understand the need for schools in the Caribbean to become more culturally responsive institutions in shaping the identities of students, framing their everyday interactions, and extending their educational opportunities.

Schools and the daily interactions of both students and educators are influenced by often unspoken cultural ideas about equality and inequality, and success and hard work, for example. But pervasive ideas can be detected, studied, and even changed, says social psychologist Hazel Rose Markus, when people are mindful of cultural forces and amend or reject them. The chapters in the final section of this volume capture the voices of students, teachers, and administrators within the culture of Caribbean schools and help readers understand that those who work daily with these young people need to provide them with a more meaningful education.

Caribbean Discourse in Inclusive Education: Historical and Contemporary Issues offers an excellent foundation on which to build future scholarship. Dr. Blackman and Professor Conrad probe past and present issues in ways that invite readers to ask important questions about the current situation in the countries of the Caribbean and to consider how cultural and organizational forces today are like or different from the past: W*here* and *when* did similar circumstances occur? *Who* dealt with similar issues previously? *How* did they respond? *What* did they do, and *why* did they make the choices they did? This is a thoughtful book for thoughtful readers seeking to arrive at a deeper, more significant level of understanding as they move toward educating traditionally marginalized children in the Caribbean more inclusively.

> Jean B. Crockett, Ph.D.
> University of Florida
> Professor of Special Education
> Gainesville, FL

Jean Crockett is internationally recognized for her scholarship at the intersection of special education policy, leadership development, and the instruction of exceptional learners. She is a past-president of the Division for Research of the Council for Exceptional Children, associate editor for the Journal of Special Education Leadership, and the special education editor for the Journal of Law and Education.

PREFACE

Stacey Blackman

Caribbean Discourse in Inclusive Education (CDIE) tells the unique story about the emergence, development, challenges, and efforts associated with achieving inclusive education in the English-speaking Caribbean. It gives voice to academics, practitioners, and other stakeholders within the Caribbean and the Diaspora who are committed to the ideals of parity, equity and the promotion of socially just practices for all.

The primary focus of this first volume on historical and contemporary issues is on providing information about the conceptualizations and origins of inclusive education within the Caribbean. It also aims to raise awareness of the critical issues that influence and impinge upon achieving socially just practices in education for all in the Caribbean. Populations that are marginalized include students who are of different ethnicities, race, and/or religion; those who are older than their peers, with differing gender or sexual orientations, and exceptionalities; and those from lower socio-economic status groups, rural or urban communities.

A number of scholars and practitioners, from the English-speaking Caribbean both *in situ* and from the Diaspora, have authored chapters that reflect critically on issues in inclusion within their respective islands or communities. While it is tempting to argue that issues are esoteric and context bound, the organization of the book sections help to provide a structure that harmonizes the stories into a

Caribbean Discourse in Inclusive Education:
Historical and Contemporary Issues, pages xiii–xviii.
Copyright © 2017 by Information Age Publishing
All rights of reproduction in any form reserved.

coherent piece and locates it within the larger body of work at the international level on inclusion.

The book is a companion reader for graduate and undergraduate students, advocates, university lecturers and teachers who study, research, teach and work in diverse educational settings. It is the first of its kind to compile research from the countries of Barbados, Grenada, Jamaica, and Trinidad and Tobago. It speaks to a newly-emerging context in the international arena on debates about inclusion and inclusive practices.

The book sections examine key questions designed to solicit new epistemes about the origins of inclusive education in the Caribbean, the structures that either facilitate or hinder the development of inclusive education and draws attention to the voices in the trenches that impact and are impacted by inclusion.

BUILDING THE STRUCTURE TO SUPPORT INCLUSIVE EDUCATION

The first section of the book is titled Building the Structure to Support Inclusive Education. It is about the vision and policies that Caribbean governments and MOEs used to establish this approach to education reform. This section traces the historical roots and underpinnings of inclusive education in the English-speaking Caribbean. The discourse centers on the key policy initiatives that have been used by governments in an attempt to reform traditional educational approaches and their relationships to international conventions that espouse a philosophy based on social justice and equality. The tensions, successes and barriers to inclusion are discussed by authors in this section.

Stacey Blackman presents a historical overview of the origins of special and inclusive education by tracing its routes from colonial times to the present day. The chapter uses this content analysis of primary and secondary documents to piece together the evolution of inclusive education in Barbados. Specifically, this account draws attention to the lack of political will needed to make inclusive education a reality despite its numerous articulations in policy documents and subscriptions to international conventions.

Joan Pedro examines the provocative question does educational vision and change lead to success? The discussion focuses on inclusion and examines Trinidad and Tobago's readiness for this educational reform and its navigation of such within a culture not quite ready for this major educational change. Joan argues that, for successful change to occur education leaders must work with their staff and the community to build a clear educational vision that is connected to teaching and learning; how to manage educational change and reform successfully is discussed.

Elna Carrington Blaides and Dennis A. Conrad explore the history of Trinidad and Tobago's inclusive education policy context. The authors explore the emergence of inclusive education since the establishment of the Special Education Unit in 1980. The discussion focuses on three questions: What are the key developments in inclusive/special education in Trinidad and Tobago over the last 30 years? What is the current state of inclusive/special education in Trinidad and Tobago? And what are the issues impinging on the future agenda for inclusive/special education in Trinidad and Tobago? Findings indicate that progress towards inclusive education has been slow despite the many historical milestones, visionaries, and exemplary educator-leaders that emerged to lead the development of inclusive/special education.

SHAPING THE LANDSCAPE OF INCLUSIVE EDUCATION

The second section of the book on Shaping the Landscape of Inclusive Education presents a multicultural perspective of issues that influence the development of inclusive education. In particular, the discussion here captures some of the challenges that principals and teachers face catering to the diversity of students in their schools and classrooms. How schools can become more inclusive is examined by the authors in this section.

Irish Bradshaw Hewitt examines the influence of language diversity on teachers' classroom pedagogy in the Caribbean. She argues that a lack of accommodation of language diversity across the curriculum can have a negative impact on the student's learning and achievement. This is especially true when teachers utilize the official language or instruction rather than Creole languages that function as vernaculars for the majority of Caribbean students in their everyday lives. The chapter suggests ways that schools can acknowledge and respond to the language and cultural resources of diverse Caribbean communities to provide quality education for all students.

Jerome De Lisle, Sabrina McMillan-Solomon, Nadia Laptiste-Francis, and Cheryl Browin investigate how Caribbean assessment systems are at variance with the ideals of inclusion. These authors highlight how education systems of the small island states of the Caribbean over-emphasize public examinations and perform a sorting function. Although recent assessment innovations such as the Trinidad and Tobago Continuous Assessment Component (CAC) Caribbean Primary Exit Assessment (CPEA) have adopted a multi-purpose design, claiming to honor assessment for learning, they still retain a high-stakes sorting function. This study gathers evidence from policy documents and interviews to highlight weaknesses and opportunities for reform and suggest pathways toward high performing and equitable education systems.

Dyanis Popova examines the relationship between micro-cultures and the academic identity of children and young adults. She argues that microaggressions experienced as a result of social pressures arise from differences in children's microcultures, be it religion, ethnicity, sexual orientation, or socioeconomic status. This creates dissonance between the student's sense of self and identity and presents a challenge to positive social and academic experiences. Using the expression "You know who is me?" indicates feelings of and resistance to being discounted. It also challenges imposed representations and acknowledges the potential inner conflict faced by Caribbean or other students as they navigate both their sociocultural and academic lives.

Sandra Richards Mayo provides a historical insight into the Jamaican government's response to the education and training of children who are orphans. The chapter begins with an etymology of social orphanhood placing this concept within a larger discussion of poverty in Jamaica and the historical processes that have shaped existing attitudes towards children in residential care. It asks, what does educational inclusion mean for Jamaica's social orphans in residential care? How can historical responses to the education and training of this population inform current realities in the field of inclusive education? Sandra argues that discourses of educational inclusion in the Caribbean region must interrogate the politics of inclusion and exclusion. In its final analysis, the stage is set for understanding how notions of child and parental rights influence directions in inclusive education.

Ian Marshall engages in an important discussion about education leadership for inclusive education. In particular, he questions Caribbean principals' roles and levels of preparedness for inclusion. He further surmises that there is a need to critically interrogate the legal, institutional and socio-cultural supports needed to implement this reform to traditional education. Lessons from the field to inform the constellation of best practices in inclusive education are suggested in this chapter.

Grace Ann Jackman and James Young investigate how Caribbean teachers define and model creativity, and what factors they believe either encourage or impede the teaching of creativity in the classroom. The study draws primarily on a sample of Barbadian and Grenadian teachers who viewed arts-based subjects as more amenable to the development of students' creativity than the sciences. A lack of resources, poor student attitudes, and an overemphasis on high-stakes testing and extensive secondary-level curricula were the main inhibitors to the growth of creativity in Caribbean classrooms. How teachers can foster creativity across both arts- and science-based curricula is discussed.

VOICES FROM THE TRENCHES

The third section of the book, Voices from the Trenches, presents the perspectives of the teachers, students and stakeholders who work in regular and special education settings. These are the persons charged with making schools more inclusive and the students who are impacted most by this thing called special and inclusive education. What more schools and teachers need to do to become more inclusive is tackled by authors in this section.

Kimberly Glasgow-Charles, Lisa Ibrahim-Joseph, and Laurette Bristol tackles teachers' perspectives on inclusive education in Trinidad. They seek to capture teachers' realities and provide insights into the current state of affairs as it relates to the issue of inclusive schooling in this context. The authors ask the following questions: What are teachers concerns about educating students with special needs in general education classrooms in Trinidad and Tobago? What do teachers perceive as the barriers to educating students with special needs in general education classrooms in Trinidad and Tobago? And what are teachers' recommendations for educating students with special needs in general education classrooms in Trinidad and Tobago? The authors found that teachers were generally anxious about their capacity to meet the needs of diverse groups of students and that person, school and system barriers hampered inclusion. Teachers' recommendations are also discussed.

Andrew Campbell engages in a courageous conversation about the schooling experiences of young men who are homosexual in Jamaica. The author rationalizes the need for engaging in a courageous conversation around the topic of homosexuality before focusing on expressions from the participants who share their lived experiences about formal schooling. He then presents the philosophies and arguments which echo the need for all stakeholders within the educational system to engage in this courageous conversation.

Dawn Marie Keaveny investigates how students who are in regular high schools and who have a learning disabilities and or attention deficit hyperactivity perceive their experiences of transitioning to high school. She found that students used their social capital, i.e. social networks, to navigate high school and access academic, emotional and social support. Key themes in this study were pedagogy, ableist beliefs, the hidden curriculum and social networks. She argues that social capital and having a sense of belonging are likely to have a significant impact on a student's transition experiences, and future outcomes. The author recommends the creation of a national transition policy to guide students' transition from primary to secondary school and suggest that teachers provide opportunities for students to build social capital in these settings.

Kirk Felix, Margaret Bruce, Suzanne Charles, Nickisha Borris-Lezama, and Myrtle Blackman present the voices of various stakeholders at one special education school in Trinidad and Tobago. This chapter is practitioner-based, and creatively enacts the fictional narrative approach to tell the stories of the teachers, the principal and a student in special education. The narrative represent the challenges faced and strategies utilized by stakeholders represented. The results reveal the need for the system to be more supportive if the rhetoric of inclusion is to become an effective experience for all stakeholders.

Keitha Gail-Martin Kerr presents a theoretical and philosophical discourse on issues facing students who are gay, transgendered and lesbian in Jamaica. She examines the role that the heteronormative discourse plays in the marginalization of these students and how an anti-oppressive approach to pedagogy can ensure the participation of all children in schools. Education for critical consciousness and liberation is needed to question elusive ideologies of heteronormativity and to work toward changing the heterosexual status quo in schools and society.

Stacey Blackman examines a selected group of Barbadian educators' narratives in special and inclusive settings to understand how the cultural milieu facilitates the participation of students with disabilities. Stacey argues that the culture of schools in the study are tokenistic and at variance with the ideal of inclusion. This is demonstrated by students with disabilities not enjoying the same level of citizenship as peers without disabilities. At the level of pedagogy, teachers maintain a support structure for students but low levels of collaboration and planning among teachers in special education units and regular classrooms maintain a state of autonomy and segregation

PART I

BUILDING THE STRUCTURE
TO SUPPORT INCLUSIVE EDUCATION

CHAPTER 1

FROM CHARITY EDUCATION TOWARDS INCLUSION

The Development of Special and Inclusive Education in Barbados

Stacey Blackman

PRE AND POST EMANCIPATION PERIODS "CHARITY BEGINS AT HOME"

The purpose of this chapter is to trace the development of special and inclusive education in Barbados in the years prior to, and after, emancipation. In order to guide the discussion a timeline has been established in Tables 1.1 and 1.2 (at the end of this chapter) that outlines the sequence of education provision from the 1600s to the modern era of the twentieth century. Education provision in Barbados has its philosophical roots in the "charity paradigm" where white plantation owners in the second half of the seventeenth century sought to bestow a type of patronage on a society still in the throes of slavery. These benefactors however, reluctantly extended the opportunity to access schooling, and by extension an education, to poor whites who shared their racial phenotype but bore no resemblance to them in terms of privilege and socio-economic status. Bacchus (1991) describes the planters as being "indifferent to the formal instruction of children of poorer whites, the colored and black population" (Bacchus 1991, p. 217) In essence, education remained largely exclusive, and served to reinforce a very rigid system of social stratification. One must also examine the role that missionary societies played in the development of education provision in the pre and post emancipation era in the island, and (Bacchus, 1991) provides one of the most extensive accounts of the work of these groups in Barbados.

During the period prior to emancipation the Anglican Church's attitude towards the black and enslaved population mirrored that of the plantocracy, and this is no surprise, since many of the clergy at that time were paid by, and dependent on, the planters for their wages. Bacchus describes their relationship like this:

> The church itself was in the grips of King Sugar. As a result, the Anglicans initially tried not to do or say anything that might conceivably offend the plantocracy which was not particularly supportive of educational activities among the black population and was strongly opposed to the education, even the religious education of the slaves. (Bacchus, 1991, p. 218)

Bacchus further cites Captain S. Hodgson, who contended that the priests were subject to the whims of the legislature of the day (predominantly white planters) and were therefore not obliged to oppose the will of this powerful group who could reduce them to a state of "beggary." Hodgson, cited in Bacchus (1991) noted that ."... their incomes can, at any moment be reduced or augmented; let them hesitate to acquiesce in any proposition submitted by the planters and they are exposed to beggary" (Bacchus, 1991, p. 218).

In fact, this reticence by the Anglican Church to advocate for the education of blacks continued right up until 1839, and the clergy likewise anaesthetized themselves into accepting that blacks should not be afforded equal access to education. The ideology of the church and civil society from the 1790s to the 1830s, according to Bacchus (1991), endorsed keeping blacks in a state of ignorance because it was viewed as their "natural state," as claimed by the Bishop of London. In addition to this, it was also believed—and noted in Blackwood Magazine—that any form of education granted to the poor population should be religious and spiritual in nature to "render them patient, humble and moral" (Bacchus, 1991, p. 219).

Unlike the Anglicans, the Quakers took a more proactive role in the provision of education for freed blacks from as early as the 1600s. These very early accounts were provided by Dr. Sporri, who noted that Quakers had taken an interest in the religious and moral education of blacks in the 1660s and 1670s. Bacchus (1991) provides an insightful account of how, when George Fox visited Barbados in 1671, he noted that the policy of the Society of Friends was that "black people should be given religious, instruction and were to be taught The Light i.e. admonish them to be sobre [sic], to fear God, to be diligent and truthful to their masters and not to rebel" (Bacchus, 1991, p. 220).

Under the Quakers, freed blacks were introduced to a rudimentary curriculum in reading, writing, "casting" accounts, and Fox's Catechism (Bacchus, 1991). Bacchus also stated that "the school books and teaching that the Quakers provided for the children of all faiths in Barbados acted as a potent proselytizing device for the society" (Bacchus, 1991, p. 221). In spite of this, efforts by Quakers to sustain education for children on the island was not supported by the white planter class, and in 1696 the legislature passed an act that restrained anyone from teaching unless they had taken "the oath of supremacy and allegiance" and possessed a licence from the Governor to teach.

In the pre-emancipation period, the focus on the spiritual education of the black population, whether slave or free, had one purpose, and that was to domesticate and ensure conformity (Bacchus, 1991) of this group to the planter class. Planters feared rebellion and through their liaisons with the various church bodies found ways to segregate, subvert and deny blacks a form of education that would make them socially conscious of their place in society or demand their freedom from their owners earlier.

An examination of a report prepared by the Planning, Development and Research unit of the Ministry of Education, Youth Affairs and Culture (2000) provides a synopsis of the early development of schooling in Barbados. Some examples of these early charity schools—funded via grants and gifts of money—as noted in the report, include: the first school for poor white children in 1686 established by John Elliott, Rowland Buckley, and then Henry Drax at a later period. Other schools for poor whites, then followed in the period from 1709–1785, with Harrison's College being the most prominent grammar school to be established in 1733, by Mr. Thomas Harrison. In 1818, a National Charity School was established by the Church of England, governed by Lord Combermere, for colored and slave children ages 5–12, who attended from 9am until 4 pm (Bacchus, 1991). Children were taught reading, writing and arithmetic as part of the curriculum, and by 1825 the enrolment of the school was 160 students. According to the report by the Planning, Development and Research unit of the Ministry of Education, Youth Affairs and Culture (2000), and Bacchus (1991), Bishop Coleridge established an elementary school near St. Mary's Church in Bridgetown, and a central school for colored girls to aid in their education development in 1827.

POST-EMANCIPATION PERIOD

The post-emancipation period saw an expansion of access to education for former slaves in Barbados, but colored children had already obtained this privilege as early as the 1600s under the Quakers. After slavery, there was a proliferation in the development of schools by the Quakers to suit the convenience of different sectors of the population: field schools, Sunday schools, evening and adult schools, trade schools, estate or plantation schools, and independent schools, as well as regular primary and secondary day schools. The main agenda of the time was the civilization of newly-freed blacks in order to maintain the social and economic stability of the island, and exposure to religious education continued to be seen as the primary vehicle to achieve that goal (Bacchus, 1991). Bacchus (1991) stated that:

A major concern of the authorities during this period was to ensure that there was a peaceful transition from a slave to a free society without any radical changes in the existing social order. For this it was necessary to get the population, including children at school to internalize those values that would lead to their willing acceptance of their ordained place in the social order. (Bacchus, 1991, p. 255)

After 1834, which marked the time of emancipation, the British government invested in the education of the former slaves by extending an annual grant to the West Indian colonies, but the Church remained the benefactor of the masses, establishing over 48 Anglican schools, 4 Moravian Schools, 4 Wesleyan schools and 149 private schools that catered to 7,452 pupils (Ministry of Education Report, 2000).

Of significance in the post emancipation period was the passage of two Education Acts (1850, 1858) that ensured a system of checks and balances were in place to monitor education provision by inspectors in the island. Between 1878 and 1894 a number of schools were reorganized, although what this entailed is not discussed in the report by the Ministry of Education (2000).

THE EVOLUTION OF SPECIAL EDUCATION PROVISION

Much of what is known about how special education provision evolved in Barbados was extracted from a now-dated UNICEF Situation Analysis compiled by O'Toole in (2000). In a book chapter written by Blackman, Richardson, and Fong- Kong Mugal (2013) it is noted that the evolution of special education provision and services for children and adults with disabilities preceded any development of policy in the area. In addition, Blackman et al. (2013) also point out the similarities in the trajectories of the development of inclusion as emerging out of a historical context that mirrors the Unites States of America and the United Kingdom, where institutionalization was the primary mode through which the state exercised its fiduciary responsibility towards persons with disabilities.

The history of the provision of services for persons with disabilities can be traced back to institutions like the Psychiatric Hospital and the Institution for Lepers, which were established in 1894 and 1945 respectively. These institutions cared for the day–to-day needs of the persons with disabilities, but it was not until 1959, with the establishment of The School for the Deaf and Blind by a charity organization called the Lions Club of Barbados (and which was turned over to the government in 1968), that one saw the emergence of a separate and concerted effort to distinguish education and social services provisions for persons with disabilities.

The thrust towards the provision of education continued in 1976 when the Albert Cecil Grahame Development Centre, formerly the Children's Development Centre, was set up to offer multidisciplinary services including speech, occupational and physical, primary health care, audiological, orthopaedic, and psychiatric counselling to children with special needs, and their parents. By the 1980s and 1990s, the government of Barbados had established another tier of education provision with the formation of special education units attached to mainstream primary schools. These units, according to O'Toole's (2000) report, catered to children with a range of other disabilities, for example, movement, autism, cerebral palsy, intellectual impairments, learning problems, and speech problems.

Private special education provision started with settings such as the Challenor School that opened in 1964, aided by government subventions (O'Toole, 2000). At the time the Challenor School catered to children with a range of disabilities such as problems with movement, autism, and developmental delays. This school continues to serve such students today (2015) but has been renamed The Challenor Creative Arts and Training Centre in recognition of the addition of services to adults with mild intellectual disabilities in the Adults Training Facility section. The adult section equips students with technical and vocational skills in the areas of woodworking, sewing and craft and culinary arts over a period of two to three years. In addition, other units and classes were also established at St. Angela's and St. Ursula's schools in 1991 and 1998 respectively, for students primarily having learning disabilities and movement problems.

GLOBAL TRENDS TOWARDS INCLUSIVE EDUCATION

At the international level, UNESCO has spearheaded the drive towards inclusive education worldwide. UNESCO defines inclusion as:

> A process of addressing and responding to the diversity of needs of all learners through increasing participation in learning, cultures and communities, and reducing exclusion within and from education. It involves changes and modifications in content, approaches, structures and strategies, with a common vision which covers all children of the appropriate age range and a conviction that it is the responsibility of the regular system to educate all children. (UNESCO, 2005)

Moreover, the development of inclusive education as a philosophy can be traced almost chronologically to a number of important conventions, standards and frameworks that are briefly outlined below.

In 1982 the UN World Programme of Action Concerning Disabled Persons published a statement which expressed a preference for these children to be educated in an inclusive setting, which noted that:

> Member states should adopt policies, which recognise the rights of disabled persons to equal educational opportunities with others. The education of disabled persons should as far as possible take place in the general school system. Responsibility for their education should be placed upon the educational authorities and laws regarding compulsory education should include children with all ranges of disabilities, including the most severely disabled. (UN General Assembly, 1982)

In 1989, the UN General Assembly recognized that although there was widespread acceptance of the notion of education as a right, there were still reports of inequitable access to education worldwide. According to a 2000 UNESCO report, 113 million children worldwide had no access to primary education, and there were 880 million illiterate adults (Fiske, 2000); a similar situation is recorded in the 2002 monitoring report with a slight increase of the number of children—115 million—who had no to access primary education (UNESCO, 2002). The 2000 report noted that "the chances of being denied schooling is much greater for persons with disabilities and girls...." Other groups of excluded children included: children at risk (including street children); children from nomadic populations; children from linguistic, ethnic and or cultural minorities; and children from disadvantaged and marginalized areas/groups.

In 1993, the UN General Assembly adopted an instrument called the United Nations Standard Rules on the Equalization of Opportunities for Persons with Disabilities (PWD). It represented an international understanding that advocated for governments to have the moral and political will to ensure equity, parity and justice by equalizing opportunities for persons with disabilities worldwide. A number of areas were targeted for equal participation and these included rules 5 to 12 on accessibility, education, employment, income maintenance and social security, family life and personal integrity, culture, recreation and sports, religion. With regard to education, the rules served to inform policy and economic development and created an agenda for member states to promote inclusive education. It also refocused the thrust from special education which, according to the rules was to prepare students for inclusive education. The rules specified a critical look at the provision of education for PWD, in particular the following areas were to be scrutinized:

- National Education Planning: in particular Structural and Systemic strategies;
- Curriculum development: provision of a flexible curriculum;
- School Organization: Teacher Training and Support for Teachers, Quality Materials; and
- Support Services: Other members of Special Education Team, Therapies and Interventions.

In addition to the above, a number of important conferences were also convened to assist with the establishment of standards to guide national priorities on inclusive education, including: The 1990 World Conference on Education for All in Jomtien, Thailand, held by the United Nations Development Programme, UNESCO, UNICEF and the World Bank, which reaffirmed the principle of integration through its theme Education for All children, including those with special needs. The focus of this conference was to extend primary education to all children and decrease illiteracy around the world. Governments from over 155 countries, along with 150 Non-Governmental Organizations (NGOs) committed themselves to achieving this vision. Through the *Framework for Action to Meet the Basic Learning Needs* (UNESCO), governments adopted a reformist agenda to meet the learning needs of all children by the year 2000. The goals articulated included:

1. Universal access to learning;
2. A focus on equity;
3. Emphasis on learning outcomes;

4. Broadening the means and the scope of basic education;
5. Enhancing the environment for learning; and
6. Strengthening partnerships by 2000.

The Salamanca Statement and Framework for Action held by UNESCO and the Ministry of Education and Science in Spain (1994) articulated the clearest support for inclusive education. About 125 countries signed the declaration, which acknowledged the uniqueness of all children and their entitlement to an education. It was at this conference that delegates agreed to a Framework of Action that recognized inclusive education as the vehicle to actualize "Education for All Children." Article 2 of the Salamanca Framework for Action states that:

> Regular schools with an inclusive orientation are the most effective means of combating discriminatory attitudes, creating welcoming communities, building inclusive societies and achieving the goal of an education for all. (Ministry of Education and Science, Madrid Spain, & United Nations Educational, Scientific and Cultural Organisation, p. 8)

This Framework called for countries worldwide to implement laws and policies that make it illegal to exclude children from school and especially those with disabilities. Under this framework, inclusive education means that:

> Schools should accommodate all children, regardless of their physical, intellectual, emotional, social, linguistic or other conditions. They should include disabled and gifted children, street and working children, children from remote and nomadic populations, children from linguistic, ethnic or cultural minorities and children from other disadvantaged or marginalized areas or groups. (Ministry of Education and Science, Madrid Spain, & United Nations Educational, Scientific and Cultural Organisation, p. 15)

The 2000 World Education Forum in Dakar, Senegal, broadened the scope the conference held in Spain, and suggested that Education for All seemed to focus too narrowly on children with disabilities. It was decided that a broader remit was needed to include all children and that full inclusion would be pursued.

THE THRUST TOWARDS INCLUSIVE EDUCATION IN BARBADOS

Barbados became a member of UNESCO in 1968, and a decade later, in 1982, a signatory to the United Nations World Programme of Action, which sought to equalize opportunities for children including those with disabilities. In response to this, Caribbean governments convened an Advisory Task Force on Education in 1989, mobilized by a steering committee of education ministers, and developed a policy entitled "The Future of Education in the Caribbean." This task force developed a 10-point plan of action that targeted:

1. Early Childhood; Primary, Secondary and Tertiary Education;

2. Education for Special Needs;
3. Language Learning;
4. Mathematics and Science Education;
5. Technology and the Curriculum;
6. School and The World of Work;
7. Adult Education;
8. Teacher Education;
9. Management and Administration of Schools; and
10. Financing of Education (Rudder, 2015, p. 19).

The Future of Education in the Caribbean report recognized, *inter alia*, that children with special education needs remained an underserved population in the region in particular those who were gifted, were slow learners, had sensory impairments or orthopaedic impairments, and children with communication disorders. Carrington (1993) argued that "a number of reasons account for this, ... that special education has no strong advocates, especially where decisions are taken about financial allocations for education" (Carrington, 1993, p. 30). He also cited additional challenges that included: 1) that special education services were mainly in the hands of private stakeholders whose service varied in quality, effectiveness and efficiency; 2) that efforts to provide special education service was too compartmentalized; 3) that there was fierce competition for scarce resources; 4) that there was a lack of coordination and continuity of effort; 5) that identification of children with special needs remained problematic owing to poorly defined criteria; 6) that special education was expensive; and 7) that negative attitudes towards children with disabilities by parents and teachers were barriers to participation and the potential development of these children.

It is interesting to note the section on future directions identified attitudes and mainstreaming as alternative strategies to combat some of the challenges that hindered the development of special education services at that time (Carrington, 1993). Carrington stated that "such attitudes and perceptions are best nurtured in situations where all children learn in the same environment" (Carrington, 1993, p. 31). He also identified the importance of providing teacher education and professional development opportunities for teachers who worked with a more diversified student population. In particular, teachers' pedagogical knowledge, and the provision of adequate support services and diagnostic centres, were to be provided to assist in this effort.

Moreover, a number of policy goals were recommended to Ministries of Education regionally that would underpin the development of special education. The five goals identified by Carrington (1993) were: 1) the provision of an appropriate education climate and curricula to develop the potential of students with special needs; 2) the adoption of a regional approach to introducing a cost-effective approach to the delivery of special education; 3) the resources of communities were to be harnessed to serve students and adults with special needs; 4) the development of advocacy to promote more positive attitudes towards persons with disabilities; and 5) the development of training programmes to provide for students with disabilities of school leaving age.

In 1991, the government of Barbados convened a National Advisory Commission on Education that would undertake a number of education initiatives in support of the goals and targets outlined at UNESCO World Conference for All in Jomtien. The commission agreed, *inter alia*, to engage in the following monitoring activities

1. An overall examination and review of the educational services and report on their effectiveness in meeting national development needs;
2. A review of the need for rationalization of the education system at the primary, secondary and tertiary level;
3. An examination of the overall cost of education in the context of the national budget and allocation at various levels of education;
4. A review of the curricula of schools and other educational institutions;
5. An assessment of the adequacy of training programmes for teachers at all levels of the system;
6. A review of the existing legislation and institutional framework; and
7. An assessment of learning and learning outcomes at primary and secondary level.

Out of this monitoring and evaluation activity, sweeping reforms of the education system were suggested, and this was followed by the development of a policy called The White Paper on Education (Ministry of Education, Youth Affairs and Culture, 1995) with its theme "Each One Matters—Quality Education for All." According to Rudder (2015) the major reform policies in this document related to:

1. Expanding access to Early Childhood Education;
2. Ensuring that all primary children achieved acceptable standards of literacy and numeracy;
3. Providing a foundation for entry into the world of work through secondary education;
4. Expanding and enhancing tertiary education;
5. Special Needs Education and at Risk students;
6. Student Assessment and Examinations;
7. Teacher recruitment, training, appraisal and empowerment;
8. Governance of schools;
9. Management of the Education system; and
10. Education cost and efficiency.

These reform policies were buttressed by another education initiative called the Education Sector Enhancement Programme or Edu-Tech 2000, which sought to integrate technology into the school system after an extensive overhaul of the civil, infrastructural works of schools, teacher training to enhance the pedagogical delivery of ICT skills and technology integration, installation of hard- and software, a shift from predominantly teacher centred models to student-centred models, and a more project-based and collaborative orientation to learning for students in primary and secondary schools.

Two years later the Education Sector Strategic Plan 2002–2012 followed EduTech. Several strategies were identified in this document to assist with achieving EFA. Among the strategies listed were:

1. Early Childhood, Primary and Secondary Education;
2. Special Needs Education;
3. Student Performance; assessment methods and instruments; and learning outcomes;
4. Tertiary Education and rationalisation of post-secondary institutions;
5. Adult and Continuing Education;
6. Teacher Training and development; teacher appraisals;
7. Establishment of a National Accreditation Agency;
8. Curriculum Reform; and
9. Education and student Support services. (Rudder, 2015, p. 22)

As it relates to Barbados, a tiered approach to the provision of special education services continues. The World Data on Education (IBE-UNESCO, 2010) commenting on Barbados states that "special needs education is addressed in three ways, in the regular education classroom, in the special classroom in the regular school and in the special unit or special education school" (p. 3). This suggests that the island endorses the philosophy that all children have a right to an education. The Ministry of Education, in articulating its principles and general objectives of education, and more specifically its commitment to inclusion noted that:

> ... an inclusive approach to the concept of inclusive education can be inferred from the Ministry's understanding of the importance of addressing the diversity of learners. The Ministry underlines that inclusive education refers to the philosophy that ensures students with varied abilities be supported in chronologically age-appropriate general education classes in their home schools and receive specialised instruction delineated by their individualized education programmes within the context of the national curriculum and general class activities. (International Bureau of Education-United Nations Education Scientific and Cultural Organization, 2007, p. 1)

According to another Barbados Report, compiled by UNESCO in 2007 at the Caribbean Symposium on Inclusive Education, the island adopted two service delivery models: a pull-out programme, and a full-inclusion model. Pull-out programmes were introduced so that special needs students could spend part of their time in regular education settings and still have their learning needs met in resource classrooms. Full-inclusion programmes, on the other hand, were utilized so that students with special needs were in regular education settings with their peers. However, it is unclear how students were assigned to both programmes, and what category of student accessed each programme. Students who were classified as mentally and physically challenged were integrated into the mainstream school system.

For example, mild to moderately mentally-challenged students, who would have previously been removed from general education classes and assigned to a special education unit at special schools across the island, now remain in mainstream education (International Bureau of Education-United Nations Education Scientific and Cultural Organization, 2007, p. 2).

The report also indicated that a "new curricular" guided schools and teacher pedagogy in the island, noting that:

> The new curricula prepares all students to be creative, numerate, and literate, while ensuring that all students understand the necessity of living and working harmoniously with others. It also prepares students for life in a technologically-advanced society, by ensuring that all school leavers have a good knowledge, adequate skills, and favourable attitudes towards information technology. (International Bureau of Education-United Nations Education Scientific and Cultural Organization, 2007, p. 2)

Pedagogically, teachers were encouraged to adopt constructivist approaches to teaching, i.e. child-centred and collaborative approaches, which would foster learner autonomy and active engagement in the classroom. The report states that:

> Such adaptation of the curricula for students with special needs is already noticeable in the Barbados education system. For example, schools may modify the curricula to meet the needs of diverse learners through alternative formats, for example Braille and assistive devices. The general education structure also includes different modes of assessment, with teachers engaging in more authentic assessments for a classroom of diverse learners, such as orals, interviews, exhibitions, portfolios, project-based work and norm referenced tests. Similarly, the curriculum has been restructured to accommodate individual students to proceed at a rate proportionate to their aptitudes and abilities. (International Bureau of Education-United Nations Education Scientific and Cultural Organization, 2007, p. 3)

With regard to teacher training, the Ministry of Education pursued teacher preparation for inclusion through training a cadre of 83 teachers in inclusive practices at the Mount St. Vincent University in Halifax, Canada, at a cost of 2 million Barbados Dollars 2003. According to the report:

> In these programmes, teachers developed skills in learner-centred strategies and practices, in teacher-facilitator modes to support the teaching/learning process, and in learner assessment strategies in the form of strategies that support and enhance programme planning. They also learnt about the delivery of alternative modes of instruction to meet the needs of exceptional learners in regular schools through individualized learning practices that enable meaningful inclusion of a range of learning styles. In addition, varying leadership, collaboration and classroom management models were introduced, as were strategies to address learners at risk in literacy

and numeracy at the elementary and secondary levels. (International Bureau of Education-United Nations Education Scientific and Cultural Organization, 2007, p. 5)

CHALLENGES TO THE DEVELOPMENT OF INCLUSIVE EDUCATION

No National Policy on Inclusive Education

Although the Ministry of Education in Barbados expresses a clear commitment to inclusive education, no clear policy guiding the implementation of inclusive practices in schools or education currently exists. The continued existence of tiers of education, where children with disabilities are in special schools rather than regular education, means that their "confinement" in segregated settings will also remain unchanged and unchallenged. In addition, no reform of the current Education Act to govern and reflect the principles of inclusion has been undertaken. This signals a need to urgently address this issue, but also ensure that a national policy on inclusion does not suffer the same fate as the stalled national policy for persons with special needs.

In 1995, a draft policy was created to address the needs of children and individuals with disabilities, called the *Green Paper on Education Reform*. It included a section on special education stating the government's vision that "all physically and mentally challenged children will receive educational instruction that is appropriate to their developmental needs" in the "least restrictive educational environment, better known as mainstreaming" (Ministry of Social Transformation, 1995, p. 52). This was followed in 2000 by the *White Paper on Persons with Disabilities,* which re-echoed the need for education reform by the Ministry of Social Transformation, through the work of the National Disabilities Unit (O'Toole, 2000; Ministry of Social Transformation, n.d.). Although these papers represented a step toward policy development, they failed to address the education needs of children with disabilities.

Although a gap existed between articulation and ratification, the *White Paper on Persons with Disabilities* reaffirmed the need to pursue the inclusion of children with disabilities. Its social justice view is evident as one of its key principle states, "provision of access to education for all Persons with Disabilities at all educational levels, in an integrated setting whenever possible, with specialised facilities for those needing such" (Ministry of Social Transformation, 1995, p. 8). By 2008, the Ministry of Education sought to outline governmental policy specific to students with special needs, but this document remained stalled at the draft stage. As of 2015, special needs education guidelines continue to be those outlined in the now 20-year-old 1995 *White Paper on Education Reform* meant for students in general education settings. The effort to move policy guidelines on special education into legislation has not been sustained.

Inadequate Support Services

At the international level, there is a consensus that for inclusive education to be effective and feasible, a system of support is needed to accommodate and facilitate the needs of students with disabilities in regular education. Support can be construed in a number of ways, but it includes the provision of specialists and resources (Deppeler, Loreman, & Sharma, 2005); teacher practices and strategies (Mumford & Chandler, 2009; Spratt & Florian, 2015); teacher attitudes and concerns about inclusion (Forlin & Chambers, 2011); and policy and school culture (Purdue, Gordon-Burns, Gunn, Madden, & Surtees, 2009).

In Barbados, according to the 2010 report on the World Data for Education, special education needs services focus on the identification of students for placement through multidisciplinary evaluation. It also notes that the education of students with special needs is guided by Individualized Education Plans. In spite of these structures, research conducted by UNICEF in collaboration with the University of the West Indies Consulting Group (UWI Consulting) on the Quality of Teaching and Learning in Special Education Settings in Barbados (UNICEF & UWI Consulting, 2012) with special education officers in the Ministry of Education, found that the evaluation and assessment procedures used in the identification process were often hampered by a number of factors including:

1. Parents provided very limited medical information at the 45-minute clinical interview conducted by education officers in the Student Services Section of the Ministry of Education. Also that the clinical interview was only 45 minutes also limited the number of assessments that could be done with the student in that period of time;
2. The small cadre of specialists who conducted and provided assessment reports to the Ministry of Education Teachers delayed the availability of those reports to schools, which in turn inhibited placement and pedagogical decisions of the principal and teachers in school; and
3. Assessment information from the Ministry of Education was not translatable into instructional practice.

Teacher Attitudes Towards Inclusion

The issue of teacher attitudes remains a critical point with respect to the success of inclusion in the region as a whole. One quantitative study on teacher attitudes towards inclusion conducted by Blackman, Conrad, and Brown (2012) in Barbados and Trinidad found that while the overall attitudes of teachers sampled (231) in Barbados was positive, the same could not be said for their counterparts in Trinidad (254). This study utilized Antonak and Larrivee's (1995) *Opinions Relative to the Integration of Students with Special Needs Scale* to assess teacher attitudes. The scale was divided into four sub-scales that measured: 1) Benefits of Inclusion; 2) Inclusion and Classroom Management; 3) Perceived Ability to

Teach; and 4) Inclusion in Special vs. General. A disaggregation of the data revealed that teachers in Barbados scored low on their attitudes towards inclusion and classroom management sub-scale and perceived ability to teach students with special needs sub-scaled. These results therefore suggest that teachers in Barbados, in spite of their overall positive attitude, felt that it would be difficult to manage and instruct students with special needs if they were integrated into regular education classrooms. It is quite possible that teachers held positive philosophies about education and the inclusion of children with disabilities and this in turn might account for their positive attitudes. These findings are congruent with those noted in a qualitative study on teacher attitudes in selected schools in Barbados by UNICEF and UWI Consulting (UNICEF & UWI Consulting, 2012).

Attitudes of Children, Teens and Youth Towards Inclusion

A recent quantitative study by Blackman (2015) utilized the Chedoke McMasters Attitude towards Children with Handicap Scale (CATCH) to collect attitudinal data on a cross section of 178 Barbadian students. The findings suggest that many students did not have contact with peers with disabilities, and less than half of the students sampled reported having a friend with a disability. There were clear differences between the attitudes of children 7–12 years, teenagers 13–18 years old, and young adults aged 19, with teens expressing more negative attitudes towards integration than children and young adults. This is critical, given that the literature has consistently noted that students with disabilities experience difficulties achieving a sense of homophily and affiliation with peers their same age at school. Moreover, these findings also suggest a need to improve the levels of propinquity between peers with and without disabilities and for teachers to foster such opportunities for meaningful direct contact to improve attitudes among students and pro-social behaviors in inclusive settings.

INCLUSIVE EDUCATION: THE WAY FORWARD

The above discussion clearly indicates that Barbados has been, and continues to be, responsive at the philosophical level to the call for all children and in particular those with disabilities to be included in schools on the island. However, there is a need to understand how inclusion translates into practice in very tangible ways at the levels of policy, schools, teachers, parents, students and administration. Moreover, legislative action is needed to lend support for the call to adopt and implement inclusive education as a whole school and system wide approach to education reform. In order to address the challenges outlined in the chapter, there needs to be a fundamental commitment on the part of The Ministry of Education, schools, parents and teachers to collaboration and cooperation in order to:

- Assist the Ministry of Education in formulating a comprehensive policy on inclusive education that clearly identifies the roles and responsibilities

TABLE 1.1. Chronological Developments of Inclusive Education in Barbados 1700–1989

Time Period	Agent of Change	Who Served	Education Provision/Policy
1600s	Church—Quakers	Freed colored	Separate school for free colored children
18th Century 1700s Pre-Emancipation	Churches	Poor whites	Separate school for whites
19th Century 1818	Church—Church of England	Colored boys	Separate school for boys governed by Lord Combermere
1827	Churches—Church of England	Colored Girls	Separate school for girls
Post-Emancipation Period 1834–45	Churches and grants from British governments	Former slaves	
1858; 1878; 1890	Education Acts		Monitoring of all schools by Her Majesty's Inspectors
1894		Persons with disabilities	Institutionalisation psychiatric hospital
20th Century 1945; 1959		Deaf and blind students	Separate school
1968	Barbados becomes a member of UNESCO	Children with developmental delays	Children's Development Centre
1975	United Nations Declaration on the Rights of Disabled Persons		
1980s–1990s			Separate classrooms and private schools for students with disabilities
1982	World Programme of Action	WPA advocates for inclusion of children with disabilities in regular schools	
1989	Standing Committee of Ministers & Advisory Task Force on Education prepare the Future of Education in the Caribbean		Inclusion

(*continues*)

TABLE 1.2. (continued)

Time Period	Agent of Change	Who Served	Education provision/ Policy
1990	Barbados becomes a Signatory to the Convention for the Rights of the Child		
1991	Jomtien, Thailand—United Nation's Framework for Action to Meet Learning Needs—Excellence For All		Inclusion
1991	National Advisory Commission on Education (NACE) convened by the Ministry of Education in response to EFA		Inclusion
1993	UN Standard Rules- access and equality of opportunity		Inclusion
1994	Salamanca Statement and Framework for Action		Inclusion
1995	White Paper on Education Reform; informed by the Future of Education in the Caribbean (Regional Education Policy Framework, and National Advisory Commission on Education)—WPE was the foundation for the programme of action to achieve EFA	All children in regular education settings	Inclusion
1997	Regional Development- Plan of Action for Education for All. Barbados's National Initiative was Education Sector Enhancement Programme	All children in regular education settings	EduTech 2000: integrate technology into classrooms
2000	Curriculum Reform		Curriculum 2000
2002	Education Sector Strategic Plan 2002–2012		
2003	Mount-St. Vincent Training in collaboration with Erdiston Teachers Training College—Bachelors and Masters Programmes Offered in Special Education	Teachers	

of schools, principals, parents and teachers in the education and development of all children but in particular those with special education needs. It is likely that structures which supported special education for example, learning support assistants, special education teachers, resource rooms, resources will need to be seen as part of a continuum of services that must now serve a larger group of students in regular education settings;
- Identify and assess children for the purpose of "diagnosing" learning needs will need to be informed by a new model. A multi-tiered approach to assessment that places teachers rather than professionals at the centre of the process will ensure that children referred for assessment have been through curriculum based assessment rather than psycho-educational testing approaches that do little to inform instruction;
- Address teacher attitudes to inclusion, as this is the fulcrum that will determine how well students with disabilities meet their educational goals and achieve their potential. Teachers professional development and training in

inclusive practices must become a priority for the Ministry of Education. In particular, teachers must attain higher level qualifications, for example, at the Masters level and be exposed to more intensive and extensive professional development opportunities that demonstrate how to impact the learning of all students and meet the needs of a diverse student population; and
- The corollary to the above argument is that the attitudes of students without disabilities must also be addressed, in particular at the adolescent stage of development. It is possible to increase the contact and time that adolescents will spend with peers with disabilities via requiring them to engage in more volunteer service, work on projects where students with disabilities are likely to experience success as well, by teachers providing opportunities for more collaborative and cooperative approaches to learning.

The picture that emerges is that Barbados is on its way towards developing a system of education that can be considered as inclusive, but it demands a commitment by all stakeholders in order to achieve the goal of being socially just and equitable as articulated so many years ago by UNESCO.

REFERENCES

Anotnak, R. F., & Larrivee, B. (1995). Psychometric analysis and revision of the opinions relative to mainstreaming scale. *Exceptional Children, 62*(2), 139–149.

Blackman, S. (April 18th, 2015). Fostering social inclusion and justice: Barbadian students' attitudes towards peers with disabilities. *A paper presented at the American Education Research Association Conference.* Chicago, Illinois.

Blackman, S., Conrad, D., & Brown, L. (2012). The attitude of Barbadian and Trinidadian teachers to integration. *The International Journal of Special Education, 27(3),* 158–168.

Blackman, S., Richardson, A. G., & Fong Kong-Mungal, C. (2013). Special educators' efficacy and exceptional students' future trajectories: Informing Barbados' education policy. In C. Z. Szymanski-Sunal & K. Muta (Eds), *Research on the impact of educational policy on teaching and learning* (pp. 163–81). Charlotte, NC: Information Age Publishing.

Carrington, E. W. (1993). *The future of education in the Caribbean: Report of the CARICOM advisory task force on education.* Castries, St. Lucia: Caribbean Community Secretariat.

Deppeler, J., Loreman, T., & Sharma, U. (2005). Improving inclusive practices in secondary schools: Moving from specialist support to supporting learning communities. *Australasian Journal of Special Education, 29(2),* 117–27. doi.org/10.1080/1030011050290204.

Fiske, E. (2000). *World education forum Dakar: Final report.* Paris, France: UNESCO.

Forlin, C., & Chambers, D. (2011). Teacher preparation for inclusive education: increasing knowledge but raising concerns. *Asia-Pacific Journal of Teacher Education, 39(1),* 17–32. doi.org/10.1080/1359866X.2010.540850.

International Bureau of Education-United Nations Education Scientific and Cultural Organization (IBE-UNESCO). (2007). *IBE-UNESCO Preparatory report for the 48th*

ICE on inclusive education: Caribbean symposium on inclusive education. Paris, France: UNESCO.

International Bureau of Education-United Nations Education Scientific and Cultural Organization (IBE-UNESCO). (2007). *Caribbean Symposium on Inclusive Education.* Fontenoy, Paris: UNESCO.

Ministry of Education, Youth Affairs and Culture. (1995). *White paper on education reform in Barbados.* Bridgetown, Barbados: Ministry of Education, Youth Affairs and Culture.

Ministry of Education, Youth Affairs and Culture. (2000a). *Curriculum 2000: Rationale and guidelines for curriculum reform in Barbados.* Bridgetown, Barbados: Ministry of Education, Youth Affairs and Culture.

Ministry of Education, Youth Affairs and Culture. (2000b). *Historical developments of education in Barbados 1686–2000.* Bridgetown, Barbados: Planning Research and Development Unit, Ministry of Education, Youth Affairs and Culture.

Ministry of Education, Youth Affairs and Sports. (2002). *Strategic plan 2002–2012.* Bridgetown, Barbados: Ministry of Education, Youth Affairs and Sports.

Ministry of Education and Science, Madrid Spain, & United Nations Educational, Scientific and Cultural Organisation. (1994). *Salamanca statement and framework for action on special needs education:* Paris, France: UNESCO.

Ministry of Social Transformation. National Disabilities Unit. (1995). *White paper on persons with disabilities.* Bridgetown, Barbados: National Disabilities Unit, Ministry of Social Transformation.

Mumford, V. E., & Chandler, J. P. (2009). Strategies for supporting inclusive education for students with disabilities. *Journal for Physical and Sport Educators, 22*(5), 10–15. do.org/10.1080/08924562.2009.10590834

O'Toole, B. (2000). *An assessment of the status of children and adolescents with disabilities in the Caribbean.* Bridgetown, Barbados: UNICEF Area Office.

Purdue, K., Gordon-Burns, D., Gunn, A., Madden, B., & Surtees, N. (2009). Supporting inclusion in early childhood settings: Some possibilities and problems for teacher education. *International Journal of Inclusive Education, 13*(8), 805–815. doi.org/10.1080/13603110802110743.

Rudder, R. (2015). *National Education for all 2015 review: Barbados report.* Bridgetown, Barbados: Planning, Research and International Relations Unit: Ministry of Education, Science, Technology and Innovation.

Spratt, J., & Florian, L. (2015). Inclusive pedagogy from learning to action: Support each individual in the context of everybody. *Teaching and Teacher Education, 49,* 89–96. doi.org/10.1016/j.tate.2015.03.006.

UNESCO. (2002). *Global monitoring report Education for all: Is the world on track?* Paris, France: UNESCO.

United Nations Educational, Scientific and Cultural Organisation & International Bureau of Education. (2010). *World data on education.* Fontenoy, Paris: UNESCO.

UNICEF & UWI Consulting. (2012). Quality of teaching and learning in the special education setting in Barbados. Bridgetown, Barbados: UNICEF.

United Nations Educational, Scientific and Cultural Organisation. (2005). *Guidelines for inclusion: Ensuring access to education for all.* Fontenoy, Paris: UNESCO.

United Nations General Assembly. (1982). *World programme of action concerning disabled persons.* New York, NY: United Nations.

CHAPTER 2

SPECIAL EDUCATION IN TRINIDAD AND TOBAGO

Does Educational Vision and Change Lead to Success?

Joan Pedro

INTRODUCTION

This chapter reviews the implementation and success of a special education initiative in Trinidad and Tobago's Education system. In the late 1990s, Trinidad and Tobago saw reforms in education with the University of Sheffield Initiative for preparing teachers to meet the special education needs of children in schools. I look at Trinidad and Tobago's readiness for navigating educational reforms within a culture not quite ready for major educational change, and the current success of this movement. This chapter shares my personal and professional experiences as a teacher educator committed to the politics of change and educational reforms. I was directly involved with this special education initiative as the second project director. Dennis Conrad was the first project director and the driving force that brought the project to Trinidad and Tobago upon completing his Master of Education at the University of Sheffield. In offering this account, I share some of the

Caribbean Discourse in Inclusive Education:
Historical and Contemporary Issues, pages 21–32.
Copyright © 2017 by Information Age Publishing
All rights of reproduction in any form reserved.

lesser-known challenges faced and the critical lessons learned by these pioneers. I consider Dennis Conrad, Errol Pilgrim, Ann Cheryl Armstrong (nee Namsoo), Launcelot Brown and myself, Joan Pedro to be the main constituents of this group.

I use a self-study methodology because of the lasting impression these experiences have made on my life as an educator and professional. Self-study is interpreted here as "reflective enquiry," leading to self-understanding and professional development in one's work (Knowles & Cole, 1996). I view the work within the theoretical framework of educational change prescribed by Fullan and Stiegelbauer (1991). The pioneers in this project had a vision that was not easily accepted by the status quo, and they actively sought to institute educational change. I start this narrative by reviewing what research has to say about vision and its importance to reform within the system of education.

THE IMPORTANCE OF VISION IN EDUCATION

Educational vision provides guidance to an institution by articulating what that institution wishes to attain. It serves as a signpost pointing the way for all who need to understand what the organization is, and where it intends to go (Nanus, 1992). Vision describes an organization's direction or goal, and the various ways to accomplish these goals. Seeley (1992) describes vision as being a goal-oriented mental construct that helps to guide people's behavior: it should be what individuals in the organization are willing to work towards. Vision involves more than just having a picture of what should be, it also has a very compelling facet that inspires, motivates, and engages individuals to move to action. Manasse (1986) contends that vision is the force that gives meaning and purpose to the work of any organization. Vision is a more than a compelling picture of the desired future that inspires commitment of individuals within the organization, it encourages people to work and to strive for its attainment (Méndez-Morse, 1993). Pejza (1985) also states that vision is a hunger to see improvement by educational leaders who implement change.

Educational change is always difficult when a country does not have the human or material resources, or when that country does not see the importance of the area in its development. The latter sums up the case for special education teacher preparation. It was my view, and other special educators at the time, that in Trinidad and Tobago in the 1980s special education was not a major component of teacher education and training at The University of the West Indies. There was no special education programme as part of its curriculum, neither was there an attempt to implement such a programme because of a lack of resources and trained personnel. My view at the time was that there was no desire or willingness on the part of the University personnel to implement special education programs although many teachers were coming back from foreign universities with the necessary special education qualifications to implement such programmes. Typical training involved being selectively sent to England, the USA, Mico Teachers College (Jamaica), and the University of the West Indies Distance Teaching Experiment

(UWIDITE). The latter provided a one year certificate via a teleconference network offering options in mathematics, social studies, literacy studies, integrated science, and deaf education.

A special education teacher education program was sorely needed because teachers in the regular schools were not knowledgeable about dealing with students with special needs, and many had become burnt-out and frustrated. It can be said that the education system included a considerable number of students with special needs in the regular classrooms (Marge, 1984). This was further complicated by inadequate resources and facilities in our traditional segregated special schools, and under-prepared and under-resourced teachers in both special and regular schools. Although there were numerous students with special needs in the school system at all levels, special education services were not considered a support for students in the regular schools. Here was a need waiting to be filled and the pioneers were ready to implement this program.

Changes occur because of political or social forces or as a result of local leadership. This statement is exceedingly true of the vision and work of Dennis Conrad who mobilized a few like-minded committed educators to develop and provide the distance programme initiative. This involved a unique collaboration between a foreign university, special education teachers, and the teachers' association to provide opportunities to acquire a Certificate, Diploma, or Master of Education in Special Education. Conrad's involvement with and support from the Ministry of Education's Special Education Advisory Committee facilitated critical engagement by these key stakeholders. This group of special educators who came from a tradition of pioneering, teamwork, and leadership were willing to take the risk and launch this special education initiative (Pedro & Conrad, 2006).

When we think about change, the leader has to visualize not just how a new programme or practice would work, but also how whole new sets of expectations, relationships, accountability structures, etc., would fit together into a coherent whole (Seeley, 1992). The vision, mission and values must align to an institution's own philosophy, and if there are collaborations and partnerships across institutions then it is important that there is a common purpose across these institutions. When partnerships are formed they should be based on trust, a common framework, a common language and collaborative inquiry with data shared within those partnerships. For successful professional development undertaken by different partners there must be the alignment of a mission at the beginning of the innovation with constant reflection, assessment and conversation on an ongoing basis.

Various approaches have been suggested for the actual development of a shared vision (Blokker, 1989; Nanus, 1992; Rogus, 1990). Four steps suggested by Méndez-Morse (1993) that facilitate the conceptualization of vision that can lead to successful change are used in this chapter to frame the vision for, and the implementation of, the special education initiative in Trinidad and Tobago. These four steps include: knowing your organization, involving critical individuals, exploring the possibilities and putting it in writing. The author suggest that these steps can be adjusted to facilitate conceptualization of your vision. In looking back on the realization of the project, it is not clear whether the vision was articulated in writing which the fourth step suggest, however, the proposal for the project was well articulated and honoured for accreditation by the University of Sheffield.

Know Your Organization

Nanus (1992) suggests that "the basic nature" of an organization can be defined by determining its present purpose and value to society. Knowing what an educational system needs should be the reason for developing a vision. Dennis, Errol, Joan and Launce were involved in the special education of students for many years and were convinced that there was a dire need for more special education teachers at all levels of the education system. There was also a collective understanding of the needs of the education system and it included the participation of constituencies and the collaboration of the three organizations that undertook the Special Education Project. For successful change to occur, education leaders must work with their staff and the community to build a clear educational vision that is connected to teaching and learning. This collective vision motivates and increases the sense of shared responsibility for student learning (Nanus, 1992). As Fullan (1993) points out, education leaders need to understand the process of change in order to lead and manage change and improvement efforts effectively. They must learn to overcome barriers and cope with the chaos that naturally exists during the complex process of change (Fullan & Miles, 1992). During the initial phase of formulating a vision, it is important to learn everything about the organization as it currently exists. This idea corresponds to the concept of organizational vision as a comprehensive picture of the existing system within its environment.

What historically existed in Trinidad and Tobago in the area of special education was a segregated arrangement that was not part of the public school system. Special education services were operated by philanthropic and religious organizations in separate special schools. In 1980, a major step in the development of this sector of education was prompted by a government mandate and a Special Education Unit was formed to establish guidelines and supervision of all special schools in the country. This move was an attempt by the Government of Trinidad and Tobago to raise the standard of education offered to these students. The Ministry of Education, although "committed" to adequate education for all, lamented that the cost of making special education teachers available was too high for the public purse. Teachers were struggling in the schools, and there were no special education teachers in the mainstream elementary and secondary schools.

The vision to change the existing system of special education came about in 1989, when the Ministry of Education completed a series of workshops under the auspices of the Canadian International Development Agency (CIDA) and the University of Manitoba. This Special Education Sensitization Project was part of its initiatives to address special education needs and demonstrated some commitment to addressing the recommendations of the Marge Report (Marge, 1984).

This report had also proposed that the Ministry of Education focus special education teacher preparation as a matter of urgency. The project was immensely successful and the workshops served to give teachers "a taste" of special education strategies and to highlight the need for more teacher education in the area of special education. However, neither the Ministry of Education nor the University of the West Indies were willing to embark on such large-scale teacher education (Pedro & Conrad, 2006).

It was in this context that in 1989 the opportunity to introduce teacher education in special education through distance learning was presented by the Association of Special Education of Trinidad and Tobago (TASETT), the Trinidad and Tobago Unified Teachers Association (TTUTA), and the University of Sheffield in England. These organizations developed a partnership that produced over 300 special education teachers in Trinidad and Tobago. As the leading figure in this initiative, Conrad talked about the coming together of three entities as a partnership that crossed distance. He stated that for the first time in the Caribbean teachers were able to shape and construct their professional development (Lavia, 1998). At that time these three organizations formed what Wenger and Snyder (2000) describe as a group of people informally bound together by shared expertise and a passion for a joint enterprise. They forged together and focused on the problems directly related to their work (Wenger & Snyder, 2000). These organizations shared a collective knowledge.

Involve Critical Individuals

Critical individuals are all the players who are essential to the process of change. These individuals or groups identified as constituencies include those that are the most critical both inside and outside the organization. The major expectations or interests of these critical constituents as well as any threats or opportunities that may originate from these groups or individuals should always be considered (Méndez-Morse, 1993)

The individuals or groups identified as constituencies include those that are the most critical, both internal and external, to an institution or district. These "critical" individuals can be those who are essential, such as a representatives of a major business in the community, (Méndez-Morse, 1993), one such organization being the Teachers Association, there were critical individuals in this organization who took on the role of facilitators along with faculty from the University of Sheffield as the external partner in this project. The role of the project management in Trinidad was undertaken by the Vice-President of the Teachers Association, and the organization became the local brokers of the project. They provided the infrastructure with accounting and secretarial personnel for fees collection and the major oversight for the day-to-day management of the project. The academic management was the responsibility of the project director, an important undertaking by Conrad as the pioneering educator. He along with others "built the ship as it was sailing." The first project experienced significant growing pains, and through lessons learned many improvements were implemented as the project continued to expand to educate future cohorts of teachers for the next six years. The University of Sheffield provided teaching expertise and the accreditation of the program, with Sheffield's faculty taking part in summer workshops and commencement activities as cohorts of teachers completed the Diploma program every two years.

There were major expectations or interests of these critical constituents as well as any threats or opportunities that originated from these groups or individuals (Méndez-Morse 1993). Each of these entities had their expectations and interests that at the time seemed to be similar, however, there were different interests and expectations that evolved over the course of the project that created some threats and opportunities. Positions changed and the project continued under the administration of the Teachers' Association for six years, with three cohorts of teachers successfully completing a Diploma in Special Education accredited by the University of Sheffield. The critical individuals remained committed to the vision and mission of educational reform and change in special education, although roles changed we continued to manage and teach in this program.

In any project, critical individuals such as teachers, leaders, and other community members should be included. They ensure the participation of advocacy groups that worked with our students and major employers of our teachers (Méndez-Morse, 1993. Not all constituents were involved in the creation and implementation of this special education project. Although formal support from the Ministry of Education and the local university were lack lustre, there were many individual faculty members from the University of the West Indies (UWI) who subsequently became involved and provided critical support. They and others participated in the administration, curriculum, and teaching on the project. They were very instrumental to the success of the special education initiative.

Many critical individuals came together to maintain the viability of this partnership, it was an experiment in a way, but more importantly, it was a real partnership. There was a commitment made and it was real innovative work. As Fletcher, Watkins, Gless, and Villarreal-Carman (2011) state, there is no secret formula, but the three factors of mutuality, clarity of purpose and roles and positive impact should be considered as important when defining the nature of the partnership. I believe that the individuals involved felt they maintained the goals of the project and that there was mutuality as we forged forward teaching and administering the work. Fletcher et al. (2011) also argue that there should be the use of mutually agreed upon language, tools and protocols which are paramount to maintaining a healthy partnership. In addition, there should not be mistrust and cross-purposes if there is a clear division of labour and roles are clearly defined (Fletcher et al., 2011). An important distinction can be made in the redefinition of mutuality as the return of the investment are equally valued by the partners. Fletcher et al. (2011) also reiterate the importance of honest respect and a mutual desire to benefit from each other's assets, and not about fixing the other's failings, so that all individual involved in the project are critical to its success.

The involvement of critical individuals often presents challenges to the development of a shared vision. Rogus (1990) suggests identifying consensus and grappling with non-consensus and discussing the factors that could impact on the system you are trying to change. It can be said, that this process was not fully established, as the special education project was initiated by three different organizations, the Trinidad and Tobago Unified Teachers Association, the Association of Special Education Teachers, and the University of Sheffield. The special education project was launched as a private responsibility without the blessings of the Ministry of Education. The curriculum was developed by the local professionals in special education and validated by the University of Sheffield and taught by both qualified teacher educators from both countries. There were discussions with the director of the University of Sheffield programme prior to, and early on in the project on how we could develop the courses to meet the needs of the local teachers and students. To meet the competing interests of all stakeholders was a huge task for the program leadership, particularly Conrad, the critical individual involved in the early implementation of this project.

The professional as well as administrative duties, and this dual leadership, proved to be overwhelming at times, leading to many quick fixes and rush decisions that did not always work. With a large enrolment of teachers from special, elementary and secondary schools, and implementation on an on-going ad-hoc basis, many problems emerged that were not addressed by the leadership. This project would not have survived were it not for the commitment and support of the pioneers (Pedro & Conrad, 2006).

We were also very mindful that there were differing agendas according to stakeholders, and were adamant that we would avoid anything in policy or practice that might suggest neo-colonialism. These actions went a long way to affirming our trust in working in a truly collaborative relationship with a foreign university. It was important to consider that the external validating agency might be insensitive, or even hostile, to openness and equity among stakeholders engaged in collaborative practice with the partner body. More importantly, this project was important to the reform of education, and as critical individuals on this project, we were attentive to the notion that the leadership in Trinidad and Tobago should own the responsibility of administering and teaching the programme, we were also responsible for accountability to the validating university and so we had to support and ensure the project's success. Much effort was extended to ensure mutuality, a clear purpose and roles and to have a positive impact (Fletcher et al., 2011) on all constituents.

Explore the Possibilities

When we think of the possibilities for teacher education in the area of special education that existed in Trinidad and Tobago in the 1990s, we believe that it was the right time to introduce the special education teacher education initiative. Manasse (1986) advocates that with any new vision there should be the consideration of future developments and trends that can influence a system. There were many factors that were uppermost in the minds of the pioneers who launched the project, knowing that there were economic, social, and political considerations that would impact the future of the education system. We considered the needs of our students and the possible future expectations that would impact these students, however, I do not believe that much attention was paid to the possible changes in social, economic, political or technical areas (Manasse, 1986) that would impact the education of a large number of teachers in the area of special education.

Evidencing the characteristics of a community of practice (Wenger & Snyder, 2000) is a necessary condition for establishing partnerships and should form the guiding principles for successful collaboration. This community of practice includes a joint enterprise that is defined with specific roles and responsibilities, mutual relationships that are respected and nurtured and a well-honed repertoire of ways of reasoning with tools and artefacts available (Wenger & Snyder, 2000). Fletcher et al. (2011) share the idea that useful evaluative tools such as a mid-year review and a self-assessment summary can be used for accountability purposes.

This partnership offered us a chance to operationalize the vision and desires of a small group of committed educators to make possible the education of teachers equipped to teach students with special needs in an inclusive system. There were many of us in the leadership who were recognized as competent people and we understood the magnitude and complexity of what we were trying to accomplish (Fletcher et al., 2011). We had an articulation that allowed us to maintain coherence of action. There was put in place a local Board of Governance and a Curriculum Advisory Board and these bodies were charged with dealing with the financial aspects and curriculum implementation. These structures were in place to ensure that the programme was embedded on a sound foundation and for the provision of adequate resources. Although there were many challenges to the successful operation of the structures to manage the project, the teachers who were the constituents were motivated to complete their programme of studies and received their diplomas.

There were many economic and social aspects of the project that should have been monitored more closely, as well as the political implications for the future of the educators being equipped for special education positions. We were engrossed in the possibilities of educating teachers to fill a need, and we did so successfully. The challenges arose when it was time to place these teachers in the school system as special educators and to compensate them for their expertise. This process took a long time before a policy was put in place to create a new system of special education and remuneration for special education teachers in the school system.

Put It in Writing

As pioneers we knew what we wanted and articulated our vision clearly to everyone who would listen. It must have been well articulated because the project was accepted and accredited by University of Sheffield. The proposed vision and subsequent plan for a Diploma in Special and Inclusive Education was well designed and implemented based on information and data collected on the need for teacher education in special education. Much of the research was centred on the absence of such programs in the regional universities. The project was a culmination of many discussions by Conrad and other committed individuals who shared their vision and went out to secure a higher education institution outside of Trinidad and Tobago to create a collaboration that would result in the education of more than four hundred teachers. This was a vision that was enacted successfully.

THE EFFECTS OF EDUCATIONAL VISION IN SPECIAL EDUCATION TEACHER PREPARATION

The utilization of the special educators who came out of this programme in key roles to meet the needs of all special needs students in our school system is a major success for this programme. The majority of teachers who hold Masters and Diplomas in Education from the University of Sheffield are being utilized in the education system in Trinidad and Tobago as part of the multidisciplinary team in the various education districts. Special education programmes sponsored by the University of Sheffield has broadened and widened in its scope. Over the last few years, there was a Distance Education Masters programme that was initiated by the University of Sheffield and recently a doctoral programme was added. Other education programmes have been added and a centre established in the Caribbean and more comprehensive system has been put in place and other people are carrying on (Pedro & Conrad, 2006).

Current practices in Trinidad and Tobago are now very different to those prior to the practices of the 1989–98 period. The utilization of the special educators who came out of this programme and placed in key roles to meet the needs of all special needs students in our school system is a major success for this programme, which did not come easily. The teachers who now hold Masters and Diplomas in Education from the University of Sheffield are being used in the system as part of the multidisciplinary team in the various education districts. Many of the persons including the authors of this article have since left Trinidad and Tobago and have found success in the United States, Canada, Australia, New Zealand, England and other countries. This in most part, because they felt that their efforts went unnoticed by the decision makers, and that they were unable to implement many of the pedagogies learned (Pedro & Conrad, 2006). Further, the opportunities for upward mobility within the entrenched bureaucracy of Trinidad and Tobago's education system were significantly limited.

CHALLENGES TO EDUCATIONAL VISION AND CHANGE AND LESSONS LEARNED

There are many challenges that are significant to the implementation of any pilot programme and this project had its fair share of birthing pains. There should be relevance, readiness and resources at the start of any implementation, but as Fullan and Stiegelbauer (1991) point out it is not always possible to sort out these three elements in advance. A significant issue was the recognition of the certificate programme as accredited by the University of Sheffield. Teachers were frustrated and demotivated because it took a long time for them to be recognized and remunerated by the Ministry of Education. Although recognition and placement of special educators in schools have now become a reality, it was very frustrating for teachers who had invested heavily in their professional development to implement the knowledge and skills in schools without the structures in place or the recognition of their work. We applaud the resolve of the Teachers' Association to provide student loans to many of the teachers completing these studies. Two groups of teachers in the programme received their Diplomas and Masters from the University of Sheffield from 1992 and again in 1997. These teachers were working in the system and were not re-numerated or promoted during this time. The accreditation of the programme came in 1998.

Another area of weakness for the programme was that the educators involved tried to do everything, administrative and educational. It is important to separate administrative from academic functions and not implement the project until the support system for the administrative aspect is put in place. Conrad for example donated his academic library as a resource for teachers in the programme, and *tried* to do everything; be student-centered lecturer, program administrator, and advocate. This, while still holding his full-time position for the Ministry of Education. According to Fletcher et al. (2011) there should be mutuality and clarity of purposes, goals and roles so as to avoid becoming overwhelmed and engaging in cross-purposes with each other. Upfront and continuous communication and ongoing monitoring must also be maintained (Fletcher et al., 2011). At the time, these practices were often done on an ad-hoc basis that proved to stall the success of the project. We always found a way to keep the vision alive and we experienced the successful culmination of the programmes and preparation of cohorts of special education teachers.

In reflecting on the mission of the project, we are reminded that the vision and the mission should be maintained by the followership. It is important to recognize that the supporting institution may not be a part of the community vision and that they will have their own interests in maintaining a relationship with the community. With respect to the Sheffield initiative, it was important to treat our relationship with this university as cordial and business like so as to ensure that our interests were addressed. We needed to be alert to the commitment of all stakeholders in the partnership.

Another lesson learnt was that change is a process that can be painful because of the lack of support, and bureaucratic red tape. It takes transformative leadership to transmit a vision and see the vision through teamwork and sharing the vision. And transformative leadership is not synonymous with administrative efficiency. A firm belief that kept the team strong throughout the process was that that the power for success lies in the people and the tool is education. Education is not just career training; it is the means to liberation from our past thinking. Our teachers are our missionaries. They are the change agents who would help to transform the education system, however, many of them believe that they must serve the bureaucracy or their own selves and not the larger community. Our people must be educated to think community and to know "globally." Just as important is commitment, advocacy, responsiveness all those noble ethics can come to naught if one idealizes the problems or ignores the threats to the community. One must become political and be aware of the implications (Pedro & Conrad, 2006).

CONCLUSION

This chapter began with the question does education vision and change lead to success? and the answer to this question within the context of this discussion is undoubtedly yes. The success of this collaborative partnership to realize a vision that was grounded in the desire for change proved to transform the education of students with special needs in Trinidad and Tobago. Armstrong (2001) states this partnership could have been "generated and informed by critical self-reflection of all involved on the politics of knowledge and its uses in relation to broader socio-political relationships between nation, cultures and post-colonial identities" (p. 49).

In presenting this story of educational vision, responsiveness, and reform, there is a celebration of the will and dynamic action of the teaching fraternity that responded to the passionate spark led by the special educators at that time. There is an enduring hope that the teachers and teacher-leaders created by this initiative would continue to explore and expand on the reform efforts needed to have a system of education that is adequate, available, and accessible to all students. I can state that the pioneers who enacted this vision in teacher education believed that the 'fire' of reform must be kept burning in our twin island republic as we continue to meet the educational needs of our children.

REFERENCES

Armstrong, D. (2001). Developing the potential for distance learning modalities for teacher education. In *Rethinking teacher education professionalism in the Caribbean context,* Conference Proceedings. UK: University of Sheffield.

Blokker, J. W. (1989). *Vision, visibility, symbols.* Everett, WA: Professional Development Institute.

Fletcher, S., Watkins, A., Gless, J., & Villarreal-Carman, T. (2011). *Partnerships for new teacher Learning: A guide for universities and school districts.* New York, NY: Teachers College Press.

Fullan, M. (1993). *Change forces: Probing the depths of educational reform.* London, UK: Falmer Press.

Fullan, M. G., & Miles, M. B. (1992). Getting reform right: What works and what doesn't. *Phi Delta Kappan, 73,* 745–52.

Fullan, M., & Stiegelbauer (1991) *The new meaning of educational change* (2nd. ed). New York, NY: Teachers College Press, Columbia University.

Knowles, G. J., & Cole, A. L. (1996). Letters and reflections on our first year as beginning professors–And a letter to deans of education. *Teacher Education Quarterly*, Summer 1996.

Lavia, J. (1998). The case of a visionary teacher; An interview with Dennis Conrad. In J. Lavia & D. Armstrong (Eds.), *Teachers' voices from the Caribbean* (pp. 14–20). Sheffield, UK: Sheffield Papers in Education.

Manasse, A. L. (1986). Vision and leadership: Paying attention to intention. *Peabody Journal of Education, 63(1),* 150–73.

Marge, M. 1984. *Report on the National Survey of Handicapped Children and Youth in Trinidad and Tobago.* OAS/National Project in Special Education and Rehabilitation of the handicapped. Port of Spain: Ministry of Education.

Méndez-Morse, S. (1993). Vision, leadership, and change. *Issues about Change, 2*(3). Southwest Educational Development Laboratory. Austin, TX.

Nanus, B. (1992). *Visionary leadership: Creating a compelling sense of direction for your organization.* San Francisco, CA: Jossey-Bass.

Pedro, J., & Conrad, D. (2006). Special education in Trinidad and Tobago: Educational vision and change. *Childhood Education, International Focus Issue, 82*(6), 324–326.

Pejza, J. P. (1985, April). *The Catholic school principal: A different kind of leader.* Paper presented at the Annual Meeting of the National Catholic Educational Association, St. Louis, Missouri.

Rogus, J. F. (1990). *Developing a vision statement—Some consideration for principals. NASSP Bulletin, 74*(523), 6–12.

Seeley, D. S. (1992, April). *Visionary leaders for reforming public schools.* Paper presented at the Annual Meeting of the American Educational Research Association, San Francisco, California.

Wenger, E. C., & Snyder, W. M. (2000). Communities of practices, the organizational frontier. *Harvard Business Review, 78(1),* 139–45.

CHAPTER 3

TOWARDS INCLUSIVE EDUCATION IN TRINIDAD AND TOBAGO

Policy Challenges and Implications

Elna Carrington Blaides and Dennis Conrad

In Trinidad and Tobago, the term inclusive and special education has emerged as an ideological compromise as the society grapples with questions of transition, fusion, and future. The compromise is a fusion of the notion that all students cannot be adequately served in the same environment, that those students diagnosed with a special need should be treated differently in a different environment. On the other hand, inclusive education in the Trinidad and Tobago context holds to the notion of strategizing so that all can be educated in the same environment. In this discourse, inclusive and special education, special education, and inclusive education are used to add clarity to issues being considered at various times in unique socio-historical contexts. This chapter reviews and highlights systemic and attitudinal changes in the policy and practice of special education in Trinidad and Tobago since 1980, and makes recommendations for future practice and research. A national survey of children with disabilities was spearheaded by Dr. Michael Marge of Syracuse University in the early 1980s under the auspices of the

Caribbean Discourse in Inclusive Education:
Historical and Contemporary Issues, pages 33–49.
Copyright © 2017 by Information Age Publishing
All rights of reproduction in any form reserved.

Organization of American States (Marge, 1984) While re-focusing on the Marge Report, some crucial questions arise—specifically, the following inquiries are addressed in this discussion: What are the key developments in inclusive and special education policy and practice in Trinidad and Tobago over the last 30 years? What is the current state of inclusive and special education policy and practice in Trinidad and Tobago? And what are the policy and practice issues impinging on the future agenda for inclusive and special education in Trinidad and Tobago? In response to these questions, developments globally will be revisited with a focus on the local environment. The current successes and challenges in the inclusive and special education environment and the future agenda for policy development, implementation and evaluation will be explored in light of what currently exists.

DEVELOPMENTS

The Global Agenda

An understanding of inclusive education in context cannot exclude awareness of its genesis in the rights-based movement. The Universal Declaration of Human Rights (1948) Article 26(1) stated that everyone has the right to education, education shall be free, at least in the elementary and fundamental stages. Elementary education shall be compulsory (Universal Declaration of Human Rights, 1948). The United Nations Convention on the Rights of the Child statement asserts that all children should receive an education without discrimination on any grounds. In 1990, the Jomtien World Conference on Education for All established the goal of Education for All (EFA). The Salamanca Statement and Framework for Action on Special Needs Education (UNESCO, 1994) reaffirmed these positions, stating that "... schools should accommodate all children regardless of their physical, intellectual, social, emotional linguistic or other conditions ... this should include disabled and gifted children, street and working children from remote or nomadic populations, children from linguistic, ethnic or cultural minorities and children from other marginalized areas or groups (UNESCO, 2005, p. 14). Inclusive education is defined, according to the UNESCO documents, as a process of addressing and responding to the diversity of needs of all learners through increasing participation in learning, culture, and communities, reducing exclusion within and from education. Inclusive education involves modifications to approaches, content, and strategies that share a common vision for all children optimally learning within the regular education system.

Globally inclusive education and special education are culturally defined. The current needs in each country, together with available resources, determine how inclusive and special education are practiced; as each context varies, so does the practice of inclusive and special education. The global north-south divide is conceptualized as a division between the wealthy more developed nations such as the United States, Canada, western Europe and developed parts of east Asia and the poorer southern countries including Africa, Latin America, and developing Asia.

In the poorer countries of the global south, one might observe the practice of inclusive education as being limited, under-resourced, and focused on individuals with disabilities. In contrast, countries of the global north, which tend to be resource rich, provide more evidence of effective inclusion and focus on overcoming barriers to participation, learning, and development for all children.

INCLUSIVE AND SPECIAL EDUCATION IN TRINIDAD AND TOBAGO

Historical Perspective

Education systems in the Anglophone Caribbean have maintained the structures of the "mother country"; it is only through radical and sustained nationalistic effort that any change in the typical post-colonial legacy emerged. Unlike Guyana, Jamaica, and Cuba; Trinidad and Tobago have mostly maintained the legacy of its former colonial ruler, a legacy that has handed down an elitist system that is deeply examination-oriented and focused on rewards for small percentages of the brightest citizens. Currently, Trinidad and Tobago remains committed to a seamless non-differentiated education system where an educational service to the population is provided by networks of government, denominational and private organizations, even as a legacy of differentiation and exclusion persists. Hence, the post-colonial legacy in Trinidad and Tobago along the path of development of inclusive and special education in Trinidad and Tobago reflects challenges and milestones related primarily to access and quality (Jules, 2008). In the transition period from colonial dominance to full self-governance, two extremely differing schools of thoughts developed. On the one hand, there was the thinking that only a primary education is required for the masses. The other view supported the notion that a highly educated workforce was needed for economic, social and political progress; education is seen as a way forward for successful decolonization (Lavia, 2008). Even though the latter view seemed to be dominant, the historical marginalization, and oppression of people with special needs persisted well into the 1980s. The continued marginalization was ample justification for gathering baseline data that would guide policy development for the nation's children and youth with special needs. There were some policy reports that impacted the development of special and inclusive education in Trinidad and Tobago. A summary of the major contents and intended impact of key policy reports follow.

The Winschel Report

This report was presented to the government in 1979, and served as a significant catalyst to national policy development for inclusive and special education in Trinidad and Tobago. James Winschel was the chairperson of a special education team comprising scholars and administrators associated with the Organization of American States (OAS), Syracuse University, Partners of the Americas, and the Ministry of Education (and Culture). The team met with and interviewed, key and exemplary educational, special educational, health, voluntary, and religious stakeholders. The report's focus was on reviewing the existing state of services to the targeted population, then identified as the "handicapped," and estimating the extent of these conditions, in particular, sensory, intellectual and orthopaedic impairments. In addition, Winschel made recommendations to government and other affiliated agencies on appropriate prevention and intervention strategies. The report argued that to invest monies into a survey to estimate populations would be professionally unfeasible, costly, and unnecessarily delay needed action (Winschel, 1979). He recommended immediate policy planning, development, and implementation to determine appropriate definitions of disabilities. Winschel argued that enhanced educational services and resources to meet the needs of ALL students including those in rural communities would create the needed database. This would comprise knowledgeable personnel, shape a service delivery system to elementary and secondary schools, special education training. In addition to, developing more inclusive curricula, the approach would engage parents as stakeholders, accelerate prevention and identification programmes, enhance planning and cooperation between related ministries and institutions.

Following the Winschel report, the government proceeded with the development of a Special Education Unit. The discouraged National Survey of Handicapped Children and Youth in Trinidad and Tobago (Marge, 1984), commonly referred to as the "Marge Report" followed soon after.

Special Education Unit

The creation of the Special Education Unit in 1981 at the Ministry of Education was a positive response to the needs of students with disabilities. The Unit served in a supervisory capacity for established special schools, most of which were receiving government assistance at that time. These schools comprised the Cascade School for the Deaf (established in 1942); the Santa Cruz School for the Blind (est. 1952); the Princess Elizabeth School for the Physically Handicapped (est. 1953); the Wharton-Patrick School (est. 1958); the Audrey Jeffers School for the Deaf (est. 1967); and the Lady Hochoy Homes/Schools for the Mentally Retarded (the first of four schools established in 1961). When the Pointe-à-Pierre Government Special School serving students with multiple disabilities was established in 1988, it was also subsumed within the Unit's authority (Conrad & Conrad, 2007).

Despite some exemplary leadership, the Unit faced many challenges, such as the lack of qualified human resources to identify and assess the level of need in students. Another factor was the inadequacy of teacher training and professional development for special education teachers. This was compounded by the categorical model of pedagogical interventions, where teachers were being prepared and expecting to teach students with Visual Impairments/Blind, Hearing Impairments/Deaf, Physical Impairments, Intellectual Impairments [then called Mentally Retarded], Emotional Disorders and so on. There were also turf issues between special education personnel and guidance officers, impacting on job mobility and incentives. Further, the economics and politics of educational reform appeared to conspire with the philosophies of some curriculum officers. As a result there was resistance to the evolving role of special educators and the Unit. The status quo seemed to reinforce a deficit model of disability, where the problems were either the students or parents, rather than a matter of educational and personnel organization resourcefulness, and sustainability. This eventually led to the subsuming of special education under student support services.

Exemplary Pioneers

The history of special education services in Trinidad and Tobago is incomplete without a clear recognition that its evolution was not shaped primarily by the state's innovations and commitment to educational equity. It is also important to highlight the efforts of individual volunteers, benefactors, parents, and educators. The following presents a sample of the persons who advocated for students with disabilities and others that were marginalized in Trinidad and Tobago.

Nesta Patrick. Dr Patrick has been a pioneer in several areas of social work including Rape Crisis in the Caribbean but is celebrated for her work with students with developmental, intellectual, and emotional disabilities. She established and later became principal of the School for the Mentally Handicapped at St Ann's Hospital [which later became the Wharton-Patrick School] and led the teaching of slow learners in the regular education system, organizing seminars for teachers in primary schools (Pidduck, 2012, "Grande Dame for All Children," para. 10).

Errol Pilgrim. Pilgrim was the second principal at the school for the blind in Santa Cruz. He characterized limitless vision and stewardship not just for students with visual disabilities but also for those with other types of impairments. Errol emphasized the importance of service delivery, the role of organization and teacher education for students with disabilities. He inspired many, including Dennis Conrad and Launcelot Brown; reminding them about the importance of service to community and that those in leadership are only there for a finite period.

Other leaders. Other stalwarts who epitomized commitment to and resilience in special education were Wallace Pedro, Special Education Supervisor and former principal of Cascade School for the Deaf; Claris Manswell, former principal of the Princess Elizabeth Centre; Beulah Byron-Reece, former principal at the Cascade School for the Deaf; the Carmelite Sisters including Sir Antoinette Dickie and Antoinette Fahey for their work with the Lady Hochoy Schools; Merle Gay, former principal Wharton-Patrick [originally School for the Mentally Handicapped] and president of the Child Welfare League. These exemplars, along with the bureaucratic skills of Kathryn Donaldson-Baptiste and Darnley Gittens special education supervisors at the Special Education Unit, each contributed in no small measure to the evolution of current special education services. Launcelot Brown and Joan Pedro are also among those who made significant contributions to special education leadership.

Exemplars however are not exclusive to those associated with the Government's special education system. In Tobago, Eileen Guilleame and other outstanding members of the Tobago Council for the Handicapped and at the Plymputh School for the Deaf pressed forward. Esla Lynch of Eshe's Learning Center; Beth Harry and the Immortelle Center; Charis Works developed by Joy Sampath; Fr. Gerry Pantin and the Servol Life Centers; and more recent advocates in Autism, Down Syndrome, Special Olympics and other agencies were instrumental in urging for reform to special education and to service delivery models.

There is need to research, document, and celebrate the many who gave, whether through voluntary associations, the Trinidad and Tobago Unified Teachers Association and its Special Education Committee, the Special Education Advsory Committee, Goodwill Industries, or others. This does not in any way represent a comprehensive list of major contributors to the development of special education services.

The Marge Report

Despite not being recommended by the Winchel Report, a National Survey was requested by the Ministry of Education in 1981. The Survey was completed in collaboration with the Organization of American States (OAS) consultant Michael Marge of Syracuse University, who was a member of the Winschel team. Marge worked along with local education exemplar Majorie Parkinson, and other stakeholders from the Special Education Unit and the Advisory Committee on Special Education. The Survey was commissioned for two primary reasons. First, it sought to shape policy for resource building, necessary for improving services for students with disabilities; and second, it sought to facilitate programme development for the prevention of disabilities in children and youth ages three through sixteen (Marge, 1984). The primary outcomes of the Survey indicated that overall some 16.1 percent of children and youth had a disability. This was disaggregated by disability type, in the following categories: Physical Disabilities, 1.7 percent; Hearing Impairments (all severities), 4.6 percent; Visual Disabilities (severe), 7 percent; Speech and Language (moderate and severe), 4.1 percent; Mental Retardation [now Intellectual Impairments], 1 percent; Learning Disabilities, 2 percent; and Mentally Handicapped [now a Mental Health Condition], 2 percent. These prevalence estimates were used to develop a plan for training special education personnel by area of disability. Some 661 special educators with expertise in various disability types were to be trained over six years. This number, it was projected would add much-needed expertise to the then 75 special education personnel. A plan was outlined to develop a national programme of primary and secondary prevention of the occurrence of new cases of disability. The plan included key personnel such as physicians, social workers, and special educators. Also included were key agencies such as the Ministry of Health, the Ministry of Education, hospitals and clinics (Marge, 1984).

Trinidad and Tobago/Manitoba/CIDA Sensitization Project

Largely through the efforts of Wallace Pedro and Winston Rampaul, the work of the Trinidad and Tobago/ University of Manitoba/Canadian International Development Agency's Sensitization Special Education Project 1987–90 was realized. This collaborative project sensitized and trained regular and special education teachers in classroom management and differentiated instruction. The project emphasized teacher attitudes, responsive teaching and school organization, and localized support. It had some positive impact on the public and teachers' attitudes toward students with disabilities. Further, it supplemented the effort and enhanced the successes of the Schools for the Blind and the Deaf as they made efforts at integration. A new set of potential educational leaders emerged, who recognized the power of collaborative practice. According to Rampaul, Freeze, and McCorkell (1991), along with this wave of enthusiasm, "two noteworthy events have occurred ... laying the foundation for long-lasting and positive changes in quality education ... a] National Task Force ... and] a National Consultation on Special Education" (p. 52).

The Sensitization Project, which targeted school supervisors, principals, special education teachers and regular education teachers, eventually served to improve skills and resource delivery to more than 477 participants over no less than 375 hours. This, despite limitations that included time constraints, restrictively centralized curricula, large school populations and resistance and reluctance by some teachers to accept peers without university evidenced qualifications in any consultative capacity (Rampaul, Freeze, & McCorkell, 1991).

The Pilgrim Report

1990 may have been the golden year for special education policy as there were sustained interest and innovative practice resulting from special education advocacy. The Pilgrim Report (Pilgrim, 1990)—also known as the Report of the National Consultation on Special Education—proposed the unification of special and general education. The Report emphasized a philosophy whereby all students with special needs have the right to "full opportunity for self-development in a wholesome educational environment" (p. 57); and equal education treatment in the "most productive and least restrictive environment" (p. 58).

The White Paper

The Education Policy Paper (1993–2003), (Trinidad and Tobago, National Task Force on Education, 1994), also referred to as the White Paper, devoted much attention to the provision of access and the opportunity to students of *all* abilities for the development of individual talents. Quoting from the earlier Education Plan 1985 to 1990, the Policy or White Paper reiterates: "our greatest hope for the future lies in the full development of the potential of its children":

This Plan [1993–2003] recognizes that individuals with Special needs, like any other person, are entitled to opportunities for education, work, happiness, and leisure. Education should enable the special needs child to overcome, minimize the effects of his/her disability and develop to his/her fullest potential. It should also prepare all others in the society to accept and to interrelate positively with the disabled (Trinidad and Tobago, National Task Force on Education, 1994, p. 62)

Overall, the White Paper endorsed the Pilgrim's report but went further towards service delivery. It recommended the establishment of Regional Diagnostic/Prescriptive Centres with multidisciplinary teams; teacher education in special education that includes parental involvement and collaboration; the retention of special schools to be used as education support centres; that regular schools be required to articulate their plans for meeting the needs of their students with special needs; and an increase in inclusive education opportunities.

TASETT/TTUTA/ University of Sheffield Project

From 1989, efforts were made to enhance teacher education opportunities associated with human capital development. Teacher Education as identified by these earlier policy documents (such as the Winschel Report and the White Paper) was a key strategy in addressing special education and the more recent inclusive education. Before 1990, training for special education teachers was the result of a few committed individuals, chief among them being Nesta Patrick. However, starting in 1990, the Association for Special Education pioneered a collaborative teacher training effort with the University of Sheffield and the Trinidad and Tobago Unified Teachers' Association (TTUTA). This project had emerged along with, and was inspired by, these same reports, initiatives, and policies—namely the Winschel, Marge, and Pilgrim Reports, The White Paper, and the pioneering spirit of earlier special educators as mentioned. Dennis Conrad, mentored primarily by Nesta Patrick, and Errol Pilgrim had a rich understanding of the education policies at that time. Conrad was both Chair of the Special Education Committee of the Trinidad and Tobago Unified Teachers Association Special Education Committee (TTUTA-SEC), as well as the president of The Association for Special Education of Trinidad and Tobago (TASETT). During his period of service on the Advisory Board for Special Education, Conrad lobbied the University of the West Indies- St Augustine for teacher education-special education programme development. Despite meaningful and collegial discussions, developing such a programme in special education was slow to come to fruition. Instead a project with Sheffield University, where Conrad had completed his Masters of Education degree was embarked upon and this lead to the creation of the Diploma in Special Education and a Master's in Education with a focus on special education. These programmes were offered by TTUTA/TASETT/Sheffield University to practising teachers and graduated more than 300 special education teachers in Trinidad and Tobago. This initiative was embraced by large numbers of teachers in all sectors of the education system in Trinidad and Tobago. Since this effort, other education programs were added including a doctorate; and a Center was established in the Caribbean (Pedro & Conrad, 2006).

Other key international developments, such as the passage of the UNESCO initiative Education for All (EFA) in 1990, began to have an impact on inclusive education in Trinidad and Tobago by encouraging the training of special education teachers and a few related services professionals. Over a five-year period, more than 100 special education teachers earned Diplomas and Masters of Education degrees across a varied spectrum of levels, from early childhood to secondary education. This initiative followed unsuccessful, although promising, efforts to create a special education training programme with the University of the West Indies. The local expectation was that students with and without special needs would be entitled to rights previously respected by only some nations (UNESCO, 1990). It was hoped that EFA would have facilitated a free and appropriate public education (FAPE), education in the least restrictive environment (LRE), and Zero Reject—for students in Trinidad and Tobago. Further, the World Conference on Special Needs Education, held in Salamanca, Spain, in 1994, adopted and detailed the EFA principles for all students with special needs. In the Trinidad and Tobago context, the realization of expectations after the passage of the EFA initiative has been slow in coming.

SUCCESSES AND CHALLENGES

Student Support Services Division

By early 2000, the efforts of the Special Education Unit were being significantly hampered by bureaucracy. There was a growing perspective of and resistance by many within the Ministry of Education that special education is a function of curricula, and that services could be delivered therein. Efforts to expand the Unit were stymied largely because of inadequate leadership—the position of coordinator was never filled. Eventually, in 2004, the Unit was incorporated into the Student Support Services Division (SSSD). The SSSD comprises of Guidance and Counselling, School Social Work, and Special Education/Diagnostic Prescriptive Services (Trinidad and Tobago, 2004). All institutional and special private schools are supervised through the SSSD.

UTT and UWI Initiatives

A major push by the government of Trinidad and Tobago to train special education teachers began in 2007 with the introduction of the B.Ed. Special Education at the University of Trinidad and Tobago (UTT). The first cohort of 24 students graduated in 2011. A Masters in Inclusive and Special Education began in 2012 at the University of the West Indies (UWI) with a cohort of 27 students. This first cohort graduated in 2014. The University of the Southern Caribbean (USC), while not offering a programme in special education does provide an introductory level course to its undergraduate BSc-Elementary Education and Education Service degrees; and an equivalent within the BSc (Social Work) and BSc (Psychology). These programmes at the tertiary level at the UTT, UWI and USC, continue to be the major source of training for teachers in inclusive and special education.

Emerging Challenges

In the post-colonial period, which started in 1962 when Trinidad and Tobago become an independent nation, up to the present time, the challenges of education reform focused on access and quality. Today's reality is that the challenge of education reform is becoming increasingly more social (Jules, 2008). There exists a dearth of data related to prevalence estimates for children and youth with special educational needs in Trinidad and Tobago. A study which examined only one area of special education need, emotional and behavioral disorders examined a random sample of 80 school-age students from 23 primary schools across Trinidad and Tobago. It was estimated that the prevalence of emotional and behavioral disorders in the school-age population in Trinidad and Tobago is currently at 36.5 percent (Carrington-Blaides, 2013). Additionally, there is a need to reassess particular obstacles to the prevention of difficulties and disabilities in children and youth. These challenges include, but are not limited to, implications of HIV/AIDS, the widespread use of illicit drugs among children and youth, and a pervasive lack of resources—both human and financial.

THE CURRENT STATE OF INCLUSIVE AND SPECIAL EDUCATION IN TRINIDAD AND TOBAGO

The initial hope was that the deficiency exposed by the National Survey of Handicapped Children and Youth in Trinidad and Tobago, Marge (1984), and the Pilgrim Report (Pilgrim, 1990), would lead to the formulation and subsequent implementation of appropriate policy initiatives in special and inclusive education. The challenge of implementing a policy to effect social change begins with the realization that the term policy is not defined in any uniform way. Guba (1984) further suggests that there are eight different definitions of policy. In summary, his suggestions were that policy can be described as goals or intents, standing decisions, a guide to discretionary action, problem-solving strategy, sanctioned behavior, norms of conduct, output of the policy-making system and construction based on experience. Guba (1984, 1985) contended that there are three types of policy into which the eight definitions of policy could be categorized: policy-in-intension (policy framers or legislators) which includes policy defined as goals or intents, standing decisions, guide to discretionary action, problem-solving strategy, policy-in-implementation (policy implementers) which includes policy defined as sanctioned behavior, norms of conduct, output of the policy making system, and policy-in-experience (policy beneficiaries) which includes policy defined as construction based on experience.

Policy Classifications

Policy-in-implementation. Even as teacher attitudes are mostly positive towards inclusive education, much work remains outstanding in the area of teacher and related services personnel development. Here, the major constraining factors being a combination of limited economic resources, the capacity and will of key professionals to develop inclusive and special education programmes.

Policy-in-experience. The preceding reality makes identifying persons with invisible disabilities an ongoing challenge because of the shortage of competent personnel to source and conduct assessments (Reynolds & Fletcher-Janzen, 2007).

Policy-in-intension. It must be noted that in spite of contextualized notions of inclusive education one should not disregard the prevailing global contention which suggests that inclusive education is a means to the attainment of a just and equitable society where fundamental human rights are upheld. Further, the principles of human rights, equity, and social justice must be recognized as critical to inclusive educational policy and practice (Armstrong & Barton, 2007; Slee & Allan, 2001).

Guba (1984) further contends that policy definition determines policy questions, data collected, data sources, methodology and policy products. An analysis of two policy initiatives, subsequent to the Marge and Pilgrim Reports, will be undertaken. A summary of this analysis is presented in Table 3.1. These reports, the Education Policy Paper (Trinidad and Tobago, National Task Force on Education, 2004) and the Draft Special Education Policy (Trinidad and Tobago, 2013) define policy as an assertion of intents or goals. Both documents speak of inclusive and special education.

The Education Policy Paper (Trinidad and Tobago, National Task Force on Education, 2004) in Section 3.30, Special Needs, recognizes that children with special needs have a fundamental right to opportunities for education, work, happiness, and leisure, while acknowledging that physical and social barriers that have their genesis in ignorance, indifference and fear have prevented children with special needs from participating fully and developing to their fullest potential. Three broad goals of the special needs policy are identified:

- To facilitate an appropriate curriculum, educational climate, as well as the requisite support services for those with special educational needs;
- To provide information and support for the immediate family of those with special needs; and
- To develop and implement public educational programmes targeting the larger society.

Similarly, the Draft Special Education policy (Trinidad and Tobago, 2013) identifies the following goals:

- To outline a clearly defined approach to special education in Trinidad and Tobago;
- To establish a framework for the efficient and cohesive delivery of services to learners/students with special education needs;
- To develop an integrated system (and effective mechanisms) for the early identification, assessment and subsequent provision of relevant interventions for learners/students with special education needs;
- To delineate the range of services and service delivery /placement options to be made available for students identified as having special education needs;
- To create a platform for continuous, meaningful dialogue and consultation with all stakeholders involved in special education service provision; and
- To provide an effective mechanism for accountability and redress for families of children with special education needs.

The objectives stated as emerging from the Draft Special Education Policy (Trinidad and Tobago, 2013) have not provided the framework to measure the success of the stated goals. Also, there is much uncertainty as to what will be done and how it will be accomplished. In contrast the earlier document, Education Policy Paper (Trinidad and Tobago, National Task Force on Education, 2004) clearly outlines the following objectives:

- Formation of Regional Diagnostic Prescriptive Centres (RDPC);
- Each centre to have a multidisciplinary team consisting of a special education officer, a psychologist, school social work and nurse;
- Regional Diagnostic Prescriptive Centres to engage in community sensitisation to prompt positive responses to students with special needs;
- The MOE and the UWI (St. Augustine Campus) to initiate a programme of training in special education which will include training in diagnosis for effective performance in specialist resource rooms;
- Mainstreaming of all children with special needs except in severe cases;
- All schools to articulate a plan for students with special needs;
- Special schools to be retained and used as resource centres; and
- The introduction of objectives as pilot projects in two selected districts

The summary presented in Table 3.1 allows for quick comparison of the two policy initiatives, there is much more content, description and detail provided by the intended policy products of the Education Policy Paper (Trinidad and Tobago, National Task Force on Education, 2004) which begs the question; has emphasis on the provision of special education resources declined in recent years, specifically from 2013 and onwards?

Today, inclusive education in Trinidad and Tobago is viewed as being not mainly about the placement of categories of students with special needs but more about the effective and sustained teaching and learning of all students (Trinidad

TABLE 3.1. Analysis of Education Policy Paper (1993-2003) and Draft Special Education Policy (2013).

Item	Education Policy Paper (1993–2003)	Draft Special Education Policy (2013)
Policy Question	What are the key products of Education Policy Paper	What are the key products of the Inclusive Education Policy Paper
Data collected	Special Education Statistics	Special Education Statistics
Data Sources	Stakeholders: education professionals, heads of agencies, community members, and staff of several ministries	Stakeholders: education professionals, heads of agencies, community members, and staff of several ministries
Methodology	Surveys, interviews, observations	Surveys, interviews, observations
Policy Product	Establishment of Regional Diagnostic Prescriptive Centres (RDPC) in each educational district	Adequate and reasonable provision for students identified as having a special educational need
	The Ministry of Education and the University of the West Indies to initiate a program that will include training in diagnosis for effective performance in specialist resource rooms for students with special educational needs	

Note: Definition of Policy: Policy is an assertion of intents or goals (Guba, 1984).

and Tobago, May 21, 2004). The current Inclusive Education Policy (Trinidad and Tobago, 2009) advanced by the government of Trinidad and Tobago states:

> Inclusive education is a developmental process of addressing and responding to the diversity of needs of all learners through increasing participation in learning, cultures and communities. (p. 3)

The policy describes a commitment to Inclusive Education in the context of a seamless education system. The emphasis is on the provision of services and support while making education "available, accessible, acceptable and adaptable" (Trinidad and Tobago, 2009).

In a national survey that focused on assessing the readiness of Trinidad and Tobago to implement inclusive education policy, Miske Witt and Associates (2008) implied that TT was not optimally ready for Inclusive Education. The report of the survey reported that:

- Teacher attitudes toward inclusive education were extremely positive, but 90 percent of teachers reported that they had no qualifications in special needs education;

46 • ELNA CARRINGTON BLAIDES & DENNIS CONRAD

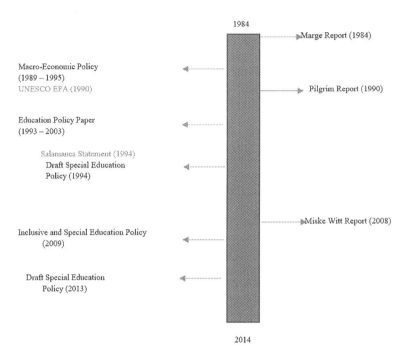

FIGURE 3.1. Trinidad and Tobago Inclusive Education Policy and Policy Research Evolution Timeline (1984 through 2014).

- Forty-one percent 'understand well,' with 45 percent of the teachers only understanding 'somewhat what is necessary to teach in an inclusive classroom';
- Many teachers cited assessment and collaboration as two skills they have already developed to work with diverse learners in their classrooms. Other survey items indicate that teachers lack other skills of inclusive education pedagogy;
- Only 3 percent of teachers had a lot of knowledge about Individualised Education Programmes (IEPs)—21 percent had some knowledge; and
- Seven percent of respondents had a lot of experience with curriculum differentiation;
- Forty percent had some knowledge.

THE FUTURE AGENDA FOR INCLUSIVE EDUCATION IN TRINIDAD AND TOBAGO

The current situation in Trinidad and Tobago underpinned by rigid conformity to an inherited post-colonial paradigm is characterized by policy instability often based on fancied notions of the government of the day. This reality raises the issue of how inclusive education can build on and expand policy frameworks, when each time there is political change there is an equal or greater change in inclusive education policy and provision. Thus, setting the future agenda for inclusive education in Trinidad and Tobago does not require definitional accuracy. Instead, issues related to practical political power must be resolved about social realities locally, regionally and globally (Armstrong, Armstrong, & Spandagou, 2011). In addition to adopting the central principles of human rights, equity and social justice (Armstrong & Barton, 2007; Slee & Allan, 2001), the future agenda for inclusive education in Trinidad and Tobago must consider that successful educational reform includes the following three characteristics: Being Strategic and sustainable; Being ongoing and thorough; and Involving all stakeholders and creating new partnerships (Jules, 2008).

Currently, the Student Support Services of the Ministry of Education in Trinidad and Tobago has outlined a draft special education policy with little mention of inclusive education and the relationship between special education and inclusive education in the Trinidad and Tobago context. There is, therefore, an urgent need to articulate a clear and focused national policy for inclusive and special education that relates to overarching visions and missions and that would position inclusive and special education in the rightful local, regional and global space. Special education provision should be recognized as fluid and dynamic. Such provision is required mainly because of the absence of appropriate and adequate resources within the education system. To successfully expand and develop inclusive and special education, the need for organizational restructuring, critical praxis, responsive community-centred leadership, and collaboration among professionals in the field, at home and in the Trinidad and Tobago, the Diaspora, must be given more than lip-service. Of greater significance, compared to more effective inclusive education practices in the global north, are the historical and cultural experiences of Trinidad and Tobago. These contexts, and these experiences, have created a unique landscape allowing opportunities to use localized approaches and innovation to address inclusive education policy and practice in Trinidad and Tobago. Among issues for consideration, one key area is rethinking initial teacher preparation to include the capacity to provide service not only to children with disabilities, but also a range of other marginalized groups. Another pressing imperative is the urgent need to manage the knowledge created and innovations made within Trinidad and Tobago, the region, and the Diaspora so that benefits redound to the Trinidad and Tobago education system; and specifically to all aspects of inclusive and special education.

REFERENCES

Armstrong, F., & Barton, L. (2007). Policy, experience and change and the challenge of inclusive education: The case of England. In L. Barton & F. Armstrong (Eds.), *Policy, experience and change: Cross-cultural reflections on inclusive education (pp. 5–18). Dordretch, NL: Springer.

Armstrong, D., Armstrong, A. C., & Spandagou, I. (2011). Inclusion: By choice or chance? *International Journal of Inclusive Education, 15(1)*, 29–39.

Carrington-Blaides, E. (2013). *Prevalence estimates of special educational needs: A focus on emotional and behaviour disorders* [PowerPoint presentation]. Retrieved from http://www.uwispace.sta.uwi.edu/dspace/handle/2139/15703

Conrad, D. A., & Conrad, D. J. (2007). Testimonies of exemplary Caribbean women educational leaders. *Advancing Women in Leadership, 24*, N_A.

Guba, E. G. (1984). The effect of definitions of policy on the nature and outcomes of policy analysis. *Educational Leadership, 42(2)*, 63–70.

Guba, E. G. (1985). What can happen as a result of a policy? *Review of Policy Research, 5*, 11–16. doi: 10.1111/j.1541-1338.1985.tb00003.x

Jules, D. (2008). Rethinking education for the Caribbean: A radical approach. *Comparative Education, 44(2)*, 203–214. doi:10.1080/03050060802041142

Lavia, J. (2008). Inclusive education in Trinidad and Tobago. In L. Barton & F. Armstrong (Eds.), *Policy, experience and change: Cross-Cultural Reflections on Inclusive Education* (pp. 107–122). London, UK: Springer.

Marge, M. (1984). *Report on the survey of the incidence of handicapping conditions in children between the ages of 3 and 16 in Trinidad and Tobago*. Trinidad and Tobago: Organization of American States.

Miske Witt & Associates. (2008). *Achieving inclusion: Transforming the education system of Trinidad and Tobago: Final report*. Saint Paul, MN: Author.

Pedro, J., & Conrad, D. (2006). Special education in Trinidad and Tobago: Education, vision and change. *Childhood Education, 82*, 324–326.

Pidduck, A. (2012, September 9). Grande Dame to all children. *Trinidad and Tobago Newsday*. Retrieved from http://www.newsday.co.tt/features/print,0,166018.html

Pilgrim, E. (1990). *Report of the collation and evaluation committee for the development and implementation of a national special education system for Trinidad and Tobago*. National Consultation on Special Education of Trinidad and Tobago.

Rampaul, W., Freeze, R., & McCorkell, V. (1991). The improvement in education in developing countries: One possible approach. *European Journal of Special Needs Education, 6(1)*, 37–55.

Reynolds, C. R., & Fletcher-Janzen, E. (Eds.). (2007). *Encyclopaedia of special education* (Vols. 1–3). Hoboken, NJ: Wiley.

Slee, R., & Allan, J. (2001). Excluding the included: A reconsideration of inclusive education, *International Studies in Sociology of Education, 11(2)*, 173–192. doi: 10.1080/09620210100200073

Trinidad and Tobago. (1989). *Macro-economic policy medium term (1989–1995)*. Port of Spain, Trinidad: Ministry of Education.

Trinidad and Tobago. (2004, May 21). *Draft national special education policy*. Port of Spain, Trinidad and Tobago: Ministry of Education.

Trinidad and Tobago. (2009). *Inclusive education policy*. Port of Spain, Trinidad: Ministry of Education.

Trinidad and Tobago. (2013). *Draft special education policy*. Port of Spain, Trinidad and Tobago: Ministry of Education.

Trinidad and Tobago, National Task Force on Education. (1994). *Education policy paper (1993–2003) (White Paper)*. Port of Spain, Trinidad: Ministry of Education.

Universal Declaration of Human Rights. (1948). Retrieved 1/12/2014 from http://www.un.org/en/documents/udhr/

UNESCO. (1990). *World declaration on education for all*. Paris, France: UNESCO. Retrieved from http://www.unesco.orgretrieved July 17, 2014

UNESCO. (1994). *The Salamanca statement and framework for action on special needs education*. Salamanca, Spain: UNESCO.

UNESCO. (2005). *Guidelines for inclusion: Ensuring access to education for all*. Paris, France: UNESCO.

Winschel, J. (1979). *OAS technical multi-national project: Special education and rehabilitation*. Syracuse, NY: Syracuse University.

PART II

SHAPING THE LANDSCAPE OF INCLUSIVE EDUCATION

CHAPTER 4

YOU KNOW WHO IS ME? CULTURALLY INCLUSIVE EDUCATION

Dyanis Popova

Culture is often thought of in terms of a national group, or the larger ethnic groups within a nation, but rarely do we consider the significance of how individuals relate to this culture as they shape their personal cultural frameworks. Culture is much more than dress, food, and other identifiers related to racial and ethnic heritage. It can be much more personal and much more connected to each individual's way of understanding the world. The symbols of cultural identity are often indicators of social position and privilege relative to others and can determine not only how individuals are perceived by others, but also their own sense of self.

Many researchers and educators—teachers and administrators—see culture as connected only to ethnicity, country of origin, and the immediate family group, and often don't comprehend how these theories can apply in pluralistic Caribbean communities where cultures are blended and where differences are often quite subtle. Born of the survival instincts of generations alongside the process of acculturation, cultural identity in the Caribbean "is produced out of those historical experiences, those cultural traditions, those lost and marginal languages, those marginalized experiences, those peoples and histories which remain unwritten"

Caribbean Discourse in Inclusive Education:
Historical and Contemporary Issues, pages 53–68.
Copyright © 2017 by Information Age Publishing
All rights of reproduction in any form reserved.

(Hall, 1995, p. 14). Because of this history, and perhaps in spite of it, an individuals' cultural identity in the Caribbean is extremely variable and can have far-reaching social, political, and economic implications.

Culture and cultural identity mean different things to different people. There are multiple cultural definitions and theories (Banks, 2015; González, 2005). Nieto and Bode (2012) define culture as consisting of

> the values, traditions, worldview, and social and political relationships created, shared, and transformed by a group of people bound together by a common history, geographic location, language, social class, religion, or other shared identity. Culture included not only tangibles such as foods, holidays, dress, and artistic expression but also less tangible manifestations such as communication style, attitudes, values, and family relationships. (p. 158)

I use the term *culture* to describe ways of "being, knowing, and doing [and their influences on] cognition, communication, motivation, language development, and behavior" (Educational Research Service [ERS], 2003, p. 5). Cultural identity is influenced by age, class and socioeconomic status (SES), (dis)ability, gender, ethnicity and race, and religion, among others. In a classroom of twenty-five students, each student has his/her[1] own cultural identity, learned from birth and shaped by each of these factors (Gollnick & Chinn, 2012).

Culture is a complex *process* (Nieto & Bode, 2012), and especially during adolescence is in a constant state of flux. Although many studies have looked at youth identity, they have rarely explored the connections between youth identity and student learning and achievement (Moje, 2006). School is, as a meeting place for different cultures, a space where cultures can be negotiated, ignored, or rejected (Korn, 2002) and the emerging cultural identity influences student learning and contributes to student learning styles and communication preferences. It is an integral part of the learning process (Nieto & Bode, 2012). Moving beyond cultural identity as part of the macroculture related to ethnicity and the nation-state, I discuss here the intricate interplay of the numerous microcultures that comprise one's sense of identity—such as religion, gender, sexual orientation, linguistic practices, socioeconomic status, and social community identification—and how these can influence academic success. In order to positively contribute to the learning experiences of all children, we need to understand which cultural funds of knowledge (González, 2005) students bring to the classroom.

In a pluralistic society that prides itself on simultaneous unity and diversity, as is found in several Caribbean countries, it is easy to ignore or overlook the often minute differences that shape student identity. Although students in these societies may share a dominant language, there may also be divergent dialectic variations used outside of school. They may also share gender, an age group, or religion, but

---

[1] This binary is used for grammatical accuracy and simplicity. It in no way excludes third genders or students with gender fluid identities.

their experiences up to that point may have shaped their ways of knowing and of performing the Self in a variety of ways. "Cultural variables influence how children present themselves, understand the world, and interpret experiences" (Educational Research Service [ERS], 2003, p. 7). These ways of knowing and understanding the world can influence multiple aspects of students' daily lives in a variety of ways.

There is no denying that learning happens in a sociocultural context (Nieto & Bode, 2012). Within an educational setting, there are numerous non-academic contributors that can shape students' world view and performance of the Self. Teachers hold an enormous amount of power in the classroom (Freire, 2005) and their actions or their response to the actions of others can have significant influence on students' academic and sociocultural development. Stereotypes regarding cultural differences, like those suggesting that specific cultural characteristics determine student ability, parental participation, and student performance, among others, can be particularly damaging. On a larger scale, these stereotypes and subsequent assumptions can become institutionalized and/or systemic and be influential in shaping educational policies, practices, and structures.

Using the Caribbean expression "you know who is me?" to indicate feelings of and resistance to being discounted (Fournillier & Lewis, 2010), I aim to explore the complex interaction between cultural identity and student learning in Caribbean schools. Directing this question at principals, teachers, and students challenges imposed representations and acknowledges the potential inner conflict faced by students as they navigate both their sociocultural and academic lives. This chapter is intended to broaden the discussion of culture as part of the learning process and to move beyond the misunderstandings and often meaningless rhetoric sometimes associated with diversity, inclusion, and multicultural education. In this space, I present a concise conceptualization of culturally inclusive education and discuss its importance and implementation in classrooms and schools. Through Hall's (1990) second view of cultural identity, which acknowledges both points of similarity and points of difference, cultural identity "is a matter of 'becoming' as well as of 'being'" (p. 225). This chapter calls for teachers and school administrators "to be cognizant of the passages their students make as they move from home to school, and [to appreciate] the role of their own perspectives and experiences and how these impact upon teaching praxis" (Korn, 2002, p. 10).

It is of course important to note that the responsibility for this process is not solely that of classroom teachers and school administration. There is significant overlap between the role of parent and that of teacher. Parents shape the cultural identity of their children, whether that identity is based on modelling or on resistance. They can shape their children's perspectives on difference and how they respond to others in social and academic settings. This piece of the puzzle can support the efforts of teachers and administration as they strive to create a welcoming and inclusive learning environment.

The presence and role of cultural variations within a nation is of particular significance because multicultural education—of marked importance in pluralistic communities—"focuses on equal educational opportunities for different groups within the national culture" (Banks, 2015, p. 74). Education beyond, and in addition to, schooling curricula is the foundation for a critically conscious and socially just population. Providing a learning environment in which all students feel welcomed and included is essential in this endeavour.

Banks (2015) identifies six major cultural elements for teaching and learning about student and teacher cultures: values and behavioral styles, nonverbal communication, languages and dialects, cultural cognitiveness, identification, and perspectives, world views, and frames of reference. Rather than focusing on cultural intangibles, this conceptualization provides a more concrete theoretical framework through which educators can explore the cultural variations present in their schools and in society at large. It emphasizes the numerous interconnected facets of individual cultural identity and the various lenses through which one's world view can be framed.

Cultural variations are numerous and, when presented in such broad terms, may be overwhelming to some teachers. To understand and be able to apply the concept, we must first recognize the components that comprise cultural identity and be conscious of how those components can affect students' educational experiences. Cultural variations exist on two interconnected levels: the macroculture—the national dominant culture—or microcultures—the smaller cultures within it—of a society.

WELL, WHO IS YOU?

Caribbean Macroculture

Macroculture, originally a sociological term, alludes to the main characteristics of a cultural group. It refers to the system of shared beliefs, symbols, and interpretations that exists within a society or nation-state. It considers the race/ethnicity, gender, sexual orientation, social class, religion, social communities, and (dis)ability of the dominant population, which we then internalize as the norm within that society. In a diverse society, some of these lines can become blurred, while others become quite dominant. Dominant culture views are normalized and it is this group that holds the power in that society or nation-state. In the United States for example, the dominant culture is identified as white, Anglo-Saxon, and Protestant—WASP (Gollnick & Chinn, 2012), which is notably different than the dominant culture in Caribbean countries. Though there may be some variation between islands, which in turn can generate sub macrocultures specific to the nation-state, the Caribbean is generally considered to be a culturally pluralistic region (Premdas, 2007) where the majority of nationals are persons of color.

Caribbean cultures are the product of colonization and globalization (Hall, 1990), characterized by negotiation and transculturation (Hall, 1995) and it is impossible to discuss or define Caribbean culture without understanding how it has been shaped by power relations. Using Trinidad and Tobago as an example of one nation-state, Premdas (2007) notes that many former colonies are framed by a history of cultural imperialism during which there was no policy of multicultural tolerance. Instead, other cultures were controlled, devalued, or ignored. Cultural control was systematic and institutionalized "through the legal system of crime and punishment and through the implanting of symbols and institutions" (Premdas, 2007, p. 79). With cultural and ethnic groups being historically pitted against each other, the remnants of this legacy linger and are visible today in intercultural relations, especially when involving politics and power itself. During the 2015 national elections in Trinidad and Tobago, social media became the platform for hateful speech and racial-ethnic stereotyping. Anthropologist Dr. Dylan Kerrigan noted this to be a "cultural manifestation of the political climate" (Rambally, 2015) and attributed this behavior in part to failing social and educational institutions, and a lack of critical thinking among the general public, especially those with low socioeconomic status. Another recent example can be found in the racialized discourse in the Dominican Republic that peaked in 2015 as that nation prepared to deport illegal immigrants from Haiti, some of whom had been born in the Dominican Republic and who knew no other home.

In the Caribbean, we speak often of our culture. We speak of the variety in our cuisine, the richness of our heritage and cultural events, and our contributions to the world stage. Each nation-state has national values that are shared by all groups and other values that distinguish groups from one another (Banks, 2015). A quick Google search of Caribbean Culture highlights several factors that are considered to be part of the regional macroculture: rhythm, celebration, folklore, heavily spiced food, racial intermixing, and multicultural influences and traditions, among others (Caribya, 2015; Diaz, 2012).

Uncovering the macroculture of your specific nation-state involves asking which groups hold the power and privilege in and across political, economic, and social institutions. What is considered normal or average? Who do we see reflected in the newspapers and on television and how are they represented? What foods or musical styles do you hear about when nationals are asked to choose one that represents their country? What types of clothing are considered national dress if asked to represent the nation among other nations? Does the society place homosexual, transgender, or gender fluid persons on the fringes? What about differently abled persons; how included are they in the national discourse? These questions and many others can be used to critically analyze the norms of any society and the ways in which segmentation and stereotyping can be enacted and perpetuated. This does not mean that each citizen reflects and is reflected in the macroculture, only that the macroculture represents the normalized majority.

As Caribbean peoples (re)construct their identities, there have been recent challenges throughout the region dealing with power, privilege, and community membership (Premdas, 2007). There are complex power relations found throughout the region. Although there is some fluidity within a national or regional macroculture, representations of domination and power touch the lives of each citizen in both hidden and obvious ways. Understanding the macroculture provides a base through which we can explore individual microcultures and develop social and educational systems, policies, and procedures which support and engage all nationals, regardless of their macro or micro identification.

Microcultures

Microcultural identifiers take the concept of macrocultures to a more personal level. Microcultures refer to an individual's ways of knowing, doing, and understanding the world. They are not always visible or enacted but are components to a person's identity and represent the groups with which the individual identifies. They include multiple variables and include small group membership—crunchy mom, military family, rock climber—along with the better known categories of gender, race, and religion, among others. Small group membership is often ignored in empirical studies but is a key factor and is quite significant regarding the ways individuals form connections outside of their ethnic or religious heritage. Although these are stand-alone variables, individuals belong to each group simultaneously, and the interactions between these variables influence daily behavior (Banks, 2015).

There is significant fluidity in a person's microcultures as they are constantly shifting due to personal experiences and growth. For example, gender identification might not play a significant role in one teenager's life but as he/she ages, it has

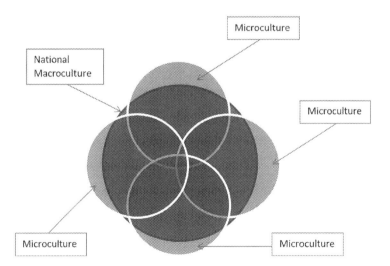

FIGURE 4.1. The Relationship Between the National Macroculture and an Individual's Microcultures.

the potential to grow and become much more important to how they understand the world and perform the Self. As another example, when considering my own microcultures, being a mother was not one of my microcultural identifiers until I became one in my late thirties. Now, it represents a major part of my world view.

Microcultures can be enacted or repressed as a response to the dominant culture. If the macroculture is perceived as being oppressive to a particular cultural group, it can impel the individual to emphasize or deemphasize that particular identifier. This can motivate students—knowingly or not—to act out either by displaying extreme representations of said identifier, by retreating into isolation, or by rejecting the identifier in an effort to fit in and be better accepted by the dominant group. Going even farther, the relationship between these microcultures is directly related to the academic identity of children and young adults who are still determining their sense of self while additionally trying to succeed academically. Social pressures can exert psychological pressure that can make it difficult to perform and succeed academically (Harter, 2012; Johnson, 2000; Spavins, 2007).

Essentially, because a group of students is from the same country or the same neighborhood, it is important that teachers and administrators do not assume that their cultural identifiers are all the same. In a class of students who all look the same and who may share multiple macrocultural identifiers, there can still be subtle, important differences that can have a meaningful influence on their social and academic performance.

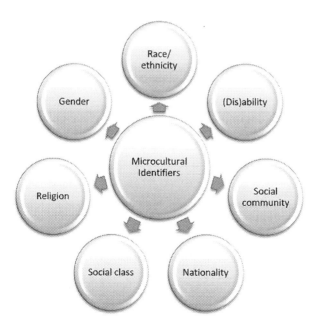

FIGURE 4.2. Some Major Components of Microcultural Identity..

Microaggressions and the Classroom

Microaggressions experienced due to difference—real or perceived—can create additional, often unexpected, pressure that challenges the possibility of positive social and academic experiences, and also creates dissonance in a student's sense of identity and self. Microaggressions are defined as "the everyday verbal, nonverbal, and environmental slights, snubs, or insults, whether intentional or unintentional, that communicate hostile, derogatory, or negative messages to target persons based solely upon their marginalized group membership" (Sue, 2010a, p. 3). They have also been described as "subtle, stunning, often automatic, and nonverbal exchanges which are 'put downs'" (Pierce, Carew, Pierce-Gonzalez, & Willis, 1978, p. 66), as subtle insults (Solórzano, Ceja, &Yosso, 2000), or as dismissive behavior that is pervasive and often normative based on a society's historical or contemporary inequities.

These often hidden messages relegate individuals or aspects of their identity to an inferior status, and can go unrecognized by the aggressor due to the norms and expectations of the dominant culture. These messages are most harmful when communicated by aggressors who do not recognize the influence of their words or actions and can perpetuate social inequities (Sue, 2010a). Sue (2010a) provides some valuable examples of microaggressive behavior: "an assertive female manager is labelled as a 'bitch,' while her male counterpart is described as 'a forceful leader' (hidden message: women should be passive and allow men to be decision makers)," and another: "A blind man reports that people often raise their voices when speaking to him [. . .] (hidden message: a person with a disability is defined as lesser in all aspects of physical and mental functioning)" (pp. 5–6). These examples demonstrate the ways in which individuals are judged and labelled based on dominant norms and expectations.

This in no way infers that aggressors intend to be offensive or hurtful. As noted above, microaggressions are often considered harmless comments/actions and recipients of these aggressions are often told to get over it or let it go. Aggressors may not recognize their position of privilege or the possibly numerous encounters with this type of behavior that the person to whom they are referring has previously had (Suárez-Orozco, Casanova, Martin, Katsiaficas, Cuellar, Smith, & Dias, 2015). When these behaviors are pointed out, aggressors may become defensive and may try to deny any bias (Sue, 2010a), which in turn intentionally or unintentionally questions the legitimacy of the past or present experiences of the person experiencing the microaggression. Not addressing and challenging these aggressions can perpetuate oppression, invalidate someone's identity and realities, and reinforce negative stereotypes. Microaggressions can not only manifest emotionally through anxiety and feelings of alienation, but can also generate stress-related physical effects, cognitive effects that influence productivity and performance, and behavioral displays like anger, hopelessness, suspiciousness, and even strength through adversity through the development of survival skills

(Suárez-Orozco, Casanova, Martin, Katsiaficas, Cuellar, Smith, & Dias, 2015; Sue, 2010a).

These effects can build up over time, and when microaggressions extend outside the classroom and become part of the systemic and institutionalized school or social climate, the effects can be magnified. Sue (2010b) defines these as environmental microaggressions and the pressure they exert can have a profound effect. A study by Suárez-Orozco, Casanova, Martin, Katsiaficas, Cuellar, Smith, & Dias (2015) found that instructors were the most frequent perpetrators of microaggressions in a school setting, which can establish a negative power dynamic in the classroom. The study also found that the most frequent type of microaggressions were those that attacked the intelligence and competence of students. These also intersected with various stereotypes based on race/ethnicity or gender, among others.

Responding to an aggressor can often be tricky due to the often unconscious or ambiguous nature of microaggressive behavior. Observing this behavior among students in actions and attitudes of their parents and family members. It is here that the relationship between home and school, parents and teachers, takes centrestage. A strong relationship between home and school can create space in which microaggressive behavior can be recognized and addressed. Of course, teachers and administrators may find that parents and extended family may themselves have biases—both recognized and unrecognized—that need to be addressed. Fostering a learning environment that encourages and supports family involvement can provide education about these issues for all persons involved. Defining and recognizing microaggressions are the first steps to any effective intervention (Sue, 2010b).

Although much of the research around microaggressions specifically addresses race and racism (Solórzano, Ceja, & Yosso, 2000; Sue, 2010a), these concepts are applicable to, and visible in, interactions with all other facets of microcultural identity. Individuals can feel discounted because of microaggressive behavior based on their religion, gender, age, sexuality, socioeconomic status, and even their identification with environmental activism or motorcycle owners, among others. As learning is an emotional and social activity (Educational Research Service [ERS], 2003), any resulting deficit notions can affect student performance (Moje, 2006).

Through all of this, how do we as teachers support student exploration and enactment of identities? How can we support students throughout their youthful development as they explore the different facets of themselves and perform the Self they identify at that moment in time? Reflective teaching practices combined with a focus on culturally inclusive education is the first step toward creating an environment in which all students, regardless of microcultural identifiers, can feel safe, respected, and heard.

Culturally Inclusive Education

Inclusive education is not a new concept. It has in fact been established as an important factor in education, particularly in special education and the discussion around (dis)ability (Slee, 2001). Inclusive education's original focus engages social justice as a pathway to equity and equality for persons with disabilities. It has since developed to embrace the concept of access for all students and now focuses on "how diverse students experience their worlds as social beings and construct realities and meanings based on their own lived experiences" (Carter-Hicks, 2015, p. 412). This pedagogical approach incorporates students' sociocultural and linguistic backgrounds into curricula design and implementation and requires differentiation and the consideration of multiple learning styles and intelligences.

Embracing this concept, I focus here on the inclusion of multiple aspects of macro and micro cultures into curricula design and implementation, acknowledging (dis)ability to be one aspect of personal culture. Culturally Inclusive Education is not intended to replace or contrast against similar concepts, like that of Culturally Responsive Education or Culturally Proficient Instruction. It is instead intended to partner with these ideas to provide a supportive and welcoming learning environment for all students.

There are those who might say that the discussion of culture should remain on a broader level related to ethnicity and large group membership. There may also be doubts about its applicability in societies or communities in which students are mostly homogenous at the macrocultural level. I assert, however, that this stance does not address the close ties between social development and academic performance. In order to facilitate a truly learner-centered environment in Caribbean schools, we must delve deeper into student understanding and performance of the Self.

Teacher Culture

While considering student culture, teachers and administrators must explore their own macrocultures and microcultures in order to determine how their performance of the Self affects classroom teaching, school policies, and student-teacher interactions. This process involves reflection and a willingness to consider multiple perspectives. Understanding teaching to be a moral and political act (Freire, 2000), teachers must continually reflect on instructional practice in order to explore how their position of power in the classroom affects student learning.

Teachers and administrators interested in culturally proficient (Nuri-Robins, Lindsey, Lindsey, & Terrell, 2012) and culturally responsive education (Gay, 2010; Ladson-Billings, 2009)—important aspects of culturally inclusive education—demonstrate awareness of both their own learning styles and those of their students, and understand the power they wield over the acknowledgement and performance of student cultural identity. This power shapes classroom interactions and can have a profound effect on student achievement. Teachers must take the time to become aware of each learner's unique backgrounds, experiences, and learning styles. They must also consider how their own culture influences instructional behavior and expectations, and the ways in which cultural differences can influence the learning environment.

Culturally inclusive teachers value and respect cultural diversity and are intentional in their pedagogy. They must constantly balance the needs of their students with the priorities of the position, all the while acknowledging the "visible invisibility" (Welch, 2006) of students who do not identify with the dominant culture. They must be willing to challenge the status quo and be vocal advocates for their students.

Learning Differences

As students explore their macrocultural and microcultural identities, there can be both internal and external conflicts as they navigate their beliefs and preferences, and develop their world view. These cultural conflicts can be misinterpreted as a lack of interest, rebellion, or a lack of ability (Educational Research Service [ERS], 2003). Teachers and administrators must endeavour to understand how this process can influence student learning and performance, while developing an understanding of their own cultures and their effect on their classroom pedagogy. These learning differences go beyond the concept of multiple intelligences (Gardner, 1983) and varied learning styles—visual, auditory, and kinesthetic—and include the differences that are presented based on cultural variations and preferences. Some of these variations can be distinctions in interpersonal communication styles, notions of leadership, notions of modesty, inferential vs. deductive or inductive reasoning, preference for verbal or non-verbal cues, top-down learning approaches rather than bottom up, group work vs. individual work, concrete vs. abstract representations, mental images to stimulate memory vs. word associations, just to name a few (Educational Research Service [ERS], 2003). This does not require teachers to master the details of each and every culture represented in the classroom, but rather prompts them to be alert and aware of cultural influences on teaching and learning and to learn as much as possible about the students in their classrooms.

WHAT NEXT?

Who Are My Students?

As educators, how can we use this information to enhance our instruction and interactions, and provide a positive, welcoming, and culturally affirming educational experience for all involved? As noted above, this process will involve reflection and begins with discovering your own and your students' microcultures. Teachers often ask how they are supposed to uncover this information in their classrooms. The answer is simultaneously simple and complex. Simply put, we must do what all good teachers do: learn about our students. We must ask questions, seek knowledge, and provide activities that will encourage students to share about themselves. The same way that we can figure out student allergies or the family structure in a student's life—siblings, pets, etc.—we must make an effort to delve even deeper into how a student sees and understands the world around him/her.

This, then, is where the complexity emerges. This process takes time and concerted effort. Designing activities that will elicit this information will involve trial and error, and can be time consuming. In all of this, it is important to remember why we teach and why we choose to work with children. It is essential that we provide the type of learning environment that is encouraging, affirming, and will encourage them to become critical thinkers and active participants in a continually shifting society. When combined with an understanding of our own microcultures and how they affect our teaching and their learning, understanding student culture is the first step in this direction.

Classroom Pedagogy

Understanding microcultures is only one step toward providing a culturally inclusive education. As noted in the section above, in their effort to respect and affirm student differences, teachers and administrators should plan a variety of activities not only to get to know students and to address learning preferences, but also to relate to students' out-of-school experiences (Nieto & Bode, 2012). The brief examples presented here are in no way exhaustive, but are intended to spark ideas that teachers can adapt for use in their classrooms.

- Use technology in the classroom to expand the curriculum and provide more culturally relevant and inclusive materials (Nieto & Bode, 2012);
- Encourage student voice and expression. Though this at times may challenge the classroom dynamic, it is important to development management practices that will allow the space for open expression;
- Use literature and music from different cultural groups;
- Include multiple perspectives with any lesson;
- Use classroom materials to actively challenge stereotypes;
- Support students' physical, mental, spiritual, and emotional growth, and volitional competence by encouraging awareness of the five elements of learning identity: self-determination, self-esteem, self-image, self-concept, and physical awareness (Brown, 2006); and
- Help students actively think about and explore how their enacted identities can shape their educational experiences.

School Culture

The classroom teacher should not be alone in this endeavour. Although a teacher can implement these ideas in an isolated classroom setting, it is far more effective when integrated into the overall school culture. When students feel culturally affirmed and respected not only in their classroom, but also throughout the school, it can have an even greater influence on their social and academic development. Both teachers and administrators must be involved in creating a culturally meaningful learning environment that incorporates the Five Cs: commitment, communication, co-responsibility, courage, and cultural understanding (Larke, Elbert, Webb-Johnson, Larke, & Brisco, 2006).

Toward this effort, teachers can form coalitions in support of different groups. Each staff member can support a specific group for LGBTQ students, anti-bullying, and students with disabilities, among many others. Rather than encouraging separatism, these coalitions can form a safe space for students to discuss issues related to their identification with the group. These groups can go beyond the mainstream identifiers and include social communities like practitioners of classical dance styles and an auto club in order to include the less often acknowledged social group identifiers that are an important aspect of personal microcultures.

For even more involvement, teachers and administrators can be encouraged to list some identifiers on their classroom or office door. Just as university professors at many institutions post a rainbow flag on their door to identify their office as a safe space for LGBTQ students, those at the primary and secondary school levels can do the same. This does not require full personal disclosure but providing three to four identifiers can encourage students to explore their own microcultures and let them know that there are other people out there that share their interests and identifiers. This list should not simply be a list of interests or hobbies, but should relate to the way the individual identifies as a member of a larger group. Providing

FIGURE 4.3. An Example of a Teacher's List of Identifiers That Can Be Posted on a Staffroom or Classroom Door.

a culturally inclusive education must be an integral part of both the formal and informal curriculum.

School administrators must reflect on their hiring practices to ensure that any new teachers are willing to be an active part of the process. Parents and families must also be included in these efforts as the learning environment extends beyond the school grounds. As with academic classes, families can reinforce what students learn at school and continue fostering their social and academic growth. Although more studies are needed to investigate how enacted cultural identities can support or constrain student achievement, schools should stop requiring students to fit unnecessary molds, which can invalidate their journey of personal discovery and learning. Instead, schools should invite students to participate in a "teaching/learning relationship and spaces of belonging" (Moje, 2006, p. 152).

TOWARD NORMATIVE CULTURAL INCLUSION

Although cultural inclusion as a theory has been researched and explored, it is often enacted at the surface level of cultural awareness. In pluralistic Caribbean societies, where surface demonstrations and integration of diversity can obscure the need for more in-depth understanding, it is important to delve deeply in order to truly understand the plurality of culture and its influence in our lives in all levels of schooling.

The benefits to including a deep understanding of macro and micro cultural identities in the curriculum extend beyond the classroom and can positively affect students' ways of knowing and being. Rather than identifying with others solely on the traditional bases of race/ethnicity, gender, and class, etc., an understanding of microcultures provides all stakeholders with the opportunity to form bonds across these lines. Being able to explore and perform the Self and be part of an in-group, no matter how small, all while engaged in academic activities, can transfer the gains of acceptance and confidence to academic performance.

Culturally inclusive education should not be an optional supplement to education, but should be entwined with teacher education, curriculum design and implementation, and overall school culture. As nation-states strive to provide political, economic, and social access and equity for all, we must look to the educational institutions to be a base of support and learning through which students can equip themselves with the tools to become critically conscious thinkers and positive, active participants within the society.

REFERENCES

Banks, J. A. (2015). *Cultural diversity and education: Foundations, curriculum, and teaching* (6th ed.). Upper Saddle River, NJ: Pearson.

Brown, L. (2006). A holistic model of learning identity. In H. R. Milner & E. W. Ross (Eds.), *Race, ethnicity, and education: Racial identity in education* (pp. 257–78). Westport, CT: Praeger Perspectives.

Caribya. (2015). *The culture of the Caribbean.* Retrieved from http://caribya.com/caribbean/culture/
Carter-Hicks, J. (2015). Inclusive education. In *Encyclopedia of diversity and social justice* (vol. 2, pp. 412–13). Lanham, MD: Rowman & Littlefield.
Diaz, C. G. (2012). Caribbean traditions and customs. In *Encyclopedia of Puerto Rico.* Retrieved from http://www.enciclopediapr.org/ing/article.cfm?ref=11112506
Educational Research Service [ERS]. (2003). *Culture and learning.* Arlington, VA: ERS.
Fournillier, J. B., & Lewis, T. (2010). Finding voice: Two Afro Caribbean immigrant members of the academy writing "home. *Studies in Continuing Education, 32(2),* 147–62.
Freire, P. (2000). *Pedagogy of the oppressed* (30th anniversary ed.). New York, NY: Continuum.
Freire, P. (2005). *Teachers as cultural workers: Letters to those who dare to teach.* Boulder, CO: Westview Press.
Gardner, H. (1983). *Frames of mind: The theory of multiple intelligences.* New York, NY: Basic.
Gay, G. (2010). *Culturally responsive teaching: Theory, research, and practice* (2nd ed.). New York, NY: Teachers College Press.
Gollnick, D. M., & Chinn, P. C. (2012). *Multicultural education in a pluralistic society* (9th ed.). Upper Saddle River, NJ: Pearson.
González, N. (2005). Beyond culture: The hybridity of funds of knowledge. In N. González, L. C. Moll, & C. Amanti (Eds.), *Funds of knowledge: Theorizing practice in households, communities & classrooms* (pp. 29–46). Mahwah, NJ: Lawrence Erlbaum Associates, Inc.
Hall, S. (1990).Cultural identity and diaspora. In J. Rutherford (Ed.). *Identity: Community, culture, difference* (pp. 222–37). London: Lawrence & Wishart.
Hall, S. (1995). Negotiating cultural identity. *New Left Review, 209,* 3–14.
Harter, S. (2012). *The construction of the self: Developmental and sociocultural foundations* (2nd ed.). New York, NY: The Guilford Press.
Johnson, K. A. (2000). The peer effect on academic achievement among public elementary students. *CDA Report No. 00– 06, May 26, 2000, Heritage Center for Data Analysis, Heritage Foundation.* Retrieved from http://www.heritage.org/research/reports/2000/05/peer-effect-on-achievement-among-elementary-school-students
Korn, C. (2002). Introduction: Cultural transitions and curricular transformations. In C. Korn & A. Bursztyn (Eds.), *Rethinking multicultural education: Case studies in cultural transition* (pp. 1–12). Westport, CT: Bergin & Garvey.
Ladson-Billings, G. (2009). *The dreamkeepers: Successful teachers of African-American children* (2nd ed.). San Francisco, CA: Jossey-Bass.
Larke, P. J., Elbert, C., Webb-Johnson, G., Larke, A. W., & Brisco, M. (2006). Culturally meaningful classrooms: The five c's of best practices. In V. Ooka Pang (Ed.), *Race, ethnicity, and education: Principles and practices of multicultural education* (pp. 161–79). Westport, CT: Praeger Perspectives.
Moje, E. B. (2006). Achieving identities: How do youth identities matter in school achievement? In R. T. Jiménez & V. Ooka Pang (Eds.), *Race, ethnicity, and education: Language and literacy in schools* (pp. 133–56). Westport, CT: Praeger Perspectives.
Nieto, S., & Bode, P. (2012). Affirming diversity: The sociopolitical context of multicultural education (6th ed.). Upper Saddle Road, NJ: Pearson.

Nuri-Robins, K. J., Lindsey, D. B., Lindsey, R. B., & Terrell, R. D. (2012). *Culturally proficient instruction: A guide for people who teach* (3rd ed.). Thousand Oaks, CA: Sage.

Pierce, C., Carew, J., Pierce-Gonzalez, D., & Willis, D. (1978). An experiment in racism: TV commercials. In C. Pierce (Ed.), *Television and education* (pp. 62–88). Beverly Hills, CA: Sage.

Premdas, R. (2007). *Trinidad & Tobago: Ethnic conflict, inequality, and public sector governance.* Hampshire, UK: Palgrave Macmillan.

Rambally, R. K. (2015, October 4). Small group "fanning the flames" of race in T&T—UWI lecturer. *Trinidad & Tobago Guardian.* Retrieved from http://m.guardian.co.tt/news/2015-10-04/small-group-%E2%80%98fanning-flames%E2%80%99-race-tt%E2%80%94uwi-lecturer

Slee, R. (2001). Social justice and the changing directions in educational research: The case of inclusive education. *International Journal of Inclusive Education, 5*(2–3), 167–77. doi: 10.1080/13603110010035832

Solórzano, D., Ceja, M., & Yosso, T. (2000). Critical race theory, racial microaggression, and campus racial climate: The experiences of African American college students. *The Journal of Negro Education, 69*(1/2), 60–73. Retrieved from http://www.jstor.org/stable/2696265

Spavins, E. A. (2007). *Friendship quality and peer attachment as predictors of adolescents' subsequent academic achievement* (Unpublished undergraduate thesis). University of Virginia, Charlottesville. Retrieved from http://people.virginia.edu/~psykliff/Teenresearch/Publications.html

Suárez-Orozco, C., Casanova, S., Martin, M., Katsiaficas, D., Cuellar, V., Smith, N. A., & Dias, S. I. (2015). Toxic rain in class: Classroom interpersonal microaggressions. *Educational researcher, 44*(3), 151–60. doi: 10.3102/0013189X15580314

Sue, D. W. (2010a). *Microaggressions and marginality: Manifestation, dynamics, and impact.* Hoboken, NJ: John Wiley & Sons.

Sue, D. W. (2010b). *Microaggressions in everyday life. Race, gender, and sexual orientation.* Hoboken, NJ: John Wiley & Sons.

Welch, O. M. (2006). Seeing with cultural eyes: Leadership for change in multicultural schools. In V. Ooka Pang (Ed.), *Race, ethnicity, and education: Principles and practices of multicultural education* (pp. 127–42). Westport, CT: Praeger Perspectives.

CHAPTER 5

INCLUSIVE EDUCATION ACROSS THE SCHOOL CURRICULUM

Providing Greater Access Through Language

Iris Hewitt-Bradshaw

This chapter explores language diversity and the impact on student learning across the curriculum in Caribbean classrooms. I argue that, historically, concerns about language education policies in the Caribbean have largely focused on the choice of language alternatives for the education of learners, appropriate educational approaches, strategies and methods to teach a Standard language, and the impact of negative attitudes to school children's native language. Here, I extend the discussion to examine, more specifically, issues related to language diversity and factors that can impact on student learning across disciplines in the school curriculum. As Nero and Ahamad (2014) observe, language is an essential component of a child's educational experience. Hence, failure to define a positive role for the vernacular languages of the majority of children to facilitate learning from their earliest level of schooling results in pedagogical practices of language exclusion and a resulting negative impact on learning across the curriculum.

Caribbean Discourse in Inclusive Education:
Historical and Contemporary Issues, pages 69–85.
Copyright © 2017 by Information Age Publishing
All rights of reproduction in any form reserved.

Under an education policy that follows accepted principles of effective inclusion, all learners have equal access to all aspects of the curriculum; there is sensitivity to individual strengths and challenges, and attention to diversity in all forms through strategies such as differentiated instruction; and links are established among school and community. Salend (2011) defines inclusion as "a philosophy that brings diverse students, families, educators, and community members together to create schools and other social institutions based on acceptance, belonging, and community" (p. 7). He further states that inclusion is based on the recognition that all students are capable of learning and enjoy opportunities for success when curriculum is appropriately delivered, using instruction that is meaningful, challenging and differentiated. Thus, effective pedagogy addresses learners' diverse and unique strengths, challenges and experiences.

If we apply these ideas to situations of language diversity in educational contexts, the language and literacy challenges that students face in learning content in school disciplines can result in their exclusion if their learning is not actively supported by educators who are aware of the centrality of language for children, as well as its importance in the process of education across the school curriculum. Further, the situation is made worse if the linguistic and cultural resources that students bring to the classroom are ignored, or under-utilized, when they are expected to acquire knowledge, develop understanding, and acquire practices in content areas.

To address the question of language inclusion in Caribbean education, I first discuss relevant historical issues and concerns in research on language in education in the Anglophone Caribbean, where Creole languages have been for a long time the first language of the majority of people, while a European standard variety, usually English, is the official language. I then discuss differences between the language required for learning in schools and students' home language, and then consider the implications of language diversity on students' learning in school subjects such as mathematics and science. This exploration is based on the premise that, in situations of language diversity, and especially when the language of instruction is different from the first language of students, there is a need to find ways to achieve congruence between students' linguistic experiences and resources, and the specific language and discourse demands of school disciplines. In the absence of this, students can be excluded from understanding and participating in disciplinary discourses, with consequences for their achievement in school subjects. The chapter concludes with recommendations for further research to make language learning and teaching more inclusive for speakers whose first language is not the variety used as the language of instruction.

LANGUAGE IN EDUCATION IN THE CARIBBEAN REGION: HISTORICAL ISSUES AND CONCERNS

Although it has long been established that Creole vernacular languages have as valid grammatical systems and patterns as Standard English (Bryan, 2010; James

& Youssef, 2002; Roberts, 2007), many people in Caribbean society, including native speakers, still believe that such languages are corrupted forms of English and cannot be considered viable means of communication. Possible reasons for this are discussed in Nero (2006). The relatively low status of Creole vernacular languages and the prevailing negative attitudes to them have traditionally resulted in such varieties playing a minor role in education throughout the region. The emergence of politically independent nation states in the 1960s and 1970s did little to change the status of European languages, primarily English or French, as the official language of instruction in schools in the Caribbean because those languages were considered superior, more cultured systems of communication. The status of English as a global language was also convenient for its use as an official language in post-colonial states. However, for a long time, the fact that the majority of the population in most Caribbean states acquired a Creole language as their first language prompted concerns about the suitability of existing education programmes, limited as these were in the post-independence period. A Creole language is any new language that develops in a sustained contact situation where two groups speak different languages and a new medium of communication evolves over time and is eventually adopted as a first language by a generation of speakers. Most of the lexicon of a Creole language is drawn from one of the contact languages, commonly called the lexifier or superstrate language (Siegel, 2008). This is usually the language of the dominant or powerful social group. Siegel further explains that:

> the meanings and functions of the lexical forms, as well as the phonology and grammatical rules of the ... creole, are different to those of the lexifier and may sometimes resemble those of one or more of the other languages in contact .... (p. 1)

In the Caribbean, colonization by European powers, slavery, indentureship, and migration brought linguistically diverse groups in contact. Pidgin and Creole languages emerged from this situation, and today, vernacular or home languages of large numbers of Caribbean nation states include English-related Creoles, French-related Creoles, and in some cases Dutch-related Creoles. In most territories, the official language used for classroom instruction is the Standard variety of a language, whereas the majority of children entering schools speak a Creole language as their first language. These are the major factors that resulted in the diversity of language in Caribbean education systems.

Language Policy and Education

In such a situation of language diversity, one of the major issues addressed by Caribbean linguists and educators was that of the adoption of appropriate language policies for educating children for whom a Creole variety was a first language (Carrington, 1976;, Craig, 1971; 1980; Robertson, 1996; Simmons-McDonald, 2004). In English-speaking Caribbean states such as Trinidad and Tobago, Jamaica, and Barbados, the education system maintained the policy of using Standard English as the official language of instruction, from primary to tertiary level. This meant that, from early in their school life, children were taught in a language in which they had limited competence. On the basis of growing research on first and second language acquisition, linguists questioned the wisdom of an approach to education that seemed to assume that Standard English was the first language of students when it clearly was not. Craig (1980), in fact, argued that for Anglophone Creole speakers Standard English was neither a foreign language nor a native language and this had implications for how such learners should be taught. In effect, policy that marginalized children's first language excluded an important and enabling educational resource. Robertson (1996) also emphasized the need for accurate description so that appropriate education policies could be established. Whether Caribbean states considered the educational goal to be the development of learners who were bi-lingual or bi-dialectal, linguists highlighted the need for informed planning and decision making with respect to the role of language in education. Rightfully, their concern was linguistic exclusion in education given their appreciation of the significance of language in education for students' educational achievement.

Robertson (1999) suggested that a shortage of informed personnel to address the needs of all levels of the education system has hampered appropriate educational policy. He further argued that a lack of awareness of the role of language in education created problems in the selection and preparation of teachers, the management of the differences between home language and school language, and, ultimately, curriculum design and the management of classrooms. To address this, he recommended that administrators make conscious efforts to promote relevant levels of knowledge and awareness about language in education given that a crucial goal of education is students' learning, which in turn relies heavily on language. This position supports the goal of language equity and the creation of school systems that are more inclusive.

Inappropriate education policies reflected insufficient concern about the role of language in promoting inclusion in education processes, and researchers linked such policies in the field of language education to the low levels of literacy recorded for most Caribbean territories. The fact that many students left secondary schools with limited proficiency in English was taken as evidence of the failure of schools to develop students' language competence throughout the region (Craig, 2006a).

Language Differences in the Classroom

Apart from concerns relating to language policies and programmes, the literature on language in education in the Caribbean also highlighted the impact that linguistic differences between Standard English and Creole vernaculars have on the teaching and learning process. Comparative descriptions of the two language systems have shown that, despite areas of overlap, there are significant lexical and grammatical differences between the two language systems. In Caribbean territories, where mesolectal or mixed varieties of language are common and are linguistically closer to the local standard variety, it would be more difficult to identify the boundaries between the different language systems. Mesolectal varieties of language in a Creole language complex are those varieties that are in the middle of the speech continuum. At one extreme of the continuum is the most extreme form of the Creole called the *basilect*. At the other extreme is the *acrolect*, the Standard variety which is used in official institutions such as schools. Bickerton (1975) used the term *mesolect* to refer to the system of intermediate language varieties that links the *basilect* to the *acrolect*. Carrington (1993), though, suggested that the relationship among the varieties is not linear, but multidimensional and complex, with a speaker's language choices determined by a range of social and stylistic factors.

Thus, early and current language researchers on dialectal varieties in the Caribbean region highlight the importance of an awareness of such social and stylistic factors in speakers' language choices, and the implications for teaching and learning language in Caribbean classrooms. Craig (2006a) reiterated the position that, in such a situation, teachers need to be aware of similarities and differences among the language varieties so that they do not assume that the unknown is known, or that they teach what is known as though it were unknown to students. He also emphasized the psychological aspects of language learning when he noted that because some forms are familiar to students, they may think they already know them, when they do not. Craig (1978) also highlighted a social dimension. He observed that the existence of a creole language and a standard language in the same speech community tends to correlate with patterns of social stratification. However, varied social factors and personal interrelationships influence a speaker's choice so that in the process of a single discourse, speakers tend to switch from one language to the other. This phenomenon is usually called *code-switching*.

Pollard (1978) examined the phenomenon of code-switching in Jamaican Creole to discover how "the classroom operation can benefit from first-hand knowledge of how actual speech situations condition an individual's choice of speech style" (p. 16). Detailed analysis of oral discourse led her to recommend that, for Creole-speaking learners, educators might find it useful to emphasize the difference between the language of school and of all official usage, and the language of what she termed "their real relating." Such language varieties are the community languages or out-of-school dialects that children commonly identify with and those that fulfil their everyday communicative needs. Even if such language varieties are tolerated in oral classroom discourse, they are typically excluded from other aspects of literacy processes in Caribbean schools and not allowed as official forms of communication in events such as examinations or education products in the form of essays and letters.

In a subsequent publication, Pollard (1993) addressed classroom pedagogy in a handbook for teachers of students whose vernacular is Jamaican Creole. In it, she identified some linguistic features that might be problematic for learners in linguistically diverse contexts. These include words that sound alike but which mean different things in the two languages; grammatical structures that are different but convey the same information; and idiomatic speech or writing. Her approach connects language, culture, and identity, and places literature and discourse styles at the forefront of students' literacy development. Like other Creole linguists, Pollard adopted the position that, instead of attempting to eradicate or ignore students' first language, language teaching should help students move from being able to use one language to use two by carefully taking language differences into account. This position connected to approaches that advocated contrastive analysis between languages as an essential component in second language teaching. An interesting theme in Pollard's research, and reflected as well in Craig (2006a, 2006b), and Winer (1982), is the usefulness of the development of students' competence in their vernacular as well as the target language, Standard English (SE). This issue raised important questions about the rationale for teaching language in schools, and the need to respect learners' first language, given the close connection between language and identity.

Other related educational research highlighted the influence of linguistic differences between SE and Creole varieties on students' writing in English (James, 1997, 2001; Narinesingh & Watts, 1992; Winer, 1982). The themes in the historic body of literature on language diversity and variation in Caribbean education pointed to possible transfer of features of students' vernacular or home language to their attempts to write using Standard varieties of language; the lack of correspondence of major grammatical features across language varieties and the effect of this on developing competence in the Standard language; and the consequence of inadequate exposure to the target language. Students' comprehension of texts written in SE would similarly be affected by these factors. It is because of such a situation that researchers emphasized the need for teachers to know the grammar of SE as well as Creole vernaculars, and use that knowledge to devise appropriate methodology to suit the requirements of learners at different levels of the school system (Craig, 2006a; James & Youssef, 2002). This is a critical issue that should be addressed in a policy to promote language inclusion in schools in all disciplines in the curriculum.

Currently, the position adopted in many Caribbean schools is perhaps similar to that described in Siegel's (2006) description of accommodation programmes where the standard language remains the medium of instruction, but students are permitted to use Creole language for speaking. Creole is generally not used for most writing activities, but is allowed to a very limited extent in story writing for the direct speech of characters being written about. Though Winer (1990) spoke of Creole being accommodated into the literature and the creative writing curriculum at the higher levels, she conceded in a later publication (Winer, 2006) that encouragement by policymakers and linguists over the years has not ensured informed practice by teachers nor the support of parents.

The Role of the Teacher

Interrogation of education policy with suitable approaches and strategies to accommodate speakers of Creole languages brings the role of the teacher into focus. As in every educational environment that aims to cater to diversity, situations where learners have different languages require teachers who are knowledgeable about language teaching and the centrality of language to learning; who are sensitive to the needs of the student population; and who respect the language of learners. Caribbean linguists and educators have always expressed concern about the impact of negative societal attitudes to Creole languages on the education of Creole-speaking learners, and the consequences for learners if teachers share the negative attitudes prevailing in their society.

Current research in methodology for successful classroom language teaching and learning suggests that teachers should help to develop students' language awareness of the differences between the official language of instruction and students' language. Craig (2006a) advocated a language awareness approach at both the primary and secondary level. His fundamental argument was that since English-related Creoles and the local Standard share linguistic features, English learners only need to acquire those English features that are absent from their vernacular. This requires both teachers and students to have knowledge of the areas of similarities and differences. However, while language awareness is unquestionably an essential goal in our language situation and a precursor to accommodate language diversity, the complexity of language acquisition and use requires more than the teaching of unknown features to engender the level of competence in Standard English that Caribbean students need to succeed in the education system as it is currently structured. This is especially true when language use across the curriculum is considered.

In summary, the literature surveyed above on language in education in the Caribbean can thus broadly be said to reflect concerns about overall language policy in the region, and the adoption of suitable policy and approaches to develop the literacy of the largely Creole-speaking population. Related issues are the way students' language is viewed, and the extent to which the vernacular is used to enable further development of their language competence. The role of the teacher and the suitability of methods in Creole socio-linguistic situations were also critical issues that educators and researchers felt it necessary to address in order to ensure that Caribbean learners become literate. In the next section, I focus on a wider body of research on the implications for education where there is divergence between language use in schools and students' communities. This presents another angle on the important question of the ways in which education systems can facilitate student learning by recognizing their home language and linking their out-of-school language skills and abilities to develop literacy in school settings.

HOME LANGUAGE AND LANGUAGE FOR LEARNING IN SCHOOL DISCIPLINES

While the question of language and language education has been well researched in the Caribbean region, there is not a significant body of literature exploring the impact of language diversity and language variation on students' learning in conventional school disciplines such as mathematics and science. The issue is important because subject content in textbooks and materials is represented in a Standard language. For most of the Caribbean region, this is Standard English (SE), the official language of instruction. A significant consequence is that teacher instruction is usually conducted in a language variety that is not the first language of many Caribbean learners. Even if it is argued that accommodation is made in some classrooms during oral classroom discourse, for official internal school examinations and standardized external examinations such as those conducted by the Caribbean Examination Council (CXC), many students are required to show their understanding using a variety that is not their first language. In this situation, students who command greater competence in reading and writing in the official language of instruction enjoy a greater advantage over those with more limited competence. However, the impact of different levels of access to the official school language on student achievement can be easily overlooked.

In international research literature on divergence between the language of school and home, different terms are used to refer to the type of language that students are required to use in order to learn in schools. This variety is most frequently referred to as "academic language" (Zwiers, 2005, 2007, 2008), though some researchers use alternative terms. Gee (2012), for example, considered the language of school a "social language," which students must acquire to develop "school literacy" (p. 76). How language use in school is described and characterized in the literature reflects an emphasis on either the linguistic or the social. Zwiers (2008) highlights the linguistic and defines "academic language" as "the set of words and phrases that describe content-area knowledge and procedures, express complex thinking processes and abstract concepts, and create cohesion and clarity in written and oral discourse" (p. 1). He argued that for English language learners, it is almost a third language, the acquisition of which is limited to the classroom.

Acquiring academic language has been identified as a critical factor in the disparity in achievement levels between high-performing and low-performing students in schools. This is due to the fact that academic language is characterized by subject-specific vocabulary, grammatical forms and structures, figurative expressions and prescribed ways of communicating (Ernst-Slavit & Mason, 2011; Fang & Schleppegrell, 2010; Gee, 2008; Nagy & Townsend, 2012; Schleppegrell, 2007). Halliday (1978) argued that language in school disciplines such as mathematics constructs knowledge in specific ways, and schools attempt to teach students to use this "register" to participate effectively in disciplinary ways of knowing. He defined "register" as "a set of meanings that is appropriate to a particular function of language, together with the words and structures which express these meanings" (p. 95). The variety serves a specific function and is characterized by domain-specific vocabulary, appropriate styles of meaning, and modes of argument. All three aspects can be more obvious to the teacher than to the student who may come to class with the knowledge of terms used in one way, and must learn the concept in a specific discipline called by the same name (Lager, 2006; Schleppegrell, 2007).

From a socio-cultural perspective, the way schools in any community require students to use language is termed "school literacy" (Gee, 2012). This required language use reflects the social practices and world views of particular social groups, usually the language of privileged mainstream culture. It indicates different ways of knowing and making sense of human world experiences, and is not a neutral, value-free language variety that is better suited for use in schools. Its use can be explained by prevailing social, cultural, and political dynamics which constrain teachers and students to act and speak in specific ways. Ethnographic studies conducted by researchers such as Brice Heath (1983), Cazden (2001), and Delpit (2006) revealed important differences in the discourse patterns of social groups; that is, the ways different groups use language to communicate in speech and in writing. Brice Heath (1983) identified specific cultural conflicts that created difficulties for working-class children in schools with value-systems that were more middle-class in orientation. Such differences were due to structural language patterns as well as discourse patterns, or what Brice Heath called "ways with words" that mark a variety of language as belonging to a particular speech community. Thus, different speech communities in a society might have different norms, and the use of non-standard varieties of a language may fill important communicative functions in particular contexts in social interaction (Adger, Wolfram, & Christian, 2007). Further, although differences among dialects of English might affect comprehension and interpretation, the source and severity of the problems are not always obvious. This includes the linguistic and textual, as well as the different "ways with words" that children have in other social contexts of their lives.

This body of research suggests that schools favour an essayist prose style that requires the use of grammatical and lexical information to make important relationships between sentences quite explicit. For some social groups, the way they are required to use language in school conflicts with their everyday, out-of-school language use. This situation can privilege one social group over others in school. Thus, the analysis of language use in schools cannot exclusively focus on linguistic and the textual factors, but must include the social and historical context in which language is used to produce educational discourse, and the value placed on the language that children bring to school.

When student achievement is measured by results in standardized examinations, the impact of language differences should be considered since there is evidence that transacting the academic language of subjects such as mathematics and science can be problematic for students in Caribbean examinations. For example, content analysis of examination reports on candidates' performance in mathematics and science examinations administered by the CXC in 2010–2011 identified four salient areas of language challenges for students—subject discipline terminology, data representation, content area reading, and content area writing—as these related to students' understanding and expression (Hewitt-Bradshaw, 2012). This investigation suggested that Caribbean students may be facing challenges in using the conventional tools of the disciplines to show their understanding of mathematics and science in examinations. A more in-depth investigation of classroom discourse in mathematics and science at the primary school level (Hewitt-Bradshaw, 2014) revealed that while primary school learners experienced challenges in understanding and expression because of morphological, syntactic, and semantic differences between Trinidad Creole English and Standard English, the language challenges were largely defined by the academic language that they were expected to use in the classroom. The process involved students' understanding and use of appropriate features of the registers of mathematics and science in classroom discourse that was linguistically and conceptually complex.

To highlight the importance of teacher sensitivity to the potential impact that language and language differences can have on student learning in school disciplines, the next section references additional literature on the impact of language on learning in mathematics and science, and illustrates this using two classroom teaching events. Both are taken from a study of learning across the curriculum in a Caribbean Creole language environment (Hewitt-Bradshaw, 2014), and the descriptions exemplify some of the language and language use issues discussed previously. They underscore the position that unless the language demands of all disciplines are understood and catered for in classrooms, and efforts made to promote meaningful levels of vernacular language inclusion in content area teaching and learning, some students would continue to be excluded from the teaching-learning process.

The Impact of Language in Mathematics and Science Learning

Studies conducted with students whose primary language was not the language in which they were instructed revealed varying degrees of difficulty with mathematical text due to language factors. Bernardo (2002) reported that Filipino-English bilingual students performed better at solving word problems when these problems were written in their first language. Similarly, Brown's (2005) investigation of differences in mathematics achievement between English language learners and fully English proficient students on a literacy-based performance assessment suggested that their underdeveloped literacy skills in English placed these learners at a disadvantage. When their socioeconomic status (SES) was factored into the study, the findings suggested that this factor had a significant impact on all students, whether their first language was English or not. Brown argued that high SES was correlated with greater proficiency with academic language, thus enabling students from more affluent backgrounds to achieve higher levels of success in mathematics. She concluded that the nature of the examination masked students' true abilities.

With respect to science, Lee, Quinn, and Valdés (2013) examined the language demands and opportunities embedded in the American National Research Council's *Framework for K–12 Science Education* and concluded that language challenges are amplified for English language learners and for other speakers with limited SE proficiency. General features of science learning that they identified included the fact that engagement involved both scientific sense-making and language use. In addition, essential classroom practices were language intensive and required scientific discourse involving all language modes: reading, writing, listening, speaking, viewing and visually representing. Lee, Quinn, and Valdés further observed that while the practices required by the Framework offer rich opportunities and demands for language learning, the classroom culture of discourse must be developed and supported, especially for learners whose first language is not the language in which they are being instructed. To do otherwise would mean that students are not given full opportunities to acquire concepts and develop crucial disciplinary discourse patterns. Consequently, as content increases in quantity and complexity at higher class levels, students would be increasingly excluded from developing knowledge and understanding in school disciplines.

Two teaching events that illustrate how important it is for teachers to attend to aspects of language use and language differences across the curriculum are among those described in Hewitt-Bradshaw (2014). This case study was conducted over one academic year at a primary school site and involved classroom observation of mathematics and science instruction in three classrooms with four participant teachers: Infants Year 1 (5–6 years old); Standard 1 (8–10 years old); and Standard 4 (10–13 years old). All 51 learners observed were from working class backgrounds and spoke Trinidad Creole English as their first language. However, the official language of instruction across the curriculum was Standard English. The study sought to determine the nature of the language challenges which this linguistic situation posed for these English language learners in the two content areas. The following descriptions of classroom teaching events connect to issues discussed in the literature on language in education. One is the need for classroom teaching to facilitate students' acquisition of the registers of school disciplines because academic language is different from every-day, out-of-school language. Another issue is the degree of teacher sensitivity to linguistic differences between the language varieties in use especially in second language or second dialect situations such as those that exist in many Caribbean territories.

The first illustrative teaching event took place in the Standard 4 classroom. At the beginning of the mathematics lesson, the teacher reviewed terms for concepts that she had taught previously. These included *angles, centre, diameter, quarters,* and *halves*. She followed this review segment with students' use of manipulatives to draw, fold, and locate different parts of the circle. Another main technique was oral questioning to ascertain whether students knew what the terms were, and how they related to each other; for example, that a diameter divided a circle in half. Analysis of transcribed discourse of the lesson revealed the difficulty some students initially experienced with the concepts during oral language activities. They were often unable to respond correctly to questions posed by the teacher. This in itself is not surprising since the process of teaching and learning involves moving from the largely unknown to the known. However, at the end of the lesson, many of the students appeared to have difficulty understanding what the teacher expected them to learn. The summative assessment for the lesson included an exercise which required students to complete two sentences on properties of the *circle*, given five preceding statements that conveyed information on the properties of *circles*, *semi-circles*, *quarters* and the relationship among them. The two additional statements for students to complete were:

1. A quarter of a circle when divided in two is _____.
2. _____ of a circle is 45°.

The fact that most of the students were unable to complete the statements correctly after extended teacher explanation and students' use of manipulatives indicated that the entire classroom discourse needed to be closely analyzed to determine the source of challenges for students. It would be incorrect to conclude that these students did not learn what many teachers would consider simple concepts in mathematics because of some intellectual deficit. Demographic information provided for the teacher indicated that she held professional qualifications and had many years of primary school teaching experience. The researcher's analysis of the context noted the high lexical density of both oral and written texts as one possible factor. This occurs when specialized terms related to a school discipline are used close to each other in speech or writing, and their relationships are often expressed using complex grammatical forms and structures. Lexical density, of course, often accompanies high conceptual density. What this teaching event suggests is that the teaching of unknown features (Craig, 2006a) and specialized vocabulary must be accompanied by other pedagogical strategies to facilitate deep understanding of disciplinary content.

In a second teaching event in the same classroom, a significant number of students experienced difficulties understanding and reproducing a diagram illustrating a *food web* in a science lesson. The teaching focus was to have students understand and represent the network of food chains reflecting feeding relationships of organisms using a diagram. At the start of the lesson, the teacher asked students to describe what they were seeing in a picture of a *food web*. She questioned them on several aspects of the diagram to elicit their understanding, focusing specifically on the direction of the arrow in the *food web* and asked students to describe what was happening in the diagram they were viewing. Students were expected to indicate which organism was eating or feeding on the other, and which one was being eaten. Through questioning, the teacher also sought to elicit what the arrow represented. This was part of a process to determine whether students understood the relationship among the organisms depicted in the diagram, and the significance of parts of the arrow. When the teacher perceived that students had difficulties using the terms *eats* and *is eaten by* in relation to the way in which organisms were displayed in the diagram, she spent time in the lesson contrasting the two terms and their use in context. The use of the two verb forms was crucial to learners' understanding and representation of the science concept and by the end of the lesson, a significant number were still having difficulty. It should be noted that for these students who were speakers of Trinidad Creole English, the passive Standard English construction *is eaten by* is different from the Creole structure that is used to express the same relationship, possibly *does get eat by*. In this instance, it would have been helpful for the teacher to make explicit the differences between the grammatical structure of Standard English and Creole as a strategy to facilitate understanding and use of the phrase in demonstrating concepts in science. The researcher noted that although the teacher recognized and responded to the challenges students faced and spent time teaching the language, at no point was this done with reference to the students' vernacular.

Based on this, and on previously discussed, research, it is reasonable to argue that language and literacy are embedded within different disciplinary-specific learning situations, and that subject-area content and the process of learning are connected. In addition, the structure and the conceptual demands of content-area texts affect the sense that learners make of those texts, how learners respond to them, and how they learn from them (Shanahan & Shanahan, 2008; Vacca, Vacca, & Mraz, 2011). Given situations where the language of learners is different from the language in which they are instructed, even greater care is needed to ensure that they are not excluded from the teaching-learning process because classroom pedagogy fails to use their language to make academic language accessible to them across the school curriculum.

CONCLUSION

Language differences between school and community can create situations of language diversity in schools and classrooms. Such diversity can result in structural inequities and affect the extent to which students participate in the school curriculum unless educators recognize the language demands of schools generally, as well as those that are required in every school subject. If a significant number of Caribbean students are not to be marginalized because their first language is significantly different from the official language of instruction, educators have to consider two broad and interrelated issues that this chapter highlighted. The first relates to language use and the fact that everyday language is different from the disciplinary discourse or academic language required for learning in content areas. The second relates to language structure, and is evident in the linguistic differences between language varieties in the classroom. If these aspects of language variation are not taken into account in teaching and learning, students suffer different degrees of exclusion from classroom discourse and this has an impact on their learning.

Language diversity should not be considered problematic nor should children's language be considered a liability. Instead, its reality should be acknowledged and accommodated in teacher classroom methodology, guided by a clear language policy. The language demands of disciplinary learning and the ways in which teacher methodology can accommodate the needs of Caribbean students is a broad area where further classroom research is needed. Too frequently, there is condemnation of the poor performance of students in regional examinations without necessary consideration of the effects of language discrimination and exclusion. More extensive investigation of classroom discourse in content areas to assess the extent to which language competence in SE is a factor in students' achievement would not only help educators to understand the nature of the language demands in school disciplines, but would simultaneously contribute to the formulation of effective language policies to support and improve learning for all students.

Although the Creole languages spoken in regional communities might overlap with Standard English, the differences in structure and use should not be taken for granted. The greater the distance between the nature and the patterns of discourse at home and at school, and the greater the linguistic variation between children's first language and the official language of instruction, the more demanding the process of learning would be for students. Many of the differences between home and school are cultural, and are often expressed in the language of the students. Where a positive role for their language is not defined in the education of Caribbean students, issues of linguistic and cultural exclusion arise. There is therefore a strong argument for educators to continue to discuss how students' language can be accommodated in classrooms to facilitate their learning.

Finally, additional research is needed into oral and written discourse processes in content area instruction. Teachers spend a lot of time explaining and questioning, and students spend as much time listening. Linguistic analysis of textbooks, learning materials, and examination questions would provide educators with critical knowledge of the way oral, written, and symbolic texts work to influence knowledge construction in school disciplines. Additionally, the values and ideologies underlying education processes in Caribbean influence how indigenous languages are treated. Access to classrooms at all levels—primary, secondary, and tertiary—would enable educators to gain insights necessary to create appropriate curricula to cater for language diversity and to improve teacher pedagogy so that the potential of all students can be developed.

REFERENCES

Adger, C., Wolfram, C., & Christian, D. (2007). *Dialects in schools and communities.* Mahwah, NJ: Erlbaum.

Bernardo, (2002). Language and mathematical problem-solving among bilinguals. *Journal of Psychology, 136(3),* 283–97.

Bickerton, D. (1975). *Dynamics of a Creole system*. Cambridge, UK: Cambridge University Press.
Brown, C. (2005). Equity of literacy-based math performance assessments for English language learners. *Bilingual Research Journal, 29*(2), 337–64.
Brice Heath, S. (1983). *Ways with words: Language, life, and work in communities and classrooms*. Cambridge, UK: Cambridge University.
Bryan, B. (2010). *Between two grammars: Research and practice for language learning and teaching in a Creole-speaking environment*. Kingston, Jamaica: Ian Randle Publishers.
Carrington, L. D. (1976). Determining language education policy in Caribbean sociolinguistic complexes. *International Journal of the Sociology of Language, 8*, 127–43.
Carrington, L. D. (1993). Creole space—A rich sample of competence? *Journal of Pidgin and Creole Linguistics, 8(2),* 227–36.
Cazden, C (2001). *Classroom discourse: The language of teaching and learning* (2nd ed.). Portsmouth, NH: Heineman.
Craig, D. (1971). Education and Creole English in the West Indies: Some sociolinguistic factors. In D. Hymes (Ed.), *Pidginisation and creolisation of languages* (pp. 371–92). Cambridge, UK: Cambridge University Press.
Craig, D. (1978). Language, society and education in the West Indies. *Caribbean Journal of Education, 7(1),* 1–17.
Craig, D. (1980). Models for education policy in Creole-speaking communities. In A. Valdman & A. Highfield (Eds.), *Theoretical orientations in Creole studies* (pp. 245–85). New York, NY: Academic Press.
Craig, D. (2006a). *Teaching language & literacy to Caribbean students: From vernacular to Standard English*. Kingston, Jamaica: Ian Randle.
Craig, D. (2006b). The use of the vernacular in West Indian education. In H. Simmons-McDonald & I. Robertson (Eds.), *Exploring the boundaries of Caribbean Creole languages* (pp. 99–117). Kingston, Jamaica: University of the West Indies Press.
Delpit, L. (2006). *Other people's children: Cultural conflict in the classroom* (2nd ed.). New York, NY: New Press.
Ernst-Slavit, G. & Mason, R. (2011). "Words that hold us up": Teacher talk and academic language in five upper elementary classrooms. *Linguistics and Education, 22(4),* 430–44.
Fang, Z., & Schleppegrell, M. (2010). Disciplinary literacies across content areas: Supporting secondary reading through functional language analysis. *Journal of Adolescent and Adult Literacy, 53(7),* 587–97.
Gee, J. P. (2008). What is academic language? In A. Rosebery & B. Warren (Eds.), *Teaching science to English language learners: Building on students' strengths* (pp. 57–70). Arlington, VA: National Science Teachers Association.
Gee, J. P. (2012). *Social linguistics and literacies: Ideology in discourses* (4th ed.). Oxford, UK: Routledge.
Halliday, M. A. K. (1978). *Language as social semiotic: The social interpretation of language meaning*. London, UK: Edward Arnold.
Hewitt-Bradshaw, I. (2012). Language issues in mathematics and science: An analysis of examiners' reports on students' performance in Caribbean Secondary Education Certificate examinations (2010–2011). *Caribbean Curriculum, 19,* 43–66.

Hewitt-Bradshaw, I. (2014). *Speakers of Trinidad English Creole taught in Standard English: Understanding the nature of the language challenges in mathematics and science.* (Unpublished doctoral dissertation). The University of the West Indies, St. Augustine, Trinidad.

James, W. (1997). Students' TAM errors in the context of the speech of Tobago. (Unpublished doctoral dissertation). The University of the West Indies, St. Augustine, Trinidad.

James, W. (2001). Explaining past for past perfect errors in a Caribbean English Creole environment. *Caribbean Curriculum, 8,* 89–110.

James, W., & Youssef, V. (2002). *The languages of Tobago: Genesis, structure and perspectives.* St. Augustine, Trinidad: The University of the West Indies.

Lager, C. (2006). Types of mathematics–language reading interactions that unnecessarily hinder algebra learning and assessment. *Reading Psychology, 27(2–3),* 165–204.

Lee, O., Quinn, H., & Valdés, G. (2013). Science and language for English language learners in relation to Next Generation Science Standards and with implications for Common Core State Standards for English language arts and mathematics. *Educational Researcher, 42(4),* 223–33. doi 10.3012/0013189X13480524

Nagy, W., & Townsend, D. (2012). Words as tools: Learning academic vocabulary as language acquisition. *Reading Research Quarterly, 47(1),* 91–108.

Narinesingh, R., & Watts, M. (1992). Literacy in education: A dual exploration of reading and writing. In O. Kuboni (Ed.), *Literacy in the modern world: Proceedings of the symposium* (pp. 29–44). St. Augustine, Trinidad: School of Education, The University of the West Indies.

Nero, S. (2006). *Dialects, Englishes, Creoles, and education.* Mahwah, NJ: Lawrence Erlbaum Association.

Nero, S., & Ahmad, D. (2014). *Vernaculars in the classroom: Paradoxes, pedagogy, possibilities.* New York, NY: Routledge.

Pollard, V. (1978, July). *Word and meaning in Jamaican Creole: Some problems for teachers of English.* Paper presented at the Conference of the Society for Caribbean Linguistics, Barbados.

Pollard, V. (1993). *From Jamaican Creole to Standard English: A handbook for teachers.* Brooklyn, NY: Caribbean Research Centre.

Roberts, P. (2007). *West Indians and their language* (2nd ed.). Cambridge, UK: Cambridge University Press.

Robertson, I. (1996). Language education policy: Towards a rational approach for Caribbean states. In P. Christie (Ed.), *Caribbean language issues: Old and new* (pp. 112–19). Kingston, Jamaica: The Press, The University of the West Indies.

Robertson, I. (1999). Educational linguistics for the Caribbean: Some considerations. *Caribbean Journal of Education, 21(1&2),* 75–86.

Salend, S. (2011). *Creating inclusive classrooms: Effective and reflective practices* (7th ed.). Boston, MA: Pearson.

Schleppegrell, M. J. (2007). The linguistic challenges of mathematics teaching and learning: A research review. *Reading & Writing Quarterly, 23(2),* 139–59.

Shanahan, T., & Shanahan, C. (2008). Teaching disciplinary literacy to adolescents: Rethinking content area literacy. *Harvard Educational Review, 78(1),* 40–59.

Siegel, J. (2006). Keeping Creoles and dialects out of the classroom: Is it justified? In S. Nero (Ed.), *Dialects, Englishes, Creoles, and education* (pp. 39–69). Mahwah, NJ: Lawrence Erlbaum Association.

Siegel, J. (2008). *The emergence of Pidgin and Creole languages*. New York, NY: Oxford University Press.

Simmons-McDonald, H. (2004). Trends in teaching standard varieties to creole and vernacular speakers. *Annual Review of Applied Linguistics, 24*, 187–208.

Vacca, R., Vacca, J. A., & Mraz, M. (2011). *Content area reading: Literacy and learning across the curriculum* (10th ed.). Boston, MA: Pearson.

Winer, L. (1982). An analysis of the errors in the written compositions of Trinidadian English Creole speakers (Unpublished doctoral dissertation). The University of the West Indies, St. Augustine.

Winer, L. (1990). Orthographic standardization for Trinidad and Tobago: Linguistic and socio-political considerations in an English Creole community. *Language Problems and Language Planning, 14(3),* 237–68.

Winer, L. (2006). Teaching English to Caribbean English Creole-speaking students in the Caribbean and North America. In S. Nero (Ed.). *Dialects, Englishes, Creoles, and education* (pp. 105–118). Mahwah, NJ: Lawrence Erlbaum.

Zwiers, J. (2005). The third language of academic English. *Educational Leadership, 62(4),* 60–63.

Zwiers, J. (2007). Teacher practices and perspectives for developing academic language. *International Journal of Applied Linguistics, 17(1),* 93–116.

Zwiers, J. (2008). *Building academic language: Essential practices for content classrooms*. San Francisco, CA: Jossey-Bass.

CHAPTER 6

STUDENT ASSESSMENT SYSTEMS IN THE CARIBBEAN AS AN OBSTACLE TO INCLUSIVE EDUCATION

The Case of Trinidad and Tobago

Jerome De Lisle, Nadia Laptiste-Francis,
Sabrina McMillan-Solomon, and Cheryl Bowrin-Williams

AN ASSESSMENT SYSTEM ALIGNED TO THE PHILOSOPHY OF INCLUSION

Worldwide, there is now growing awareness of the need to adopt a system perspective when analyzing student assessment reform in education (Berry, 2010; Black & Wiliam, 2007; Clarke, 2012). A student assessment system may be considered as all the policies, structures, practices, and tools needed for generating and using information on student learning within a nation state (Clarke, 2012). The student assessment system of a nation state therefore provides a complete framework for gathering information on student learning for multiple purposes. A high-quality

Caribbean Discourse in Inclusive Education:
Historical and Contemporary Issues, pages 87–105.
Copyright © 2017 by Information Age Publishing
All rights of reproduction in any form reserved.

student assessment system will facilitate three key procedural tasks: (1) eliciting and interpreting different kinds of evidence; (2) making credible judgments; and (3) taking different kinds of actions based on the evidence (Harlen, 2007). Such information is needed for key decisions in inclusion,[1] such as diagnosis, placement, and the provision of additional support and resources.

Despite differing architectural designs, many student assessment systems include three distinct types of tools: public examinations for selection and certifying learning; large scale assessments for monitoring and accountability; and classroom assessments for supporting and promoting learning (Black & Wiliam, 2007). Although different student assessment systems might emphasize specific tools, different tools are required in a comprehensive, coherent, and balanced student assessment system. The comprehensive dimension implies that a full range of assessment tools are available (Gallagher, 2010). Coherence means that the tools in the assessment system inform each other, and also that assessment and instructional purposes connect (Herman, 2010). A balanced system means that no one assessment tool is given inordinate emphasis. High quality student assessment systems, then, are essentially about providing valid data for making different kinds of inferences or decisions in an education system (Black & Wiliam, 2007).

From this data-centric perspective, a quality student-assessment system might be measured by the sufficiency and appropriateness of the information available to make key decisions (Mislevy, 2010). The first criterion of sufficiency relates to adequate amounts of high-quality information and the second criterion of appropriateness relates to the assessment's fitness for purpose or suitability of the data for particular uses (Clarke, 2012; Mansell, James, & the Assessment Reform Group, 2009). These criteria imply that some tools may provide insufficient or inappropriate information. The criteria of sufficiency and appropriateness can be illustrated by the current practice in Trinidad and Tobago of using the capricious cutscore of 30 percent on the Secondary Entrance Assessment for judging schools and individuals in Trinidad and Tobago. The questions then become: (1) Is this information sufficient and of high quality? (2) Is a large-scale, high-stakes placement examination the best tool for providing this kind of information?

Promoting and supporting learning are the critical goals in a comprehensive, coherent, and balanced assessment system (Gallagher, 2010). It is this purpose (and not sorting and certifying) that is truly supportive of progress towards a high-performing and equitable education system (Darling-Hammond et al., 2013; Pellegrino, 2014). A high-performing equitable education system is one that combines quality with equity (Ainscow, Dyson, Goldrick, & West, 2012). This is a necessary and appropriate goal for postcolonial education systems in the Anglophone Caribbean. Equity as a goal demands greater fairness and inclusion in the education system. For example, evidence from both PISA and PIRLS suggests

---

[1] Vislie (2003) talks about an observed policy shift from integration to inclusion in Western societies after Salamanca. Such a shift may not have occurred in the education systems of the small island states of the Caribbean with both approaches strongly resisted in policy implementation.

that the Trinidad and Tobago education system reports high levels of inequality linked to gender and socioeconomic status (De Lisle, Seecharan, & Ayodike, 2010). In contrast, inclusion implies that all students are able to reach a basic minimum skill level (Field, Kuczera, & Pont, 2007; OECD, 2012). This broad definition extends the meaning of inclusion beyond the integration of special education needs students to processes targeting full access by all groups to high quality educational experiences (UNESCO, 2008). Inclusion, then, represents an overall ethic of care and concern for the most vulnerable of groups of learners, including but not exclusive to those with designated special education needs.

In an inclusive system, a compatible assessment system must emphasize tools for promoting and supporting learning rather than prioritizing instruments meant to select and place vulnerable and diverse learners. This is because the system will be focused on helping diverse learners reach a minimum level of competence in core areas. These supportive student assessment tools will be varied, and include formative assessment in the teaching-learning process, general diagnostic assessments to identify learning needs, and psychoeducational assessments for identifying students with specific special education needs. The term "formative assessment" here is equivalent to assessment for learning with assessment as learning as a subset. The latter focuses upon the development of higher order skills by providing challenging cognitive tasks with self-regulation as an outcome (Earl, 2013). Diagnostic assessments include both informal teacher made instruments and specialized instruments. Psychoeducational assessments include a broad range of specialized instruments use to identify students in need of special services.

Perhaps it is notable that these different tools function entirely within the boundary of the school and classroom. In contrast, public examinations and monitoring systems are large-scale assessments that are administered by an agency external to the school. These tools are designed by technocrats in Ministries of Education and enter the classroom and schools as boundary subjects (Moss, Girard, & Haniford, 2006). When they cross the boundary, some system rules are distorted, and data may be misused. For example, in Trinidad and Tobago the National Tests in primary school are explicitly designed to monitor learning at a system level. However, some school sites and classrooms misuse the information on performance standards to label individual students (De Lisle, 2015). Many principles of good school and classroom practices are embedded within systems such as Response to Intervention (RTI) (Wixson & Valencia, 2011). The multiple uses of assessment in such systems include screening, diagnosis, formative progress monitoring, benchmark progress monitoring, and summative assessment (Lipson, Chomsky-Huggins, & Kanfer, 2011). However, RTI systems remain rare in the Anglophone Caribbean. Nevertheless, it is through the use of formative, diagnostic and psychoeducational assessments that diverse learners are able to experience inclusion.

Assessment Types/ Quality Drivers	Classroom Assessment Public Examinations National Learning Assessments
Enabling Context *Overall framework of policies, leadership, organizational structures, fiscal and human resources in which assessment activity takes place in a country or system and the extent to which that framework is conducive to, or supportive of, the assessment activity.*	• Policies • Leadership and public engagement • Funding • Institutional arrangements • Human resources
System Alignment *Degree to which the assessment is coherent with other components of the education system* **Assessment Quality** *Degree to which the assessment meets quality standards, is fair, and is used in an effective way*	• Learning/quality goals • Curriculum • Pre and in-service training opportunities • Ensuring quality (design, administration, analysis) • Ensuring effective uses

FIGURE 6.1. The System Approach to Better Results Evaluation (SABER) framework for student assessment systems (Clarke, 2012).

Judging Caribbean Education and Assessment Systems

The World Bank project, *Systems Approach to Better Education Results* (SABER), provides one useful framework for evaluating student assessment systems. As illustrated in Figure 6.1, this framework includes two major dimensions: (1) assessment types and purposes, focusing upon classroom assessments, examinations, and large scale, system-level assessments; and (2) quality drivers, focusing upon enabling context, system alignment, and assessment quality. The enabling context refers to governance, legislative and policy frameworks along with resources and structures that support educational assessment. System alignment refers to the level of coherence between elements in the system, including goals. Assessment quality refers to the validity and reliability in instruments, processes and procedures. Both dimensions are assessed on a four-point scale varying from latent (absence of), emerging (partial), and established (acceptable) through advanced (best practice).

Currently, there is no student assessment system in the Anglophone Caribbean which has been evaluated in SABER. However, there are evaluations of student assessment systems in similar postcolonial contexts. Two examples cited here are Sri Lanka and Zambia. Sri Lanka was judged as emerging in classroom assessments, established in public examinations, emerging in national learning assessments, and latent in international large scale assessment. Zambia's evaluation is similar, except that international large scale assessments are emerging. Therefore, in both contexts the public examination system appeared much more developed than the other components. The weakness of classroom assessment and the dominance of public examinations in these systems is very apparent and is a part of all postcolonial student assessment systems.

Perhaps what has been neglected in SABER evaluations is the washback effect of high-stakes public examination on teaching, learning and assessment at the classroom level as captured in the historical study of wash back in Sri Lanka "O" Level examinations (Wall & Alderson, 1993). The implications for student assessment systems in the Caribbean are obvious. Any evaluation must consider the possibility of assessment misuse. For example, current evidence suggests that school-based assessments have frequently been misused even in high-performing assessment systems such as Hong Kong (Qian, 2014). This misuse is only partially reported in the SABER report for Sri Lanka, which discusses the presence of continuous and school-based assessments, but notes the absence of system-level guidance or monitoring systems. Likewise, in Zambia, the focus of classroom continuous assessments is mainly administrative, rather than acting as a pedagogical resource. A similar judgement might be made of classroom assessment in Trinidad and Tobago. Although protocols for SBAs and CAC are formerly prescribed, the quality of practice is universally poor. For the now-discontinued continuous assessment programme (CAC) of the secondary entrance assessment (SEA) in Trinidad and Tobago, there are similar issues with the fidelity of implementation. Moreover, training for formative assessment in teacher preparation programmes remains limited as is monitoring.

Another notable deficiency of the SABER evaluation framework is the failure to acknowledge the socio-historical context of education. This context strongly influences existing assessment policies and practice in postcolonial states. Thus, this is an important analytical tool for better understanding the architecture and functioning of current assessment systems in the Anglophone Caribbean. For example, current education and assessment systems have retained many institutionalized features of colonial systems. For example, De Lisle (2012) has explored the historical development of the Secondary Entrance Assessment (SEA) from the Common Entrance Examination (CEE) installed at Independence. The SEA and CEE have retained many design and purpose features of the College Exhibition Examination from the colonial era.

De Lisle (2012) described the system for secondary school selection as stable in purpose despite sporadic tinkering (incrementalism) in the assessment design by policymakers. Such a pattern of long periods of stability spiked with occasional disequilibrium is perhaps better regarded as an example of punctuated equilibrium theory in policy change (Petridou, 2014). Such a pattern of policy change reflects perhaps the hidden concerns of policymakers or what issues are brought to their attention. If the concern of policymakers is to maintain the elitist system, then even when appropriate data is brought to their attention, the required policy change might still be ignored. Indeed, there are significant attentional deficits among policymakers in the Anglophone Caribbean (Jones & Baumgartner, 2012).

The explicit focus on public examinations in the student assessment system of Trinidad and Tobago is evident in the placement of high stakes certification and selection tests at multiple points in the system: 11+, 16+ and 18+. These selection systems operate to ensure that the educational system is highly stratified with different school types arranged hierarchically (London, 1989). This is most evident in the secondary school system, where there are four distinct school types as illustrated in Figure 6.2. However, even at the primary school level, there is a complex pattern of stratification with increasing numbers of private schools and prestigious government and denominational public primary schools often located in urban areas (De Lisle, Smith, & Jules, 2010).

The outcome of early selection leading to stratification is shown in Figure 6.2. The outcome is high levels of horizontal and vertical differentiation. A differentiated school system is the exact opposite to a seamless system. Vertical differentiation means that some students are repeating grades or are being excluded from some tracks. Horizontal differentiation means that advantaged and disadvantaged students attend different schools. High levels of vertical and horizontal differentiation imply that the education system is not inclusive and does not accommodate all learners in high quality learning. The high levels of both vertical and horizontal differentiation may be related to continued early selection at eleven plus despite the provision of universal access to secondary education in 2001.

Class	ACADEMIC UNIVERSITIES		COMMUNITY/ TECHNICAL COLLEGES		>18
TERT-IARY					AGE
F 6.2	TRADITIONAL PUBLIC SECONDARY SCHOOLS (BUILT BEFORE 1950)	MODERN PUBLIC SECONDARY SCHOOLS (BUILT 1950-1970)	NEW SECTOR PUBLIC SECONDARY SCHOOL (BUILT 1970-1990)	SEMP PUBLIC SECONDARY SCHOOLS (BUILT AFTER 1990)	18
F 6.1					17
F5					16
F6					15
F3					14
F2					13
F1					12
S5	PRIVATE PRIMARY	GOV'T-ASSISTED (DENOMINATIONAL) PUBLIC PRIMARY		GOV'T PUBLIC PRIMARY	11
S4					10
S3					9
S2					8
S1					7
I2					6
I1					5
Y4	PRIVATE CENTRES	OLD GOV'T CENTRES	SERVOL CENTRES	NEW GOV'T CENTRES	4
Y3					3

FIGURE 6.2. The Education System of Trinidad and Tobago Showing Horizontal Differentiation in all Sectors.

OECD (2010) data suggest that the level of horizontal differentiation in the secondary school system of Trinidad and Tobago is high, and similar to that of school systems in Germany and Argentina. Unlike Germany, with three separate secondary school tracks—the *Gymnasium*, the *Realschule* and the *Haptuschle*—Trinidad and Tobago has four models of high school that have been implemented over time.[2] Figure 6.2 shows these models as: (1) the traditional schools built prior to 1950; (2) the Government 5-year schools built after 1959; (3) the new sector schools built during 1970–1990; and (4) the SEMP schools built after 1990. The perceived prestige and SEA scores of students assigned are ranked as follows: (1) traditional schools; (2) Government 5-year schools; (3) Secondary Education Modernization (SEMP) schools; and (4) new sector schools. This ranking is maintained by the 11+ selection and placement system (De Lisle, 2012; De Lisle, Smith, Keller, & Jules, 2012).

The Trinidad and Tobago Assessment System as a Barrier to Inclusion

Caribbean student assessment systems such as in Trinidad and Tobago still emphasize sorting as a predominant purpose to the exclusion of other assessment purposes such as accountability and support of learning. Lavia (2007) correctly identified this pervasive enthusiasm for, and belief in, the efficiency of examinations as a notable barrier to the development of inclusive structures in the Caribbean. This emphasis on sorting may be fuelled by a pervasive philosophy of elitism inherited from colonial education. Such an emphasis may be founded on the widespread belief that differences in "natural ability" exist, are unchangeable, and are measurable in achievement tests. This is related to an ability belief-system that Li and Lee (2004) called an entity conception of ability.[3] It might be this belief-system that amounts to a philosophical mind-set with an elitist logic that influences both the design of the education and assessment systems.

There are several implications of this hypothesized philosophical mind-set for inclusive thinking, practice, and policy. One consequence for policymakers might be silences or pauses in the policy on inclusion. For example, local policy documents rarely speak of barriers to learning, as if they do not exist. Indeed, some policy documents appear to conflate differences in student performances due to ability with achievement differences due to context (Government of the Republic of Trinidad and Tobago, 2012). Recent policy on the Continuous Assessment Component (CAC) of the Secondary Entrance Assessment (SEA) is also notable in that it regards sorting as inevitable even when claiming to focus upon improved learning through feedback and multiple intelligences. This assessment innova-

---

[2] London (1991) argued that in the postcolonial development of secondary education, there is no one single model of the secondary school, but instead multiple conceptions that have been separately developed and implemented over time.

[3] This belief-system is also considered a theory of intelligence (See Bonne & Johnston, 2016)

tion is designed as a multi-purpose instrument and claims to honour assessment for learning while at the same time privileging the high stakes sorting function (Stobart, 2009).

Elitist philosophical mind-sets often lead to misuse of assessment results, as in the use of a 30 percent cutscore in the high stakes SEA to designate students as "remedial." There is little doubt that this is the wrong assessment tool, and the wrong information for making such a decision. The absence of radical changes in the student assessment system is another perverse outcome of elitist philosophical mind-sets. Indeed, unlike the high-performing systems of Hong Kong and Singapore (OECD, 2011), no radical reform in high-stakes testing at age eleven has been attempted in Trinidad and Tobago. The purpose of the current system reform initiative, called the seamless education project, is to ensure lower levels of vertical and horizontal differentiation. Despite these policy intentions, the focus on high-stakes public examinations at age eleven has been retained and even expanded. The irony of further expanding a high-stakes examination positioned at the transition of primary and secondary schooling in an era of seamless education has somehow been lost on the policymakers.

Additionally, despite several funded evaluations, there remains an absence of authentic assessment for learning in the classroom, and few opportunities for sustained diagnostic assessment or accommodations in the Trinidad and Tobago education system (Northey, Bennett, & Canales, 2007). Authentic assessment for learning is embedded assessment on cognitively challenging tasks in which there is a focus on feedback and performance of understanding (Brookhart, Moss, & Long, 2008; Swaffield, 2011). Arguably, radical reform of Caribbean student assessment systems is now needed to facilitate inclusion. This study is designed to provide an evaluation of the student assessment system in Trinidad and Tobago in terms of facilitating or hindering inclusion and integration processes. Judgment is based on the sufficiency and appropriateness of the information available to make key decisions related to these processes. The key research questions were:

1. How is the relationship between the assessment system and the goals and outcomes of inclusion conceptualized in policy documents related to general and special education?
2. What are stakeholders' perspectives on the role of the assessment system and student learning in inclusion?

DESIGN OF STUDY

This is a qualitative study using data obtained from content analysis of policy documents and individual interviews conducted with key stakeholders. The stakeholders were education leaders at different levels of the special education needs system. These included a former government minister, a university lecturer, a district administrator, and a former principal of a special school. Document analysis is a systematic procedure for evaluating documents in order to elicit meaning and gain understanding of key issues (Bowen, 2009). Content analysis is the primary process used to identify major themes in document analysis. The content analysis was primarily inductive with a focus on identifying latent content, including silences and pauses in policy (Elo & Kyngäs, 2008). The inductive method used was akin to applied thematic analysis (Guest, MacQueen, & Namey, 2012). Broad sub-themes were first identified and these sub-themes were then coalesced and organized into the major themes.

The policy documents were selected from recent policy papers associated with the seamless education project. The five documents from 2007 to 2010 were used to inform the intervention phase of the seamless education project. These included:

1. Gender issues in education and intervention strategies to increase participation of boys (George, Quamina-Aiyejina, Cain, & Mohammed (2009));
2. Language and language education policy (Robertson, 2010);
3. Achieving Inclusion: Transforming the Education System of Trinidad and Tobago (Peters et al., 2008);
4. Curriculum and instruction, testing and evaluation, and Spanish as the first foreign language (Northey, Bennett, & Canales, 2007);
5. Evaluation of the 2000 Continuous Assessment Programme in Trinidad and Tobago (De Lisle, 2010).

FINDINGS

The three themes identified from the documents and interviews were: (1) the need for a comprehensive and balanced assessment system; (2) pervasive, negative influence of high-stakes testing; and (3) the neglect of assessment tools and policies for inclusion.

A Comprehensive and Balanced Assessment System?

Several of the policy documents identified the need for a comprehensive and balanced assessment system to provide greater support for twenty-first-century learning in a seamless education system. This was most explicitly stated by De Lisle (2010) where the issue provides a backdrop for several of the key recommendations:

> The key recommendations focused on the need to develop a coherent and balanced comprehensive assessment policy and a simplified, targeted and restructured CAP, with an emphasis on formative assessment. (p. 4)

As a matter of fact, recommendation 7 is very specific in this regard, identifying the need to "develop a nation-wide overall policy for the primary school that promotes a balanced, coherent, comprehensive assessment system that provides continuous data, but with an emphasis on formative assessment practice" (p. 166).

De Lisle's (2010) focus on the use of formative assessment in the classroom is consistent with the original planners' conception of the 2000 Continuous Assessment Programme, which was intended to improve students' readiness for learning according to the planners. However, the Peters et al. report (2008)—popularly called the Miske Witt and Associates report—also considered some assessment functions as the cornerstone of reform for inclusion. It identified: (1) assessment and early intervention; and (2) monitoring and evaluation as two of the six major goals in making the system more inclusive. In terms of reform they had argued for the following reform goals:

> All Diagnosticians and Special Education Teachers will receive training in how to use informal diagnostic instruments as a way of accurately understanding students' current level of functioning and achievement. Likewise, all teachers will participate in technology-based training aimed at improving assessment literacy. As part of this training, teachers will learn how to best use classroom assessment data to improve education for their students. The overall aim of Diagnostician, Special Education, and General Education teacher training is to provide school-based personnel with data from which to make decisions on how to best support student learning. (Peters et al., 2008, p. 21)

This report therefore saw assessment as a critical tool facilitating inclusion by providing information or data to both the general and specialist teacher. Implied in this focus on training personnel to teach all students is understanding that there are a variety of assessment tools, currently absent in the system, which are necessary to ensure inclusion and integration.

The Pervasive, Negative Influence of High Stakes Testing

The concern over the high-stakes testing environment in Trinidad and Tobago was expressed in four out of the five reports. The most expansive criticism is found in the work of Northey, Bennett, and Canales (2007), who identified "national examinations as having a distorting effect on both curriculum and pedagogy. They noted that:

> While a number of curriculum guides contain aspects of a modern constructivist approach such as encouragement of continuous assessment and engagement of students, classroom practice emphasizes a more transmissive approach. One key influential factor has been the national exams, which strongly influence what content teachers emphasize, the amount of curriculum time spent in preparing for exams and the teaching/learning strategies utilized. This has led to a more teacher-centred, rather than a student-centred, approach, which means less focus on, and adaptation to, student-oriented approaches to learning. (p. 4)

Therefore, Northey, Bennett, and Canales (2007) pointed to possible perverse wash back effects from high-stakes testing on pedagogy. De Lisle (2010) also theorized on the possibility of negative wash back if high stakes were associated with the continuous assessment programme. It seems more likely, however, that the pervasive beliefs associated with the traditionally elitist education system acted to exert a strong influence on curriculum, pedagogy, and assessment. Peters et al. (2008), in the Miske Witt and Associates report, alluded to such a belief pattern, observing that:

> When parents and students described students, they invariably used test scores as a barometer. "Results are up" and "results are good" were common responses, indicating that "..." high-stakes testing plays a dominant role in the ethos of general education schools. Special school parents were not concerned with test scores in their children's current schools, but of the high stakes of general education schools. Concerns over test results and the lifelong implications of high or low marks led some parents to question inclusive education policy. One parent expressed his desire for students to be together under the same roof, but not to compete for attention in the same classrooms. "They should be in the same school, but not in the same classroom," he said. (p. 20)

These observations point perhaps to this more general influence, evident in the pervasive penchant for labelling among stakeholders. Such a misuse of test scores will likely be a strong inhibitor of inclusive practice.

Despite this concern for results from tests and testing, paradoxically, both classroom and national tests were reported to be of low quality. Indeed, one of the concerns in at least three of the five policy documents was the lack of assessment validity coupled with a penchant for testing low order skills. George et al. (2009), for example, observed that the content and cognitive level of curriculum tended to favour lower order skills but felt that the National Tests also de-emphasized broader skills that might be expected given a focus on the holistic aspect of a child's development. However, this weakness was not only observed for national large scale assessments. De Lisle (2010) also judged classroom performance assessments to be uncommon and when practiced by the teacher, the quality was invariably low. More specifically, he noted that there was "wide variation in practice, universal absence of training, and general lack of support at building sites" (p. 4).

Despite these observations on the pervasive lack of quality assessment practices and the absence of appropriate assessment skills, De Lisle (2010) also theorized that:

> The place to experiment with large-scale performance assessment might be in the national tests where it is possible to introduce a writing portfolio at this stage. The assessment task would be in response to a standardized prompt and would involve several writing products illustrating the process of writing over a two-week period. Scoring would be [by] a trait rubric. This would remove writing from the high stakes

SEA but reinforce writing as a process in the accountability system. The benefit of removing the high stakes writing from the national assessments is the disadvantage experienced by males, low SES students, and students from low quality schools. (p. 175)

Thus, even in this work, there seems to be an inordinate emphasis on the role of large-scale assessments in the system. Although large-scale assessments are needed for monitoring, selection and certification, problems in curriculum and pedagogy within classrooms can rarely be solved by such data, or instructionally sensitive large scale assessments.

Robertson (2010) supported the adverse judgments on the quality of assessment and testing by George et al. (2009) and De Lisle (2010). He felt that, given the language situation in Trinidad and Tobago, most test score inferences were unfair because they assumed that the first language of the child was the standard rather than the creole. He therefore advised:

There are clear implications here for how test scores are understood and interpreted as well as for evaluation of the student based on test scores. The student for whom the language of the test is not the first and for whom control of the language of the test is restricted, has to approach the assessment exercise through the mediation of the native or first language. (p. 11)

Thus, there are implications for test use and interpretation related to the diversity of learners in Trinidad and Tobago. Since learners come from a wide variety of cultural and socioeconomic contexts, high-stakes tests in Trinidad and Tobago inevitably capture some aspect of construct irrelevant variance.

The majority of interviewees also perceived evidence of unfairness in the system, especially for students with special needs. This observation was related to the fact that students with special education needs often did not have the opportunity to learn, but were still expected to take national monitoring tests and high stakes assessments. For example, one respondent noted:

The risk of bias emerging in those situation[s] is very real because ... we have to make sure that the curriculum that these children are exposed to is aligned to the test. That is one of the key issues with the use of formal standardized tests which are sometimes purchased off the shelves. Another thing is our local high stakes test here also carry the same or similar challenges for students because even though there is a written curriculum, when we speak of children with special needs a lot of the time the curriculum doesn't get covered for one reason or another.

The issue with the lack of opportunities to learn was widespread through the system and some respondents felt that this invalidated the use of the 30 percent benchmark since many students in this category did not have opportunities to learn. Thus another interviewee admitted that:

30 percent is what we use as a benchmark. It was used since Student Support started. That was the flag that they used out of the National Test. Anybody who was scoring under 30 percent may need to be investigated. What we have recognized over the years though is that that 30 percent is not always indicative of the child's natural ability totally. Because we have had incidences of absenteeism which would have contributed to the 30 percent. If you are not coming to school you can't learn, right. Of the majority of students scoring under 30 percent we have found that the majority of them require remediation, not special education.

The Neglect of Assessment Tools and Policies for Inclusion

One of the interviewees believed that the system was not truly cognizant of the needs and purposes of inclusion. For her, then, the changes that had been made were mostly symbolic, a token admission in the midst of persistent neglect. She noted that the losers were the students, especially the most marginalized. She commented:

> The child is being left behind and we're using all these terms that we hear from North America but in terms of putting things in place to ensure that the children are not left behind, we are sadly lacking. So I say, you know, get it right. First of all, understand disability. I am not sure that the powers that be understand anything about disabilities, special needs and inclusive education.

One of the reasons for such policy stasis was the lack of capacity in the areas of diagnostic tests and psychoeducational assessments. Thus, Peters et al. (2008) called specifically for training of diagnosticians and special education teachers in assessment practice. The report argued that this was necessary for these teachers to assess students' current level of functioning and achievement. The consultants in this report were moved to develop a local diagnostic tool because they felt that standardized instruments from the global North were culturally and linguistically inappropriate. However, they did not offer evidence for this claim of inappropriateness or lack of validity. Although the CAP evaluation report claimed to call for a coherent balanced assessment system, it was strangely silent on the use of specialized psychoeducational assessments. This report was also somewhat vague on the nature of diagnostic assessments, a policy reminiscent of the 2000 CAP.

In terms of an assessment system catering for inclusion, Peters et al (2008) called for the establishment of a two-tiered system of assessment in which diagnoses of "invisible disabilities" in learning, behavior and cognition would be followed by informal instruments to better understand these needs. The report warned against the unhelpful practice of labelling students, but does not explain how this is to be avoided in their two tier system. The possibility of misuse was in fact raised by one of the interviewees who functioned as an education leader at district level. He noted that:

> Recently we would have done teacher training where we would have distributed certain screeners to teachers with the verbal warning "do not diagnose." But that

does not stop the teacher from using knowledge because many teachers are also furthering their studies so they begin to feel confident that they have given the screener, without realizing it they begin to diagnose and that becomes very dangerous. So that is the major issue that we have within the referral process with teachers using screeners—misuse.

Any system that ignores the teacher is likely to promote such misuse. This suggests that extensive system wide training is needed, including neglected areas such as accommodations since this was inappropriately applied.

De Lisle (2010) included several useful recommendations as target goals towards developing a comprehensive balanced student assessment system applicable to inclusion. These included a clear data route for information from diagnostic assessments to individualized education plans and school-based special education needs teams. The benchmarks also included changes in the governance structure for assessment, private service providers and a focus on site based learning. De Lisle also suggested that long-cycle formative assessments be introduced in some districts.

DISCUSSIONS AND IMPLICATIONS

The evaluation provided by the analysis of the policy documents and interviewees points to a student assessment system in Trinidad and Tobago that is fundamentally and fatally flawed. Further tinkering with such a system to cater to the needs of diverse learners in an inclusive system may not at all be possible. Indeed, recent innovations such as the CAC meant to improve learning likely resulted in perverse effects, further exaggerating the loss suffered by marginalized students. The policy reports associated with seamless education suggest that the current student assessment system is characterized by low assessment literacy and the absence of key tools for inclusion. The lack of training and tools mean that information to guide inclusion is not available.

However, the analysis also suggests that the reluctance to move the education system forward towards greater equity derives not just from the absence of assessment tools or misuse of these assessment tools, but from fundamental societal understandings and core beliefs that drive assessment purposes and use. It is these beliefs and (mis)understandings that appear to drive policy formulation and implementation. The relationship between belief and policy actions is illustrated in Figure 6.3, which shows that stakeholders' philosophical mind-sets may have a central role, guiding action and thinking. The current mind-set includes several beliefs that are opposed to inclusive thinking. As shown, the mind-set or belief structure is the centerpiece of policy change, influencing practice and the design of assessment and the education system. The philosophical mind-set influences what policy is implemented. The meanings and understandings captured in philosophical mind-sets may reflect the past experiences in a postcolonial society. Some of these beliefs are strongly held myths.

Student Assessment Systems and Inclusion • 101

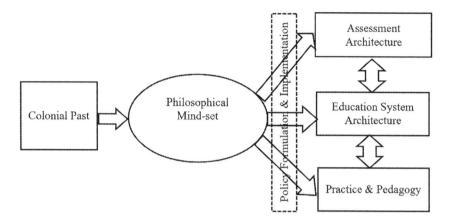

FIGURE 6.3. Hypothesized Operation of Philosophical Mind-Sets Opposed to Inclusive Thinking in the Caribbean.

Midgley (2004) provides an understanding of the role of these beliefs. For her, "myths are not lies. Nor are they detached stories. They are imaginative patterns, networks of powerful symbols that suggest particular ways of interpreting the world. They shape its meaning" (p. 4). Myths about student assessment in Caribbean society include beliefs about the utility and effectiveness of testing in a society, including perceptions of what is fair and just (Olmedilla, 1992). In the analysis, this hypothesized mind-set was best seen in the Peters et al. (2008) where it was reported that practitioners felt inclusion to be unfair to other children not assessed as having a need (Peters et al., 2008).

Although the seamless education project was designed to remove the weaknesses in the education system, very little change has occurred despite an abundance of policy reports from consultants. Perhaps, then, substantive reform will require a more critical and reflective exploration of the current belief structure rather than further tinkering with assessment structure and tools. One important focus of that reflection might be an exploration of how the socio-historical context gave rise to the current student assessment architecture. Benveniste (1999) has described the act of testing in some societies as a ritualized myth with social consequences more important than actual results. Therefore, it is through public examinations that societies such as Trinidad and Tobago achieve its intention and goal, which for the most part remains elitist in the extreme.

Once there is widespread stakeholder consensus on moving forward towards developing a high performing and equitable education system, then appropriate curriculum, pedagogy, and assessment sub-systems can be put in place. Achieving widespread consensus is a part of the meaning making needed for implementing inclusive practice as described by Ainscow (2005):

The methodology for developing inclusive practices must, therefore, take account of these social processes of learning that go on within particular contexts. It requires a group of stakeholders within a particular context to look for a common agenda to guide their discussions of practice and, at much the same time, a series of struggles to establish ways of working that enable them to collect and find meaning in different types of information. The notion of the community of practice is a significant reminder of how this meaning is made. (p. 115)

The current student assessment sub-system will require extensive reconstruction. One of the goals will be a reduced focus on public examinations and installation of a range of short and long cycle formative assessments. This reconstruction cannot be done in isolation. Research into testing, assessment and psychoeducational assessment is needed. Universities must then support diagnostic centres, including further development of local measures and validation of commercially available tools. Sadly, there is still little such work in University departments and faculties supporting evidence-based teacher preparation programmes in the Caribbean (Jennings, 2001). In Trinidad and Tobago, many teacher preparation programmes are constructed on successful teaching in the traditional schools rather than on an explicit model of inclusive practice (Florian & Rouse, 2009).

The seamless education consultancy reports have shown that the absence of tools, training, and services in the current student assessment system means that students with special needs are rarely formally assessed. The SEN system therefore becomes suspect and very unreliable. However, what is needed in reform is a broader focus on barriers to learning in teacher preparation programmes. With the pervasive penchant for transmission teaching, it is perhaps not wise to locate courses in inclusion only in special or restricted programmes. Given the resource stringent environment in the Anglophone Caribbean, some may even consider reform unlikely or impossible given the lack of awareness or political will among some policymakers and technocrats. What might be needed now is collective and concerted action by academics and practitioners in the field inclusion to advocate and influence policy. In an era of evidence-informed policy making, greater use of data and benchmarking best practice is needed to guide policy choices.

REFERENCES

Ainscow, M. (2005). Developing inclusive education systems: What are the levers for change? *Journal of Educational Change, 6(2),* 109–24.

Ainscow, M., Dyson, A., Goldrick, S., & West, M. (2012). *Developing equitable education systems.* London: Routledge.

Benveniste, L. (1999). *The politics of student testing: A comparative analysis of national assessment systems in southern cone countries.* (Unpublished doctoral thesis). Stanford University, Palo Alto, California.

Berry, R. (2010). Assessment reforms around the world. In R. Berry & B. Adamson (Eds.), *Assessment reform in education: Policy and practice (pp. 89–102).* London: Springer.

Black, P., & Wiliam, D. (2007). Large-scale assessment systems: Design principles drawn from international comparisons. *Measurement: Interdisciplinary Research and Perspectives, 5(1),* 1–53.

Bonne, L., & Johnston, M. (2016). Students' beliefs about themselves as mathematics learners. *Thinking Skills and Creativity, 20,* 17–28.

Bowen, G. A. (2009). Document analysis as a qualitative research method. *Qualitative Research Journal, 9*(2), 27–40.

Brookhart, S., Moss, C., & Long, B. (2008). Formative assessment. *Educational Leadership, 66*(3), 52–7.

Clarke, M. (2012). *What matters most for student assessment systems: A framework paper. SABER–Student Assessment Working Paper No.1.* World Bank: Washington, DC.

Darling-Hammond, L., Herman, J., Pellegrino, J. W., Abedi, J., Lawrence Aber, J., Baker, E., Steele, C. M. (2013). *Criteria for high-quality assessment.* Stanford, CA: Stanford Center for Opportunity Policy in Education. Retrieved from http://edpolicy.stanford.edu/publications/pubs/847

De Lisle (2010). *Final report for the consultancy to determine the status of the continuous assessment programme (CAP) in the 60 full treatment schools under the SES project.* Port of Spain, Trinidad and Tobago: Seamless Education Project Unit.

De Lisle, J. (2012). Secondary school entrance examinations in the Caribbean: Legacy, policy, and evidence within an era of seamless education. *Caribbean Curriculum, 19,* 109–43.

De Lisle, J. (2015). Installing a system of performance standards for national assessments in the Republic of Trinidad and Tobago: Issues and challenges. *Applied Measurement in Education, 28*(4), 308–29.

De Lisle, J., Seecharan, H., & Ayodike, A. T. (2010, March). *Is the Trinidad and Tobago education system structured to facilitate optimum human capital development? New findings on the relationship between education structures and outcomes from National and International Assessments.* Paper presented at the 11th Annual SALISES conference, "Turbulence and Turmoil in small developing states: Going beyond survival" Hyatt Hotel, Port of Spain, Trinidad and Tobago.

De Lisle, J., Smith, P., & Jules, V. (2010). Evaluating the geography of gendered achievement using large-scale assessment data from the primary school system of the Republic of Trinidad and Tobago. *International Journal of Educational Development, 30*(4), 405–17.

De Lisle, J., Smith, P., Keller, C., & Jules, V. (2012). Differential outcomes in high stakes eleven plus testing: Gender, assessment design, and geographic location in secondary school placement within Trinidad and Tobago. *Assessment in Education: Principles, Policy, & Practice, 19*(1), 45–64.

Earl, L. (2013). *Assessment as learning: Using classroom assessment to maximize student learning.* Thousand Oaks, CA: Corwin Press.

Elo, S., & Kyngäs, H. (2008). The qualitative content analysis process. *Journal of Advanced Nursing, 62(1),* 107–15.

Field, S., Kuczera, M., & Pont, B. (2007). *No more failures: Ten steps to equity in education and training policy.* OECD Publishing. Retrieved from http://dx.doi.org/10.1787/9789264032606-en.

Florian, L., & Rouse, M. (2009). The inclusive practice project in Scotland: Teacher education for inclusive education. *Teaching & Teacher Education, 25*(4), 594–601.

Gallagher, C. W. (2010). Keeping the focus, expanding the vision, maintaining the balance: Preserving and enhancing formative assessment in Nebraska. In G. L. Cizek & H. L. Andrade (Eds.), *Handbook of formative assessment (pp. 328–43).* New York: Routledge.

George, J., Quamina-Aiyejina, L., Cain, M., & Mohammed, C. (2009). *Gender issues in education and intervention strategies to increase participation of boys.* St Clair, Port of Spain: Trinidad and Tobago Ministry of Education.

Government of the Republic of Trinidad and Tobago. (2012). *Education sector strategic plan 2011–2015.* Port of Spain, Trinidad and Tobago: Ministry of Education.

Guest, G., MacQueen, K. M., & Namey, E. (2012). *Applied thematic analysis.* Thousand Oaks, CA: Sage.

Harlen, W. (2007). *Designing a fair and effective assessment system.* Paper presented at the 2007 BERA Annual Conference as part of the ARG Symposium, Future Directions for Student Assessment. University of Bristol, UK.

Herman, J. L. (2010). *Coherence: Key to next generation assessment success (AACC Report).* Los Angeles: University of California.

Jennings, Z. (2001). Teacher education in selected countries in the Commonwealth Caribbean: The ideal of policy versus the reality of practice. *Comparative Education, 37(1),* 107–34.

Jones, B. D., & Baumgartner, F. R. (2012). From there to here: Punctuated equilibrium to the general punctuation thesis to a theory of government information processing. *Policy Studies Journal, 40(1),* 1–20.

Lavia, J. (2008). Inclusive education in Trinidad and Tobago. In L. Barton & F. Armstrong (Eds.), *Policy, Experience and Change: Cross-Cultural Reflections on Inclusive Education* (pp. 107–22). New York: Springer-Verlag.

Li, W., & Lee, A. (2004). A review of conceptions of ability and related motivational constructs in achievement motivation. *Quest, 56(4),* 439–61.

Lipson, M. Y., Chomsky-Higgins, P., & Kanfer, J. (2011). Diagnosis: The missing ingredient in RTI assessment. *The Reading Teacher, 65(3),* 204–8.

London, N. A. (1989). Selecting students for secondary education in a developing society: The case of Trinidad and Tobago. *McGill Journal of Education, 24(3),* 281–91.

London, N. A. (1991). The concept of the high school in an emerging society: An analysis of major trends. *Canadian & International Education, 20(2),* 54–70.

Mansell, W., James, M., & the Assessment Reform Group. (2009). *Assessment in schools. Fit for purpose? A commentary by the Teaching and Learning Research Program.* London: ESRC, TLRP.

Midgley, M. (2004). *The myths we live by.* London: Routledge.

Mislevy, R. J. (2010). Design under constraints: The case of large-scale assessment systems. *Measurement, 8(4),* 199–203.

Moss, P. A., Girard, B. J., & Haniford, L. C. (2006). Validity in educational assessment. *Review of Research in Education, 30,* 109–62.

Northey, D., Bennett, L., & Canales, J. A. (2007). *Support for a seamless system: Curriculum and instruction, testing and evaluation and Spanish as a foreign language.* Port of Spain, Trinidad and Tobago: Trinidad and Tobago Ministry of Education.

Olmedilla, J. M. M. (1992). Tradition and change in national examination systems: A comparison of Mediterranean and Anglo-Saxon countries. In M. A. Eckstein & H. J.

Noah (Eds.), *Comparative and International Studies* (pp. 135–47). Oxford, UK: Pergamon.

Organisation for Economic Co-operation and Development (OECD). (2010). *PISA 2009 Results: Overcoming social background: Equity in learning opportunities and outcomes (Volume II)*. Paris, France: OECD.

Organisation for Economic Co-operation and Development (OECD). (2011). *Shanghai and Hong Kong: Two distinct examples of education reform in China. In Lessons from PISA for the United States: Strong Performers and Successful Reformers in Education* (pp. 83–116). Paris, France: OECD Publishing. Retrieved from http://dx.doi.org/10.1787/9789264096660-en.

Organisation for Economic Co-operation and Development (OECD). (2012). *Equity and quality in education: Supporting disadvantaged students and schools*. Paris, France: OECD.

Pellegrino, J. W. (2014). Assessment as a positive influence on 21st century teaching and learning: A systems approach to progress. *Psicología Educativa, 20*(2), 65–77.

Peters, S., Miske, S. J., Johnstone, C., Harris, D. P., Wolbers, K-A., Trotman, A., & Sales, G. (2008). *Achieving inclusion: transforming the education system of Trinidad and Tobago. Final report for the inclusive education component of the seamless education project*. Saint Paul, MN: Miske Witt & Associates.

Petridou, E. (2014). Theories of the policy process: contemporary scholarship and future directions. *Policy Studies Journal, 42*(S1), S12–S32.

Qian, D. D. (2014). School-based English language assessment as a high-stakes examination component in Hong Kong: Insights of frontline assessors. *Assessment in Education: Principles, Policy & Practice, 21*(3), 251–70.

Robertson, I. (2010). *Language and language education policy*. Port of Spain, Trinidad and Tobago: Seamless Education Project Unit.

Stobart, G. (2009). Determining validity in national curriculum assessments. *Educational Research, 51*(2), 161–79.

Swaffield, S. (2011). Getting to the heart of authentic assessment for learning. *Assessment in Education: Principles, Policy & Practice, 18*(4), 433–49.

UNESCO. (2008). *Defining an inclusive education agenda: Reflections around the 48th Session of the International Conference on Education*. Geneva, Switzerland. Retrieved from http://unesdoc.unesco.org/images/0018/001868/186807e.pdf

Vislie, L. (2003). From integration to inclusion: Focusing global trends and changes in the western European societies. *European Journal of Special Needs Education, 18*(1), 17–35.

Wall, D., & Alderson, J. C. (1993). Examining washback: The Sri Lankan impact study. *Language Testing, 10*(1), 41–69.

Wixson, K. K., & Valencia, S. W. (2011). Assessment in RTI: What teachers and specialists need to know. *The Reading Teacher, 64*(6), 466–69.

CHAPTER 7

HISTORICAL CONUNDRUMS

Extending Inclusivity to Jamaica's Children in State Care Education in Jamaica: Inclusive of Whom?

Sandra Richards Mayo

Discussions of inclusive education in the Caribbean region until now have focused almost exclusively on children with disabilities. One of the goals of this chapter is to broaden perspectives of inclusivity to address educational provisions for all children who are at risk of exclusion and marginalization. Specifically, this chapter provides a historical framework for examining educational responses to children in Jamaica who have fallen outside traditional social safety networks and who are living in a variety of private and state-run facilities, including children's homes, places of safety, and remand and correctional centres.

The first section provides a critical, historical analysis of nineteenth-century Jamaican legislation in relation to the development of children's homes and industrial reform schools set up to serve the needs of vulnerable youth. Drawing on Jonathan Simon's (2007) work on governing through crime as a conceptual framework, this chapter argues that the use of crime metaphors in response to issues of homelessness and lack of family contributed to the development of a less than adequate system of reformatory and industrial schools, and existing negative

Caribbean Discourse in Inclusive Education:
Historical and Contemporary Issues, pages 107–121.
Copyright © 2017 by Information Age Publishing
All rights of reproduction in any form reserved.

attitudes towards children who are wards of the state. Throughout this analysis, emphasis is placed on legislative responses to youth vagrancy, both in terms of how the issue of vagrancy was defined, and how it was managed in response to Jamaica's changing economic climate following emancipation.

The second part of the chapter provides an overview of educational services made available to children who are wards of the state, by exploring findings of existing studies that address conditions within residential care facilities and remand centres. Overall, this discussion seeks to demonstrate the need for more focused attention on ensuring equal educational opportunity. Furthermore, it illuminates how historical responses to the education and training of Jamaica's children in state care inform current realities in the field of inclusive education.

Throughout this chapter, educational inclusion is envisaged through a human-rights paradigm that considers notions of full participation, self-representation, and self-determination as core principles of equity (Neufeldt & Enns, 2003). It also draws on broader features of inclusion that place primacy on "supporting the achievement and participation of all pupils who face learning and/or behavior challenges of any kind, in terms of socio-economic circumstances, ethnic origin, cultural heritage, religion, linguistic heritage, gender, sexual preference, and so on" (Topping & Maloney, 2005, p. 5). This broader conceptualization of inclusive education is consistent with international proclamations, such as the Salamanca Statement and Framework for Action on Special Needs Education (UNESCO, 1994) and the Dakar Declaration (UNESCO, 2000). A central philosophical underpinning of these global calls to action is the need to account for all learners, including children in residential care who remain largely invisible in regional and global policy and reform efforts.

Implementation of Jamaica's Task Force on Education Reform in 2004 further paved the way for a more expansive framework of inclusive education. In addition to addressing the material resource needs within Jamaica's educational system, the Task Force set its vision on providing pathways for all students to reach their full potential. Tantamount to this comprehensive reform programme was a commitment to affirm the "human rights" and "dignity of all persons" (UNESCO, 2007, p. 2). In recent decades, Caribbean scholars have also signalled an imperative to broaden existing schema for understanding and producing inclusive practice. Conrad, Paul, Bruce, Charles, and Felix (2010) and Blackman, Conrad, and Brown (2012) situate the notion of inclusion within a larger context of social justice education and education for democratic citizenship. Similarly, Barton points out that "questions of social justice, equity, human rights, and non-discrimination are central to the issue of inclusion" (as cited in Lavia, 2008). Building on the foundational work of these scholars, this chapter calls for a critical reframing around issues of inclusion to remain responsive to larger societal issues of homelessness, lack of family, and poverty in Jamaica.

HISTORICAL CONTEXT: INCLUSION THROUGH A CRIMINAL JUSTICE PARADIGM

Historical responses to Jamaica's homeless and family-less children must be understood within a framework of Jamaica's changing political and economic climate in the decades following emancipation, with particular emphasis on the years 1845–1879. Economic strain characterized this period, as British manufacturers faced intense competition in the world market. Following the Sugar Duties Equalization Act of 1846, the British market opened to international competition. As such, Jamaica lost its favoured status as the primary supplier of sugar—the basis of the nation's economy. Along with economic decline in the mid-nineteenth century, Jamaica experienced increasing unemployment rates and low wages, followed by social rebellion. With the crash of the sugar trade, racial and religious tensions came to a head, culminating in a working-class uprising in 1865, known as the Morant Bay Rebellion (Black, 1991). This rebellion became a defining moment in Jamaica's history and in the history of black resistance to white hegemony. John Edward Eyre, governor of Jamaica, feared the spread of the rebellion to other parts of the island. Because the ruling planter class perceived a threat to the island's stability, they made considerable changes in the governance of Jamaica. Most significant among those changes was the move from a representative assembly to a system of direct rule by the Colonial Office in Britain.

In addition to prompting political change, the uprising stood as a reminder to the Jamaican government of the need to provide some form of education for the masses to maintain political stability in the region (Bacchus, 1993). Throughout the last quarter of the nineteenth century, government incentives spurred vocational training in conjunction with a pervasive ideology that deemed industrial education an ideal solution to the growing population of poor and vagrant youth (Whyte, 1977).

Increased economic hardship and heightened unemployment throughout the Caribbean led to escalating numbers of young people living in poverty and neglect, particularly in the urban centres where social and economic decline was most prevalent. In an 1858 statement to the secretary of state, Governor Darling described the situation in Kingston, which served as a primary justification for the development of industrial and reformatory schools in Jamaica:

> The want of some Institution in the nature of a "Reformatory" or "Industrial School," where better habits should be taught to a large portion of the Juvenile Population, is more particularly felt in the City of Kingston, which I deeply regret to say, swarms with vagrant and destitute children, or children utterly abandoned or neglected by their Parents, practicing every species of vice to which idleness combined with the absence of a religious and moral training can possibly give birth. (Cited in Gordon, 1963, p. 71)

This statement echoed sentiments later reflected in various government reports and parallel legislation. Among the most influential of these documents was the

1879 *Report Upon the Condition of the Juvenile Population of Jamaica.* Although not designed as an investigation into the education system, the findings of the Commissioners' Report guided Jamaica's educational policy and shaped future educational reforms including the establishment of reformatory and industrial schools. So great was the concern surrounding the idleness and unsupervised activities of adolescents from the poor class—a perceived threat to the stability of urban society—that the colonial government appointed the commissioners to inquire into the condition of the youth "with a view to the devising of means for the protection of the destitute, the training of the ignorant, and the reclaiming of the idle and criminal" (Report of the commissioners, 1879, p. 1). As historian Shirley Gordon (1963) notes, "At a time when the Trinidadian Government and the Barbados Legislature both called for reports on their education system, the Jamaican government instituted instead, an enquiry into the social problem amongst young people of school age" (p. 17). The emphasis of the 1879 inquiry highlights the historical precedent of addressing homeless and family-less children in Jamaica through a criminal justice paradigm that shaped educational responses to poverty.

A large portion of the 1879 Commissioners' Report focused on the condition of parents as the leading cause of juvenile vagrancy:

> We must take account also of the vicious and debased condition of the parents themselves. Ignorant, undisciplined, and lacking in moral sense, they know nothing of the value of protection or education for their children, and do not care to make provision for it, even when they might be able to do so with small effort. (p. 1)

It is this very issue of parental absence and neglect that was central in the development of reformatory and industrial schools. Within the context of the 1879 inquiry, these institutions served to eradicate concerns about Jamaica's vagrant youth—an issue that was foremost in the minds of Jamaica's white ruling class.

As a direct response to what was seen as a pervasive ill among the poor, the commissioners focused on the issue of industrial training. Citing the Industrial Schools Act of 1857 (Old Industrial Schools Law) as a basis for their argument, the commissioners urged a system of reformatory and industrial schools that could help address concerns about social stability following emancipation. The Industrial Schools Act made it lawful for children who appeared to have "no settled place of abode," or those having "no visible means of sustenance," to be taken into custody and ordered to an industrial school (The National Archives, 1857, p. 2). Under the provisions of the law, any individual—law enforcement agent or civilian—could bring a vagrant child before a justice, whether or not that child had parents, or any guardian or adult relative, living.

The framing of the issue of homelessness as a crime placed Jamaica's poor youth under the watchful gaze of the colony's officials. What is particularly striking is the manner in which legislators used crime metaphors to both define the problem and move toward solutions. This emphasis on patrolling homelessness can be understood within Jonathan Simon's (2007) theoretical exposé of governing through crime. Simon makes it clear that the way we think about crime influences the way in which we conduct our daily affairs in communities and seek guarantees of security against perceived threat. Simon draws a distinction between "governing crime" and "governing through crime," pointing out that the latter is more about giving primacy to crime as a state interest, and as a way of extending power and control. According to Simon (2007), governing through crime as a paradigmatic approach ultimately distorts institutional priorities, such that crime becomes a "locus of governance" above other normative elements central to civil society, including education, health care, and food security (p. 27). Although focused on the United States context, Simon's work has relevance to other nation-states whose efforts to lessen the crime rate have ultimately resulted in policies for managing the poor.

Throughout legislative acts in the late nineteenth century, the use of the term "inmates" to refer to children who were to be detained in industrial schools serves as one indicator of the criminalization of poverty in nineteenth-century Jamaica. The methods of discipline employed against youth in Jamaica's industrial schools serves as another. Examples of this appear in an amendment to the 1857 Industrial Schools Act, which endorsed corporal punishment and other punitive sanctions for children who ran away from industrial schools:

> In case of any child absconding, or repeatedly deserting from any such certified industrial school, it shall be lawful for the managers to cause to be inflicted on such child such moderate whipping at any time, as in their judgment may be advisable, or to confine such child in solitary confinement, and to place him on a diet of bread and water, for such period as managers may think advisable. (The National Archives, 1859, p. 2)

Addressing youth vagrancy within a criminal justice paradigm is not exclusive to post-emancipation Jamaican society. In fact, the language used to discuss poor children in Jamaica during this period emerged from British Poor Laws established in the early seventeenth century and revised in 1834—the year of the emancipation of slaves in Jamaica—to address the specific moral failing of the able-bodied poor (Roper, 2012). Consequently, the legacy of this legislation must be understood within the unique colonial experience in Jamaica, the remnants of which continue to shape educational responses to Jamaica's children who face unfortunate circumstances.

The use of crime metaphors is evident in subsequent amendments to the Old Industrial Schools Law in 1869 and 1872. These amendments influenced the establishment of a government-funded reformatory (Stony Hill Reformatory) and clear articulation of the categories of youth who were to be detained there. Children under the age of 16 who were found begging in a public space, wandering the streets without proper supervision or care, orphaned or having a surviving parent in the penal system, or those who took company with reputed thieves, could be sent to the reformatory under application for Poor Relief. Out of a concern about mixing criminal and non-criminal children together, the commissioners for the 1879 inquiry recommended that the law under which vagrant and destitute children were sent to the government reformatory be modified, with the establishment of industrial schools apart from the reformatory. Criminal children would be sent only to the latter, with vagrant and destitute to the former. It is important to note that until 1892 industrial schools housed both criminal and non-criminal children. In that year, industrial schools were removed from the oversight of the police and the prison department (Bryan, 2000).

Additional legislative acts during the late nineteenth century showed a continued thrust toward the criminalization of youth. Jamaica Law 34 of 1881, also known as the Reformatories and Industrial Schools Law, defined criminal children as those "apparently above the age of ten, and below the age of sixteen, duly convicted of any crime punishable with penal servitude, or imprisonment, with hard labour without the option of a fine" (The National Archives, 1881, pp. 1–2). The law also specified the types of offences for which children could be detained in reformatories and industrial schools. Children found "begging or receiving alms" and those found wandering "in any street or public space for purposes of begging or receiving alms," as well as children found without any apparent "home or settled place of abode, or proper guardianship or visible means of sustenance," could be brought before two justices and ordered to an industrial school or government reformatory (The National Archives, 1881, p. 5). These categories of criminal offences were not discrete, and certainly children who met the description in one category would be at risk of unlawfulness in other categories, since all were linked to the underlying problem of poverty.

Once ordered to carry out their sentence in an industrial school or reformatory, children were also subject to indentured labour. The Reformatories and Industrial Schools Law specified that children could be let out on licence to any "trustworthy and respectable person" (The National Archives, 1881, p. 9). As a response to the growing numbers of homeless youth, the goal was to apprentice children out to ensure the development of long-term habits of work. Inmates of the government reformatory who were not apprenticed during their sentence were required to provide evidence of both their residence and occupation for two years after leaving the reformatory:

> Any male child not having been apprenticed…shall, for a period of two years after he shall have ceased to be an inmate of any Reformatory, be deemed to be under the supervision of the Superintendent of the Reformatory, and shall report to such Superintendent the place of his residence and the nature of his occupation, and if he shall change the same any change thereof. (The National Archives, 1881, p. 10)

Anyone failing to comply with this law could be sentenced to prison as a vagrant, with up to three months of hard labour.

The 1881 law also defined sanctions for children who did not conform to the rules of reformatory or industrial schools. Those ordered to be detained in a reformatory that had committed an offence could be imprisoned with or without hard labour for between 14 days and three months. Any child detained in an industrial school who did not maintain proper discipline could be ordered to a reformatory for the rest of his "term of detention" (The National Archives, 1881, p. 10). Furthermore, children who escaped or attempted to escape from a reformatory could be "apprehended without warrant" and sentenced to prison "with or without hard labour" and "if male, with or without whipping" (The National Archives, 1881, p. 11). Children who absconded from an industrial school could be ordered to a reformatory school. Individuals who knowingly abetted a child's escape were also liable to penalty or imprisonment.

In the imagination of Jamaica's colonial ruling class, poverty was regarded as a moral problem and personal deficit, rather than a product of a long and deliberate history. Within a criminal justice paradigm, laws were instituted to uproot the apparent social ills associated with poverty, with children becoming a focal point in an emerging political effort to establish and maintain social order following emancipation. By applying crime metaphors to non-criminal acts related to conditions of homelessness and lack of family, legislators who shaped the system of industrial and reformatory schools in Jamaica effectively brought criminal justice functions into the realm of schools, thereby shaping the direction of educational provisions for children from disadvantaged circumstances. This historical context is important for understanding contemporary educational responses to Jamaica's youth in state care within a framework of inclusion.

CONTEMPORARY REALITIES: EDUCATION FOR JAMAICA'S CHILDREN IN STATE CARE

A total of 4,370 of Jamaica's children are in state care. Of those, 203 are in custodial care—85 in remand centres and 118 in correctional centres (Hanna, 2015). While these numbers represent less than 6 per cent of Jamaica's total child population, a small percentage proportionally, they are significant in terms of their social impact. As former South African president Nelson Mandela (1995) once said, "There can be no keener revelation of a society's soul than the way in which it treats its children." In allowing Mandela's words to serve as a guide, this section explores contemporary educational responses to Jamaica's homeless and family-less children, demonstrating the need to understand both historical precedents for exclusion and current opportunities for providing more equitable opportunities for all children.

In her opening statement to the Committee on the Rights of the Child in Geneva, Switzerland, Youth and Culture Minister Lisa Hanna (2015) offered a promising glimpse into the experiences of Jamaica's children based on traditional measures of health and well being, including infant mortality, school attendance rates, and life expectancy. According to Hanna, children in Jamaica have a 97 per cent chance of surviving beyond the age of five, with nearly 100 per cent of children having the opportunity to participate in school through the secondary level, and living an average of 73 years. To summarize, based on standard measures of human well being, the majority of Jamaica's children are thriving. Unfortunately, however, these measures fail to capture the unique experiences of children living outside traditional social safety networks. While the majority of Jamaica's children do have an opportunity to participate in some form of schooling, a better indicator of well-being, as conceptualized within a human-rights framework, would be the extent to which all children have the opportunity for full participation, self-representation, and self-determination.

Under the purview of the Ministry of Youth and Culture, the Child Development Agency (CDA) carries out the provisions of the Jamaica Juveniles Act of 1951. The Juveniles Act is the principal legislation in Jamaica that sets forth all rights recognized by the United Nations on the Convention on the Rights of the Child and other international guidelines that protect children from abuse and neglect. The Juveniles Act establishes a series of measures designed to protect children from birth to 18 years who are wards of the state, juveniles accused of criminal offences, and youth who are deemed beyond parental control. Depending on the needs of the child, the CDA can facilitate court proceedings, provide temporary shelter for a child in a place of safety (pending trial or long-term placement), communicate with the child's parents or guardians, or provide long-term supervision for the child through foster care, adoption, or placement of the child in a children's home.

All institutions run by the CDA provide education to varying degrees. Children who are housed in places of safety are educated on-site by specially trained teachers. In addition to academics, the children receive training in various crafts and skills including woodwork, agriculture, basketry, home economics, and sewing. Children who are housed in more permanent children's homes may go to school on-site or in the community, and also participate in skills training. Although these educational services are available, little is known about the range and quality of services provided. The few reports that do exist present a picture of gross neglect with regard to the educational and developmental needs of children in Jamaica's institutions of care. This neglect, while particularly acute for those identified as having special educational needs, appears to be a fairly pervasive experience for children who find themselves outside the traditional safety networks of family.

No studies to date have focused specifically on the education of Jamaica's youth in state care. However, in response to public concern about the treatment of youth in need of care and protection, several reports over the last two decades have examined the conditions within residential care facilities and remand centres, the analysis of which provides insights about educational offerings within these institutions. Drawing on primary and secondary source documents, in the following pages I present findings from existing studies on the care of youth in Jamaica's children's homes, places of safety, and juvenile detention centres. These findings highlight the need for more expansive definitions of inclusion that not only consider the particular needs of children with disabilities, but that also broaden perspectives of educational access and equity for all young people who experience limiting educational opportunities because of socio-economic circumstances, or other conditions beyond their control.

A 1999 study, *Faces of Residential Care in Jamaica,* commissioned by the Ministry of Health and carried out jointly by the Children's Services Division, UNICEF Jamaica, and NCH Action for Children UK, examined a number of factors, including the reasons children were admitted to the homes and places of safety, demographic characteristics, behavioral and health status of the youth, and standards of care across institutions. The study included survey responses from the then 52 institutions in operation, as well as interviews with more than 200 children and their caregivers (Two-Year-Old Report, 2003). Data from the study indicated that 55 per cent of children were admitted to institutions because they were beyond parental control; 35.7 per cent were placed in care because of physical and sexual abuse and neglect; 20.3 per cent were in care because of the unavailability of their parents (due to death, illness, abandonment, or other life circumstances); and 9.9 per cent were reported as having delinquent behavior problems (as cited in Ministry of Health, 2003).

Despite the high percentage of children who were placed in care because of incidents of abuse, the study found that homes and places of safety did not provide adequate and continuing services for children who experience abuse. From the sample surveyed, there was little or no evidence of any clear policies for the management of cases for abused children. With regard to children who were abused prior to admission to care, "There appears to be a near total disregard for the emotional consequences, the educational underachievement and the capacity for abusing other children by these children" (Two-Year-Old Report, 2003, p. 1). Although the data do not give clear insight into the extent of this disregard, the statement does suggest that education in youth homes, in this case for children with a history of abuse, might be inadequate. This claim is further supported by data from interviews with the children in care, which yielded a mix of positive and negative responses to questions about their experiences in youth homes and places of safety. According to data from the report,

> Many children say staff are loving, kind and nurturing and that they are respected and valued. Yet some children report that their rights to privacy are violated, that the quality of care they receive suffers from a lack of coordinated planning, that staff members are sometimes abusive and that they frequently have difficulties accessing secondary education and advanced skills training. (Thomas, 2003, p. 1)

According to Thomas (2003), the study found that standards of care in Jamaica's homes and places of safety were inadequate, and that standards of care "varied from institution to institution" (p. 1). Overall, most of the problems identified were attributed to "inadequate physical resources, too few staff, and a lack of training" (Thomas, 2003, p. 1).

Another report, *"Nobody's Children": Jamaican Children in Police Detention and Government Institutions* (Human Rights Watch, 1999), also revealed that standards of youth care varied by institution. Findings from this study, based on research conducted by Human Rights Watch from late August to early September 1998, indicated that provisions for youth in state custody were inadequate. Researchers interviewed more than 30 children from six police lockups (Spanish Town, Kingston Central, Gun Court, Ewarton, Matilda's Corner, and Portmore). All of the children interviewed were males ranging in age from 13 to 17. Researchers from Human Rights Watch also visited a children's home for girls and two places of safety—one for boys and one for girls—and Jamaica's only remand centre, which is for boys only. In addition to site visits to places in which children were held, background interviews were conducted with ministers, attorneys, representatives of nongovernmental organizations (NGOs), police officers, judges, and social workers, as well as several government officials including the commissioner of police, the commissioner of correctional services, and the director of children's services.

Data from this study suggest that educational provisions for youth in police detention centres are inadequate. In particular, the study found that educational opportunities within the remand centre are "hardly a substitute for the standard elementary school or high school education in that it is limited" (Human Rights Watch, 1999, p. 72). Additional studies are needed to determine the type of education provided to children in Jamaica's correctional facilities, and to assess how it compares to the educational programmes offered in the formal system of primary and secondary education.

One of the most comprehensive studies, which begins the work of assessing educational programmes offered to Jamaica's youth in need of care and protection, is the *Review of Children's Homes and Places of Safety*, also known as the Keating Report (Ministry of Health, 2003). In December 2002, the prime minister of Jamaica, P. J. Patterson, mandated a review of all children's homes and places of safety in order to determine whether Jamaica was meeting its obligations under the United Nations Convention on the Rights of the Child. The study used a mixed-methods approach, which included three separate survey instruments, focus groups, interviews, observations, and a review of data included in institutional files and records.

Although the 2003 review is not a direct study of education in Jamaica's youth homes and places of safety, it does make some critical statements about educational offerings within these institutions. First, the study provides descriptive data about the educational facilities, which vary by institution. According to the review, a select number of homes have on-site educational facilities, ranging from extensive school facilities with all the required grades to some homes combining children of mixed ages in one classroom. Data from the second survey indicated that 38.9 per cent of the students were receiving full-time education, and 11.1 per cent were receiving part-time education on site. Respondents to the same survey reported that 28.6 per cent of students were receiving full-time education off-site, while none of the respondents indicated that students were receiving part-time education outside of the institution. Additionally, 22.9 per cent of students were receiving vocational training at the children's homes/places of safety, but, according to survey responses, none were receiving vocational training elsewhere. Through observation, "the schoolrooms appeared neat and well tended" (Ministry of Health, 2003, p. 30).

The review also reported on the educational attainments of youth in institutional care. Using data from the surveys, focus groups, and observations, the review team found that most of the children in the children's homes and places of safety "were not learning and could not fit into the regular school system" (Ministry of Health, 2003, p. 30). It is not clear from the report, however, how learning was being measured; although it did appear that most of the children were "enrolled in some educational institution before they came into care and so had been at some stage part of the established school system" (Ministry of Health, 2003, p. 30).

In the institutions observed, there appeared to be no remedial programmes for children who were below grade-level achievement. Furthermore, in the home with the most extensive school system, researchers were informed that the children do not go on to secondary school since their academic performance is below required levels. For instance, "In spite of being told on more than one occasion that the Homes/POS had children with GSAT [Grade Six Achievement Test] and CXC [Caribbean Examination Council] levels, nothing was seen to suggest that such curricula were being pursued by any of the children" (Ministry of Health, 2003, p. 30). Further evidence from focus group data suggested that "Children are not encouraged to participate in external examinations or are unable to because of lack of proper documentation" (Ministry of Health, 2003, p. 111).

Based on findings from the *2003 Review*, access to adequate education appears to be even more limited for students with disabilities. Data extrapolated from visits to the institutions, a review of files, and focus group interviews indicated that there are no standards for minimum levels of education to be provided to children with disabilities. According to the review, "There are no requirements for the education of these children" (Ministry of Health, 2003, p. 44). In the absence of standards, the provisions made for children with disabilities may vary greatly by the institution. For instance, one home that cared for 40 children with moderate to severe developmental and/or physical disabilities was asked about their education programme for the children, and the response was that "the children cannot learn—we just take care of them" (Ministry of Health, 2003, p. 45). Furthermore, there were no individual developmental plans for these children. A visit to this site confirmed that less than one per cent of the children were in a structured education programme.

At another home, where 40 per cent of the children had some form of disability, those with mild to moderate disabilities attended a school on-site and appeared to be doing fairly well. At a third institution, where the population included students with moderate to severe disabilities, 23 per cent of the children were in a formal learning environment and attended schools within the community. At a fourth site, which served 77 children with moderate to profound levels of developmental and physical disabilities, 15 students were attending school, some on-site and some off-site.

The results of the second survey revealed that 89 per cent of all children in the available sample group were receiving some form of formal education, training, or occupational therapy. Visits to the homes and reviews of records indicated that children with no disabilities were generally mainstreamed into traditional primary and secondary schools. According to the review, "The challenge these children face is less one of access to school and more one of quality of education they are receiving and the appropriate support once back in homes to undertake after school assignments and ongoing study" (Ministry of Health, 2003, p. 62). Overall, for children with disabilities, less than 10 per cent were in a structured off-site education programme.

With regard to staffing and preparation of teachers, focus group data indicated that many teachers had not received formal training and were not appropriately prepared to address the particular needs of students with learning difficulties. Of those surveyed, 28.6 per cent of the children's homes/places of safety did not employ full-time teachers; this percentage is consistent with the number of institutions that did not operate on-site schools.

All three existing reports point to the need for in-depth studies that examine the educational programme offerings within institutions providing care to children in need. As the literature here suggests, the education and skills training historically provided to Jamaica's youth in state care has been largely inadequate. And although recent reports point to significant improvements in the care and protection of Jamaica's children who have fallen outside of traditional social safety networks (see, for example, Reckford, 2014), the available data are limited and further research is needed to determine the extent to which children in state care have the opportunity to be integrated into established school systems and receive quality educational provisions on par with their peers within the traditional population.

CONCLUSION: REFRAMING INCLUSIVITY—A WAY FORWARD

Drawing on evidence from primary and secondary source documents, this chapter demonstrates how legislation in the second half of the nineteenth century reinforced public perception of children who, due to conditions of poverty or abuse, fell outside traditional social safety networks. Throughout the nineteenth century and into the twentieth century, children who lacked access to familial networks remained vulnerable to legislative efforts to control societal ills of vagrancy and homelessness. An analysis of legislative acts concerning industrial and reform schools during the second half of the nineteenth century provides a historical narrative of social and economic reform that is missing from discussions of inclusive education in the Caribbean region. The current work seeks to make an important contribution to this arena by illustrating the specific relationship between conditions of poverty, the governance of crime, and educational policy.

This chapter argues that the goals of inclusion must be re-examined in the context of Jamaica's system of education, which was established within prevailing colonial structures. Given this historical context, successful implementation of inclusive education cannot simply be envisioned as an add-on to existing educational arrangements. Instead, meaningful change will necessitate radical reconceptualization and broadening to address features of neglect that have persisted throughout Jamaica's institutions of care. Furthermore, it will require formulation of a framework of human rights to include issues of full participation, self-representation, and self-determination. Central to this effort is the facilitation of access and equity in a manner that is multi-pronged—one that is shaped by national policy; school climate, pedagogy, and curriculum; and cultural norms and practices that inculcate a valuing of children who are in state care.

Throughout this discussion, I have sought to demonstrate the economic and political circumstances in which education for wards of the state was defined in post-emancipation Jamaica. On a broader scale, this work provides insight into the features of educational exclusion that emerged during this period. In so doing, this work contributes to a larger body of scholarship on colonial education and post-slavery social reform, highlighting the distinct features of neglect that arose in this context.

This analysis not only calls for greater attention to educational provisions for children in residential care, but also highlights the need for a more acute focus on providing a full spectrum of family and child welfare services including, but not limited to, early intervention and mental health counselling and therapeutic treatment. Children in state care often face a complexity of issues that negatively affect their ability to take full advantage of educational services, even when those services exist. Consequently, discussions of inclusion must not only be broadened to address the educational needs of children who are wards of the state, but must also consider the ways in which issues of educational opportunity are linked to other aspects of child welfare. Furthermore, they must interrogate the politics of inclusion to examine the very nature of what it means to be *included*. Such critical engagement holds the potential to expand opportunities for participation through a paradigm of human rights and social justice.

REFERENCES

Bacchus, M. K. (1993). Consensus and conflict over the provision of elementary education. In H. Beckles & V. Shepherd (Eds.), *Caribbean freedom: Economy and society from emancipation to the present* (pp. 296–312). Princeton, NJ: Markus Wiener Publishers.

Black, C. V. (1991). *History of Jamaica*. London, UK: Longman Group UK.

Blackman, S., Conrad, D., & Brown, L. (2012). The attitude of Barbadian and Trinidadian teachers to integration. *International Journal of Special Education, 27*(3), 158–168.

Bryan, P. (2000). *The Jamaican people, 1880–1902: Race, class, and social control.* Kingston, Jamaica: University of West Indies Press.

Conrad, D. A., Paul, N., Bruce, M., Charles, S., & Felix, K. (2010). Special schools and the search for social justice in Trinidad and Tobago: Perspectives from two marginalized contexts. *Caribbean Curriculum, 17,* 59–84.

Gordon, S. (1963). *A century of West Indian education.* London, UK: Longmans, Green and Co.

Hanna, L. (2015, January 19). *Jamaica's opening statement to the committee on the rights of the child.* Geneva, Switzerland. Retrieved from http://tbinternet.ohchr.org/Treaties/CRC/Shared%20Documents/JAM/INT_CRC_STA_JAM_19272_E.pdf

Human Rights Watch. (1999). *Nobody's children: Jamaican children in police detention and government institutions.* Washington, DC: Author.

Lavia, J. (2008). Inclusive education in Trinidad and Tobago. In L. Barton & F. Armstrong (Eds.), *Policy, experience and change: Cross-cultural reflections on inclusive education* (pp. 107–122). New York, NY: Springer-Verlag.

Mandela, N. (1995, May 8). *Speech at the launch of the Nelson Mandela Children's Fund.* Pretoria, South Africa. Retrieved from http://db.nelsonmandela.org/speeches/pub_view.asp?ItemID=NMS250&txtstr=Mahlamba&pg=item

Ministry of Health. (2003). *Review of children's homes and places of safety.* Kingston, Jamaica: Author.

The National Archives of the UK (TNA). (1857). *Industrial Schools Act, 1857,* ff. 350–56 of CO 139/92.

The National Archives of the UK (TNA). (1859). *Amendment to the Industrial Schools Act, 1857,* ff. 165–66 of CO 139/93.

The National Archives of the UK (TNA). (1881). *The Reformatories and Industrial Schools Law, 1881,* ff. 123–31 CO 139/104.

Neufeldt, A. H., & Enns, H. (2003). *In pursuit of equal participation: Canada and disability at home and abroad.* Toronto, Canada: Captus Press.

Reckford, E. H. (2014, January 14). *Major focus on the safety of children in 2013.* Retrieved from http://jis.gov.jm/major-focus-on-the-safety-of-children-in-2013/

Report of the commissioners of inquiry upon the condition of the juvenile population of Jamaica. (1879). Kingston, Jamaica: Government Printing Office.

Roper, S. (2012). *'A almshouse ting dat': Developments in poor relief and child welfare in Jamaica in the interwar years* (Doctoral dissertation). Retrieved from Proquest dissertation and theses (umi no. 3577324).

Simon, J. (2007). *Governing through crime: How the war on crime transformed American democracy.* New York, NY: Oxford University Press.

Thomas, P. (2003, January 5). Who's taking care of the children? *Jamaica Gleaner.* Retrieved from http://old.jamaica-gleaner.com/gleaner/20030105/lead/lead4.html

Topping, K., & Maloney, S. (2005). Introduction. In K. Topping & S. Maloney (Eds.), *The Routledge Falmer reader in inclusive education* (pp. 1–14). New York, NY: Routledge.

Two-year-old report damns state care. (2003, January 12). *Jamaica Gleaner.* Retrieved from http://old.jamaica-gleaner.com/gleaner/20030112/lead/lead3.html

UNESCO. (1994). *The Salamanca Statement and Framework for Action on Special Needs Education.* Paris, France: UNESCO. Retrieved from http://unesdoc.unesco.org/images/0009/000984/098427eo.pdf

UNESCO. (2000). *The Dakar Framework for Action: Education for all—Meeting our collective commitments*. World Education Forum. Dakar, Senegal: UNESCO. Retrieved from http://www.unesco.at/bildung/basisdokumente/dakar_aktionsplan.pdf

UNESCO. (2007). *Jamaica country report*. Caribbean Symposium on Inclusive Education. Kingston, Jamaica: UNESCO. Retrieved from http://www.ibe.unesco.org/fileadmin/user_upload/Inclusive Education/Reports/kingston_07/jamaica_inclusion_07.pdf

Whyte, M. (1977). *A short history of education in Jamaica*. London, UK: Hodder and Stoughton.

CHAPTER 8

INCLUSIVITY OR EXCLUSIVITY

An Educational Leadership Perspective

Ian Marshall

In the 1990s, the Government of Barbados through the White Paper on Education Reform (1995), with the theme "Each One Matters," signalled its intention to pursue a policy of inclusion or mainstreaming. The policy, grounded in the principle of the least restrictive educational environment—consistent with the 1975 authorization of the law that in 2004 became known in the United States as the Individual with Disabilities Education Act (IDEA)—sought to promote the integration of those students who were mentally and physically challenged. To this end, Special Education was legally defined as education suitable to the requirements of persons who were mute, deaf, blind or otherwise physically or psychologically disabled or intellectually impaired; and included education suitable to the requirements of pupils who were gifted or had exceptional ability (White Paper on Education Reform, 1995). The intention of the Government of Barbados found expression in two inclusionary models, the pull-out programme and the full inclusion programme. In the case of the former, students identified as experiencing special education needs, spent part of their time in general education and part of their time in the resource centre engaged in small group instruction, focused on their particular needs (Browne, 2007). In the case of the latter, students with special needs remained in their classrooms all of the time. They participated either with adaptations or modifications to the curriculum (Browne, 2007). The Government of Barbados also facilitated the training of more than 105 teachers at the Masters and Bachelors level in inclusionary practices, Special Education and Educational Psychology, to the tune of two million dollars. It must be noted; however, that the Barbadian concept of inclusive education targeted four categories of students: category 1, those who were not benefiting from the delivery of education; category 2, those who were "at risk" for grade retention and dropout; category 3, mild to moderately mentally challenged students, who previously would have been removed from the general education classes and assigned to a special education unit; and category 4, students with physical and mobility challenges (Browne, 2007).

Yet the way in which inclusion has evolved in Barbados is not unusual. Inclusion is tightly bound to context. As such, the culture and history of a country will strongly mediate the manner in which inclusion is defined, implemented and achieved within respective countries (Ruairc, Ottesen, & Precey, 2013). In the Barbadian context, inclusion emerged as a response to four key events at the international level. The first was the United Nations Declaration on the Rights of Disabled Persons (1975) which stated that all persons with disabilities are entitled to the rights stipulated, without respect to race, color, sex, language, religion, political or other opinions, nation or social origin, state of wealth, birth or any other situation. The second was the Education for All Goals (EFA) which emerged out of a meeting in Jomtien, Thailand in 1990. These goals included expansion of early childhood care and education for all, the provision of free and compulsory primary education for all children, especially girls and those children from ethnic minorities, promotion of life skills, and achievement of gender parity and adult literacy. The third was the Salamanca Statement (UNESCO, 1994), which reaffirmed that education was a human right. It called on governments and non-governmental organizations to focus specifically on the provision of special needs education within mainstream schools, in short, inclusive education. The fourth event was the Dakar Framework for Action 2000, which simply reaffirmed a commitment to the realization of the Education for All (EFA) goals by the year 2015.

The above events spawned a number of top-down policy initiatives at the national level. As a result, inclusive education in Barbados took on a characteristic that made it appear, paradoxically, exclusive. As a consequence, those leaders who were trained in special education were deemed to be the ones most capable of facilitating the process of inclusive education, in their respective schools. From the inception, therefore, inclusive education was deemed to be the reserve of a select few. The point to be made, however, is that inclusive education must be driven, not by a few leaders who have acquired the qualifications in special and inclusive education, but by principals and school leaders who understand that successful inclusive education requires a whole system approach. This brings us to the first discussion point in this chapter, whether or not principals are aware of the nexus between inclusive education and instructional leadership.

THE PRINCIPAL AS INSTRUCTIONAL LEADER OF INCLUSIVE EDUCATION

According to Villa & Thousand (2003), successful promotion and implementation of inclusive education require the following five system-level practices: (a) connection with organizational best practices; (b) visionary leadership and administrative support; (c) redefined roles and relationships among adults and students; (d) collaboration; and (e) additional support when needed. Although all of the above are important, at this juncture a more focused look at what constitutes visionary leadership is warranted. But what exactly is meant by visionary leadership? According to Ambrose (1987), visionary leaders recognize that changing any organization, including a school, is a complex act. They know that organizational transformation requires ongoing attention to consensus building for the inclusive vision. It also requires skill development on the part of educators and everyone involved in the change; the provision of extra common planning time and fiscal, human, technological, and organizational resources to motivate experimentation with new practices; and the collaborative development and communication of a well-formulated plan of action for transforming the culture and practice of a school (Ambrose, 1987).

If one were to look at the role of the instructional leader as posited by Hallinger and Murphy (1985), it would be clear that there is great overlap with Ambrose's definition of the visionary leader. Put another way, it is virtually impossible to embark on any educational initiative that is as systemic as inclusive education, without having an instructional leader to drive the process. Let us delve a bit further to strengthen the point. According to Hallinger and Murphy (1985) the Principal Instructional Leadership Management Rating Scale (PIMRS) identifies three key dimensions of the instructional leadership construct as follows: defining the school mission, managing the instructional programme, and developing a positive school learning climate. When these areas are further expanded, they all underscore the role of the principal as chief architect of the processes both directly and indirectly. For example, in order for the school to engage in effective inclusion, there must be a clear vision for what the school ought to look like when it is fully inclusive. This is particularly important since the literature is divided on what is meant by inclusion. According to Fuchs and Fuchs (1998), the inclusionists believe that regular classroom teachers and special educators, using an assemblage of research-backed instructional methods, can help children with disabilities acquire important skills, knowledge, and behaviors that would results in college graduations and a good job: however, they argue that some children with disabilities typically fail to respond to such instructional methods, and that even knowledgeable and dedicated teachers cannot address the special instructional needs of all children in the regular classroom (Fuchs & Fuchs, 1998). On the other hand, the full inclusionists believe that the primary job of educators is to help children with disabilities to establish friendships with non-disabled persons, change stereotypic thinking about disabilities among normally developing children, and help children with disabilities develop social skills: however, like their inclusionist counterparts, this full inclusionist approach is also fraught with challenges, especially when one considers children with severe disabilities in mainstream classrooms (Fuchs & Fuchs, 1998). It is absolutely critical, therefore, for the leadership of schools to collaboratively determine what vision of inclusion would be adopted. This implies that there must be meetings and sessions where the principal seeks to get buy-in and generate support for the concept of an inclusive school.

Operationalizing the Vision

In the context of Barbadian schools this could be quite challenging for several reasons. First of all, there is the hurdle of stakeholder perceptions, including parents, teachers and members of the community. Historically, students with special needs in Barbados were educated in separate settings, and in some cases persons were not even sure if it was safe to have children with disabilities or atypical development in schools at all. Therefore if the leaders of the schools are not themselves convinced that inclusion is appropriate, how then can they lead such an initiative? Further, if they themselves are convinced of the value of inclusion, the other hurdle would be to get buy-in from teachers and the parents of the children with typical development. Such a task requires leadership with vision: leadership that is synonymous with instructional leadership. The point is, inclusive schools do not simply emerge as a result of random processes and actions but through purposeful principal leadership. In a secondary school, the principal should be the key professional leading others through the process of change (Parker & Day, 1997). Research conducted by Waldron, McLeskey, and Redd (2011) identified five themes that pointed to the role of the principal in developing an effective inclusive school. More specifically, the themes spoke to the fact that the principal was substantially engaged with teachers and provided leadership in setting the direction for the school, redesigning the school organization, improving working conditions for school staff, providing high quality instruction in all settings, and ensuring that data were used to drive decision-making.

Managing the Curriculum, Shaping School Climate

Facilitating the development of buy-in is simply the first step for the instructional leader. The second and third steps are managing the instructional programme, and creating a conducive school climate, which are, arguably, more challenging. As instructional leader, the principal must not only be aware of the current instructional approaches in the field of special education, but must also be aware of what it takes to facilitate the delivery of such approaches. Questions that surround what will be taught, how it will be taught, to whom it will be taught, and at what time it will be taught, are just a few. As one looks at assessment, similar questions surrounding the what, how, when, and purpose will also have to be addressed. This in this author's opinion is the core of the instructional leader's role. The instructional leader must manipulate, revise, expand and contract the curriculum to motivate students and teachers alike to achieve their maximum. To achieve this, the instructional leaders would be expected to have systems in place for monitoring the progress of students, rewarding students, motivating teachers, and engaging the support of the parents, business community and other service organizations. Research by Blackman (in press) examined the role of the principal in managing assessment, curriculum and instruction and found that principals utilized teachers as experts and critical partners in curriculum development and planning; that principals mediated roles in assessment and placement or grouping of students with disabilities; and that principals played a role in checking up on and checking in with teachers when monitoring instruction.

In the words of Blackman (in press), the principals were engaging in some semblance of "distributive leadership," which according to Spillane (2006) is a vital component of instructional leadership. This speaks to process and not product, collaboration and not insularity. Learning communities are not built overnight, therefore when one is seeking to create inclusive educational institutions, the financial, resource, and manpower outlays could increase exponentially. If inclusive schools are to be successful, indeed, if *schools* are to be successful, they must be well-oiled engines of collaboration. Achievement of inclusive education presumes that no one person would have all the expertise required to meet the needs of all the students in a classroom. Therefore, for inclusion to work, educators must become effective and efficient collaborative team members, they must develop skills in creativity, collaborative teaming processes, co-teaching, and interpersonal communication that will enable them to work together, to craft diversified learning opportunities for learners, who have a wide range of interest, learning styles and intelligences (Thousand & Villa, 2000; Villa, 2002; Villa & Thousand, 2003).

CHALLENGES WITH THE DELIVERY OF INCLUSIVE EDUCATION

Preparing or developing an educational system that is more inclusive is theoretically easy, that is, if it begins and ends with articulation in a policy document. However, the operationalization of such a goal is fraught with myriad challenges ranging from principal preparation, stakeholder perceptions, and teacher preparation. These will be discussed in turn. Garrison-Wade, Sobel, and Fulmer (2007) note that while every teacher must be prepared for the vast diversity of today's student population, principals face additional challenges leading special education initiatives. They conclude that given the complexity and demanding nature of inclusive education, the practice of inclusion is often misunderstood and sometimes resisted by teachers, and not fully understood or supported by school administrators. Research by Kim (2013) in the Korean educational jurisdiction echoed similar sentiments. This researcher noted that in the practice of inclusive education, two major barriers were insufficient understanding and inactive participation from principals of the regular schools, and the quality of the 8,600 inclusionary classes relied greatly on the interest and support of the school principals (Kim, 2013). Strong principal leadership, therefore, was deemed necessary for the successful practice of inclusive education in Korea.

The Challenge of Principal Preparation

This raises another question: if principals are so critical to the process, how adequately prepared are they? According to the literature, many administrator preparation programmes provided principals with a minimum amount of knowledge deemed by special education experts to be relevant in the implementation of inclusion (Angelle & Bilton, 2009; DiPaola & Walther-Thomas, 2003; Osterman & Hafner, 2009; Pazey & Cole, 2013). Further, while characteristics of disabilities, special education law, and behavior management may be covered in preparation programmes, specific topics that present authentic strategies and processes to support inclusion appear to be lacking (Praisner, 2003). To address the issues related to administrator preparation, Billingsley, McLeskey, and Crockett (2014) suggest that leadership preparation must acknowledge that successful school leadership is not about a leader's direct intervention with students, but more so about leadership practices that affect the social context in which teachers and students work. Therefore, effective leadership in inclusive education is about the extent to which school leaders share leadership to improve student learning through the following six core leadership dimensions: academic press, disciplinary climate, high quality instruction, progress monitoring, working conditions, and professional learning opportunities (Billingsley et al., 2014). If one accepts the forgoing argument, then the leadership preparation paradigm must now shift from the one-off to the continuous professional development model, framed within the context of shared leadership.

THE CHALLENGE OF PRINCIPAL PREPARATION IN BARBADOS

In Barbados, our principal preparation programmes tend to prepare future leaders for leadership in mainstream rather than inclusive schooling. For example, the Masters in Educational Leadership does not include specific modules for inclusive education. The programme indirectly addresses the topic in a cursory way through the module on social justice education. This is again consistent with research by Christensen, Siegel-Robertson, Williamson, and Hunter (2013), who found that 32 per cent of principals in their study received no special education training in their principal preparation programmes. It must be noted; however, that persons are free to pursue a Masters in Special Education Inclusionary Practices for Special Needs Students, although, the programme tends to attract individuals who work in special needs schools. This anomalous situation is the genesis of the problem for principals in the Barbadian educational system. On the one hand, there is the rhetoric that declares the country's commitment to inclusive education, while on the other there is the perpetuation of the separatist ideology for students and for the training of school leaders. For example, in Barbados there are three dedicated public special needs schools—one caters for children up to 13 years of age, the second for children from ages 5 to 18, and the third for children from age 13–18. There are four special needs units which are situated on the compound of mainstream schools but operate as autonomous entities with their own leadership and staff. There are also seven other schools which deliver what is known as partial inclusion or "dual settings" instruction. Special needs students received instruction in literacy and mathematics by special education teachers and joined their mainstream counterparts for instruction in physical education, art, social studies, and general science. The fact is that with the exception of the first three dedicated specialist schools mentioned earlier, there is no requirement for principals in mainstream schools to be trained in special education before assuming their leadership positions. Neither is there any requirement for principals, having assumed the positions, to access in-service training. It is common practice to have principals leading mainstream schools which are supposed to be inclusive without the requisite training, knowledge or competencies. Principals cannot lead what they do not know, so you can appreciate the challenges with inclusion in such contexts. This point was underscored by Garrison-Wade et al. (2007), who pointed out that beliefs and attitudes that principals hold towards special education are key factors in implementing inclusive school programmes. Implicitly, then, if inclusion is to be successful in Barbadian schools, there is a strong case for revamping the principal preparation programs to be more consistent with inclusionary best practices.

Stakeholder Attitudes

Another challenge to the delivery of inclusive education are stakeholder attitudes in general, and teacher attitudes specifically. According to Meijer, Soriano, and Watkins (2003), positive teacher attitudes nurture belongingness, and may directly affect behavior with and by students, and, by extension classroom climate and student outcomes (Blackman, Conrad, & Brown, 2012). Moreover, there is still the tendency or sentiment to view disabilities as an individualized pathology or disease. As a consequence, regular education teachers have a strong tendency to avoid or ignore the responsibilities of providing education for children with special needs, passing their responsibilities to special education teachers (Kim, 2013). This tendency also emerged in research on teacher attitude to integration, conducted in Barbados and Trinidad by Blackman, Conrad, and Brown (2012). More to the point, teachers in Trinidad did not feel confident in their ability to teach students with disabilities who were in their classrooms, while the teachers in Barbados were of the view that only those students who could be successfully accommodated should be in the regular education setting. The only difficulty with the latter position is this: Who would determine those who could be successfully accommodated? Further: What would be the criteria for selection? Such a stance by teachers, signals that they are still locked in the mind-set that says that students with disabilities are seen as problem students, rather than the mind-set that is premised on the fact that education is a human right. The implication, therefore, is that teachers, and, by extension, the teacher training institutions, must approach teacher training for inclusive education, not as an adjunct course or module. It must be part of the core curriculum of what teacher training institutions deliver. The attitude therefore, of the tutors and instructors and indeed the leadership of such institutions must align with the human rights and social justice paradigms of inclusive education. Put more bluntly, for models of effective inclusion to move from idealism and rhetoric towards equity, advocacy, and socially just practices, there must also be change in school organization and leadership (Conrad & Brown, 2011).

Later research by Hunter-Johnson, Newton, and Cambridge-Johnson (2014) examined the issue of teacher attitudes in the context of the Bahamian school system. They also identified teacher attitudes as a challenge to implementing inclusive education in the public primary schools. Their research findings indicated that 90 per cent of teachers interviewed expressed negative perceptions of inclusive education (Hunter-Johnson, Newton, & Cambridge-Johnson, 2014). So how then should one deal with the issue of teacher attitudes? According to Avramidis and Norwich (2002), teachers' attitudes could become more positive if more resources and support were provided. At first glance, this may seem like a workable solution, although this author is of the view that while resources and support are important, the more fundamental factor that could impact the success of inclusion is teachers' philosophical orientation. It borders, to some extent, on teacher efficacy: if teachers believe that children have the right to be educated and that they, the teachers, have the capacity to facilitate that education, then resources and support will be found, both within and without the school. Implicitly, the role of the principal and his/her staff as advocates for student outcomes would come to the fore.

Compounding the challenge of teacher attitudes is what Forbes (2007) called the misconception that inclusion refers to a place and not a process. A place called school where everybody belongs, is accepted, and where special education-needs students are supported and cared for by their peers and other members of the school community. As far as Forbes (2007) is concerned, such a view is utopian and does not take cognizance of the processes and learning environments needed to achieve authentic educational outcomes for all students. One can argue that such utopian ideals are present in Barbadian schools for two reasons. As was indicated earlier, teachers, like principals, are exposed to general principles of special-needs education; however, the specialized training that is required for a truly inclusive programme is not included in the teacher training programmes offered by the two major teacher training institutions in Barbados. In fact, one parent of a special-needs student suggested that what is being offered by the training institutions is remedial education, which focuses on students with mild-to-moderate learning difficulties. The special knowledge and skills that would be required to deal with severe learning difficulties, and other more challenging special needs, along with support personnel like psychologists and social workers, are not part of the inclusionary package.

Teacher Preparation

The level of utopia also has its effect on the supply of suitably qualified special-needs teachers. The Barbadian educational system operates on an in-service rather than a pre-service teaching training programme. This means, therefore, that you can have novice teachers in inclusive schools interacting with special-needs students. Put differently, you have students included in mainstream schools with significant special needs for which the teacher has not been prepared (Forbes, 2007). This point is well supported in the literature. In a comparative study involving Australia and Singapore by Sharma, Ee, and Desai (2003) the findings pointed to the role of teacher training in special education as a factor in reducing pre-service teachers' concerns regarding inclusive education. This situation appears even more dire when one considers that some teachers could be in the system for 4 or 5 years before they are able to access training. Additionally, more and more students who attend mainstream schools are presenting with special needs. One must hasten to add that while there is also a one-year special-needs programme on offer, it is an optional programme at one of the main teacher training institutions in Barbados, and consequently attracts only teachers who have an interest in the area of special needs.

Another aspect of teacher training that is a cause for concern is the over-emphasis on children with mild-to-moderate disabilities. It seems as if teachers and principals alike forget that the special-needs spectrum includes children who are gifted. Again, there is little training available to meet the needs of gifted learners in the public school system. In response to this inertia on the part of the public sector, private providers have emerged to fill the void, albeit at prohibitive rates to parents. So the question that needs to be asked, therefore, is what is the quality of inclusive education being provided by public schools? Which in turn points to another question, that of accountability for educational outcomes.

LEGAL, INSTITUTIONAL AND SOCIO-CULTURAL SUPPORTS

In order for there to be an effective inclusive education model, there must of necessity be a legal framework which undergirds any policy initiatives. According to the Barbados Education Act (1982, Cap. 41), there are 5 sections which in the most basic way speaks to special education. The ones that are relevant for this paper are Section (53.1), which states that "the Minister may for the purpose of ascertaining which children of compulsory school age require special education treatment, carry out such investigations as he considers necessary and after the investigations the minister may provide for the education of any child requiring special education treatment"; Section (53.2), which states that "the minister may, where practical, provide special schools appropriate for the education of children requiring special education treatment, but where it is not practical to do so the minister may provide facilities for special education at any school," and Section (53.5), which states that "the Minister may provide transport and other facilities as he considers necessary to enable children receiving special treatment to attend school." From the foregoing, it is reasonable to argue that the legislative framework is an extremely paltry attempt at facilitating effective inclusive education.

Contrast this with Japanese system of education, which specifies the types of schools that are available for children with visual impairment, hearing impairment, mental disorder, physical disabilities, and health-related needs. It goes further and indicates that in regular kindergarten, elementary schools, and secondary schools, education service can be provided to children with disabilities, who fall into the categories outlined above.

The United States, through the Individual with Disabilities Education Act (IDEA, 1997), the Individual with Disabilities Improvement Education Act (IDEA, 2004) and many other pieces of legislation, took inclusive education to another level. It made provision for children with disabilities to be educated to the maximum extent appropriate with children who are not disabled. As noted by Howard (2004), before a student can be removed, it must be considered whether the student is unable to achieve satisfactorily in the regular classroom environment with supplemental aids and services.

From the foregoing, it is clear that there is much ground to be covered if the provision of inclusive education in Barbados is to meet international standards and best practices. Importantly, the Ministry of Education, Science, Technology and Innovation (METI) through funding from the European Union, is in the process of creating a policy framework for special needs inclusive education. It is hoped that this policy framework would make provision for appropriate, rather than practical, education for all children in the least restrictive environment.

LESSONS FROM THE FIELD

In the literature, there is ongoing discourse around the notion of schooling for most and some; and schooling for all, between mainstream and special, and inclusive education; between bell-curved education and social justice education (Florian, 2008). Looking beyond the intellectual discourse, there is also ample evidence of some educational best practices that are worthy of further examination. In this vein is the work of Florian (2008), who argued for a tripartite approach as follows: (a) teacher professional development that rejects the deterministic views of ability and embraces discursive practices (Peters & Reid, 2006); (b) evidence-based practice that takes into account the impact of socio-cultural factors, such as biology, culture, family, and school on individual differences; and (c) the use of collaborative teaching as suggested by Thousand, Nevin, and Villa (2007). All of the best practices mentioned have enjoyed varying levels of success and are good for benchmarking what is done in Barbadian schools.

Components of Effective and Sustainable Schools: American Context

Additionally, the findings of case studies on inclusive education conducted by Dyson et al. (2004) and Hehir and Katzman (2012) underscore three key components for an effective and sustainable school. These include strong active principal leadership to ensure that teachers share core values and institutional commitment to developing an effective inclusive school; a data system that monitors student progress; and a school-based system of learner-centred professional development to improve instruction. Importantly, all of these components speak to the concept of instructional leadership built on a type of distributed leadership platform. Hallinger and Murphy (2013) are in accord with the previous sentiments. They assert that principals must find time to engage their instructional leadership role. They further maintain that when we consider the expertise needed to lead learning, the normative pressures that draw principals away from the classrooms, and the conflicting demands on principal time, it becomes clear that instructional leadership cannot be a solo performance (Hallinger & Murphy, 2013). To this end, they have suggested that if principals are to be effective instructional leaders they must ensure that they clarify their personal visions and supporting "habits"; articulate a collective instructional leadership role; and enable others to act.

Components of Effective and Sustainable Schools: European Context

Researchers also looked at the issue from the European context, and came to similar conclusions as their counterparts in the United States. For example, Meijer (2010) while underscoring the role of principal leadership, made the point, first of all, that what was good for pupils with special education needs was good for all pupils. Seven features of effective inclusive education practice were identified as follows: cooperative teaching, cooperative learning, collaborative problem solving, heterogeneous grouping, effective teaching, home area systems, and alternative ways of learning (Meijer, 2010). These features, notably, are to some extent in accord with the principles of Universal Design of Instruction, as espoused by Burgstahler (2005), the central goal of which is to maximize the learning of students by taking cognizance of and catering to the heterogeneous nature of student populations. It must be noted, however, there are some limitations to the aforementioned seven features, and as such should not be regarded as a panacea. Indeed, there is also research that points to the role of flexible grouping in inclusive classrooms (Chorzempra & Graham, 2006).

The point being stressed here is the one made by McLeskey and Waldron (2015), that effective leadership is what makes schools truly inclusive. In other words, you can have all the legislative frameworks in place, the institutional strengthening, in terms of support personnel such as psychologists, psychiatrists, teaching assistants, training initiatives and opportunities and all the other supports that the literature suggests should be present in an inclusive school, but if the educational institutions are led by leaders who are unclear about the pivotal role of effective instructional leadership, then the potential for student learning outcomes would be significantly undermined. This idea finds support within the Barbadian context. An analysis of the schools that are deemed to be effective in delivering student outcomes indicates that effective principal leadership is the key driver of student outcomes. There is therefore a case to be made for a renewed emphasis in this area.

CONCLUSION

Having examined the Barbadian case of inclusive education, one would have to conclude that there were efforts made by the educational authorities in Barbados to deliver some semblance of inclusive education: nonetheless, there are some enduring themes that need to be underscored. The first is that inclusion is still conceptualized by the educational authorities and educational leaders in a particularly narrow and restrictive manner. The second is that at the policy level, there is much work to be done to facilitate the emergence of truly inclusive schools. The third is that there needs to be a paradigmatic shift in the approach by principals to the facilitation of inclusive education. The UN General Assembly, Convention on the Rights of People with Disabilities (2006) has clearly articulated through Article 24 that all states/parties shall ensure an inclusive education system at all levels. The extent to which countries are able to fulfil the spirit and letter of this convention is directly related to the quality of instructional leadership that is provided in schools. An indication of how this can be operationalized is captured in the Education Agenda for post-2015 posited by UNESCO (2005). It argues for a continued focus on quality education for all, by recruiting and retaining well trained and motivated teachers with an assemblage of skills, abilities and dispositions. More specifically teachers must: (a) be inclusive in their orientation; (b) be gender-responsive; (c) employ child-centred pedagogical approaches; (d) provide content that is relevant to all learners and to the context in which they live; (e) establish learning environments that are safe, gender-responsive, inclusive and conducive to learning; (f) encompass mother tongue-based multilingual education; and (g) ensure that learners reach sufficient levels of knowledge and competencies according to national standards at each level (UNESCO, 2005). This is a Herculean task to say the least, but one that can be accomplished, if principals as instructional leaders are core facilitators of the myriad processes aforementioned. Core facilitators, one may add, who understand and employ the principles of shared leadership to deliver learning outcomes for all students.

REFERENCES

Angelle, P., & Bilton, L. (2009). Confronting the unknown: Principal preparation training in issues related to special education. *AASA Journal of Scholarship & Practice, 5*(4), 5–9.

Ambrose, D. (1987). *Managing complex change.* Pittsburgh, PA: The Enterprise Group.

Avramidis, E., & Norwich, B. (2002). Mainstream teachers' attitudes towards inclusion/integration: A review of the literature, *European Journal of Special Needs Education, 17*(2), 129–147. doi:10.1080/08856250210129056

Barbados Education Act of 1982, Chapter 41.

Billingsley, B., McLeskey, J., & Crockett, J. (2014). *Principal Leadership: Moving toward inclusive and high-achieving schools for students with disabilities* (Document NO.IC-8). Retrieved from University of Florida, Collaboration for Effective Educator, Development, Accountability, and Reform Center website, http://ceedar.education.ufl.edu/tools/innovation-configurations/

Blackman, S. (in press). School Principals' roles in managing assessment, curriculum and instruction in mainstream and special education in Barbados. *Journal of Education and Development in the Caribbean.*

Blackman, S., Conrad, D., & Brown, L. (2012). The attitude of Barbadian and Trinidadian teachers to integration. *International Journal of Special Education, 27(3),* 1–11.

Browne, J. (2007, 5). Barbados Country Report. *Caribbean Symposium on Inclusive Education.* UNESCO, International Bureau of Education, 5–7 December, 2007, Kingston, Jamaica.

Burgstahler, S. (2005). *Universal design of instruction (UDI): Definition, principles, guidelines, and examples. DO-IT disabilities, opportunities, internetworking, and technology. University of Washington College of Engineering.* Retrieved from http://www.washington.edu/doit/universal-design-instruction-udi-definition-principles-guidelines-and-examples.

Chorzempa, B., & Graham, S. (2006). Primary grade teachers use of within-class ability grouping in reading. *Journal of Educational Psychology, 98(3),* 529–41. doi:10.1037/0022-0663.98.3529

Christensen, J., Siegel-Robertson, J., Williamson, R., & Hunter, W. (2013). Preparing educational leaders for special education success: Principals' perspectives. *The Researcher, 25(1),* 94–107.

Conrad, D., & Brown, L. (2011). Fostering inclusive education: principals' perspectives in Trinidad and Tobago. *International Journal of Inclusive Education, 15(9),* 1017–1029.

DiPaola, M., & Walther-Thomas, C. (2003). *Principals and special education: The critical role of school leaders* (COPSSE Document No. IB-7). Retrieved from University of Florida Center on Personnel Studies in Special Education website, http://copsse.education.ufl.edu/copsse/library/executive -summaries.php

Dyson, A., Farrell, P., Polat, F., Hutcheson, G., & Gallannaugh, F. (2004). *Inclusion and pupil achievement.*(Research Report RR578). Retrieved from London, United Kingdom: Department for Educational Skills, www.education.gov.uk/publications/eOrderingDownload/RR578.pdf.

Florian, L. (2008). Towards an inclusive pedagogy. In P. Hick, R. Kershner, & P. T. Farrell (Eds.), *Psychology for inclusive education: New directions in theory and practice* (pp.38–51).London,UK: Routledge.

Forbes, F. (2007). Towards inclusion: An Australian perspective. *Support for Learning, 22*, 66–71. doi: 10.1111/j.1467-9604.2007.00449.x

Fuchs, D., & Fuchs, L. (1998). Competing visions for educating students with disabilities: Inclusion versus full inclusion. *Childhood Education, 74(5)*, 309–16.

Garrison-Wade, D., Sobel, D., & Fulmer, C. (2007). Inclusive leadership: Preparing principals for the role that awaits them. *Educational Leadership and Administration, 19*, 117–32.

Hallinger, P., & Murphy, J. (1985). Assessing the instructional leadership behavior of principals. *The Elementary School Journal, 86(2)*, 217–48.

Hallinger, P., & Murphy, J. (2013). Running on empty? Finding the time and capacity to lead learning. *NASSP Bulletin, 97(1)*, 5–21. doi:10.1177/0192636512469288

Hehir, T., & Katzman, L. (2012). *Effective inclusive schools: Designing successful schoolwide programs*. San Francisco, CA: Jossey-Bass.

Howard, P. (2004). The least restrictive environment: How to tell? *Journal of Law and Education, 33(176)*, 1–13.

Hunter-Johnson, Y., Newton, N., & Cambridge-Johnson, J. (2014). What does teachers' perception have to do with inclusive education: A Bahamian context. *International Journal of Special Education, 29(1)*, 1–15.

Individuals with Disabilities Act, 20 U.S.C. Section 1400. (1997).

Kim, Y. (2013). Inclusive education in Korea: Policy, practice and challenges. *Journal of Policy and Practice in Intellectual Disabilities, 10(2)*, 79–81. doi: 10.1111/jppi.12034

McLeskey, J., & Waldron, N. (2015). Effective leadership makes schools truly inclusive. *Phi Delta Kappan, 96(5)*, 68–73. doi:10.1177/0031721715569474

Meijer, C. (2010). *Special needs education in Europe: Inclusive policies and practices.* Zeitschrift für Inklusion, [S.l.], April 2010. Retrieved from http://www.inklusion-online.net/index.php/inklusion-online/article/view/136/136.

Meijer, C., Soriano, V., & Watkins, A. (2003). Special needs education in Europe: Inclusive policies and practices. In *Special needs education in Europe, Thematic publication.* Middelfart, Denmark: European Agency for Development in Special Needs Education. Retrieved from https://www.europeanagency.org/sites/default/files/sne_europe_en.pdf

Osterman, K., & Hafner, M. (2009). Curriculum in leadership preparation: Understanding where we have been in order to know where we might go. In M.D. Young, G. M. Crow, J. Murphy, & R. T. Ogawa (Eds.), *Handbook of research on the education of school leaders* (pp. 269–317). New York, NY: Routledge.

Parker, S., & Day, V. (1997). Promoting inclusion through instructional leadership: The roles of the secondary school principal. National Association of Secondary School Principals. *NASSP Bulletin, 81*(587), 83–9. doi:10.1177/019263659708158712

Pazey, B., & Cole, H. (2013). The role of special education training in the development of socially just leaders: Building an equity consciousness in educational leadership programs. *Educational Administration Quarterly, 49*, 243–71. doi:10.1177/0013161X12463934

Peters, S., & Reid, D. (2006, April). *Resistance and discursive practice: Promoting advocacy in teacher undergraduate and graduate programs.* Paper presented at the American Educational Research Association Annual Meeting, San Francisco, CA.

Praisner, C. (2003). Attitudes of elementary school principals toward inclusion of students with disabilities. *Exceptional Children, 69(2),* 135–45.

Ruairc, G. M., Ottesen, E., & Precey, R. (2013). Leadership for inclusive education: Setting the context. In G. Ruairc, E. Ottesen, & R. Precey (Eds.), *Leadership for Inclusive Education: Vision, Values and Voices* (pp. 1–6). Rotterdam, The Netherlands: Sense Publishers.

Sharma, R., Ee, J., & Desai, I. (2003). A comparison of Australian and Singaporean pre-service teacher attitudes and concerns about inclusive education. *Teaching and Learning, 24(2),* 201–17.

Spillane, J. (2006). *Distributed leadership.* San Francisco, CA: Jossey Bass.

Thousand, J., Nevin, A., & Villa, R. (2007). Collaborative teaching: Critique of the scientific evidence. In L. Florian (Ed.), *The SAGE handbook of special education* (pp. 418–29). London, UK: SAGE Publications. doi: 10.4135/9781848607989.n32

Thousand, J., & Villa, R. (2000). Collaborative learning: A powerful tool in school restructuring. In R. A. Villa & J. S. Thousand (Eds.), *Restructuring for caring and effective education: Piecing the puzzle together* (2nd ed., pp. 254–91). Baltimore, MD: Paul H. Brookes.

UNESCO. (1994). *The Salamanca statement and framework for action on special needs education.* Paris, France: UNESCO.

UNESCO. (2005). *Guidelines for inclusion: Ensuring access to education for all.* United Nations Position Paper on Education Post-2015. ED-14/EFA/POST-2015/1. UNESCO, Paris, France.

UN General Assembly. (1975). *United Nations Declarations on the rights of disabled persons* (U.N. General Assembly, 30th session, 1975). Retrieved 21st December 2016.

UN General Assembly. (2006). *Convention on the Rights of Persons with Disabilities.* 13 December 2006, A/RES/61/106, Annex I. Retrieved from http://www.refworld.org/docid/4680cd212.htm

Villa, R. (2002). *Collaborative planning: Transforming theory into practice.* Port Chester, NY: National Professional Services.

Villa, R., & Thousand, J. (2003). Making inclusive education work. *Educational Leadership, 61(2),* 19–23.

Waldron, N., McLeskey, J., & Redd, L. (2011). Setting the direction: The role of the principal in developing an effective, inclusive school. *Journal of Special Education Leadership, 24(2),* 51–60.

White Paper on Education Reform Preparing for the 21st Century Each one Matters. (1995). Bridgetown, Barbados: Ministry of Education Youth Affairs and Culture.

CHAPTER 9

A COMPARISON OF BARBADIAN AND GRENADIAN TEACHERS' BELIEFS ABOUT CREATIVITY

Grace-Anne Jackman[1] and James E. J. Young

> My feeling is that the concept of creativeness and the concept of the healthy, self-actualizing, fully-human person seem to be coming closer and closer together, and may perhaps turn out to be the same thing.
> —*Maslow (1963, p. 4)*

The universal debate on creativity and its interconnectedness to psychology theories such as Maslow's humanistic theory of self-actualization and Freud's psychoanalytic theory of the conscious and unconscious have been part of the educational research discourse since the 1950s. However, regardless of the lens used to explain creativity, its importance on a global scale to the economic, educational, and political landscapes cannot be underestimated. In today's environment, the ever-increasing demands to develop a workforce that can drive innovation and

---

[1] Corresponding Author

Caribbean Discourse in Inclusive Education:
Historical and Contemporary Issues, pages 139–157.
Copyright © 2017 by Information Age Publishing
All rights of reproduction in any form reserved.

boost economic growth underscore the need to understand and encourage creativity in all its forms. Ongoing discussions about its definition, and the means of fostering and measuring creativity continue. In the Caribbean, even as far back as the 1980s, the failure of the education system to produce creative individuals was recognized, and an argument was made that a shift toward embracing a culture of creativity was necessary (Richardson, 1986). Further, Richardson (1986) supported the earlier sentiments of Rogers (1951) who critically analyzed aspects of society and purported that education tended to produce persons who would only conform to the norms of society and whose prospects for further growth, exploration and learning were severely limited.

Globally, organizations such as The Partnership for 21st Century Skills (P21), have advocated for the development and integration of 21st Century Skills in the curricula and in the classrooms. These are skills and competencies that prepare students not just for success in their core courses in the classroom but, more importantly, are also required for them to thrive beyond the walls of the classroom and into their future careers and lives. The P21 model encompasses four specific areas: (a) Core subjects and 21st Century themes; (b) Information, Media and Technology Skills; (c) Life and Career Skills; and (d) Learning and Innovation Skills. Included in the latter category is a focus on the development of skills such as creativity, critical thinking, communication and collaboration, which P21 describe as "*skills that are increasingly being recognized as those that separate students who are prepared for a more and more complex life and work environments in the 21st Century, and those who are not*" (P21, Framework Definitions, 2015). The Caribbean Community (CARICOM) Heads of Government has emphasized that the goal of education in the region should be to ensure that each citizen is groomed to becoming the "Ideal Caribbean Person," a concept that has also been endorsed by United Nations Educational, Scientific, and Cultural Organization (UNESCO). One of the characteristics of the "Ideal Caribbean Person" is that of being a creative individual who is able to contribute positively to the region through novel means of problem-solving as new issues and challenges take center stage. Šorgo et al. (2012) argued that "the world we live in is overpopulated with problems on a global, large, small or individual scale" (p. 285), hence the need for individuals who are able to create and evaluate solutions. It is, therefore, imperative that our societies develop individuals who are capable of producing novel solutions or adapting existing solutions to the pervading issues, within which the education system is to play a major role (Beghetto, 2013; Hargrove, 2012; Šorgo et al., 2012).

Undoubtedly, the teachers to whom students are exposed on a daily basis are a significant influence in forming and shaping students' means and outlets for creative expression. Cheung (2012) identified several studies which suggested that teachers can encourage creativity in students by themselves "modelling creative thinking and behavior" (p. 45). However, even though teachers agree with this observation, their conceptions of and beliefs about creativity will inevitably affect their practice and can either encourage or impede the development of students' creativity within the classroom.

Some researchers argue that a correct view and understanding of creativity should lead to better classroom practices (Hong & Kang, 2010; Newton & Newton, 2010; Quek, Ho, & Soh, 2008). However, empirical research has found teachers to be lacking in their knowledge of the nature of creativity and in understanding how to nurture the creative potential of their students (De Souza Fleith, 2000; Renzulli, 1976; Sak, 2004; Shaughnessy, 1991). Previous research has corroborated the positive effects of fostering creativity in the classroom, particularly in the areas of improved academic outcomes (Atkinson, 2004; Pishghadam, Khodadady, & Zabihi, 2011; Rubenstein & Ehlinger, 2011), demonstrating increases in students' long-term knowledge retention and intrinsic motivation (Conti, Amabile, & Pollak, 1995), and optimistic academic beliefs and college aspirations (Beghetto, 2006).

The Commonwealth Caribbean consists of seventeen English-speaking developing territories, the majority of which, although having attained political independence from Britain, still maintain an educational system modeled on that of its former colonial masters. Historically, this system has tended to focus on teacher-centred strategies, the acquisition of content knowledge, and examination success. However, if the region is to boost its level of competitiveness in this fast-paced, increasingly global environment, then a transformation is needed in our classrooms, at all levels. Teachers must be encouraged to create more dynamic student-centred environments that facilitate and are supportive of creative expression.

The purpose of this study was to investigate how secondary school teachers in Barbados and Grenada, two small-island Commonwealth states, conceptualize creativity and to unearth their beliefs about their ability to foster creativity in their respective classrooms. While there have been Caribbean studies (Fearon, Copeland, & Saxon, 2013; Richardson, 1986, 1988) that have focused on the area of creativity, this study provides a complementary perspective of how twenty-first century teachers view creativity and how the results can assist in developing strategies that teachers can use to integrate more creativity-fostering practices in their classrooms.

LITERATURE REVIEW

Creativity is a complex, multifaceted concept that has been widely defined, thus, making it difficult for consensus on one definition to be attained (Runco, 2007; Sak, 2004). Some credit the existence of over one hundred contemporary definitions of creativity to cultural differences particularly between Eastern and Western cultures, while others attribute the multiplicity of definitions to the constructivist nature of the concept, with individuals constructing their unique meanings based on their personal experiences (Mann, 2006; Sak, 2004). Reber (1995) defined creativity as an "ability to generate solutions, ideas, conceptualizations, artistic forms, theories or products that are *unique and novel*" (p. 172). Runco's (1993) definition included the aspects of "*divergent* and *convergent thinking*, problem-finding and problem-solving, self-expression, intrinsic motivation, a questioning attitude, and self-confidence" (p. ix). Furthermore, Plucker, Beghetto, and Dow (2004) defined creativity as "the interaction among aptitude, process, and the environment by which an individual or group produces a perceptible product that is both novel and useful *within a social context*" (p. 90). However, even in the absence of consensus, some fundamental principles emerge.

Firstly, creativity involves generating a product or process that is both original and useful for a particular purpose or context. The second core element is the association with both divergent thinking—the generation of ideas through processes such as brain-storming and convergent thinking—the evaluation and synthesis of ideas which is the essence of higher order thinking. Thirdly, the importance of the social context cannot be understated. Henessey (2003) theorized that conative, situational factors such as motivation (particularly intrinsically-oriented motivation) and environmental factors, such as parental practices and the learning environment, have a direct impact on the expression of creativity of individuals (Barbot, Besançon, & Lubart, 2011; Glück, Ernst, & Unger, 2002; Rogers, 1954; Runco, 2007; Sternberg, 2006). In providing support for this perspective, Dean Keith Simonton, Professor of Psychology at the University of California, Davis, stated the following:

> ...[c]reativity is not just an individual phenomenon. It occurs in a specific social context—the cultural, political, military, and economic milieu. Without taking these circumstances into account, it would be impossible to explain why some times and places are more creative than others. (Moore & Shaughnessy, 2008, p. 597)

Teachers and Their Conceptions of Creativity

Guilford's (1967) observation that "creativity is the key to education in its fullest sense and to the solution of mankind's most serious problems" (p. 13) underscores the importance of creativity as an essential element in the teaching and learning process. Therefore, if our teachers are charged with creating supportive environments in which creativity can flourish, then it is important to understand teachers' conceptions and beliefs of creativity, which in turn can influence their classroom practices.

Overall, the research suggests that while teachers generally tend to perceive themselves as being creative, their conceptualizations of creativity may be limited and narrowly focused. For example, Rubenstein and Ehlinger (2011) conducted a qualitative study in which 384 teachers were asked to describe their own levels of creativity using both rating scales and open-ended questions. The researchers noted that the majority of teachers felt confident about their creativity and rated themselves as creative or extremely creative (a rating of 6 and above on a 10-point scale). While, for some, this justification was based on several factors such as the generation of creative products in teaching and their thought processes, others claimed that it was simply part of their identity (Rubenstein & Ehlinger, 2011).

The findings of Hong and Kang's (2010) study, which examined conceptions of creativity and teaching for creativity of 44 South Korean and 21 US secondary science teachers revealed that while the teachers readily associated creativity with novelty and originality, they were less likely to identify appropriateness or usefulness as elements of creativity. These findings corroborated those of a Diakidoy and Kanari (1999) study in which the beliefs about creativity and creative outcomes of 49 Cypriot pre-service teachers were examined. Results indicated that the majority of teachers tended to perceive creativity as representing novel outcomes but again omitted references to the appropriateness in a social context (Diakidoy & Kanari, 1999).

Limitations in conceptions of creativity were also highlighted in Bolden, Harries, and Newton's (2009) study, which explored 38 primary school teachers' conceptions of creativity in mathematics through the administration of a questionnaire that solicited both closed- and open-ended responses. The findings revealed that teachers were most likely to associate their use of resources and technology, applying content to everyday examples, and having students undertake practical activities and the development of student computational flexibility in the classroom, with the fostering of creativity. However, the authors described this narrow view of creativity as being more characteristic of "teaching creatively" rather than "teaching for creativity," a distinction also promoted by Jeffrey and Craft (2004). They suggest that "teaching creatively" refers to the novel use of strategies to assist in the delivery of content whereas "teaching for creativity" focuses on the development of creativity in students. Lin (2011) in developing a framework for considering the fostering of creativity in educational settings includes both "teaching creatively" and "teaching for creativity," since "teaching creatively" can increase student interest in the subject which correlates highly with student creativity (Rinkevich, 2011).

Cheung (2012) conducted an in-depth qualitative study with 15 early childhood teachers in Hong Kong in order to examine their beliefs about creativity and their corresponding classroom practices. This study used interviews to provide insight into what teachers consider to be characteristics of a creative teacher and the creative environment. Through classroom observations, the consistency between what teachers mentioned as creative teaching practices and their actual classroom practices was also examined. The small sample size, and the fact that this study was carried out with early-childhood teachers, does not allow for generalization to secondary school teachers or the wider population of teachers. Nevertheless, the information presented is still insightful as it provides a backdrop on how teacher's conceptions and practices could be compared. For example, while teachers considered concepts such as flexibility in thought and willingness to change as important characteristics of the creative teacher, only one in five teachers observed, demonstrated flexibility in their teaching and thinking; instead the majority tended to stick to their lesson plans and used close-ended questions and whole-class teaching strategies.

Another pervading belief among teachers is that arts-based courses are inherently more creative than science-based subjects (Andreasen & Ramchandran, 2012; Diakidoy & Kanari, 2009; Marquis & Henderson, 2015). Results from a study by Diakidoy and Kanari (2009) revealed that arts-based subjects are perceived to be more likely to elicit creativity. However, results from an Andreason and Ramchandran (2012) study which explored this claim from a neurological perspective, found no differences in the brain's responses of creative individuals in the arts and those of the Sciences during activities. It thus appears that creative individuals, despite their specific disciplines undergo similar cognitive processes in the production of original and useful processes and products.

Constraints to Fostering Creativity in the Classroom

Previous research has focused on the obstacles or constraints that teachers face when implementing strategies to foster creativity in their classrooms. Some have even argued that rather than being encouraged, creative teaching is actually discouraged in the classrooms (Rinkevich, 2011). Therefore, while the theoretical benefits of creativity continue to be acknowledged, there remains what Makel (2009) referred to as a "creativity gap" between what is valued and what is actually practiced, a proposition endorsed by Brown (2004) who noted that teachers' beliefs, though positive, may not always translate into practice. In researching some of the hindrances to facilitating and developing creativity in the classroom, Rubenstein and Ehlinger (2011) surveyed 314 teachers. Three major categories of obstacles emerged in their findings, namely school constraints, student characteristics and teacher characteristics. In the category of school constraints, teachers mentioned factors such as a heavy reliance on standardized testing, the limited time spent in class and the large class sizes as prevailing issues that hamper their efforts to teach creatively. Some also felt that their ability to teach creativity was impeded by the students they teach, particularly by students' lack of openness, maturity, motivation and an overall poor sense of self. Interestingly, teachers did not exclude themselves from blame and concurred that the fostering of creativity in the classroom suffered as a result of their own lack of openness, a fear of failure and fear of others' perceptions (Rubenstein & Ehlinger, 2011).

Findings from Kim (2008) highlighted a lack of teacher training and pressure to prepare students for standardized tests as two significant barriers to creativity in the classroom. It stands to reason that if teachers are not well trained to be able to appreciate and facilitate creativity in the classroom then they would be unable to effectively do so. Across several studies, teachers readily mentioned the overreliance on standardized testing and assessment and the pressure this places on teachers to complete the syllabus in the limited time allotted (Cheung, 2012). As a result, some teachers tend to resort to more traditional teacher-centred methods of delivery of instruction. However, Schacter, Thum, and Zifkin (2006) provided a contrasting view. They argued that accountability through standardized testing and creativity complement each other and suggested that teachers should, in fact, be able to increase their arsenal of creative teaching strategies even while teaching within a system that is focused on standardized assessments.

Given the global importance of creativity and the fact that this is an under-researched area within the Caribbean, a study of this nature is both necessary and timely. Therefore, the primary purpose of this study was to gain a deeper understanding of teachers' conceptualizations of creativity and the characteristics that define a creative teacher. More specifically, the study sought to answer the following research questions:

1. What do secondary school teachers in Barbados and Grenada perceive to be the main characteristics/qualities of a creative teacher? And are there any differences in teachers' perceptions by country, gender or subject area taught?
2. How do secondary school teachers in Barbados and Grenada rate their own levels of creativity?
3. What subjects do teachers believe most encourage creativity?
4. What do teachers believe are the main hindrances to fostering creativity in the classroom?
5. What are teachers' beliefs about their creativity practices in the classroom?

METHODOLOGY

Sample

Participants in this study were drawn from the population of secondary school teachers in both Barbados and Grenada. A total of 350 questionnaires were distributed to secondary teachers of nine secondary schools in Barbados and eight secondary schools in Grenada. In each school, the principal was contacted and permission was sought for the teachers to participate in the study. Graduate teachers enrolled in the Masters of Education degree programme at Cave Hill, UWI, assisted in the administration of the questionnaire and acted as the points-of-contact to ensure the timely completion and collection of questionnaires from the teachers. Teachers were assured that their participation was voluntary and that the confidentiality of their responses would be maintained. Two hundred and ten questionnaires were completed: 110 from Barbados and 100 from Grenada, resulting in an overall response rate of 60 percent. Table 9.1 presents the demographic characteristics of the sample.

TABLE 9.1. Demographic Distribution of Participating Teachers

Demographics	Barbados N	Barbados %	Grenada N	Grenada %
Sex				
Male	45	40.9	34	34.0
Female	65	59.1	66	66.0
Age				
Under 29	31	28.2	56	56.0
30–39 years	44	40.0	24	24.0
40–49 years	21	19.1	16	16.0
50+ years	14	12.7	3	3.0
Highest Educational Level				
O Level/CSEC	0	0.0	1	1.0
A Level/CAPE/Associate Degree	7	6.7	51	52.0
Bachelors	73	69.5	40	40.8
Masters	23	21.9	6	6.1
Doctoral	2	1.9	0	0.0
Subject of Specialisation				
Arts & Humanities	49	44.5	48	48.0
Business	6	5.5	0	0.0
STEM	39	35.5	48	48.0
Vocational	16	14.5	4	4.0

Instrument

Teachers' beliefs about creativity were assessed using a questionnaire consisting of three sections. Section A comprised seven questions which solicited details on the participants' demographics such as age, gender, highest level of academic qualification, primary subject taught, and form levels to which this subject was taught.

Section B consisted of six questions: four open-ended and two close-ended. The open-ended questions required teachers to describe the defining characteristics/qualities of a creative teacher as well as identify the subjects or courses that teachers deem to most encourage creativity. The two close-ended questions required the teachers to rate their own level of creative ability on a Likert scale of 1 to 10.

Section C measured the teachers' perceptions of their creative ability using a subset of the teacher self-efficacy scale developed by Rubenstein, Mc Coach, and

Del Siegle (2013). Teachers stated their level of agreement to each of 13 statements using a five-point Likert scale (from *completely disagree* to *completely agree*). Examples of statements that were to be rated on this scale included: "*I am capable of helping my students to see the world from new perspectives*" and "*I am capable of teaching my students to find connections in seemingly unconnected ideas.*" In this study, the reliability of this scale was satisfactory (α = 0.84) given the acceptability benchmark of 0.70 as suggested by Pallant (2001) and Field (2005). Prior to its final administration, the instrument was piloted with twenty secondary school teachers in order to determine its ability to reliably gather the required information.

Data Analysis Procedures

After the questionnaires were checked for errors, the data were entered in IBM SPSS Statistics V22. The quantitative variables were analyzed using simple descriptive and inferential statistics (e.g., Independent samples t-test) while the textual data from the open-ended responses were reviewed, compared and coded using an iterative, thematic process.

RESULTS

Research Question 1. What do secondary school teachers in Barbados and Grenada perceive to be the main characteristics/qualities of a creative teacher?

Table 9.2 shows the categories of responses to this question. The largest group (18 percent) indicated that creative teachers are those who are "*innovative*," and are willing to incorporate new, original ideas in their classes to stimulate students. Just about 15 percent identified the "*use of different teaching strategies in order to reach all students*" as a defining characteristic while 13 percent believed that creative teachers enhance their students' learning experiences by *integrating technology and other teaching tools and resources* in their classrooms. Another group of teachers (12 percent) characterized creative teachers as being "*risk takers*" who both practice and encourage "*out of the box thinking*" in the classroom. Other commonly mentioned teacher characteristics included *an open-minded/unbiased teaching* approach (10 percent), the ability to *make learning fun and relatable to all students* (8 percent) and generally being *enthusiastic and having a love for teaching the subject area* (7 percent). An analysis of these comments by categories such as country, age, gender and main subject taught revealed no significant differences across these demographic variables.

Research Question 2. How do secondary school teachers in Barbados and Grenada rate their own levels of creativity?

Teachers were asked to rate their own level of creativity, on a scale from 1 (*Not at all creative*) to 10 (*Extremely Creative*). Analysis of these results revealed that overall, teachers felt moderately positive about their levels of creativity as evidenced by the mean rating of 6.97 (SD=1.49). Two thirds of teachers rated

TABLE 9.2. Teachers' Perceptions of the Defining Characteristics/Qualities of a Creative Teacher

Defining Traits/Characteristics	N	%
Innovative/New, original ideas	34	17.9
Use of different teaching strategies	28	14.7
Integration of technology/resources	25	13.1
Willing to take risks/Thinking outside the box	22	11.6
Flexibility/Open-mindedness	19	10.0
Makes learning fun/relatable/engaging	15	7.9
Enthusiasm/Love for subject	14	7.1
Excellent Knowledge of content	10	5.3
Having a vivid imagination	8	4.2
Can get students to think creatively on their own	3	1.6

themselves with at least a score of 6 and 38 percent a score of 7 or higher. Interestingly, teachers both in Barbados (Mean=6.98) and Grenada (Mean=6.96) rated themselves similarly and these results showed no significant differences by either gender or area of teaching specialization (refer to Table 9.3).

Research Question 3. What subjects do teachers believe most encourage creativity?

The results in Table 9.4 reinforce the traditional perception that arts- and humanities-related subjects tend to elicit more creativity, three in four of the teachers in

TABLE 9.3. Teachers' Ratings of Their Levels of Creativity

	N	Mean	Std Deviation
Overall	208	6.97	1.49
Barbados	109	6.98	1.62
Grenada	99	6.96	1.34
Male	79	7.18	1.49
Female	129	6.84	1.48
Arts & Humanities	97	6.89	1.56
STEM	85	6.89	1.35
Vocational	20	7.35	1.39
Business	6	8.17	2.14

TABLE 9.4. Results of Chi-Square Test for Subjects Most Eliciting Creativity by Teachers' Country and Sex

	Overall N=194		Barbados N=102		Grenada N=92		Male N=71		Female N=123	
	N	%	N	%	N	%	N	%	N	%
Arts & Humanities	145	74.7	80	78.4	65	70.7	42	59.1	103	83.7
STEM	35	18.0	12	11.8	23	25.0	22	31.0	13	10.6
Vocational	12	6.2	8	7.8	4	4.3	7	9.9	5	4.1
Business	2	1.0	2	2.0	0	0.0	0	0.0	2	1.6
			$X^2(3) = 7.848, p>.05$				$X^2(3) = 17.369, p<.05$			

the sample held this belief. On the other hand, only 18 percent of the teachers viewed STEM-related subjects as being the most creative. Smaller groups of teachers credited the Vocational (6 percent) or Business related (1 percent) subjects as being those which most encourage creativity. This pattern of results was consistently seen both across the two countries and by gender. However, the chi-square test revealed significant differences by gender with notably higher proportions of female teachers crediting the Arts as more creativity fostering. Also of interest was the finding that even among science and mathematics teachers, approximately two-thirds reported that the arts-based subjects were more likely to elicit creativity that the Science/Math subjects which they themselves teach (refer to Table 9.5).

Research Question 4. What do teachers believe are the main hindrances to fostering creativity in the classroom?

An analysis of these results, shown in Table 9.6, revealed that approximately 40 percent of teachers cited a lack of resources as their main challenge. One female Biology teacher from Grenada complained that "*[not] having the materials necessary for creating and carrying out creative ideas*" was her greatest impediment. In addition, about three in ten teachers believed that the poor attitudes of students severely hampered teachers' efforts to foster a creative classroom environment. The comments listed below echo this sentiment:

TABLE 9.5. Results of Chi-square Test for Subjects Which Most Elicit Creativity by Subject Taught and Country

	Subject Taught				Country			
	Arts & Humanities		Sciences & Math		Barbados		Grenada	
	N	%	N	%	N	%	N	%
Arts & Humanities	73	90.1	38	65.5	47	88.7	64	74.4
Sciences & Math	8	9.9	20	34.5	6	11.3	22	25.6
	$X^2(1) = 4.146, p<.05$				$X^2(1) = 12.721, p<.05$			

TABLE 9.6. Teachers' Perceptions of the Challenges to Fostering Creativity in the Classroom

	Overall N=201		Barbados N=105		Grenada N=96	
	N	%	N	%	N	%
Lack of resources	80	39.8	33	31.4	47	49.9
Attitude of students	59	29.4	36	34.3	23	24.0
Exam Pressure/Extensive Curriculum	17	8.5	14	14.3	2	2.1
Limited class time	16	8.0	7	6.7	9	9.4
Large class sizes	11	5.5	7	6.7	4	4.2
Teachers' lack of creativity	11	5.5	5	4.8	6	6.3
School culture	5	2.5	2	1.9	3	3.1
Other	2	1.0	0	0.0	2	2.1

- *"Laziness of students. Some students are turned off by the mental rigors following a creative process to excellence"* (Barbados, male teacher, 20–29, technical drawing).
- *"Children's attitude. Even though one may motivate them to be creative, there are those who are lax"* (Grenada, female teacher, 20–29, chemistry).
- *"The students' attitudes toward school. Even though the classroom environment may be creative, the students' attitude determines how receptive they will be"* (Barbados, female teacher, 20–29, geography).
- *"When students lack passion for the subject and have no drive for learning. Lack of appreciation for the contents of the subject"* (Grenada, female teacher, 20–29, physics).

Teachers also suggested that the examinations-oriented culture and extensive secondary-level curricula in the Caribbean were factors that also thwart the growth of creativity in the classroom. This, however, seemed to be more of a concern for teachers in Barbados than in Grenada. One teacher reinforced this view by stating that *"Since most of the requirements for teaching the subjects for an exam CSEC/CAPE are fairly strict, it takes away from individuality and downplays the need for creative thinking."* (Barbados, Female Teacher, 20–29, Biology)

Research Question 5. What are teachers' beliefs about creativity practices in the classroom? Results from the analysis of the data revealed that overall the teachers reported positive beliefs about their ability to foster creativity in the classroom (M = 49.7, SD = 6.4). This was evident for both the Barbadian (M = 49.9, SD = 5.9) and the Grenadian sample (M = 49.5, SD = 6.8) of teachers. Further exploration of the data showed no significant difference in teachers' beliefs either by gender or main subject taught (see Table 9.7). Segmenting the data with respect to the

TABLE 9.7. Descriptive Statistics for the Overall Creativity Scale by Teachers' Country, Gender and Subject Taught

	N	Mean	SD
Overall	210	49.71	6.35
Barbados	110	49.86	5.92
Grenada	100	49.54	6.83
Males	79	50.25	5.88
Females	131	49.38	6.63
Arts & Humanities	97	50.19	7.24
Math/Sciences	87	49.51	5.00
Vocational	20	48.30	7.48
Business	6	49.67	5.05

individual items on the Creativity scale (see Table 9.8) revealed that teachers were being most positive with respect to their ability to assist students in *"becoming more flexible in their thinking," "seeing the world from new perspectives,"* and *"elaborating on the students' unique ideas."* Conversely, it was surprising to note that teachers were not as optimistic and convinced about their *"strength in teaching creative problem-solving"* and *"teaching creative thinking"* since these two statements received the lowest mean ratings.

TABLE 9.8. Descriptive statistics for the Items on the Creativity Scale

	Mean	SD
I am capable of helping students to become more flexible in their thinking.	4.17	0.61
I am capable of helping my students to see the world from new perspectives.	4.15	0.58
I am capable of helping students to elaborate on their own unique ideas.	4.11	0.57
I am capable of developing a classroom atmosphere that welcomes imagination.	4.08	0.56
I am capable of fostering creative problem-solving in my classroom.	4.00	0.56
I am capable of promoting flexible thinking.	3.99	0.57
I am capable of teaching my students to find connections in seemingly unconnected ideas.	3.98	0.56
I am capable of increasing the quantity of original thoughts my students have.	3.86	0.62
I have helped many students to become more creative.	3.82	0.61
I am capable of enhancing my students' abilities to take meaningful academic risks.	3.78	0.63
I am capable of increasing my students' abilities to create unique solutions.	3.74	0.63
Teaching creative problem-solving is one of my strengths.	3.58	0.85
Teaching creative thinking is one of my strengths.	3.56	0.78

DISCUSSION

Creativity, though complex (Runco, 2007) has been considered to be very important to education (Guilford, 1967; Hargrove, 2012). The conceptions of creativity embraced by teachers within the Barbadian and Grenadian contexts bear similarities with those communicated in the literature. Similar to Cheung's (2012) findings, the teachers in this study identified innovation as a main defining characteristic of a creative teacher, thus acknowledging that creative individuals are expected to develop novel ideas and practices; a belief in keeping with that espoused by Reber (1995). Another point of similarity was teachers' references to *"openness to ideas," "using various techniques to deliver instruction," "willing to take risks,"* and *"seeking to make learning enjoyable"* as key indicators of creative teachers. However, according to Bolden et al. (2009) and Jeffrey and Craft (2004), these views may be considered narrow and limiting. These authors maintain that these types of conceptualizations align more closely with "teaching creatively" than "teaching for creativity" since they focus more on the practices in delivering content instead of encouraging learners to be more creative. However, in the light of Lin's (2011) framework, the conceptions of the teachers may not be considered as lacking, because, as the author argued, through the process of "teaching creatively" one can foster the ability of students to become creative. These views, held by both Barbadian and Grenadian teachers, are encouraging and should be capitalized on in advancing the creativity agenda and ensuring that CARICOM's vision of the "Ideal Caribbean person" is realized.

Secondly, this sample of teachers rated themselves, similarly to those in the Rubenstein and Ehlinger (2011) study, with most of the ratings (68 percent) above six (out of ten) thus reflecting positive views of their creative abilities. This positive rating of teachers' ability to be creative remained consistent in the reported data provided by teachers from both Barbados and Grenada, with neither group of teachers viewing themselves to be more creative than the other. The absence of any differences in the ratings according to gender and subject taught indicates that these variables had no particular influence on the way in which the respondents rated themselves.

Interestingly, however, the teachers' comments reinforced the stereotypical view that arts-related subjects are more creativity-fostering (Diakidoy & Kanari, 2011; Marquis & Henderson, 2015) than maths/science related subjects. These views, propagated by teachers in both countries, is a cause for concern as it may impede the fostering of creativity within the subject areas that are viewed as less capable of promoting the development of creativity. It can be considered a reflection of deficient views or understanding of creativity held by teachers which, as purported by De Souza Fleith (2000), Renzulli (1976) and Sak (2004) can be a hindrance to any further development of creativity among the students for whom the teachers are responsible. Additionally, the finding that female teachers were more likely to embrace this view than males highlights some of the gender differences regarding subjects and subject preferences. It suggests that while female teachers are more inclined to this "art bias," male teachers hold a more balanced perspective. Notably, this partiality may limit female teachers' ability to be creative within the context of other subject areas within the classroom.

Overall, the teachers, both in Barbados and Grenada, scored highly on the self-report measure of the creativity scale, a finding similar to that in the Rubenstein and Ehlinger (2011) study. While encouraging, this self-reported rating must be considered with caution, since the results also revealed that, despite having these general positive dispositions about their creativity-fostering abilities, "teaching creative problem-solving," and their ability to "teach creative thinking" are their main areas of weakness. This finding should resonate with Brown (2004) and Cheung (2012) who argued that teachers' beliefs, though positive, are not always congruent with their classroom practices.

With respect to the perceived hindrances to fostering creativity within their classroom, teachers are of the view that a lack of resources is the main limitation to the fostering of creativity in the classroom. This can be understood in the context of teachers believing that using innovative methods such as incorporation of technology in the classroom as explored by Bolden et al. (2009) is characteristic of the creative teacher. Indeed, with the absence of these materials, as the biology teacher from Grenada suggested, teachers may feel constrained in their teaching for creativity. However, as governments in small island developing states such as Barbados and Grenada struggle with the fiscal realities of the ongoing recession, teachers will need to be more resourceful and find inventive ways to encourage creativity in schools with limited funding and resources. Environmental challenges such as large class sizes and limited class time identified as hindrances to creativity within the classroom were similarly mentioned in Rubenstein and Ehlinger's (2011) study. Not surprising, large class sizes and fewer productive contact hours with students may negatively impact on teachers' ability to cope and may lead to a strain on their ability to foster creativity within the classroom.

Additionally, the findings within this study support those of Kim (2008) and Rubenstein and Ehlinger (2011) in which teachers reported student-oriented challenges, as well as the pressure of high-stakes examinations and teachers' own limitations as hindrances to fostering creativity. Hennesy (2003) noted that motivation, specifically intrinsic motivation, is important to the practice of creativity and should not only be a characteristic of the teachers who should encourage creativity, but also of the students who are to develop creativity. In the absence of such, manifested through poor attitudes and lack of motivation as reported by the teachers, the fostering of creativity can be hindered. Furthermore, the examination-oriented culture of the two countries, which tends to be reflective of that of the Commonwealth Caribbean, is seen as negatively influencing the creativity developing process. The heavy reliance on external, high-stakes exams and pressure to have students ready for these exams may lead teachers to use the more didactic, teacher-centred approaches to instruction and hamper their efforts to diversify their classroom practices. However, considering the proposition of

Schacter, Thum, and Zifkin (2006), it appears that teachers may in fact also be lacking the creativity to produce within such a socio-cultural context (Moore & Shaughnessy, 2008). How? Why? What would fix this?

CONCLUSION AND IMPLICATIONS

The value of creativity to the development of any country, Caribbean nations not excluded, has been recognized and reiterated (Beghetto, 2006; Fearon, Copeland, & Saxon, 2013; Hargrove, 2012; Šorgo et al., 2012). Emphasis on teaching for the development of creativity of tomorrow's global citizens is, therefore, an imperative and not an option within the Barbadian and Grenadian contexts and the Caribbean region as a whole. The study sheds light on teachers' conceptions of creativity, their beliefs about their practices and provides a basis for future research in the area of creativity. Due to the self-report nature of the instruments, there is a possibility that some "superficial" data was reported and thus the findings must be considered with this possibility in mind. Studies that include observation of teachers within their classroom contexts complemented with the views of the students can shed further light on the reality of creativity and the practice of developing creativity within the classroom. Additionally, the purposiveness of the sampling of the teachers limits the generalisability of the findings to the wider population of Caribbean secondary school teachers.

While teachers' positive beliefs about creativity represent a promising finding, the study also highlights two primary areas of concern. Firstly, there is an urgent need for teachers to reorient their thinking and to use the "lack of resources" as an opportunity to be more resourceful and inventive so that the true concept of creativity is not just taught but is brought to life in the classroom. In "The Boy Who Harnessed the Wind," William Kamkwamba (2010), a Malawian teenager, used his meager resources to build a windmill. Kamkwamba (2010) recounted:

> I didn't have a drill, so I had to make my own. First I heated a long nail in the fire, then drove it through a half a maize cob, creating a handle. I placed the nail back on the coals until it became red hot, then used it to bore holes into both sets of plastic blades. (p. 160)

Though extreme, this illustrates the message of a true spirit of inventiveness and reinforces the old adage that "necessity is the mother of invention."

Secondly, the misconception, particularly held by female teachers in this study that the arts lend themselves to more creative teaching that the sciences, is a view that must be discussed. If our Caribbean students are to fully realize their potential in the areas of science, technology, engineering and mathematics (STEM), then teachers must be challenged to find ways to encourage innovative and creative thinking in these classrooms. The view that science labs and practical exercises are merely "*follow the instructions*" experiments that are designed using only one procedure, and lead to only one outcome, must be revisited. Instead, a refocusing on more open-ended investigations in which students can choose their own equipment, and write up their procedures and results on an individual basis, is needed. This approach encourages more student-based inquiry, discovery learning and problem-solving skills, all necessary twenty-first-century skills. If we are to ensure that CARICOM's vision of the "Ideal Caribbean person" is realized, then teachers' weaknesses must be addressed. Therefore, continuous professional development interventions are needed to assist teachers in learning the skills related to "teaching creatively" and "teaching for creativity," particularly in the area of STEM education. Recently, there has also been a focus on the integration of Arts into STEM education result in a new integrated STEAM approach. By capitalizing on the strengths of both fields, this melding provides more opportunities for innovative and creative thinking in the classroom.

As educators, we owe it to the children of the Caribbean to ensure that they are adequately prepared for this new global economy. Therefore, no efforts should be spared by our Ministries of Education, teacher training colleges, and other educational institutions, to provide curricula that engage students in thinking creatively and being creative, regardless of the subjects being taught or studied.

REFERENCES

Andreasen, N. C., & Ramchandran, K. (2012). Creativity in art and science: Are there two cultures? *Dialogues in Clinical Neuroscience, 14*, 49–54.

Atkinson, S. (2004). *A comparison of the relationship between creativity, learning style preference and achievement at gcse and degree level in the context of design and technology project work.* Paper presented at the DATA International Research Conference DATA International Research Conference on Creativity and Innovation, Sunderland University, Sunderland, England.

Barbot, B., Besançon, M., & Lubart, T. I. (2011). Assessing creativity in the classroom. *The Open Education Journal, 4,* 58–66.

Beghetto, R. A. (2006). Creative self-efficacy: Correlates in middle and secondary students. *Creativity Research Journal, 18*(4), 447–57. doi:10.1207/s15326934crj1804_4

Beghetto, R. A. (2013). Nurturing creativity in the micro-moments of the classroom. In K. H. Kim, J. C. Kaufman, & J. Baer (Eds.), *Creatively gifted students are not like other gifted students: Research, theory, and practice* (pp. 3–15). Rotterdam, Netherlands: Sense Publishers.

Bolden, D. S., Harries, T. V., & Newton, D. P. (2009). Pre-service primary teachers' conception of creativity in mathematics. *Educational Studies in mathematics, 73*(2), 143–57. doi: 10.1007/s10649-009-9207-z

Brown, G. T. L. (2004). Teachers' conceptions of assessment: Implications for policy and professional development. *Assessment in Education, 11*(3), 301–18.

Cheung, R. H. P. (2012). Teaching for creativity: Examining the beliefs of early childhood teachers and their influence on teaching practices. *Australasian Journal of Early Childhood, 37*(3), 43–51.

Conti, R., Amabile, T. M. & Pollak, S. (1995). The positive impact of creative activity: Effects of creative task engagement and motivational focus on college students learning. *Personality and Social Psychology Bulletin, 21,* 1107–16.

De Souza Fleith, D. (2000). Teacher and student perceptions of creativity in the classroom environment. *Roeper Review, 22*(3), 148–53.

Diakidoy, I. N., & Kanari, E. (1999). Student teachers beliefs about creativity. *British Educational Research Journal, 25*, 225–43.

Fearon, D. D., Copeland, D., & Saxon, T. F. (2013). The relationship between parenting styles and creativity in a sample of Jamaican children. *Creativity Research Journal, 25*(1), 119–28.

Field, A. (2005). *Discovering Statistics using SPSS* (2nd ed.). London: SAGE Publications Ltd.

Glück, J., Ernst, R., & Unger, F. (2002). How creatives define creativity: Definitions reflect different types of creativity. *Communication Research Journal, 14*(1), 55–67.

Guilford, J. P. (1967). Creativity: Yesterday, today, and tomorrow. *Journal of Creative Behavior, 1*, 3–14.

Hargrove, R. A. (2012). Assessing the long-term impact of a metacognitive approach to creative skill development. *International Journal of Technology and Design Education. 23*, 489–517. doi: 10.1007/s10798-011-9200-6

Hennessey, B. A. (2003). The social psychology of creativity. *Scandinavian Journal of Educational Research, 47*(3), 253–271.

Hong, M., & Kang, N. H. (2010). South Korean and the US secondary school science teachers' conceptions of creativity and teaching for creativity. *International Journal of Science and Mathematics Education, 8*(1), 821–843.

Jeffrey, B., & Craft, A. (2004). Teaching creatively and teaching for creativity: Distinctions and relationships. *Educational studies, 30*(1), 77–87.

Kamkwamba, W. (2010). *The boy who harnessed the wind: Creating currents of electricity and hope.* New York: Harper Perennial.

Kim, K. H. (2008). Underachievement and creativity: Are gifted underachievers highly creative? *Creativity Research Journal, 20*(2), 232–42. doi: 0.1080/10400410802060232

Lin, Y. (2011). Fostering creativity through education—A conceptual framework of creative pedagogy. *Creative Education, 2,* 149–55. doi: 10.4236/ce.2011.23021

Makel, M. C. (2009). Help us creativity researchers, you're our only hope. *Psychology of Aesthetics, Creativity, and the Arts, 3*(1), 38.

Mann, E. L. (2006). Creativity: The essence of mathematics. *Journal for the Education of the Gifted, 30*(2), 236–60.

Marquis, E., & Henderson, J. A. (2015). Teaching creativity across disciplines at Ontario Universities. *Canadian Journal of Higher Education, 45*(1), 148–66.

Maslow, A. H. (1963). The creative attitude. *Structurist, 3,* 4–10.

Moore, T. L., & Shaugnessy, M. F. (2008). A reflective conversation with Dean Keith Simonton. *North American Journal of Psychology, 10,* 359–602.

Newton, L., & Newton, D. (2010). Creative thinking and teaching for creativity. *Gifted and Talented International Journal, 25*(2), 111–24.

Pallant, J. (2001). *SPSS survival manual* (3rd ed.): *A step by step guide to data analysis using SPSS for Windows.* Sydney, Australia: Allen & Unwin.

Pishghadam, R., Khodadady, E., & Zabihi, R. (2011). Learner creativity in foreign language achievement. *European Journal of Educational Studies, 3*(3), 465–72.

Plucker, J. A., Beghetto, R. A., & Dow, G. T. (2004). Why isn't creativity more important to educational psychologists? Potentials, pitfalls, and future directions in creativity research. *Educational Psychologist, 39*(2), 83–96.

Quek, K. S., Ho, K. K., & Soh, K. C. (2008). Implicit theories of creativity: A comparison of student-teachers in Hong Kong and Singapore. *Compare, 38*(1), 71–86.

Reber, A. S. (1995). *Dictionary of Psychology*. London: Penguin Books Ltd.

Renzulli, J. S. (1976). The Enrichment Triad Model: A guide for developing defensible programs for the gifted and talented. *Gifted Child Quarterly, 20,* 303–26.

Richardson, A. G. (1986). Sex differences in creativity among a sample of Jamaican adolescents. *Journal of Creative Behavior, 20,* 147.

Richardson, A. G. (1988). A factor analytic study of creativity in Caribbean adolescents. *Journal of Psychology in Africa, 1*(1), 71–6.

Rinkevich, J. L. (2011). Creative teaching: Why it matters and where to begin. *The Clearing House, 84,* 219–223. doi: 10.1080/00098655.2011.575416

Rogers, C. R. (1951). *Client-centered therapy: Its current practice, implications, and theory*. Boston, MA: Houghton Mifflin Co.

Rogers, C. R. (1954). Towards a theory of creativity. *ETC: A review of general semantics, 11,* 249–60.

Sternberg, R. J. (2006). The nature of creativity. *Creative Research Journal, 18,* 87–98.

Rubenstein, L. D., & Ehlinger, J. (2011). *Teaching between the lines: An examination of teachers' perceptions of creativity.* Paper presented at the American Education Research Association Conference, New Orleans, Louisiana.

Rubenstein, L. D., McCoach, D. B., & Siegle, D. (2013). Teaching for creativity scales: An instrument to examine teachers' perceptions of factors that allow for the teaching of creativity. *Creativity Research Journal, 25*(3), 324–34.

Runco, M. A. (1993). Divergent thinking, creativity, and giftedness. *Gifted Child Quarterly, 37*(1), 16–22.

Runco, M. A. (2007). *Creativity: Theories and themes. Research, development and practice*. Burlington, MA: Elsevier Academic Press.

Sak, U. (2004). About creativity, giftedness, and teaching the creatively gifted in the classroom. *Roeper Review, 26*(4), 216–22.

Schacter, J. S., Thum, Y. M., & Zifkin, D. (2006). How much does creative teaching enhance elementary school students' achievement? *Journal of Creative Behavior, 40*(1), 47–72.

Shaughnessy, M. F. (1991). *The supportive educational environment for creativity.* (ERIC Document Reproduction Service NO. ED 360 080).

Šorgo, A., Lamanauskas, V., Sasic, S. S., Kubiato, M., Prokop, P., Fancovicova, J., Bilek, M., Tomazic, I., & Erdogan, M. (2012). A cross-national study of prospective elementary and science teachers' creativity styles. *Journal of Baltic Science Education, 11*(3), 285–92.

CHAPTER 10

EXPLORING THE TRANSITION INTO HYBRID AND ONLINE COLLEGE TEACHING THROUGH COLLABORATIVE SELF-STUDY

Dennis A. Conrad, Elna Carrington-Blaides, and Dyanis A. Popova

Using positioning theory, narrative inquiry, and self-study of teaching, two special education professors share the catalysts and conflicts encountered as they consider the implications of responding to the increased demand for online courses. Using music, poetry, fiction and personal stories, they illustrate their positions on and reflections of transitioning towards online and hybrid courses within an inclusive milieu.

As asserted by Bair and Bair (2011), and supported by Fain (2014) among others, it appears that online instructional technology is pushing faculty rather than being driven by them. Hill (2014) asserts that higher education institutions need to note this significant shift, impacted on by fully online "for profit" along with some non-profit institutions. Through the development of master courses, ownership has shifted from individual faculty members to the institution itself.

Smaller colleges and progressive faculty need to reflect and review their policy and be responsive to this dynamic with a view to more effective use of resources. The "push" by administrators reflects the increasing trend towards online and hybrid instruction resulting from a push by higher education administrators (Rhoads, Camacho, Toven-Lindsey, & Berdan Lozano, 2015); institutional competition (Daniel & Cox, 2002; Olson & Werhan, 2005); changing learner needs (Willis, Tucker, & Gunn, 2003); and the increased willingness of faculty to use technology even if reluctantly (Conrad & Pedro, 2009). However, Garrison and Anderson (2003) warn that the influence of online instruction on educational institutions has only resulted in minimal enhancement of practices.

This chapter brings the voices of two college instructors committed to inclusive practice. They, along with a "critical friend," monitor their own learning and teaching through the process of balancing the push and drive towards hybrid and online courses. The study aims to also add to the discourse as to how some educators navigate the process, to motivate and sustain themselves. The findings could also bring some insight to higher education administrators as to their role in facilitating a supportive instructional environment (McNeal, 2015).

EDUCATION FOR INCLUSIVE PRACTICE

The Process

Inclusive education, according to UNESCO (2009) is a process of providing quality education for all while respecting the diversity of, and differences in, the "needs and abilities, characteristics and learning expectations of the students and communities, [and] eliminating all forms of discrimination" (p. 3). This definition extends beyond a traditional deficit model where learners are seen as having problems. The enhanced model recognizes that inclusive education concerns issues of class, ethnicity, gender, health human rights, and social conditions. Further, it encompasses universal involvement, access, participation and achievement. The key principles underlying inclusive education as stated in the Salamanca Statement (UNESCO, 1994). have been reinforced through various international conventions, declarations and recommendations including the UN Convention on the Rights of Persons with Disabilities, in 2006, which makes explicit reference to the importance of ensuring inclusive systems of education.

The Rationale

Three key justifications are used for working towards inclusive practices in education: Educational, Social, and Economic (UNESCO, Policy Guidelines on Inclusion in Education, 2009). Educationally, inclusive contexts develop ways of teaching that respond to individual differences and benefit all learners. Socially, inclusive learning contexts are able to change attitudes towards diversity and form the basis for a just, non-discriminatory society. Economically, inclusive learning contexts cost less to establish and sustain than segregated systems for different groups. Such teacher education programmes should facilitate candidates' understanding that they are key to the success of inclusive education that will improve educational attainment, and that key competencies for all are essential to economic growth, poverty reduction, and social inclusion (Council of the European Union, 2010).

There have been sustained efforts by education policy makers worldwide to provide more socially just education and inclusive education for all citizens. In the USA, this is accommodated largely through the Individuals with Disabilities Education Act, Title IX of the Elementary and Secondary Education Act, and No Child Left Behind, (2002). In Trinidad and Tobago, the Education Policy Paper (1993–2003) emphasized the provision of access and opportunity to students of all abilities. Inclusive education has also been influenced by the sterling efforts of the United Nations through Education for All (EFA) in 1990. At the World Conference on Special Needs Education, the Salamanca Statement (UNESCO, 1994) was formulated, which adopted and detailed the EFA principles for all students with special needs. These were to provide equitable education warranted education reform initiatives that redefined the role of all teachers, including those in special education.

Teacher Education

This is a key factor in developing and maintaining inclusive practices. These might be facilitated through programmes that prepare candidates who: 1) can create classrooms and schools that address social justice issues, including gender discrimination, poverty, and racism (Ballard, 2003); 2) understand the historical, socio-cultural and ideological contexts that create discriminatory and oppressive practices—and not limited to the isolation and rejection of students with disabilities (Ballard, 2003); and 3) be comfortable with assistive technology and online approaches to teaching and learning. Programmes should also utilize e-learning and learner-directed learning (Bartolo, 2010). And Steinweg et al. (2005) contend that there are no significant differences between traditional and online courses, which should facilitate more innovative access. An important area related to social justice and issues of respect, fairness and equity, is that of advocacy. To accomplish this, programmes will need to facilitate a shift from the dominant technical-rational and the medical/deficit discourses to a socio-political discourse and the need for societal, disability/diversity, and school reform (Peters & Reid, 2009).

The redefinition of the role of educators in the field of special education and rehabilitation has meant that these professionals are working more closely with regular education teachers in classroom settings. As a result, the focus of special education has broadened to encompass inclusive education and teacher candidates need to learn to work in regular education settings, access the regular education curriculum standards, and collaborate with regular education teachers (Conrad, 2010). Since special education continues to maintain its more traditional aspects of providing modified and accommodative services in more restrictive environments, such as resource rooms and self-contained special education classrooms, special education teachers also need to learn to access alternative curriculum standards, assessments and interventions that are available within their school districts. In Trinidad and Tobago this is through the Student Support Services Division (SSSD) and in New York State through the Boards of Cooperative Educational Services (BOCES).

Teacher Education in Special Education, then, involves knowing about inclusive education and special education issues, contexts, and practices. The programmes of studies offered by the departments of Inclusive and Special Education at the two institutions involved in this study reflect this new reality. The institutions being referred to are the University of the West Indies-St. Augustine and the State University of New York at Potsdam.

The curriculum for special education teacher candidates should aim to optimally prepare candidates for teaching students with mild/moderate disabilities in regular/inclusive education and or more specialized settings; and other students at risk of disabling curricula. Such students face diverse educational needs and challenges, including factors related to geography—urban, rural, socioeconomics, language, race and ethnicity, gender, school governance and resources (government, government assisted, denominational), and academics that limit their opportunities for equal access to education. By developing both inclusive and special competencies, teachers are more likely to: 1) see their role as change agents and advocates for ALL students; 2) be valued by, and value, other educational specialists; and 3) effectively work in varying collaborative roles (Council for the European Union, 2010).

HYBRID AND ONLINE HIGHER EDUCATION

Research has revealed learners who took some portion of a course online performed better than those who took more traditional classroom-based courses (Smith & Tyler, 2011). There is also research indicating that instructors who taught using a combination of online and face-to-face instruction earner higher success rates than when they taught using only direct instruction or online teaching (Bore, 2008; Means, Toyama, Murphy, Bakia, & Jones, 2009).

Online and hybrid, also called blended learning, courses are designed to make education more accessible and flexible for busy students, particularly working adults. Such courses offer potential solutions to colleges in rural communities or challenged with constraints of space and having trouble finding classroom space for large influxes of students. However, there are some key differences in how these classes are run. Online courses are completed entirely over the Internet. College students log into their university's course management system with a username and password and access all of their lectures online in video or audio files.

Compared to online courses, where students are generally not required to meet with the professor, hybrid courses comprise both online and face-to-face sessions. According to the SUNY Potsdam's guidelines hybrid courses may utilize 25–89 per cent of their teaching online. Hybrid course design provides time flexibility for both students and faculty; particularly graduate and continuing education programmes targeting working professionals and parents. Hybrid programmes allow students time to complete work at their own convenience, providing they have the technology and connectivity. The option for asynchronous communication in most hybrid courses allows students time to consider responses and submit work with improved written communication. Conrad and Pedro (2009) report an increase participation of less assertive students.

A study of online learning revealed that while Virginia Community Colleges System had increasing enrollment in online courses over a four-year period, its completion rates were consistently lower for online courses than for face-to-face courses (Smith-Jaggars & Xu, 2010). It also reported that students in online courses were more likely to fail or withdraw than students enrolled in face-to-face courses. The analysis also revealed that fully online students struggled with technologically related difficulties, a sense of social distance, and isolation. The researchers contend that hybrid classes could be a short-term answer for bridging the completion rate gap. Other noteworthy issues related to online and hybrid instruction include that: many instructors merely import traditional pedagogy and materials to the web (Cox, 2006; Zemsky & Massey, 2004); instructors typically have neither the training nor the time to implement radical course redesigns and sustain these and there is need for more research on effective online pedagogical techniques (Conrad & Pedro, 2009); as well as the role of institutional contexts in facilitating and sustaining online environments (McNeal, 2015).

THEORETICAL FRAMEWORK

We frame the exploring of our challenges with online teaching and how these have influenced our teaching, using positioning theory, narrative analysis, and self-study.

Positioning Theory

As developed by Harré and van Langenhove (1991), positioning theory explains relationships as a flexible, qualitative factor in enabling or limiting change in communities. As contrasted with static roles, stakeholders see positioning as a flexible, dynamic, interplay. Ling (1998) broadens the concept introducing notions of parity and power, with parity being associated with deliberative positioning. Power on the other hand rather than deliberative is related to forced positioning. In positioning ourselves as learners, instructors, administrators, and "critical friend" we change our lens of experience from one to another vantage point. This allows us to embrace and connect particular metaphors, storylines, and concepts (Harré & van Langenhove, 1998). Boxer (2001) further contends that positioning theory can be used to explain how we engage in discourse to establish and balance parity and power, when we face change.

Positioning theory acknowledges that people constantly adopt and defend their positions, and accept or confront those of others. Further, it asserts that such positioning roles nurture give-and-take/win-win approaches that facilitate power and parity, negotiating change through continuous improvement.

Parity is associated with deliberative positioning, either of self or other; while power is linked to forced positioning of self or other. Deliberate self-positioning is an expression of self-identity resulting from talking about other people. It may or may not be accepted by the person being spoken about. Forced self-positioning linked to complex situation, occurs as a reaction to positioning by another, for example accepting a specific description. *Forced* positioning of others tends to result from complex situations, where one person is positioned against another, for example as in the relationship between a professor and undergraduate student.

Narrative Inquiry

We used narrative inquiry to voice and enrich our positions as instructors, administrators, and learners, as we explore how the move towards hybrid and online instruction impacted on our pedagogy and us. Narratives have been used for generations and across nations to explore lived experiences and convey values (Taylor, 1996). The use of stories, according Carter (1993) is particularly appropriate for revealing and enriching the issues and meanings relevant to education.

We believe that the evoking and sharing of the complex positions and relationships that we choose in exploring our experiences of online instruction is enhanced with narrative inquiry.

We further contend that narrative inquiry goes beyond telling, affording another frame or window into one's beliefs and experiences, thus facilitating the emergence of themes and the analysis of the underlying insights we hope to determine (Clandinin & Connelly, 2000).

For this paper, we use three sets of narratives. The first set consists of the personal stories that share the direct views of the instructors, also referred to as the primary participants. To facilitate deeper critical inquiry and verification through crystallization, the primary participants will provide a second set of narratives that identify reading materials, and a third set, which focuses on music. These three narratives exemplify the challenges and catalysts experienced by the primary participants.

Self-Study

Samaras (2010) describes self-study of teaching as a personal, systematic inquiry situated within one's teaching. It requires critical and collaborative reflection to generate knowledge that informs the broader audience. Self-study facilitates insights into the intricacies of teaching and learning about teaching, helping us to explore practices and emergent teacher identities. It [self-study] generates interplays between scholarship of teaching and practice with the focus on teacher learning and learner teacher. McNiff and Whitehead (2010) summarize the process as "mining" one's personal history, delving into the professional literature and converses with colleagues to make sense of living contradiction. In summary then, self-study involves identifying contradictions, taking risks, and admitting to weaknesses, fears and biases.

We incorporate the use of a critical friend. This "friend" provides a means of collegial member-checking, and offers alternate perspectives and interpretations of the journey and findings. Through this critical friend we aim to add to the knowledge base (Loughran, 2007). According to Schuck and Russell (2005), critical friends serve as sounding boards who ask challenging questions, facilitate the reframing of events, and join in the professional learning experience.

CONTEXTS

Trinidad and Tobago and UWI

The evolving and close-knit relationship between technology and pedagogy in Trinidad and Tobago is evidenced by government's provision of 17,300 laptops in 2011 to all students entering high school (Pickford-Gordon, 2010; Trinidad Guardian, 2011). In 2010, the first year of government benevolence, 20,400 were distributed, along with appropriate training. Through its eConnect and Learn Programme Policy, the government aims at leveraging the potential of Information and Communication Technology (ICT) to significantly enhance the Trinidad and Tobago education system through the provision of laptop computers to secondary school students (Ministry of Education, 2010).

Beyond high school, undergraduate and graduate programmes are being developed aggressively through the University of the West Indies Open Campus (OC), which was inaugurated in 2008. The OC is an amalgamation of the previous Office of the Board for Non-Campus Countries & Distance Education, the School of Continuing Studies, the UWI Distance Education Centre and the Tertiary Level Institutions Unit. OC provides multi-mode teaching and learning services that include virtual and physical site locations across the Caribbean region. It services 16 countries in the English-speaking Caribbean (University of the West Indies, Open Campus, 2012).

At the school of education, where one of the co-authors of this paper is based, the use of hybrid and blended approaches is encouraged. This co-author teaches graduate level special education courses.

USA and SUNY at Potsdam

The Potsdam college of the State University of New York through its dedicated Office of Extended Education and a Director for Distance education supervises the development of and the delivery of both online and hybrid courses. Professional development sessions, support, and fiscal incentives are afforded. The co-author at this college has developed at least three online courses and one hybrid to date. As with the co-author at UWI, this researcher also teaches special education graduate courses at the graduate level.

METHODOLOGY

Essential Questions

This collaborative self-study involved two college professors and one doctoral candidate across three universities. The study sought to determine the challenges and catalysts of two professors, one at the University of the West Indies in Trinidad and Tobago and the other at the State University of New York-Potsdam campus, as they transitioned from face to face to hybrid courses in special education.

Guiding Questions

These comprised two research questions: (1) How do these two professors identify and balance the contradictions experienced in teaching face to face and hybrid or online courses in special education?; and (2) How does this information enhance their teaching?

The two questions as addressed by the professors, comprise various prompts. For the first question comprises four prompts or supporting questions. These are: (1.1) What are the conflicts or challenges that I am experiencing or anticipating in moving towards hybrid and/or online special education courses?; (1.2) What are the catalysts I am experiencing or anticipating in moving towards online and/or hybrid special education courses?; (1.3) What arts-based medium (song, a poem, fiction) best represents any or all of these challenges and catalysts?; and (1.4) What personal narrative can I identify that exemplifies a conflict/challenge and a catalyst? Narratives are developed that relate to the specific positions of teacher-educator, learner, and administrator; direct responses to questions 1 and 2; and the participants' identification of literature and music that remind them of, or represent their perspectives.

Primary Participants and Critical Friend

There are two primary participants. The first is Elna, who is the coordinator and a lecturer in graduate special education at the School of Education, UWI, and St. Augustine. The second is Dennis, a professor, and the Chair of the Department of Inclusive and Special Education at SUNY-Potsdam.

A third co-researcher is Dyanis, who is at Virginia Tech. She serves as "critical friend." She is a doctoral candidate, completing studies in Multicultural Education, and the Teaching of English as a Second Language. She has an avid interest in qualitative studies, particularly as these relate to critical pedagogy, and ethnographic studies. As collaborative partners, we as primary participants [Elna and Dennis] initially wrote responses to the essential questions, discussed these in a face-to-face session, responded to clarifying questions via emails, phone calls, and had one face-to-face discussion with our critical friend and co-researcher [Dyanis],

The primary participants have known each other for eight years and have co-authored earlier research. The critical friend while new to one co-researcher is a family member of the other.

ANALYSIS

The critical friend serves to address the trustworthiness and verifiability of the primary participants' narratives by challenging or seeking clarification to their initial and ongoing responses. These narratives comprised initial and modified responses to the guiding questions; lyrics of songs, poems, and extracts from literature that supported the testimonies of the primary participants,

The critical friend's contributions also included alternate perspective and facilitated the identifications and harmonizations of apparent contradictions. This serves to emphasize the trustworthiness of the narrative (Hamilton & Pinnegar, 2000).

The primary participants and the critical friend through an iterative process, critique, interrogate, positioning the narratives and self, to facilitate a clear understanding of challenges, catalysts, and learning experience. Using Maykut and Morehouse's (1994) Constant Comparison model of data analysis, critical themes were elicited from the narratives.

RESULTS

The Challenges EC

Elna presents her challenges through the differing lenses of positioning and narrative.

Positioning. In her self-positioning as teacher-educator, Elna identifies her challenges of transitioning as complex. She acknowledges a conflict in accepting the notion of effective hybrid and particularly online teaching based on her lived experience. Her dramatic shift in professional role from coordinator at one institution to lecturer/coordinator at UWI required an adjustment to a new order of things. This poses a challenge to her time-management skills: she needs more time to assimilate the new responsibilities as well as acquire the new skills warranted with the hybrid push. This is further complicated by the continuum of technological change taking place on her campus. As a teacher-educator, still building her sense of confidence in adult education, Elna remains concerned that students at UWI are decidedly more mature and experienced than at her last place of employment and this may require new skills.

As she takes the position of learner and, by extension, student, she recognizes that there is a technological divide between those who are older and the younger college students who seem to ease smoothly between: "the world of the computer, the mobile/smartphone, the social networking worlds of Facebook and Twitter." She also contends that there is a need for more visible, consumer friendly support systems and computer labs.

As leader and administrator, Elna remains skeptical of what is actually driving technology and education generally and more specifically higher education.

> Is this about bringing education and knowledge more efficiently to the populace ... the average citizen? Is this about being dollars, competition, and selling the status of global tertiary education like that of the University of P? Or is this even about improving the quality of education...better teaching? This is MY concern.

Personal narrative. Elna's developed narratives reveal that her main challenges center on her immediate responsibility of developing and implementing a single graduate programme within a limited time period. The fact that while she has worked with Blackboard, she has no working experience with the Moodle platform being used by her new employer. Elna describes the challenges:

> While UWI has been using Moodle for at least 3 years now, there are still ongoing challenges with system reliability, limitations and malfunctions. To complicate issues, some irregularities have emerged, with students who had completed the registration process not being able to log on to the course site. Consider too that many students do not access critical information placed on the course site and come to class in the "tabula rasa" state. Very often handouts are not downloaded or read. As a matter of fact we need a comprehensive orientation for new students to prepare them for blended courses, in terms of hardware and software requirements.

Elna acknowledges that as a new member of faculty she has been frustrated with not having much time to become familiar with MyE-learning (Moodle) and actually adapt and upload course data. She continues: "Further, training in instructional design, media and technology is very basic and considered secondary to other duties."

While it is anticipated that faculty capacity and effectiveness would develop over time, there are areas, which she feels should be priority. She shares: "One such area is strategies for evaluating these hybrid or online courses. Student capacity is building quickly. How can we evaluate our students when they are ahead of us in more ways than one."

Narrative Fiction

Asked to identify a poem that portrays her concerns, Elna choose Dereck Walcott's *A Far Cry from Africa*, (1962) from which she quotes:

> Again brutish necessity wipes its hands upon the napkin of a dirty cause,
>
> Again a waste of our compassion, as with Spain, The gorilla wrestles with the superman.
>
> I who am poisoned with the blood of both, Where shall I turn, divided to the vein? I who have cursed the drunken officer of British rule, how choose between this Africa

and the English tongue I love? Betray them both, or give back what they give? How can I face such slaughter and be cool? How can I turn from Africa and live?
She comments:

> Ahhh, yes...the eternal struggle with self and "other." In this case the hybrid and the "online" agendas...face to face versus superman as technology. Except that my "self" continues to evolve, though being heavily influenced by the traditional. I guess this also applies to you eh Dennis? So what is the driving force behind these agendas? Better teaching or is this just business?

Music

Elna choose Rudder's "The Hammer" (1986) to affirm what motivates her. This song celebrates the resilience of one of the pioneers of the soca/calypso mix. Here is an excerpt: the song itself can be accessed on YouTube.

> I want to hear the hammer ringing out
> From every pan yard
> From Europe to Africa
> Just like here in Trinidad
> This hammer must never die
> Let me tell you why
> Anytime the music dead
> Is then life go buss we head [wound/hurt us]
> So the children start singing the refrain
> Begging me to ask the question again

Elna comments:

> And, yes, that "hammer" shaped and empowered not in a brutalizing sense but as a tool for shaping...strengthening...All part of a clear plan and mission...acknowledging the need for flexibility yet affording structure. Even the concept of hybrid and online remains elusive... the research about efficacy still emerging. Who's really in charge...who's with the hammer...What are we shaping?

The Challenges: DC

Positioning. From his position as teacher-educator, Dennis identifies time as his greatest challenge. This is not helped by the move from Blackboard to Moodle platforms at his institution.

> I had reached that zone where all my core material was organized and uploaded; and I was feeling ready to explore the use of hybrids models with my special education courses. Not that I have any problem with the rationale behind the change. Reorganizing material for Moodle takes time...my quizzes and clips are not as readily transferable as I had hoped. Added responsibilities also consume my time.

While Dennis acknowledges that the campus has a fairly good support system, he contends that making the best use of these also warrant having time to do so. Dennis has been using film to stimulate discussion and make connections to the research and personal experiences in his courses. Often these are not readily accessible in DVD format. Or streaming from sites like Netflix.

> As such, I have to identify other material in ways that are accessible and not costly to students or library services. I'm proud to say that our library is helping to explore alternatives.

As learner/student, Dennis also acknowledges the need to be more visible on the discussion board without disrupting the conversations. While he has had positive feedback from participants with the use of student moderators, a challenge remains as to how to allow his presence to not get in the way of the discussions.

Taking the position of course leader and administrator, Dennis remains challenged by how with a small department he can build a strong sense of community and facilitate dynamic consensus in response to campus policies on hybrid and online courses. He asserts his view that his role includes seeking the best interest of students.

> I need the ongoing benefits of a community that truly looks at education from the perspective of the student. Am I a gatekeeper protecting the interests of the status quo? Am I a facilitator of their learning? What is most convenient for my students without compromising quality?

Personal narrative. In response to the first guiding question Dennis's personally developed narratives reveal that his main challenges are centered on time with new responsibilities, time needed for transitioning from BlackBoard to Moodle platforms, and the question of presence through online discussions. While he is generally comfortable with the change to Moodle, transferring his archive of video clips, and test banks to Moodle posed significant challenges.

> Thanks to a colleague who helped me significantly in identifying and selecting material when I just started online courses, I have developed quite a level of confidence with Blackboard. The move to Moodle was difficult for me. Particularly now with a whole new set of responsibilities I am facing professionally and personally. What I need is a support person to facilitate a smooth and quick transition. The support might even be there, but time to utilize it is also a challenge.

As for his presence through the discussion, Dennis acknowledges his own resistance. He shares a reluctance to be the authoritarian as moderator. He confides that once students become conscious of his presence in the discussion, the quality becomes questionable and there is more of a risk of students saying what they believe the professor wants to hear. As such, he uses students as moderators for asynchronous discussions, while he monitors the discussion covertly. Should there be an issue, he communicates with the moderator directly. At the end of each discussion he posts a participating grade comprising his and the student moderator's scores. Dennis readily acknowledges that the emphasis on his "presence" through the discussion underscores how much he misses the face-to-face interaction and emergent relationships that consequently emerge. This, he contends, compromises the satisfaction he gets in his online courses as it contrasts with the anticipation that online classes could and should foster relationships and engage in positive and meaningful teaching and learning experiences (Fletcher & Bullock, 2014).

Narrative Fiction

Dennis also identifies a poem, "Lament for Apodocca," (Russel, 1922) that personifies his understanding of the challenges he faces. He recalls it being recited by his father on many an early morning.

> Up, up, my lads!
> 'Tis broad daylight,
> This is no time for slumber;
> Here be our dreaded foes in sight.
> And more than thrice our number.
> Tis vain to fly, to fight is vain;
> Was ever such a sore fix?
> Their ships are all about us here,
> And twenty-four to our six.

As a child, and contrary to his father's intention, these words did not motivate him. Instead, it made him alert to the reality that there is a battle in which he is doomed to lose. However his awaking, and his consciousness of the battle, can provide him a means of survival. Thus, for Dennis, this poem resonates with his sense of survival, that he needs to find the time to adjust to the changing needs of education and the move towards the online environment if he is to stay afloat, even if it is only a strategy of survival until he can make the best use of the evolving situation for the well-being of his students.

Music

Dennis struggles to identify a song that describes his sense of the challenges faced. Eventually he decided to go with Salt, sung by the rapso group 3Canal. A glimpse at the lyrics shares the story of recognizing that a battle wages and that it goes beyond the physical to even the spiritual. That, as teacher, he must be able to restrain himself, and keep a low profile as needed until he can navigate between the conflicts and paradoxes.

> Dis [this] rounds yuh [you] have to be ready
> Ready to deal with the vampire [oligarchy], steady
> Boy Dis rounds yuh have to be strong

> Able to decipher de right from de wrong,
> ah [I] say Dis rounds yuh have to be able
> Gird yuh [your] loins, get ready fuh [for] de battle,
> cause Dis rounds dem [them] boys ain't joking
> So yuh got to keep yuh chalice smoking [incense]
> Vampire [predatorial politicians] coming in all kinda guises
> Not to mention a range of sizes
> Utilizing de latest devices [including the technology] (3Canal, 2011)

The Catalysts EC

Positioning. For Elna, her positioning, as teacher-educator is one of privilege, which itself serves as a catalyst. She identifies five catalysts that motivate her. These include:

1. Access to open access materials;
2. Collaborative opportunity;
3. Discovering teacher tube and YouTube;
4. Her recognition that many of the more mature students see it as literacy issue;
5. Evidence of more undergraduate students with technology experience or readiness.

Elna is excited about these new discoveries that rejuvenate her teacher identity, recognizing that her challenges of transitioning are mostly related to environment and space.

As a learner, she is also enthused about using these new technologies and the potential they offer of being more convenient and limiting her need to be driving late at night from the campus.

As leader and administrator, Elna celebrates the school's positive responsiveness to her needs and the commitment to Institutional support afforded. She is proud to be part of the Caribbean's foremost university, and is appreciative of the opportunity given to contribute to the school's marketability and the development of the nations' teaching resources for an inclusive society.

Personal narrative. Elna's personal story reflects the excitement that she absorbs from her students' responses.

> I feel the students' appreciation for the flexibility the blended approach provides. Students too value the ready access to course documents and course updates; with course material could be sourced and organized and made accessible long before the actual session.

Because this provides students with increased access to information and more flexibility with class time, many have improved their class preparation affording "deeper and richer discussions." This has been helped too by the students' prior experience with technology.

Exploring the Transition Into Hybrid and Online College • 173

> I do acknowledge that a large number of students have been exposed to the my eLearning system either through another course at undergraduate or graduate level or the university orientation programme.

This, Elna contends, sustains her sense of growing tolerance or respect for all students as learners and to facilitate a context that balances between the experienced and inexperienced.

Narrative Fiction

Elna identifies Michael Anthony's *All that Glitters* (1981) as the text that best motivates her in the present situation as he prepares for hybrid teaching. The story is based on the account of Horace, a 13-year-old boy, sharing about the return from Panama of his favorite aunt. Her joyous arrival in Trinidad is complicated with the disappearance of her gold chain. Mistrust and distress is the subsequent result. A lesson for Elna is that we should be mindful of initial perceptions and be open to new experiences.

> Anthony reminds me [ever so often since I began this on-line exploration] that we must be able to move between the challenges and conflicts wherever and whenever we face change and diverse expectations. Find the humour…laugh…do not personalize. Focus on what's real.

Music

Ella Andall's (2007) music is earth music, music that speaks to the soul. The song chosen is "Bring Down the Power." This is a song that celebrates the power of love to save and heal the many challenges, which confront Trinidad and Tobago at this time.

> Bring down the power of love I say, bring down the power . . .
> The power of love I say is the greatest power; Stop hell and damnation, bring down the power …
> Love to heal a nation, is the greatest power
> A wind of destruction is blowing over this land
> …over this land…
> And now the earth is a-trembling with man's oppression of man (bring down the power
> Now the time come to sit down and rediscover what's life . . . what's life . . .
> "Show the world the true meaning of real love power not strife
> For Elna, this song speaks to the core of change, the willingness to search out our key roles in the teaching/learning process and boldly effect the needed change. (Andell, 2007)

The Catalysts DC

The catalyst. Positioning himself as teacher-educator, Dennis identifies three catalysts. These comprise: Reasonableness and accessibility of instructional support; the many opportunities provided by for training; and the rich feedback provided by the Director of Distance Education, "So while I might complain of having very little time to attend workshops, they are available."

As a learner, Dennis applauds the readiness of his students to show him their "tricks" and strategies; even involving them in helping him to make the course sites more accessible, and enjoying the sense of community that emerges.

> I thrive on the enthusiasm and hunger for innovation that often is manifested in my students. So much so, I have to resist jumping into their discussion as I monitor their engaging conversation. Each student is also given a responsibility to serve as moderator, which enriches his or her experiences as learner/teacher.

Dennis, in his administration of hybrid and online courses, shares that he has no issues demonstrating flexibility without compromising his expectations. He enjoys being a facilitator of learning, challenging students without being uncaring.

> I often see myself at another stage in my development. I know what it is like to want to reshape my life to get back to school, without the means of giving up my day job. In those days it was correspondence courses. Yet these give me the confidence to move forward. I am only too willing and excited at the prospect of making education accessible to those who are serious.

Personal narrative. Dennis's personal narrative underscores the role of distance education in his early career and his commitment to doing all that is possible to make education accessible to working and middle-class students.

> I remember being a young elementary education teacher yearning to get to university. [His first education certification was accomplished at a two-year residential teacher college]. As a single parent, with minimal funds…I needed just tne opportunity to improve myself. I got it through correspondence courses that eventually paved the way to promotion and my first scholarship.

Narrative Fiction

Salt written by Lovelace (2004) was chosen by Dennis as the story that best motivates him to use hybrid or online. The story centers on the life journey of a "slow learner," who despite hardships strives to grow professionally and personally.

> This story reminds me of the magic bean that lies within each of our students. It reminds me that being flexible is not compromising my standards. That I can choose to see the positive in my students and that they need us to see who they can become.

Lovelace's character the teacher Mr. Alford…in his hunger for helping his students to succeed through education has became overzealous in his quest for meeting the highest standards, so directive that he is inflexible, and unable to recognize that his teaching has become dictatorial and disrespectful to learners as well as a threat to his own well-being. This reminds me of the need to strive to be partners not necessarily equals in the learner-teacher relationship…

Music

The music that sustains Dennis is that of the Calypsonian David Rudder (1999). The chosen song is "Ganges and the Nile." It celebrates the multiculturalism that is Trinidad and Tobago.

> Let me tell you a story
> 'Bout their pain and their glory…
> Many rivers flowed to this naked isle
> Bringing fear and pain
> But also a brand new style.
> And of all these rivers that shaped this land
> Two mighty ones move like a sculptor's hand.
> And there's no doubt we go work it out, there is no escaping.
> And today those hands, across the
> land, man, they're still landscaping.
> As the river flows there are those who would change its passage.

For Dennis, the song celebrates the diversity of learners and teachers alike on a common mission for change and changing with the times.

Self-Study in Teaching Lessons

We [Elna and Dennis] celebrate that both the collaborative experience and the self- study of teaching approach helped us to build community, sustain our spirit, and remind us of the reason why we teach.

> I had not heard much about self-study and the early set of questions and style did put me off. I felt I was expected to open up myself too much and that as a new faculty on my campus I felt I was setting myself up. While Dennis did try to reassure me I felt that he was not in my position and I didn't feel ok. I noticed he backed off a bit, which allowed me time to review the material he sent me and this helped me enough to try. The process up to now is invigorating. I have built my sense of trust with my co-researchers. Now I am excited and I embrace this opportunity to improve my teaching and professional objectivity through subjectivity [Elna].

Dennis reaffirms his belief in the use of self-study of teaching.

> While I have been exploring self-study for a few years now, I am just beginning to address the deeper issues of my teaching style. My mission is extending to finding

ways to fire up my students with a hunger for teaching, by handing them the lighter and setting a context where they can locate the material they need to sustain themselves educationally. Yet I have to be alert to an emerging tendency to be a little too flexible to the point where I can be charged for disorganization. There will always be students even at the graduate level who need more direction yet not comfortable enough to assert this.

DISCUSSION AND IMPLICATIONS

There is no doubt that technology, whether as a means of content delivery in courses or via online education, will continue to have an impact on teacher education (Smith & Kennedy, 2014). Teacher-educators committed to inclusive practices will need to be further engaged with and utilize technology for either of these purposes. The exploration of the perspectives and experiences of teacher-educators, addressed in this chapter therefore hold merit and the emergent themes warrant consideration.

Three themes were identified from the narratives developed through positioning, direct narrative, and the identification of literature and music that represents these perspectives. The first theme is the instructors' need for a dynamic support system involving multiple stakeholders. A second theme is the instructors' need for building community where learners see themselves as agents of change and where education and academic achievement is more than just mastery of content. The third theme is that the attitudes and motivators of both primary participants seem to be linked to journeys where education proved to be personally liberating. Both the materials they cited and their search for meaning in education reflect their own schooling.

Need for Support

A dynamic support system helps faculty to meet their own and the institutions' instructional goals (Marek, 2009). This goes beyond just providing professional development opportunities and content specialists. Further, the need for support systems is underscored by the fact that, often, students are more advanced in the use of online technologies and interfaces than faculty. Support systems should thus provide training, collaborative assistance, resource identification, and resource development. It should also allow for the time to attend these courses; and to ensure that there is an adequately sized and trained team of support staff to scaffold the appropriate learning.

Building Community

A responsive approach to the support needs of faculty sharing a commitment to inclusive practice, will, according to Smith and Tyler (2011) include professional development in the use of web-based materials (WBM). Faculty need opportunities and support to objectively recognize the benefits to their learning and teaching using WBM. Appropriate support will encourage reluctant faculty to consider and explore the benefits of using WBM. This approach facilitates more appeal and learner motivation through interactivity and enhanced engagement. Beyond appeal and motivation through interactive learning, these benefits include consistent current data-driven content (Jones, 2009) that are conveniently accessed by all (Bullock et al., 2008; Cady & Rearden, 2009). WBM affords engagement There is also research indicating that instructors who taught using a combination of online and face-to-face instruction achieve higher success rates than when they taught using only direct instruction or online teaching (Bore, 2008; Means, Toyama, Murphy, Bakia, & Jones, 2009).

The primary co-researchers also reveal a need for learning communities to minimize the sense of isolation being experienced by more traditionalist instructors (face to face) who are novices in the ease of technology or online teaching. According to the Southern Educational Regional Board (SERB, 2009), faculty who teach online courses need a space and place to share information and ideas with each other. Further, faculty should experience that critical role of building community also. While synchronous online discussions and faculty presence might be effective in some instances, these are not magical formulae. As such, faculty should be afforded some leeway in determining what works best for their learning and teaching philosophies and practice (Fletcher & Bullock, 2014). However, this might be elusive, as faculty remain divided and even oppositional as to the mission of the administrative push for higher education through online provision (Rhoads, Camacho, Toven-Lindsey, & Berdan Lozano, 2015).

We note also that community is not static, but alive with all the complexities of difference, especially in the Caribbean, where diversity in opinion, resources and populations is reality. Community, then, is not just about being "part of"—it is also about valuing and sustaining each other, where one's cultural identity is recognized and valued.

Ess (2009) argues that communities associated with online teaching are fluid, epitomizing a cultural identity that goes beyond nationality or language. Ess views online contexts as themselves culturally coded spaces that invite the formation of "third cultures." Indeed, Goodfellow and Lamy (2009) contend that there is no separation between an indefinable complex notion of culture and education. The importance of cultural identity as shared by Elna and Dennis is also supported by work from Gunawardena, Alami, Jayatilleke, and Bouchrine, (2009). These researchers posited that cultural identity itself is so changing that it continues to be influenced by, and to influence, the online context. Their findings demonstrate the possibility of hybrid cultural identities are enacted or concealed in the process of negotiating norms and identities in the online environment.

Education and Teacher Identity

The third key emergent theme revolved around the role of both formal and informal education in the lives of the primary researchers. Elna and Dennis, as teacher-educators in inclusive and special education programmes, continue to frame and negotiate their own personal and professional identities. This reflects a change or readiness to change from the teacher as sage in face-to-face sessions to the facilitator of more independent learning in online or hybrid courses. This readjustment is particularly evident in responding to the need to develop online and hybrid courses and the interactions with other members of this group through online or face-to-face discussion (Wheeler, Kelly, & Gale, 2005). As with Wheeler et al., we acknowledge the positive influence of online and hybrid engagement, but hesitate to assert that this has significantly influenced our professional practice. The challenge thus seems to be that we have to develop courses that serve local, regional, and global interests where students from all contexts and needs can share equal opportunities for advancement in an inclusive and interactive learning environment (Simon, Jackson, & Maxwell, 2013).

The co-researchers acknowledge their roles of challenging the perspectives of, and facilitating transformative experiences for, teacher candidates. It is accepted that for many teacher candidates, their cultural histories, practices and values are different from those of their students.

Both Elna and Dennis celebrate the role of critical thinking on memorable experiences, music, and literature required in this study. This process, they contend, reveals the connections between their identities and responses to the challenge of online and hybrid teaching. Further, it reinforces that they are part of an evolving community of learners recognizing the unique challenges of administrators, professors, and students alike. This bodes well for them as negotiators of learning spaces that are culturally responsive and responsive to the diverse needs of all (Gay, 2010).

PERSPECTIVES FROM THE CRITICAL FRIEND

Dyanis, as critical friend, comments:

> This role allowed me to collegially seek connections between the lived experiences as positions and direct testimonies, and the chosen literature. It provided me with opportunities to verify or challenge perspectives; and, to share in lessons learned. As an emerging scholar and novice college instructor, this type of scholarship reverberated with my sense of knowledge construction and critical pedagogy. The self-study of teaching approach and my role as critical friend offers a unique opportunity to appreciate qualitative research as well as the practice of teaching in educational research.

Serving a critical friend for this paper encouraged Dyanis to reflect on her current roles as both instructor and student. While face-to-face comprised the majority of her college courses, the vast majority of these incorporated some form of online practice or activity. Indeed, the absence of technology often seems old-fashioned or awkward. At the same time, she also acknowledges that the issue of time noted by both co-authors is a major factor into why she herself does not hybridize her courses beyond the use of YouTube. Hybrid courses are highly useful as instructional tools for students with non-traditional learning styles or needs, but can add an additional layer to planning that can sometimes be temporally prohibitive. The major theme that stands out to Dyanis in her role as critical friend is the need for teachers to use online and hybrid courses *effectively* to enhance student/teacher learning, and as more than a storage space for print resources.

> I have always assumed the rush toward online courses to be about business. Whether we want to admit it or not, contemporary life is often about the bottom line. I see my role as instructor as that of an educational advocate for my students. How can I best use these materials, resources etc. to enhance my students' educational experiences? I'm still working on finding the time to get it all incorporated.

Dyanis comments further:

> I can already unequivocally claim the benefits of such critical thinking on my own teaching and research. I recognize the benefits of healthy dialogical relationships, to effective teaching and I appreciate the opportunity to enter "the conversation" of hybrid and online teaching. When the primary participants describe their struggles and strategies, I see myself too as both student and instructor striving to grow academically, share spiritedly, and remain real.

Dyanis recognizes the role of the critical friend in respecting both the readiness of the primary participants to be vulnerable and to improve their teaching. She shares that this deeper look at why we do what we do as teacher-educators in inclusive education should be ongoing effort. Inclusive education can be a vehicle for examining and challenging these tacit assumptions. "This inspires me as an individual and collectively as a member of the team to remember that education is about community."

CONCLUSION

This study explored the challenges and catalysts that revolve around the efforts of Elna and Dennis to accommodate the demands in transitioning towards the use of hybrid and online teaching in their inclusive and special education teacher education. The analysis of narratives developed through positioning theory and critical reflection reveal ongoing elasticity between the co-participants' identities as teacher-learner-administrator and their sense of mission, driven by their cultural selves, which we glimpse through their narratives and significant fictions.

Challenges include the search for time. This is, as much to benefit from training when it's available, as to develop, modify, and sustain the courses (McNeal, 2015). Further, proactive and sustained technical support by their institutions, and the facilitating of an engaged community of learners are needed. Experiences are shared, and the purposes behind such initiatives are reconnoitered. One trusts that the discussion with community would help to navigate the skepticism that both faculty members wrestle with as to whether the energy behind hybrid and online learning is about instructional interests of faculty and students.

The role of relationships and the sense of mission and flexibility to change serve as key catalysts for the co-participants. They both recognize that change is a means of survival, the importance of education for economic success, and both embrace a hope of change for the better even, if cautiously, with a concern about who/what is driving the change, and where it is headed.

The critical friend Dyanis celebrates the opportunity to appropriately appraise the paper and challenge findings and conclusions. She acknowledges that she was motivated to critically reflect on 1) her experiences as learner and teacher; 2) her readiness to utilize web-based learning; and 3) how such teaching might be influenced by and improved through the use of fiction and music. As a recently appointed, Caribbean-born, assistant professor at a mid-western university in the US, she believes that serving as a critical friend was most timely and invaluable.

REFERENCES

3canal. (2011). *Salt.* Retrieved from http://www.youtube.com/watch?v=vKDrh8tNCKQ

Andall, E. (2007). *Bring down the power.* Retrieved from http://www.youtube.com/watch?v=-DQpfo65ctI

Anthony, M. (1981). *All that Glitters.* Jamaica: Ian Randle.

Bair, D. E, & Bair, M. A. (2011). Paradoxes of online teaching. *International Journal for the Scholarship of Teaching and Learning, 5(2).* Retrieved from: http://www.georgiasouthern.edu/ijsotl

Ballard, K. (2003) The analysis of context: Some thoughts on teacher education, culture, colonization and inequality. In T. Booth, K. Nes, & M. Stromstad (Eds.), *Developing inclusive teacher education.* London: Routledge Falmer.

Bartolo, P. A. (2010) Teacher education online. Towards inclusive virtual learning communities. In C. Forlin (Ed.), *Teacher education for inclusion. Changing paradigms and innovative approaches.* London: Routledge.

Bore, J. C. K. (2008). Perceptions of graduate students on the use of Web-based instruction in special education personnel preparation. *Teacher Education and Special Education, 31*, 1–11.

Boxer, L. (2001). *Using positioning theory to make change happen.* Retrieved from http://www.cmqr.rmit.edu.au/publications/lbpositi.pdf

Bullock, L. M., Gable, R. A., & Mohr, J. D. (2008). Technology-mediated instruction in distance education and teacher preparation. *Teacher Education and Special Education, 31*, 229–242.

Cady, J.A., & Rearden, K.T. (2009). Delivering online professional development in mathematics to rural educators. *Journal of Technology and Teacher Education, 17*(3). 150–166.

Carter, K. (1993). The place of story in the study of teaching and teacher education. *Educational Researcher, 22(1),* 1–12.

Clandinin, D. J., & Connelly, F. M. (2000). *Narrative inquiry: Experience and story in qualitative research*. San Francisco, CA: Jossey-Bass.

Conrad, D. A., Paul, N., Bruce, M., Charles, S., & Felix, K. (2010). Special schools and the search for social justice in Trinidad and Tobago: Perspectives from two marginalised contexts. *Caribbean Curriculum, 17*(2010), 59–84

Conrad, D. A., & Pedro, J. (2009). Perspectives and practice of novice online instructors. *International Journal of Scholarship in Teaching and Learning, 3(2)*, 1–17.

Council of the European Union. (2010). *Council conclusions on the social dimensions of education and training*. 3013th Education, Youth and Culture Meeting. Brussels, Belgium: Council of the European Union.

Cox, R. D. (2006). Virtual access. In T. Bailey & V. S. Morest (Eds.), *Defending the community college equity agenda* (pp. 110–131). Baltimore, MD: Johns Hopkins University Press.

Daniel, G., & Cox, K. (2002). *Can technology reduce education expenditures without compromising teaching?* Web tool Newsletter. Retrieved from http://webtools.cityu.edu.hk/news/newslett/costeffectiveeducation.htm

Ess, C. (2009). When the solution becomes the problem. In R. Goodfellow & M. Lamy (Eds), *Learning Cultures in Online Education (*pp 15–30)*. New York: Continuum Studies in Education.

Fain, P. (2014). *Less prescriptive in California*. Retrieved from https://www.insidehighered.com/news/2014/08/28/online-learning-push-continues-california-approach-faculty-groups-appreciate

Fletcher, T., & Bullock, S. (2014). Pedagogies and identities disrupted: A collaborative self-study of teaching about teaching online. *Changing Practices for Changing Times: Past, Present and Future Possibilities for Self-Study Research*, 79–82.

Garrison, D. R., & Anderson, T. (2003). *E-learning in the 21 century. A framework for research and practice*. London, UK: Routledge Falmer.

Gay, G. (2010). *Culturally responsive teaching (2nd ed.) (Culturally Responsive Teaching: Theory, Research, and Practice (Multicultural Education)*. New York, NY: Teachers College Press.

Goodfellow, R., & Lamy, M. (2009). *Learning cultures in online education*. New York: Continuum Studies in Education.

Gunawardena, C. N., Alami, A. I., Jayatilleke, G., & Bouchrine, F. (2009). Entering the world of online foreign language education: Challenging and developing teacher identities. In R. Goodfellow & M. Lamy (Eds), *Learning Cultures in Online Education (*pp 30–51.)*. New York: Continuum Studies in Education,

Harré, R., & van Langenhove, L. (1991). Varieties of positioning. *Journal for the Theory of Social Behaviour, 21*(4), 393–407.

Hamilton, M. L., & Pinnegar, S. (2000). Trustworthiness in teacher education, *Journal of Teacher Education, 51(3), 234–240*

Harré, R., & van Langenhove, L. (Eds.). (1998). *Positioning theory: Moral contexts of intentional action*. Oxford, UK: Wiley Blackwell.

Hill, P. (2014). Online educational delivery models: A descriptive view. *Educause Review,* 85–97. Retrieved from https://net.educause.edu/ir/library/pdf/ERM1263.pdf.

Jones, M. L. (2009). A study of novice special educators' views of evidence-based practices. *Teacher Education and Special Education, 32*(2), 101–120.

Ling, I. M. (1998) *The role of the curriculum coordinator: An exploration through discursive practice*. Unpublished thesis, Melbourne University, Melbourne, Australia.

Loughran, J. (2007). Researching teacher education practices: Responding to the challenges, demands, and expectations of self-study. *Journal of Teacher Education, 58(1)*, 12–20.

Lovelace, E. (2004). *Salt. A novel*. New York, NY: Persea.

Marek, K. (2009). Learning to teach online: Creating a culture of support for faculty. *Journal of Education for Library and Information Science, 50(4)*, 275–292.

Maykut, P., & Moorehouse, R. E. (1994). *Beginning qualitative research: A philosophic and practical guide*. London, UK: Falmer.

McNeal, R. B. (2015). Institutional environment(s) for online course development and delivery. *Universal Journal of Educational Research, 3*, 46–54.

McNiff, J., & Whitehead, J. (2010). *You and your action research project*. New York: Routledge.

Means, B., Toyama, Y., Murphy, R., Bakia, M., & Jones, K. (2009). *Evaluation of evidence-based practices in online learning: A meta-analysis and review of online learning studies*. Washington, DC: U.S. Department of Education, Office of Planning, Evaluation, and Policy Development.

Ministry of Education, Trinidad and Tobago. (2010). *E- Connect and Learn Programme Policy*. Retrieved from http://www.moe.gov.tt/laptop_info/eConnect_and_Learn_Policy.pdf.

Olson, S. J., & Werhan, C. (2005). Teaching preparation online: A growing alternative for many. *Action in Teacher Education, 27*(3), 76–84.

Peters, S., & Reid, D. K. (2009). Resistance and discursive practice: Promoting advocacy in teacher undergraduate and graduate programmes. *Teaching and Teacher Education, 25*(4), 551–558.

Pickford-Gordon, L. (2010). $83m for school laptops. *Trinidad Newsday*. Retrieved from http://www.newsday.co.tt/news/0,126408.

Rhoads, R. A., Camacho, M. S., Toven-Lindsey, B., & Berdan Lozano, J. (2015). The massive open online course movement, xMOOCs, and faculty labor. *The Review of Higher Education, 38(3)*, 397–424.

Rudder, D. (1986). *The Hammer*. Retrieved from http://www.youtube.com/watch?v=JjV4lNu7kOg

Rudder, D. (1999). *Ganges and the Nile*. Retrieved from http://www.youtube.com/watch?v=KHH_YKWKjJg&feature=related

Russell, A. D. (1922). Lament for Apodocca. In *Legends of the Bocas*. London: Kelina.

Samaras, A. P. (2010). *Self-study teacher research: Studying your practice through collaborative inquiry*. Thousand Oaks, CA: Sage.

Schuck, S., & Russell, T. (2005). Self-study, critical friendship, and the complexities of teacher education. *Studying Teacher Education, 1(2)*, 107–121.

Simon, S., Jackson, K., & Maxwell, K. (2013). Traditional versus online instruction: Faculty resources impact strategies for course delivery. *Business Education & Accreditation, 5(1)*.107–116.

Smith, D. D., & Tyler, N. C. (2011). *Effective inclusive education: Equipping education professionals with necessary skills and knowledge*. Prospects, *41*(3), 323–339.

Smith-Jaggars, S., & Xu, D. (2010). *Online learning in the Virginia Community College System.* New York: Community College Research Center, Teachers College, Columbia University.

Smith, S. J., & Kennedy, M. J. (2014). Technology and teacher education. In P. T. Sindelar, E. D. McCray, M. T. Brownell, & B. Lignugaris-Kraft (Eds.), *Handbook of research on special education teacher preparation.* New York: Routledge.

Southern Educational Regional Board (SERB). (2009). *Guidelines for Professional Development of Online Teachers.* Retrieved from: http://publications.sreb.org/2009/09T01_Guide_profdev_online_teach.pdf

Steinweg, S. B., Davis, M. L., & Thomson, W. S. (2005). A comparison of traditional and online instruction in an introduction to special education course. *Teacher Education and Special Education: The Journal of the Teacher Education Division of the Council for Exceptional Children, 28*(1), 62–73.

Taylor, D. (1996). *The healing power of stories.* Dublin, Ireland: Gill & Macmillan.

Trinidad Guardian. (2011). *Form one students to get laptops from Wednesday.* Retrieved from:http://www.guardian.co.tt/news/2011/09/24/form-one-students-get-laptops-wednesday

UNESCO. (1994). *The Salamanca statement and framework for action on special needs education.* Paris, UNESCO, Ministry of Education, Spain.

UNESCO. International Bureau of Education. (2009). *International conference on education, inclusive education: The way of the future* (28th session). Geneva 25–28 November 2008.

University of the West Indies—Open Campus. (2012). *About the open campus.* Retrieved from: http://eportfolio.open.uwi.edu/about.php

University of the West Indies. (2012). *Welcome to the UWI open campus.* Retrieved from: http://www.open.uwi.edu/about/welcome-uwi-open-campus

Walcott, D. (1962). *A far cry from Africa.* Retrieved from http://www.wwnorton.com/college/english/nap/A_Far_Cry_From_Africa_Wallcot.htm

Wheeler, S., Kelly, P., & Gale, K. (2005). The influence of online problem-based learning on teachers' professional practice and identity. *ALT-J, Research in Learning Technology, 13(2),* 125–137.

Willis, E., Tucker, G., & Gunn, C. (2003). Developing an online Master of Education in educational technology in a learning paradigm: the process and the product. *Journal of Technology and Teacher Education, 11(1),* 5–21.

Wolfe, P. D. (2006). Best practices in the training of faculty to teach online. *Journal of Computing in Higher Education, 17(2),* 47–78.

Zemsky, R., & Massey, M. F. (2004). *Thwarted innovation: What happened to e-learning and why.* Retrieved from: http://www.thelearningalliance.info/WeatherStation.html

PART III

VOICES FROM THE TRENCHES

CHAPTER 11

VOICES FROM THE TRENCHES

Teachers' Perspectives On Inclusion

Kimberly Glasgow-Charles, Lisa Ibrahim-Joseph, and Laurette Bristol

Inclusive education remains a major educational goal as evidenced by its integration into Agenda 2030 for sustainable development. The journey to accomplishing this goal is fraught with a number of challenges, and full implementation across cultures remains elusive (Mafa 2012; Mitiku, Alemu, & Mengsitu, 2014). Arguably, the successful implementation of inclusion is contingent on the commitment of all key stakeholders, particularly teachers. According to Donohue and Bornman (2015), teachers are expected to be one of the primary drivers of inclusive policies because they are the gatekeepers for the classroom climate and activities. Therefore, the main thesis of this chapter is the understanding that teachers are the most important players in the implementation of inclusion.

Teachers are regarded as key informants who can provide insight into the barriers to inclusion and recommendations for the successful implementation of inclusive practice. This chapter includes a brief background to inclusion from international and local perspectives and draws upon data derived from a pilot case study. The case study served as a preliminary investigation into the perspectives of teachers on the issue of inclusion in schools in Trinidad and Tobago. The findings of this study reveal that factors at the level of the person, school and educa-

Caribbean Discourse in Inclusive Education:
Historical and Contemporary Issues, pages 187–208.
Copyright © 2017 by Information Age Publishing
All rights of reproduction in any form reserved.

tion system, such as the lack of a coherent inclusive policy and deficiencies in teacher professional development, militate against inclusion. These suggest the need for targeted interventions aimed at capacity building if the goal of inclusive education is to be realized in this context.

Inclusion and Inclusive Education

Education reform and innovation is a dynamic element of education systems across the globe, even in Small Island Developing States (SIDS) such as ours here in Trinidad and Tobago. Engaging in reform represents attempts to renew the system so that it is responsive to its changing context; it also represents an attempt to respond to global imperatives for which we have signaled our commitment to either abide by or be a part of. Such has been the genesis of inclusive education in the education discourse of Trinidad and Tobago.

The movement towards an inclusion paradigm in education in Trinidad and Tobago originated with the Education for All (EFA) agenda first established in Jomtiem, Thailand in 1990, and reaffirmed in 2000 at Dakar, Senegal. At the meeting of the World Education Forum in Dakar, Senegal, six educational goals were identified to be achieved by 2015. Goal 2 addressed inclusion, "ensuring that by 2015 all children, particularly girls, children in difficult circumstances, and those belonging to ethnic minorities, have access to, and complete, free and compulsory primary education of good quality" (UNESCO, 2000, p. 8). In alignment with this goal was the indicator that required national education systems to "create safe, healthy, inclusive and equitably resourced educational environments conducive to excellence in learning, with clearly defined levels of achievement for all" (UNESCO, 2000, p. 9).

The Education for All goals were further complemented by the Millennium Development Goals (MDGs), Goal 2 of which spoke specifically to education to "ensure that, by 2015, children everywhere, boys and girls alike, will be able to complete a full course of primary schooling" (UNESCO, 2000, p. 15); again, the language of inclusion that speaks to all children: children in poverty, the marginalized and excluded, including children with disabilities. It is evident that the topic of inclusion remains high on the international agenda: forming part of the post-2015 discourse on development, as represented in Sustainable Development Goal 4—"Ensure inclusive and quality education for all and promote lifelong learning" (United Nations, n.d.).Trinidad and Tobago is a signatory to all these initiatives, signaling its intention and commitment to address the goals laid out.

In addition to the EFA, MDGs and SDGs, there were other global imperatives that called for action towards the creation of more inclusive societies, and the provision of inclusive education. Included among these are the Salamanca Statement and Framework for Action on Special Needs Education (UNESCO, 1994) and the United Nations Convention on the Rights of Persons with Disabilities (United Nations, 2006). The Salamanca Statement was the outcome of the World Conference on Special Needs which took place in Salamanca, Spain in 1994.

The meeting was organized to "consider the fundamental policy shifts required to promote the approach of inclusive education, namely enabling schools to serve all children, particularly those with special education needs" (UNESCO, 1994, p iii). Moreover, the Salamanca Statement espoused the goal of schools for all which it described as "institutions which include everybody, celebrate differences, support learning and respond to individual needs" (UNESCO, 1994, p. iii).

The thrust towards including children with special needs within regular education settings was founded on the assumption that regular schools with an inclusive orientation that embraced the diversity represented by children with special needs are the most effective means of combating discriminatory attitudes, creating welcoming communities, building an inclusive society and achieving education for all (UNESCO, 1994). Among the various policy positions presented for adoption was that teacher preparation (both pre-service and in-service) for inclusion should form part of any systemic change aimed at providing for special needs education within the regular classroom.

To make the foregoing a reality, the Framework for Action which accompanies the Salamanca Statement promotes the development of child-centered schools—schools that recognize human differences as normal. It proposes that rather than seeing children and youth with disabilities as being deficient, schools need to develop a child-centered pedagogy in which learning is adapted to the needs of the child; schools need to move away from a" one-size-fits-all" approach based on predetermined assumptions about learners and learning (UNESCO, 1994, p. 6). This will require curriculum flexibility, leadership and resources among other provisions to make inclusive education a meaningful reality (UNESCO, 1994).

Article 24 of the United Nations Convention on the Rights of Persons with Disabilities (CRPD) addresses the right to education for persons with disabilities. It begins by stating, "With a view to realizing this right without discrimination and on the basis of equal opportunity, State Parties shall ensure an inclusive education system at all levels" (United Nations, 2006, p. 16). The CRPD also outlines conditions under which inclusion/inclusive education shall occur: the provision of free, inclusive, compulsory primary and secondary education in regular education settings; accommodations and supports tailored to their specific needs within these settings; and individualized support (United Nations, 2006).

Moreover, recognizing the role that teachers must play if inclusion is to be successfully implemented at the level of the classroom, the CRPD advocates the employment of adequately trained staff prepared to address the diverse abilities represented by children with special needs. The training of such personnel must encompass such areas as disability awareness, use of appropriate augmentative and alternatives modes, means and formats of communication, educational techniques and materials to support persons with disabilities (United Nations, 2006).

The orientation to inclusive education outlined above has several implications for teachers in the regular education classroom. They have to be willing to adopt the philosophy that indeed all children can learn despite their prevailing differences and challenges. Teachers must see themselves as being capable of responding to these diverse needs. They must also feel assured that the support systems to facilitate their efforts are available and accessible. In instances where they come to the task without the necessary skill set to make inclusion happen, there must be opportunities provided by the system for continuous professional development to facilitate the development of the competencies they will need to promote and support inclusive education practices.

But how do we define inclusion and inclusive education? Like many constructs in education, universally agreed upon definitions for inclusion and inclusive education are elusive (DEC/NAEYC, 2009; Ellis, Tod, & Graham-Matheson, 2008). These constructs are usually defined in the literature by their characteristics and the contexts in which they are used. Inclusive education is defined as "a process that involves the transformation of schools and other centres of learning to cater for all children—including boys and girls, students from ethnic and linguistic minorities, rural populations, those affected by HIV and AIDS, and those with disabilities and difficulties in learning and to provide learning opportunities for all youth and adults as well" (UNESCO, 2009, p. 4).

From the perspective of UNESCO, and within the context of the various conventions addressing the role of education in the international development agenda (EFA, MDGs, SDGs), inclusion is recognized as "being central to the achievement of high-quality education for all learners and the development of more inclusive societies" (UNESCO, 2009, p. 4)—indeed a social construct. UNESCO (2009) further declares that "inclusive education is essential to achieve social equity and is a constituent element of lifelong learning" (p. 4). In the light of international data identifying high numbers of marginalized and excluded groups, inclusion and inclusive education are promoted on the basis that all children should not only have access to education, but they must also be able to take full part in school life and achieve desired outcomes from their education experiences. Moreover, these outcomes must not merely be defined in terms of academic performance, but from a more broad-based perspective in which learning achievement is defined as "the acquisition of the values, attitudes, knowledge and skills required to meet the challenges of contemporary societies" (UNESCO, 2009, p. 6).

Inclusion and inclusive education also find resonance in conventions and policy frameworks aimed at addressing the education of people with disabilities, including children and youth. The 1993 Standard Rules on the Equalization of Opportunities for Persons with Disabilities adopted by the United Nations General Assembly, forty-eighth session, lays out twenty-two rules under three broad headings aimed at promoting full participation and equality for persons with disabilities: (a) Pre-conditions for equal participation—Rules 1 to 4; (b) Target areas for equal participation—Rules 5 to 12; and (c) Implementation measures—Rules 13 to 22. Rule 6 specifically addresses education and proposes that "states should recognise the principle of equal primary, secondary and tertiary educational opportunities for children, youth and adults with disabilities, in integrated setting [and] ensure that the education of persons with disabilities is an integral part of the educational system" (United Nations, 1993). It goes on to advocate the conditions under which educational provisions for persons with disabilities in the mainstream should occur (United Nations, 1993). State provisions for inclusion should include a clear stated policy that is understood and accepted at the school level and the wider community, curriculum flexibility, addition and adaptation, and quality materials, on-going teacher training and support teachers (United Nations, 1993).

These propositions are reinforced in the Salamanca Statement which states that "special needs education…cannot advance in isolation. It has to form part of an overall educational strategy and, indeed, of new social and economic policies. It calls for major reform of the ordinary school" (UNESCO, 1994, p. iii). Furthermore, "an 'inclusive education' system can only be created if ordinary schools become more inclusive—in other words, if they become better at educating all children in their communities" (UNESCO, 2009, p. 8).

Advancing inclusion and inclusive education depends on a common vision supported by decisive, specific actions (UNESCO, 2009). Drawing on the work done within the EFA frameworks and the articulated positions within the Salamanca Statement (UNESCO, 1994) and the Standard Rules (United Nations, 1993), the UNESCO's Policy Guidelines on Inclusion in Education reiterates the foregoing positions from a systems perspective. It advocates a shift from viewing the child as a problem to a vantage point that promotes reorganization of the ordinary school within the community, through school improvement and a focus on quality which ensures that all children can learn effectively, including those categorized as having special needs.

The Salamanca Statement summarizes it best:

> The fundamental principle of the inclusive school is that all children should learn together, wherever possible, regardless of any difficulties and differences they may have. Inclusive schools must recognise and respond to the diverse needs of their students, accommodating both different styles and rates of learning and ensuring quality education to all through appropriate curricula, organisational arrangements, teaching strategies, resource use and partnerships with the communities. (UNESCO, 1994, p. 11)

This is the challenge to which Trinidad and Tobago must rise, a challenge that may not be easily overcome given the number of complex, intersecting barriers complicated by "well-entrenched practices of school management which have been centrally controlled by an education bureaucracy" (Lavia, 2008, p. 116).

INCLUSION IN CONTEXT—TRINIDAD AND TOBAGO

Historical Overview

Historically, government involvement in the provision of services for persons with disabilities, including children and youth gained some measure of prominence during the 1980s. The foundation for this was set with the inclusion of "Provision for Special Schools" in the Education Act of 1966, which "advocated the establishment of special schools, classes and services, either as separate units or in connection with approved public institutions, and brought special education under the aegis of the Ministry of Education" (Ribeiro, 1994, p. 64). According to Lavia (2007), "prior to 1981, voluntary, non-governmental organizations provided programmes for disabled individuals and in many cases, special schools were set up to provide for their education" (p. 110). The decade of the 1980s represented an era in which the education of children with special needs received attention and attempts were made to ensure opportunities were provided, with a particular emphasis on persons with disabilities in the first instance. However, the language of inclusion had not yet started to permeate the national discourse.

Increased state attention to the education of persons with disabilities during the 1980s arose out of "international concerns about education as a human right and educational expansion in the developing world based on the development of human resources" (Lavia, 2008, p. 110). This attention to education for persons with disabilities on the state front manifested itself in the incorporation of "Institutional Schools" in 1980 into the educational system. These schools were re-designated special schools, and covered a range of disabilities (blindness, deafness, physical handicaps and mental handicaps). Special education became the language of the day and full responsibility for the management and operation of these schools was assumed by the Ministry of Education in collaboration with their respective boards of Management (Williams, 2007).

By Cabinet Minute 3901 of October 03, 1980, the government signalled its intentions through its decision to establish a Special Education Unit within the Ministry of Education, the functions of which were to coordinate special education throughout Trinidad and Tobago, supervise and develop curricula for special schools and regular schools where students with special education needs were enrolled, and collaborate with other Government Ministries in the prevention of disorders and disease (Williams, 2007).

There were several other initiatives during this period aimed at addressing opportunities for children with special needs. These included the establishment of the Advisory Committee on Special Education in 1982, the 1984 National Survey of Handicapped Children and Youth in Trinidad and Tobago which sought to identify the prevalence of children with disabilities within the society (16.1 percent of the population), and training for teachers funded by the Canadian International Development Agency (CIDA) (Lavia, 2008; Ribeiro, 1994; Williams, 2007).

The Government's intent was further signaled by the provisions included in the draft Education Plan, 1985–1990. One of the measures identified to support the outlined thrusts in education was "the inclusion of programmes of basic Guidance and Special Education in the Teacher Training programmes to better enable teachers to cope with children in need of special attention" (Ministry of Education Trinidad and Tobago, 1985, p. 15). This provision was critical to the role that regular teachers would have to play in the education of children with special needs. The philosophy espoused at this time was that "Special Education must make the child aware of his/her handicapping condition and should provide opportunities for him/her to become disciplined, self-reliant, productive citizen through acceptance of his condition and the use of his ability to its highest potential" (Ministry of Education, 1985, p. 38).

Furthermore, the Government, having accepted its "role as the responsible agent for providing Special Education at all levels of the Education System" identified regular public schools (with additional supporting services) as one of the modes of provision which would occur either in the form of mainstreaming, special classes or special programs (Ministry of Education, 1985, p. 38). It did sound a note of caution, however, on the way in which mainstreaming was to be addressed. While acknowledging the popularity of this approach to special education in Europe and North America, it also recognized that it lacked the capacity to approach mainstreaming on a grand scale and recommended "gradually adjusting the mainstream schools to meet the needs of those special children already in them" (Ministry of Education, 1985, p. 39). Although this recommendation was made, the ministry, at that time, did not articulate how they intended to operationalize this recommendation.

As we approached the 1990s, there were clear signals that the language of inclusion was becoming an endemic feature of the special education narrative. Education as a fundamental human right was the rallying cry. A number of international conventions and commitments identified inclusion as a way of ensuring that all people everywhere received an education with the principles of equity, access and quality as policy pillars. The forerunner to the policy shifts that were about to take place was signaled by the 1990 Pilgrim Report "which had seen inclusion as development of special education and which had called for one system of education for all children" (Lavia, 2008, p. 110).

Policy Shifts

Shifts in policy perspectives that represented a contemporary view of special education with a focus on inclusion had started to develop by 1991. The focus had moved away from labeling children by their disability to identifying what the child needs to learn and the teaching methods and arrangements required to enable the child to access the curriculum (Williams, 2007). In this context, children with special educational needs were described as "those who have characteristics that affect their ability to the extent that specially adapted conditions are necessary if they are to be appropriately and effectively educated" (Williams, 2007, p. 6).

The Education Policy Paper 1993–2003 (National Task Force on Education (NTFE), 1993) clearly illustrated this shift in its philosophy statements among which included the belief:

- that every child has an inherent right to an education which will enhance the development of maximum capability regardless of gender, ethnic, economic, social and religious background;
- that every child has the ability to learn, and that we must build on this positive assumption; and
- that students vary in natural ability, and that schools, therefore, should provide, for all students, programmes which are adapted to varying abilities, and which provide opportunity to develop differing personal and socially useful talents.

In keeping with this philosophy, several recommendations pointed to the changes that were needed to support the integration of children with special needs including: the establishment of Regional Diagnostic Prescriptive Centres with multidisciplinary teams consisting of a special education officer, a psychologist, school social worker and a practical nurse; public awareness and education; training in special education; and mainstreaming except in severe cases (NTFE, 1993). Some of these recommendations came into effect first with the commencement of a pilot Diagnostic Programme in 1999 and the subsequent establishment of the Student Support Services Division in 2004 which combined Guidance and Counselling, Special Education and School Social Work to provide ongoing support to all students in the education system (Williams, 2007). Additionally, the Ministry of Education embraced UNESCO's definition on inclusion and adopted the posture that inclusive education was first and foremost about school reform.

Within the broader national policy framework, a National Policy on Persons with disabilities was adopted in 2005 which further emphasized the movement towards the development of an inclusive education system. Moreover, the development of the Seamless Education Project witnessed the deepening of this policy perspective on the education front with the Ministry of Education, through the Student Support Services Division, commissioning a research study on inclusive education in Trinidad and Tobago during the period January 2007 to January 2008, the report on which is contained in *Achieving Inclusion: Transforming the Education System in Trinidad and Tobago* (Miske Witt & Associates, 2008).

As these movements were occurring, in 2010 there was a mid-stream change in political administration, and a consequent slowdown in the inclusion thrust. Instead, a policy on Special Education reappeared on the national agenda with general statements on inclusion as part of its narrative, drawing on the international perspectives previously described herein. Throughout our national engagement with inclusion and inclusive education, however, we have primarily witnessed an emphasis on policy posturing more than on practical implementation at the level of the school; a possible rationale for teachers' ambiguity towards inclusion—further interrogation of which is beyond the scope of the current discussion.

Whatever the prevailing trend, however, the movement from policy to practice resulting in implementation at the level of schools can only occur successfully through teacher action. Teachers must be willing to embrace the philosophy and practice if inclusion and inclusive education are to be institutionalized and result in transformation of the education system. It is against this backdrop that the authors have inquired into teachers' perspectives on inclusion in Trinidad and Tobago.

In this section, we positioned inclusion and inclusive education within the international and local policy frameworks by examining the ways in which notions of this ideology have evolved internationally and within our local context here in Trinidad and Tobago. The subsequent segment reports on the findings of a pilot, case study conducted in Trinidad and Tobago. The fundamental question the study attempted to address was: *What are teachers' perspectives on inclusion?* Thus, the study's purpose was to understand teachers' perspectives on inclusion, as well as elicit their recommendations for the advancement of this practice within the local education system.

INQUIRY INTO SELECTED TEACHERS' PERSPECTIVES ON INCLUSION IN TRINIDAD AND TOBAGO

Agreeably, the topics of "teacher attitudes," "teacher perceptions" and "teacher beliefs" regarding inclusion are internationally well-trodden paths (Ahmmed, Sharma, & Deppeler, 2012; Beacham & Rouse, 2012; Bhatnagar & Das, 2014; Blackman, Conrad, & Brown, 2012; Donohue & Bornman, 2015; Forlin, Kawai, & Higuchi, 2015; Forlin, Keen, & Barret, 2008; Gal, Schreur, & Engel-Yeger, 2010; Leatherman, 2007; McGhie-Richmond, Irvine, Loreman, Cizman, & Lupart, 2013). However, in Trinidad and Tobago, it appears that this issue remains under-researched, as evident from the dearth of local research on this topic. A general search of the literature on "teacher attitudes toward inclusion" produced 710 hits. Conversely, without surprise, the results of a refined search, "teacher attitudes toward inclusion in Trinidad and Tobago" yielded one article—"The Attitude of Barbadian and Trinidad Teachers to Integration," which was authored by Blackman, Conrad, and Brown (2012). It is clear that a gap in the local body of research on teacher attitudes toward inclusion exists; highlighting the need for studies aimed at exploring and documenting the perspectives and experiences of teachers relative to inclusion in Trinidad and Tobago.

Furthermore, this research gap gives rise to the question: "What are the issues confronting the field locally with regards to inclusion?" More critically, this lag in the local body of work raises concerns about the extent to which decisions regarding inclusive education in Trinidad and Tobago are empirically driven. Consequently, the dearth of local literature contributes to the relevance of the work reported in this chapter as it reveals teachers' perspectives on inclusion in schools in Trinidad and Tobago, and further advances our understanding of possible barriers to inclusion implementation

THE INQUIRY

A genuine interest in the development of Trinidad and Tobago's education system, in which the researchers function, coupled with the identified gap in the research provided the impetus for this study. The study was a preliminary investigation into teachers' perspective on inclusion. Though a pilot study, the researchers thought that the findings were significant enough for publication. The following three questions were addressed in this study:

1. What are teachers concerns about educating students with special needs in general education classrooms in Trinidad and Tobago?
2. What do teachers perceive as the barriers to educating students with special needs in general education classrooms in Trinidad and Tobago?
3. What are teachers' recommendations for educating students with special needs in general education classrooms in Trinidad and Tobago?

A case study design was the approach selected to conduct the investigation. A case study is described as an in-depth exploration of a bounded system (e.g., activity, event, process, or individuals) based on extensive data collection (Creswell, 2014). The researchers' focus on context, the small number of cases, and the boundary of the study provide justification for the selected methodology. The main unit of analysis is the particular experiences of a selected group of teachers.

Context of the Study

Trinidad and Tobago, a developing country, is situated northeast of Venezuela and northwest of Guyana. It is the southernmost of the Caribbean islands, with an estimated population of 1.3 million. Trinidad and Tobago has an oil and gas economy. Five levels of education have been identified within this context: early childhood, primary, secondary, post-secondary, and tertiary (National Report, 2008). These levels exist within seven pre-established, geographical, educational districts; namely: Caroni, North Eastern, Port of Spain and Environs, South Eastern, St. George East, St. Patrick, and Victoria, with the sister island of Tobago recognized as an eight district. There are approximately 14,500 public school teachers. Secondary school teachers account for 43 per cent of this figure, while primary school and ECCE teachers account for 50 per cent and 7 per cent respectively.

To date, the Marge Report (Marge, 1984) remains the only comprehensive study on Special Education Needs in Trinidad and Tobago. According to this report, 16.1 percent of children aged 3 through 16 years were found to have special education needs (Marge, 1984). The Ministry of Education has highlighted the urgent need for current, comprehensive research on the incidence of disability and special education needs in Trinidad and Tobago (Ministry of Education, 2013). Not only is there an absence of data on the prevalence and incidence of special education needs, but "Trinidad and Tobago is currently in the untenable position where there is no comprehensive system for monitoring and evaluating the progress and achievement of student with disabilities" (Paul, 2011, p. 195). Moreover, like many developing countries, "Trinidad and Tobago engages in the transferring of special education policies and practices from developed nations such as the USA, UK, and Canada but implements these practices with limited practical knowledge, experience and inadequate infrastructure" (Paul, 2011 p. 195).

Selection of Participants

The participants were selected from among 105 teachers who attended a two-week professional development workshop during the July/August school break. The researchers were involved in the workshop and issued an invitation to the workshop's participants. They were provided with details of the project such as the purpose of the study, intended method of data collection and use of data. Interested persons were asked to provide their names and contact information on the form provided. Of the 105 workshop attendees, 49 teachers expressed an interest in the research project and subsequently signed the "research consent form."

The respondents are 49 teachers from various education levels—ECCE, primary, secondary—within the Trinidad and Tobago education system. They are assigned to schools located in the eight geographical, education districts identified earlier. All 49 respondents attended a two-week professional development workshop: "Educating ALL IV—Embracing Inclusive Practices." The workshop was co-hosted by the Canadian Teachers Federation (CTF) and the Trinidad and Tobago Teachers' Association (TTUTA). The respondents have some knowledge of special education and inclusion, having been exposed to the following contents at the workshop: types of disabilities, educational considerations and strategies for addressing the needs of these students within the regular classroom setting. The authors felt that teachers' exposure to these topics, coupled with their personal and professional experiences, would have provided a useful frame of reference for them to think about and address the issues being discussed.

Data Collection

The researchers' original intent was to conduct group interviews. However, accessing participants and synchronizing meeting times proved difficult, even impossible. This was due primarily to the fact that data collection took place during the July/August school break; a 'sacred time' for teachers in this context. Consequently, the researchers had to resort to using a short questionnaire as the main method of data collection.

The questionnaire comprised a mixture of open and closed items. The first set of items elicited school and academic background data such as: school district, level currently teaching, highest level of academic qualification, special education training. The second set of items, which were open-ended and required respondents to state their concerns about inclusion and identify perceived barriers to and supports needed for inclusion. The instrument was generated using Survey Monkey and the link forwarded to the participants via their email addresses.

Survey Monkey generated descriptive statistics for closed questions while the researchers used an inductive approach to analysis of data gathered through the use of open items. This process involved: (1) reading of responses several times to become familiar with data; (2) highlighting meaningful units of data; (3) assigning and subsequently revising codes; (4) clustering codes; and (5) developing of themes.

FINDINGS

A hundred percent of the participants accessed and completed the survey. Analysis of the background data showed that 16 per cent, 55 per cent and 29 per cent of the respondents served at the preschool, primary, and secondary level respectively. This was reflective of the distribution of teachers across level, as primary schools account for the largest percentage of the teacher population in Trinidad and Tobago. Although, teachers were from different levels of the education system the data was treated as a single case—teachers.

Sixty-nine percent of respondents indicated that their highest level of education was the Bachelors in Education, while 29 per cent and 2 per cent selected the Masters/MSc and Diploma respectively, as their highest level of educational attainment. 57 percent of respondents indicated that they have training in Special Education, while 76 percent of respondents indicated that there were students with special needs enrolled in their classes.

There's a need for further investigation into the finding that 76 percent of participants perceived that there were students with special needs enrolled in their classes. This investigation will allow for an understanding of the criteria teachers use to identify students as having special needs or the basis of their claim. It brings to the fore one of the major limitations of the data collection method used in the study. However, the finding suggests that some level of inclusion was taking place in the schools participants are assigned to. Secondly, this finding reveals that some teachers were faced with the responsibility of catering to the needs of a student(s) with special needs despite not having training in special education. The issue of lack of training emerged as a main theme and is discussed later.

Closely tied to the issue of training is teachers' level of preparedness. The majority of teachers, 61 percent, rated their level of preparedness for inclusion as "somewhat prepared," while 14 percent rated themselves as "unprepared." On the contrary, 6 per cent and 18 per cent of the teachers rated themselves as "very prepared" and "adequately prepared," respectively.

Voices From the Trenches—Selected Teachers Speak

The first research question the study attempted to address was: *"What are teachers' concerns about educating students with special needs within general education classrooms?"* The purpose of this question was to identify existing fears or anxieties teachers may have regarding this practice. Concerns were treated as an a priori theme and refer to personal attitudes.

Concerns About Inclusion

Professional concern. "Professional concern" was the single, main theme that emerged from the data relative to teachers' concerns about inclusion. Professional concerns relate to participants' ability to perform the duties effectively and to be viewed as competent by others. Analysis of the data revealed that the majority of respondents, 71 per cent, seemed anxious about not being able to effectively perform their roles and their ability, or perceived inability rather, to meet the needs of students with special needs. According to the participants, this concern stemmed from their lack of preparedness including training in special education and knowledge about disabilities. In response to the question, "What are your concerns regarding educating children with special needs in general education classroom?" one participant commented:

> If I would be able to handle it. I believe in it but I am afraid I don't think I have the know-how ... you know how to really teach and help students with disabilities.

Another participant stated:

> My greatest concern is my own level of readiness. I have very little knowledge and training in special education.

Another issue related to the theme "professional concern" was teacher image. Although this concern was raised by a few participants it appeared significant. 10 per cent of the respondents raised concerns about the impact of inclusion on their teacher image. The following comment made by one of participants captures this sentiment:

> My concern is that I am being judged by the same standards as the teacher in another school who gets scholarships but they don't enroll those kinds of students ... but we who have these students are seen as "non-performers."

These teachers, from both primary and secondary schools, felt that inclusion might limit the level of academic success they experience within the classroom. Students' academic success was important to teachers because it was used to evaluate their competence. This finding was significant and highlights the strong emphasis placed on academic excellence within the Trinidad and Tobago education system. In fact, academic excellence is seen as the benchmark or qualifier for high-performing schools and teachers in this context. Additionally, it points to negative attitudes towards students with special needs who are often viewed as low achievers. Teachers alluded to the implications of this culture, correctly identifying it as a barrier to inclusion, as it contributes to teachers' unwillingness to accept students with special needs in their class

Barriers to inclusion. In addition to identifying their concerns, participants were asked to pinpoint potential barriers to inclusion in schools in Trinidad and Tobago. This question sought to elicit participants' ideas about structural and other factors that can prevent students with special needs from accessing education in the general education classroom. Three themes that emerged from the analysis of data relative to this issue are: person barriers, school barriers, and system barriers.

Person Barriers

Person barriers refer to individual characteristics and/or dispositions that can impede inclusion. Two sub-themes related to this main theme were student level of disability and negative attitudes.

The Student's severity of disability: 30 percent of the participants opined that students' 'level' of disability was a decisive factor in inclusion and a potential barrier. They felt that students with more severe conditions might not be accepted. One participant commented: "Teachers may accept pupils who are mild but not severe or profound." Sharing a similar sentiment, another participant wrote: "Depending on the severity inclusion will be counterproductive." One respondent was very specific and identified categories of special needs that teachers may avoid based on their needs. This participant stated: "students who are blind and deaf might not get accepted in a normal classroom." Participants seemed to refer to high incidence disabilities as 'mild disabilities' and low incidence as 'severe or profound.' This issue has been noted for further investigation.

Negative attitudes: The data revealed that "negative attitudes" was seen as a barrier to inclusion by participants. 57 percent of the respondents were of the view that both teachers and principals held negative beliefs and perceptions about inclusion and were unwilling to enroll students with special needs in their schools and classrooms. Additionally, participants asserted that protection of the school image contributed to principals' reservations about inclusion, while they believed that teachers' protest, against this practice, was due to beliefs such as: inclusion was too difficult, impossible, meant an increased workload and that it is the responsibility of specially trained teachers to instruct students with special needs. The desire for academic excellence came to the fore again as a perceived contributor to prevailing negative attitudes toward inclusion. This view was expressed when one participant commented: "School principals feel that inclusion will negatively impact their schools' performance."

School-Level Barriers

Sixty-three percent of the teachers identified issues such as crowded classrooms, lack of resources, little support from principals and enrolment practices as factors that can hinder inclusion. Most of these variables were viewed by participants as integral to addressing the needs of students with special needs. One teacher asked: "In a class of 45 students, how do I give individual time and attention to students with disabilities." Another participant pointed to the issue of resources in the statement: "We don't have the resources in classrooms to do the kinds of hands-on work these students need." Participants' responses indicate that they have some understanding of what is required to facilitate the practice of inclusion.

Regarding support from principals, some participants felt that administrators were not knowledgeable about special needs and were therefore unable to provide assistance to teachers. One participant opined: "Some principals are clueless about special education and cannot support teachers ... principals need training in special education." Although the data collection method did not lend itself to probing so as to determine what kinds of support teachers expect from their principals, this finding indicates that teachers saw support from the school's leadership as necessary for inclusion.

Another significant issue emerging from the data was enrolment practices. Participants alleged that some schools, described as "prestige" (high performing) schools, avoided enrolling students with special education needs. In the Trinidad and Tobago context, some schools are dubbed "prestigious." This finding, similar to an earlier finding, highlights the strong emphasis on academic success within Trinidad and Tobago's education system. Additionally, it indicates that teachers' perspectives on special needs are limited to students with cognitive deficiencies. While there are no tangible penalties such as a reduction in salary or the demotion of teachers whose students have not excelled academically, the tacit consequences appear impactful, even associated with negative attitudes toward inclusion. The following view expressed by one of the participants captures it well: "Teachers and schools are singled out when their results are not good so some teachers prefer not to have students like that."

System-Level Barriers

"System level barriers" refers to factors for which the ministry of education has a direct responsibility. These include teacher development, policy and resources/support. Ninety-five percent of the respondents perceived deficiencies in teacher development as a major barrier to inclusion in schools in Trinidad and Tobago. Teachers also argued that teachers' lack of training and knowledge relative to special education contributed to negative attitudes. One participant commented: "Teachers never did any real training to deal with students with special needs so they are not willing to have these students." Another participant made reference to teachers' lack of knowledge. This respondent claimed that "Many teachers do not understand disabilities."

Support emerged as another issue relative to "system-level barriers." Analysis of the data showed that 73 percent of the participants made reference to support. This finding highlights teachers' expectations of the Ministry of Education to provide necessary materials, resources and personnel to facilitate inclusion. Participants saw the Ministry's failure to make such provisions as a "lack of support." The following quote from one of the participants best illustrates this: "[The] Ministry of Education keep[s] demanding more from teachers without providing support, I think that is a hindrance to inclusion." Some respondents sought to pinpoint another variable they believe has added to the complexity of this issue. They cited an under-staffed Student Support Services division.

A final factor that surfaced from the data as a system-level barrier was policy. Sixty-three percent of the respondents cited "lack of policy" as a barrier to inclusion. Participants felt that inclusion had to be mandated for it to become a reality in some schools. One respondent submitted: "Unless the ministry puts it in black and white certain schools are not going to enroll students with disabilities." A similar comment made by another participant supported this assumption. This respondent stated: "It's not policy so that means schools have a choice that's why they are not in certain schools." This finding again highlights perceived ambivalent attitudes towards inclusion. It also suggests that participants see policy as a necessary structure for inclusion. More critically, the finding indicates that inclusion is still seen or treated as a privilege rather than a right in the local context.

Teachers' Recommendations for Inclusion

In addition to identifying concerns about, and the perceived barriers to, inclusion, participants were asked to provide recommendations for the implementation of inclusion in schools in Trinidad and Tobago. Their recommendations included: professional development, policy, and provision of resources. These recommendations were closely aligned with the barriers or challenges they identified. 92 percent of participants recommended education and training in special education for teachers and principals. Some respondents suggested that professional development in special education should be mandatory. Similar to professional development, 92 per cent of respondents were of the view that, personnel, (for example, special education teachers and other support staff), infrastructure and materials, and equipment were needed to make inclusion happen in schools in Trinidad and Tobago. Seventy percent of respondents highlighted the need for a policy on inclusion. One participant delineated the expected contents of such as policy. The respondent submitted:

> "Implementation of a new educational policy on inclusion, including the concept of inclusion, accommodations, budget for resources, which group of students and the number of students with disabilities per class."

DISCUSSION

The discussion addresses the research question: "*What are selected teachers' perspectives on inclusion in schools in Trinidad and Tobago?*" The aim is to understand participants' perspectives based on insights garnered from the findings of the study. Teachers involved in this study were anxious about their competence in meeting the needs of students with disabilities and their "image." The issue of teacher competence in addressing students' special education needs has also been cited in other studies as concerns to teachers (Bhatnagar & Das, 2014; Forlin, Keen, & Barrett, 2008; Sharma, Forlin, Loreman, & Earle, 2006). However, participants' concern about their image, that is, whether they are labeled as "performing or non-performing teachers" as judged by the academic success of their students, could not be found in previous studies on inclusion. Locally, the number of scholarships won by secondary school students and the placement (e.g. top one hundred) and percentile ranks of students on national high stake exams, like the Caribbean Secondary Examination Council and Secondary Entrance Assessment, are used by parents and other stakeholders, as a benchmark for teacher competence. This finding, which appears contextual, has implications for the successful implementation of inclusion, since teachers' concern may foster attitudinal barriers. However, a deeper probe into this issue is needed to disentangle teachers' beliefs regarding this perceived implication of inclusion for teachers. Nevertheless, this result seems to tie into the finding that "achievement of the objective of education for all is seriously undermined by the very narrow focus of education in the region around academic attainment" (Armstrong, Armstrong, Lynch, & Severin, 2005, p. 76).

Person, school and system barriers were deduced from the data. With respect to "person barriers," participants identified student characteristics and negative teacher attitudes as two factors that can impede inclusion. They felt that teachers were unwilling to accept students with special needs in their classes, especially those students whose needs are greater. This finding can be supported by early and recent work on inclusion (Armstrong et al., 2007; Avramidis & Norwich, 2002; Bhatnagar & Das, 2014; Booth & Aniscow, 2002; Leatherman, 2007). Although an investigation into the factors contributing to the alleged teacher antipathy to inclusion did not form part of this study, some of the study's findings, for example, the lack of training and resources, point toward variables associated with negative attitudes toward inclusion in the extant literature (Donohue & Bornman, 2015; Forlin, Keen, & Barrett, 2008; Gal, Schreur, & Engel-Yeger, 2010).

At the level of the school and classroom, participants highlighted inappropriate teacher-student ratios, little or no administrative support, unavailable resources and enrollment practices as variables that hindered inclusion. These barriers identified by participants, with the exception of enrollment practices, were common to the literature on inclusion (Bhatnagar & Das, 2014; Forlin, Keen, & Barrett, 2008; Sharma, Forlin, Loreman, & Earle, 2006; Talmor, Reiter, & Feigin, 2005). With respect to enrollment practices, participants accused some schools of discriminating against academically struggling students in their selection process, as only those students of high academic standing are admitted. Similar to that of teacher image, this finding appears contextual, as comparable findings could not be located. This too has been noted for further research. Nonetheless, the reappearance of issues such as class size, administrative support and materials in the findings as barriers to inclusion points to a failure to utilize the results of previous research, such as research on developing inclusive systems (Ainscow & Sandill, 2010; Alborz, Slee, & Miles, 2013; Lindqvist & Nilholm, 2013) to create conditions that will facilitate the implementation of inclusion. It also indicates that teachers involved in this study have a heightened awareness of some of the requirements for successful inclusion.

Regarding barriers within the system, participants identified deficiencies in teacher development, lack of support, and lack of a coherent policy as barriers to inclusion. Insufficient teacher training in special education and lack of support as impediments to inclusion can be found in previous studies (Forlin, Kawai, & Higuchi, 2015; Leatherman, 2007; Sharma, Forlin, & Loreman, 2007). However, participants' views that the absence of an inclusion policy was a hindrance, while understood in the context of other issues highlighted e.g. enrolment practices in this study, could not be found in other studies. This is another area that requires further investigation. Both school and system barriers identified by participants bring to the fore the existing need for structural adjustments and system readiness for inclusion in schools in Trinidad and Tobago.

In terms of recommendations for inclusion in schools in Trinidad and Tobago, teachers saw the need for professional development, resources and policy. These recommendations are aligned with the concerns and barriers identified by teachers and reveal their expectations of principals and the state and their ideas of the structures needed to support inclusion. Interestingly, coming out of participants' recommendations was the suggestion that policy should mandate inclusion. Participants seem to have viewed this as one way of making all, rather than some, schools inclusive. This recommendation appears impractical, particularly when evaluated against other issues raised by participants such as negative attitudes, insufficient training and lack of support and resources. However, it raises two questions:(1) To what extent is inclusion understood by teachers as a fundamental human right premised on the principles of equity and social justice? (2) Is there a conviction by teachers that it is their responsibility to educate all children? These questions provide a basis for further research. Nonetheless, judging from the study's findings, the researchers are doubtful that these ideals are generally supported or upheld.

Revealingly, through their recommendations, teachers are suggesting that the current system lacks the capacity for this change and needs to engage in capacity building. Capacity building involves the development of several factors, inclusive of collective ability, dispositions and skills, knowledge, motivation and resources, to bring about change (Fullan, 2005).

CONCLUSION

A review of international literature on inclusion and inclusive education revealed a prevailing trend towards transforming education systems for accomplishing the goals of education for all, including children with special needs. The main thrust is for all children to be educated together in ordinary classrooms within their communities. Trinidad and Tobago, as a signatory to a number of international conventions related to assuring education for all, has also adopted this philosophical position with several examples of policy posturing.

The researchers deemed the findings of this pilot study significant. However, we acknowledge that as a result of the small sample size these findings cannot be generalized. The findings of our inquiry into teachers' perspectives on inclusion in Trinidad and Tobago seem to suggest that while the language of inclusion is pervasive in our policy statements, concerns raised and barriers identified by participants suggest that concomitant changes within the education system, sufficient enough to effectively translate policy into practice, have not been implemented.

This snapshot of teachers' perspectives left the researchers reflecting on the question "Is successful inclusion in schools in Trinidad and Tobago within reach?" Arguably, the answer to this question lies in empirical proof; inter alia, an extensive evaluation of the education system. However, based on the findings of this pilot study, which is underpinned by the assumption that participants' views are grounded in their reality, and our experiences within the education system of the practice of inclusion in Trinidad and Tobago appear elusive. By "inclusion" we mean students with special needs being afforded equality in access to and participation in the general education curriculum and classroom. Undoubtedly, a great deal of work is needed to translate our many policies into targeted courses of action.

In the light of the findings from this pilot study, the authors recommend firstly, that the authorities concerned engage teachers through ongoing consultations on the topic of inclusion, so as to better understand and address their related concerns. The call by participants for an inclusion policy highlights the need for greater awareness of existing frameworks. It also points to the need for more definitive statements and legislation on inclusion of students with special needs in regular schools. This issue underscores the importance of ongoing conversations with teachers on inclusion as suggested by the writers, as these forums provide the opportunity to educate teachers about current policy documents. They also allow for teachers' contribution to policy development and direction.

Secondly, the researchers recommend training of all teachers and principals in special and inclusive education; development of support structures in schools inclusive of the assignment of personnel; monitoring of schools' enrollment practices; and revising existing inclusion policy making them more definitive.

Thirdly, in light of teachers' view that they were constrained from being inclusive by the notion of being seen as "non-performing," we recommend an intensive evaluation of the education system, inclusive of culture, to locate and eradicate competing and potentially counterproductive ideologies.

The main implication of this pilot study is that the need for further local research is great. Particularly, qualitative research aimed at a deeper understanding of teachers' attitudes toward and perspectives on inclusion.

REFERENCES

Ahmmed, M., Sharma, U., & Deppeler, J. (2012). Variables affecting teachers' attitudes towards inclusive education in Bangladesh. *Journal of Research in Special Educational Needs,* 12(3), 132–40. DOI: 10.1111/j.1471-3802.2011.01226.x.

Ainscow, M., & Sandill, A. (2010). Developing inclusive education systems: The role of organisational cultures and leadership. *International Journal of Inclusive Education,* 14(4), 401–16.

Alborz, A., Slee, R., & Miles, S. (2013). Establishing the foundations for an inclusive education system in Iraq: Reflection on findings from a nationwide survey. *International Journal of Inclusive Education,* 17(9), 965–87.

Armstrong, C., Armstrong, D., Lynch, C., & Severin, S. (2005). Special and inclusive education in the Eastern Caribbean: Policy, practice and provision. *International Journal of Inclusive Education,* 9(1), 71–87.

Avramidis, E., & Norwich, B. (2002). Teachers' attitudes towards integration and inclusion: A review of the literature. *European Journal of Special Needs Education,* 17(2), 129–47.

Beacham, N., & Rouse, M. (2012). Student teachers' attitudes and beliefs about inclusion and inclusive practice. *Journal of Research in Special Educational Needs,* 12(1), 3–11.

Bhatnagar, N., & Das, A. (2014). Regular school teachers' concerns and perceived barriers to implement inclusive education in New Delhi, India. *International Journal of Instruction,* 7(2), 89–102

Blackman, S., Conrad, D. A., & Brown, L. (2012). The attitudes of Barbadian and Trinidadian teachers to integration. *International Journal of Special Education,* 27(3), 158–68.

Booth, T., & Aniscow, M. (2002). *The index for inclusion: Developing learning and participation in schools.* Retrieved from http://www.eenet.org.uk/resources/docs/Index%20English.pdf

Creswell, J. W. (2014). *Research design: Qualitative, quantitative, and mixed approaches (*4th ed.). New York, NY: SAGE Publications.

DEC/NAEYC. (2009). *Early childhood inclusion: A joint position statement of the Division for Early Childhood (DEC) and the National Association for the Education of Young Children (NAEYC).* Chapel Hill, NC: The University of North Carolina FPG Child Development Institute.

Donohue, D. K.. & Bornman, J. (2015). South African teachers' attitudes toward inclusion of learners with different abilities in mainstream classrooms. *International Journal of Disability Development and Education,* 62(1), 42–59. http://dx.doi.org/10.1080/1034912X.2014.985638.

Ellis, S., Tod, J., & Graham-Matheson, L. (2008). *Special education needs and inclusion: Reflection and renewal.* Retrieved from http://www.nasuwt.org.uk/TrainingEventsandPublications/NASUWTPublications/AccessiblePublications/Education/ReflectionandRenewalSENandInclusion/

Forlin, C., Kawai, N., & Higuchi, S. (2015). Educational reform in Japan towards inclusion: Are we training teachers for success? *International Journal of Inclusive Education, 19(3),* 314–331.

Forlin, C., Keen, M., & Barrett, E. (2008). The concerns of mainstream teachers: Coping with inclusivity in an Australian context. *International Journal of Disability, Development and Education, 55(3),* 251–264.

Fullan, M. (2005). The meaning of educational change: A quarter of a century of learning. In A. Lieberman (Ed.), *The roots of educational change* (pp. 202–216). The Netherlands: Springer.

Gal, E., Schreur, N., & Engel-Yeger, B. (2010). Inclusion of children with disabilities: Teachers' attitudes and requirements for environmental accommodations. *International Journal of Special Education, 25(2),* 89–99.

Lavia, J. (2008). Inclusive education in Trinidad and Tobago. In L. Burton & F. Armstrong (Eds.), *Policy, experience and change: Cross-cultural reflections on inclusive education* (pp. 107–122). Dordrecht, The Netherlands: Springer

Leatherman, J. (2007). "I just see all children as children": Teachers' perceptions about inclusion. *The Qualitative Report, 12(4),* 594–611.

Lindqvist, G., & Nilholm, C. (2013). Making schools inclusive? Educational leaders' views on how to work with children in need of special support. *International Journal of Inclusive Education, 17(1),* 95–110. doi: 10.1080/136033116.2011.580466.

Mafa, O. (2012). Challenges of implementing inclusion in Zimbawe's education system. *Online Journal of Education Research, 1(2),* 14–22. Retrieved from http://onlineresearchjournals.org/IJER/pdf/2012/may/MAFA.pdf.

Marge, M. (1984). *Report on the National Survey of Handicapped Children and Youth in Trinidad and Tobago.* OAS/National Project in Special Education and Rehabilitation of the Handicapped. Ministry of Education, Trinidad and Tobago.

McGhie-Richmond, D., Irvine, A., Loreman, T., Cizman, J. L., & Lupart, J. (2013). Teacher perspectives on inclusive education in rural Alberta, Canada. *Canadian Journal of Education, 36(1),* 195–239. Retrieved from http://www.cje-rce.ca/index.php/cje-rce/article/viewFile/1155/1470

Ministry of Education, Republic of Trinidad and Tobago. (1985). *Education plan 1985–1990 (Draft).* Port of Spain, Trinidad and Tobago: Author.

Ministry of Education, Republic of Trinidad and Tobago. (2008). *National report on the development of education in Trinidad and Tobago: Inclusive education.* Retrieved from: http:// www.ibe.unesco.or/en/ice/48-session-2008/national-reports.html

Ministry of Education, Republic of Trinidad and Tobago. (2013). *Draft Special Education Policy.* Port of Spain, Trinidad and Tobago: Author.

Miske Witt, & Associates (2008). *Achieving inclusion: Transforming the education system of Trinidad and Tobago: Final report on inclusive education component of the seamless education project.* Retrieved from http://miskewitt.com/assets/miske_witt_-_associates_2008_achieving_inclusion_transforming_the_education_system_of_trinidad_and_tobago.pdf

Mitiku, W., Alemu, Y., & Mengsitu, S. (2014). Challenges and opportunities to implementing inclusive education. *Asian Journal of Humanity, Art and Literature, 1(2),* 118–35. Retrieved from http://publicationslist.org/data/ajhal/ref-11/AJHL%202.5.pdf

National Task Force on Education. (1993). *Education policy paper (1993—2003) White Paper*. Port of Spain, Trinidad and Tobago: Ministry of Education, Government of the Republic of Trinidad and Tobago.

Paul, S. (2011). Outcomes of students with disabilities in a developing country: Tobago. *International Journal of Special Education, 26(3),* 194–211.

Ribeiro, M. L. (1994). Development of one education system for all school children: The significance of teachers' attitudes. *Caribbean Curriculum, 4(1),* 63–77.

Sharma, U., Forlin, C., & Loreman, T. (2007). What concerns pre-service teachers about inclusive education: An international viewpoint? *KEDI Journal of Educational Policy, 4*(2), 95–114.

Sharma, U., Forlin, C., Loreman, T., & Earle, C. (2006). Pre-service teachers' attitudes, concerns and sentiments about inclusive education: An international comparison of novice pre-service teachers. *International Journal of Special Education, 21*(2), 80–93.

Talmor, R., Reiter, S., & Feigin, N. (2005). Factors relating to education teacher burnout in inclusive education. *European Journal of Special Needs Education. 20*(2), 215–229. ISSN-0885-6257

United Nations. (n.d.). *Sustainable development goals: 17 goals to transform our world*. Retrieved from http://www.un.org/sustainabledevelopment/sustainable-development-goals/

United Nations. (1993). *The standard rules on the equalization of opportunities for persons with disabilities*. Adopted by the United Nations General Assembly, forty-eighth session. Retrieved from http://www.un.org/esa/socdev/enable/dissre00.htm

United Nations. (2006). *Convention on the rights of persons with disabilities*. Retrieved from http://www.un.org/disabilities/convention/conventionfull.shtml

UNESCO. (2000). *The Dakar Framework for Action Education for All: Meeting our collective commitments*. Adopted by the World Education Forum. Dakar, Senegal 26th–28th April, 2000.

UNESCO. (1994). *The Salamanca statement and framework for action on special needs education*. Paris, France: Author. ED-94/WS/18

UNESCO. (2009). *Policy guidelines on inclusion in education*. Paris, France: Author. ED-2009/WS/31

Williams, S. (2007). *Trinidad and Tobago: Caribbean Symposium on Inclusive Education*. Retrieved from http://www.ibe.unesco.org/fileadmin/user_upload/Inclusive_Education/Reports/kingston_07/trinidad_tobago_inclusion_07.pdf

CHAPTER 12

THE INVISIBLE STUDENT

Engaging in A Courageous Conversation About Homosexuality and Formal Schooling in Jamaica

Andrew Campbell

WHY ENGAGE IN A COURAGEOUS CONVERSATION?

We must tell our own stories. Too often, we have allowed others to tell our story and when this happens, the characters are not given the credit they deserve. Not many of us have the ability and opportunity to speak up and speak out. I felt obligated as a researcher, lecturer of diversity studies in education and leadership and a person of influence to speak out. I believe it is my duty to give voice to others and to advocate for those who cannot do so for themselves. It is, therefore, my obligation as a scholar to use my platform to address issues and concerns of this vulnerable population: homosexual students within our Jamaican classrooms.

This work does just that—it gives a voice to Jamaican gay men who have been marginalized, ostracized, pushed aside for years within the setting of formal schooling. It gives a voice to the many young men in our schools today who are presently going through fear and intimidation each time they walk through the halls of their educational institution.

This work not only gives a voice but it offers a call to action—a call to action by parents to first love and accept their children and to foster trust and ensure the safety of home that many of our gay children have been denied. It calls to action educational stakeholders at all levels to stand as robust leaders, change agents, and advocates to provide quality education in a safe environment for all students, through the implementation of policies, authentic inclusive educational practices, and a genuine passion for student engagement. It is a call for our school agents—administrators, teachers, guidance counselors, parents, and students—to help in the creation and maintenance of school culture and climate that respects difference and diversity and ensure that all students are included in the educational process in formal schooling.

Many people are not ready to engage in a discussion on the issues of homosexuality. From my many disappointing interactions and conversations with present educators, I am even more stunned as I am again given the gruesome reminder that many of our educators are nowhere near prepared, open or willing to engage in such conversations. They are of the silly myth that if they don't talk about it, it is not a problem. Boxill et al. (2011) in research into homosexuality conducted in Jamaica, speak of the difficulty in getting Jamaicans to engage in a formal conversation around the issues:

> There are some challenges that sought to impede the process of gathering worthwhile information for the subject being investigated. It became progressively more difficult to organize the FGDs not only because of logistical issues as perhaps is a normal functionality, but more importantly because of the topic that was up for discussion. Many of the potential participants upon hearing of the topic were less than eager and some very adamant that they wanted no part of any discussion with homophobia and homosexuality as the headline. (p. 11)

More and more through global discussions, many school systems around the world are inviting stakeholders to discuss this issue: "Regrettably, there is no such public acknowledgment in Jamaica, or in the Caribbean where constructive conversations about sexual orientation are rare. There is also no discernible support in either the private or public sectors for ending discrimination and violence against LGBT people" (Fletcher, 2010, p. 12).

Let me state clearly that the intention of this chapter is not to promote a "gay agenda" as some would want to argue. The intention is to encourage Jamaicans to engage in a conversation, a needed conversation, a global conversation. So why is this conversation necessary? As Fletcher (2010) stated, "there has been a conspiracy of silence across generations that has rendered gays, lesbians, and bisexuals invisible. I am ashamed to admit that families, including my own, and social institutions, including churches, mosques, synagogues, schools, and the judicial/legal system, participated in this conspiracy of silence" (p. 4).

Many times, during this project, I wondered if a conversation was necessary or needed at this point. There are hundreds of blogs and articles about homosexuality easily accessible on the Internet. There is also always something in the news. But two things made me realize that this conversation was indeed necessary: there was not much literature available about the lived experiences of actual Jamaican gay men, and most of what is written comprises news articles, editorials and commentaries; and many of the available articles, blogs, commentaries that I have read in the past, writers and contributors were mostly preaching about homosexuality, talking at homosexuals, arguing about homosexuality—no one was having the needed conversation.

For years, we have not allowed a conversation. What we have instead are people who have the luxury of a platform such as local newspapers, blogs, and televisions to shout across the room. We shout across the room at each other using our freedom of religion, conviction and affiliation to make our voices heard. We shout across the room using our political voices. We shout across the room using our socializations, social locations, social status, social safety nets and social profile to defend who we are and establish what is socially acceptable and permissible by our own standards. We shout across the room using our lived experiences to assure others of what we know to be right, acceptable, valuable and moral. We shout across the room with our knowledge and education to inform and educate others about who we are, what they are and who we should be. We shout across the room and bring value to some and cheapen the lives of others. We shout across the room and when these voices collide, there is no real conversation. We shout words of hate, threats, condemnation, suspicion, and accusation. Where is the conversation? Where are the voices of actual young gay men who are directly affected by the voices living in a homophobic country such as ours?

This chapter is divided into three parts. Part one speaks of the purpose of engaging in a courageous conversation around the topic of homosexuality. Part two will focus on the conversations, which will be the response from the voices of the participants as they share their lived experiences during formal schooling. And part three will focus on the philosophy and arguments which echo the need for all stakeholders within the educational system to engage in this courageous conversation. In this chapter, there will be a number of strategic questions scattered among the findings for the purpose of reflection. I choose to leave these questions unanswered as they do not have a definite answer. Moreover, it is the intention that these questions will form a basis for which readers and educational stakeholders will invite and engage their peers in the conversation, as they reflect on their own actions, especially in regards to advocacy leadership, leading in a diverse educational environment and interrogating the terms of inclusive leadership.

PART I: THE PURPOSE OF A COURAGEOUS CONVERSATION

> I did not feel a lot of security. Most often than not I was often told I was not allowed to be the only person I knew how to be. I could not express myself through all the feminine energies. I had to be self-checking all the time. I also come from a family of five older brothers. My father tried to get me to not be so effeminate. So he just

avoided me. That itself brought on another set of emotions. I had to try to prove I was good enough. Wanting his approval was something that happened throughout my childhood. (Mike)

The motivation for engaging in this research emanated from an experience I had as a course writer and online lecturer for the University of the West Indies Open Campus in 2010. In order to understand the concept of diversity, difference and "otherness" in the Caribbean, I ventured to speak with a number of educators about the topic. I was shocked at the level of difficulty I had in getting educated individuals to engage in the conversation or share their honest opinion on issues affecting our students that may be perceived as being of a certain sexual orientation—homosexuals. I was taken aback as I had foolishly assumed that, since they were educators, they would have been more open-minded to such a conversation. Instead, what I found was much bitterness and poison.

This continued as I engaged a group of over 100 students online from over 14 different Caribbean countries. It became clear to me that there was a real concern. These were the very educators who had students in their classrooms who others may have perceived as being gay or others had excluded because of their effeminacy. These were teachers who had influence over these invisible students. So many refused to engage and when they did, it was full of dread and biblical damnation rants. For the first time, I really thought how "hostile" school could be for one of our marginalized and excluded population, particularly homosexuals.

Students who are perceived to be gay are often marginalized and excluded not only in the social interactions of school, but also in the formal dynamics of the learning process. A review of arguments revealed that, generally, researchers accept that between 3–10 percent of any given population are gay or lesbian. There is no such data on the Jamaican population, but in a study conducted by the Department of Sociology, Psychology and Social Work, at the University of the West Indies, Boxill et al. (2011) stated:

> Most Jamaicans (89 percent) believed that homosexuality is somewhat or very prevalent in Jamaica. Respondents also alluded to an association with this orientation and one's social class, as 66.8 percent felt that it was most prevalent among some social classes more than others. A significant 57.7 percent felt that it was most prevalent among the upper class, while 9 percent said it was most among the middle class and another 2 percent said it was most among the working class. (p. 2)

We should be reminded that our schools are indeed microcosms of our society. This would then mean that there is a significant number of gay, lesbian, bisexual and transgender (LGBT) youth in the education system. Because they are considered invisible, they have sat passively through school, having their identities ignored or denied. They remain invisible due to the fear of hostility. They have seen what others have experienced and the internalized fear they live with. The topic of homosexuality is taboo, rooted in fear and controversy, guarded by the "preaching of the gospel," and nurtured by the society's homophobia. They remain invisible.

One would think that there would be more engaging discussion, sensitization, tolerance and respect for diversity in a sex education class, Health and Family Life Education or a guidance session. In fact, these sessions can be some of the most uncomfortable and unsafe environments for homosexual students. Hunter (2012) states:

> There are some (guidance counselors) who, because their church doesn't believe in homosexuality, don't deal with the situation properly. But the stakeholders in education need to come on board and assist," said the teacher. In a letter to the editor of *The Gleaner*, the teacher argued that the Government and civil society have failed to adequately address the negative impact on human development, caused by the discrimination against youth who are perceived to be homosexuals. (para. 20–21)

Jamaica has been widely viewed as one of the most hostile places in the world for homosexuals.

Padgett (2006) opines:

> Rampant violence against gays and lesbians has promoted human-rights groups to confer another ugly distinction: the most homophobic place on earth ... Jamaica may be the worst offender, but much of the rest of the Caribbean also has a long history of intense homophobia. Islands like Barbados still criminalize homosexuality, and some seem to be following Jamaica's more violent example. (para. 2–4)

Homophobia is widespread and can be easily identified in the messages delivered in our political, religious, social, educational and general arena. The school is no different. In fact, many self-identified homosexuals today can give painful and disheartening reflection on their experience as a student in the Jamaican classroom. These experiences are filled with ways in which they were abused, marginalized and excluded solely based on the fact that they were perceived to be homosexual due to effeminacy or other actions deemed to be non-heterosexual. Homosexual students live in fear of their lives. They have a deep secret and must try, by all means, to protect it. This task is a full-time task for any child and involves loads of emotional stress and fatigue. They cannot share how they feel with peers, parents or school agents. They must remain invisible to survive. They must deny self to survive. They must become someone else to survive. They are one of the most "at risk" groups within our formal school system and the most ignored. Campos (2005) shares:

> No other group of youth suffers more than gay and lesbian youth. Indeed, the list for their potential risks is long. Imagine the psychological distress they experience when their peers use gay and lesbian epithets to humiliate one another, or when gay and lesbian issues are discussed in a pejorative way. Being gay and lesbian is a stigma in society, and gay and lesbian persons are rarely affirmed in schools. A boy who scribbles his name with another boy's name on his book cover to signify a romance is bound to be condemned, ridiculed, and ostracized at best, and verbally and physically assaulted at worst. (p. 19)

There is a lot of speculation about what happens to gay students or students who are perceived to be gay, in the Jamaican context. There are many shared experiences recorded through books and research from North America. To my knowledge, there is no research that speaks directly to the lived experiences of Jamaican gay men while in formal schooling. There are strong debates and statements launched through the media, most of which is opinion based. These articles are mostly commentary and often times do not draw upon local/national data. There is therefore a need for a more informed discussion and more importantly a need to give voices to those who have been directly affected by the dynamics of formal schooling. I chose to focus and situate this research in the formal school context, as these formative years are pivotal in the formation of character and self. Many of the decisions homosexual Jamaican men make today, whether they live in Jamaica or abroad, are still based on their lived experiences during formal schooling.

The reality for many of these young men is that school becomes a dangerous place. Many of them have attended school in fear, and have dropped out due to that same fear. These students are often abused by peers, teachers, administrators and other school agents, for displaying abnormal gender behavior. This has led to depression, decline in academic performance, truancy, lack of interest in school and suicide. Hussey-Whyte (2012) writes about a victim of schoolyard homosexual bullying:

> Things got worse in grade eight when the older students realized he wasn't like the other boys in school. His grades fell drastically and he became a truant, skipping classes and skipping school to avoid run-ins with bullies. "I knew what I was doing was wrong, but I didn't want to be in that hostile environment that I thought I had created for myself," he said. "I blamed myself for the situation I was in. I used to pray to God and ask him—and beg him—to change who I am. Most mornings I got up to go to school and stayed in bed and cried." John tried to assimilate into his school by paying close attention to the guys who were teasing him and mimicking them. He dressed the way they did, spoke the way they spoke and even copied how they did their hair. "I endeavored to emulate them," he said. "I wanted to belong, so I bleached my face. I started wearing tight pants. I curled my hair and dyed it jet black—ironically, isn't that how gays dress? Because that's how the 'popular' boys carried themselves" .... It was when I was in grade 11—my final year—that the school finally did something. This was after I was attacked on the street by a group of boys ... a group of boys who had in hand sticks and stones. This was after I learnt that students were taking knives to school to have fun with me." (para. 8–15)

Many of these young men have failed to blossom and to reach their true potential. Formal schooling for many of them has been one of the most hostile environments. They encountered a gendered curriculum where girls took home economics and boys were supposed to naturally gravitate to wood work and metal work. That same gendered environment instructed girls to join dance troupes and boys to become members of the football teams. That same gendered environment prescribed the Brownie Packs for girls and Scout Troops for boys. Woe unto the boy who dared to cross the gender line? The dynamics of formal schooling for homosexuals is a terrain to be negotiated. Who can they turn to? What help and refuge can be given by qualified, educated, licensed school agents, all classified as "caregivers?"

One writer posits:

> Also making schools unsafe places for gay and lesbian youth is the silence and homophobia of teachers and administrators. Because students look to teachers and administrators for guidance on information, attitudes, knowledge, and feelings, educators have a significant impact on the feelings and experiences of students—including homosexuality. Students perceive their teachers' attitudes and feelings through verbal and non-verbal cues… Some teachers and administrators harass, ridicule, or unfairly punish gay and lesbian students. However, the most prevalent type of discrimination within the school systems is the failure of school officials and teachers to protect gay and lesbian students from harassment and violence. (Diversity in Public Schools, n.d.)

We, however, continue to wish and hope that if we don't talk about it, they will remain invisible and even disappear. The reality is that many of these students are getting the information they need from other sources. In an age of Facebook, Twitter, and YouTube, nothing is too far from access. Our children are already exposed to various ideas through mass media, the internet, their families and peers, and pop culture. They will make their choice. If we continue to pretend that homosexuals do not exist it will not make them disappear. We must engage in healthy conversations about homosexuality in formal school and not sweep these matters of sexual orientation under the carpet; we cannot wish them away. For years we have attempted to hide information from our children, but many educators can share a story or two of children coming to school with X-rated magazines, photos, and videos. In an age where access is easy, these conversations should not be that hard.

Our society, being very homophobic in nature, has perpetuated this reality within formal schooling and society at large. Fire and destruction on the homosexual is preached from pulpits across the island. Our major newspapers are laden with bitterness, condemnation, and mockery at the homosexual lifestyle. The popular culture, in particular dancehall music, beckoned the masses to violence against homosexuals. This can be seen in the lyrics of one of Jamaica's most famous artist Buju Bonton (1992):

Boom bye
Inna batty bwoy head
Rudebwoy no promote no nasty man
Dem haffi dead…
Send fi di matican
Di Uzi instead
Shoot di batty boy

This same call for killing of homosexuals through the use of the very impactful dancehall music genre was followed by another hit by Jamaican dancehall group T.O.K. in 2001, with their song Chi Man, which speaks of burning of homosexuals:

> From dem a par inna chi chi man car
> Blaze di fire mek we bun dem!!!! (Bun dem!!!!)
> From dem a drink inna chi chi man bar
> Blaze di fire mek we dun dem!!!! (Dun dem!!!)

In the international scene, Jamaica is known to be very homophobic and a dangerous place for homosexuals. Padgett (2006) writes:

> In 2004, a teen was almost killed when his father learned his son was gay and invited a group to lynch the boy at his school. Months later, witnesses say, police egged on another mob that stabbed and stoned a gay man to death in Montego Bay. And this year a Kingston man, Nokia Cowan, drowned after a crowd shouting "batty boy" (a Jamaican epithet for homosexual) chased him off a pier. "Jamaica is the worst any of us has ever seen," says Rebecca Schleifer of the U.S.-based Human Rights Watch and author of a scathing report on the island's anti-gay hostility. (para. 3)

Many people are not ready to engage in a discussion on the issues of homosexuality. From my many disappointing interactions and conversations with present educators, I am even more stunned as I am again given the gruesome reminder that many of our educators are nowhere near prepared, open or willing to engage in such conversations.

PART II: EXPRESSIONS FROM THE CONVERSATION

Who Is Invisible?

This chapter seeks to share experiences of self-identified homosexual Jamaicans on their formal schooling experience from age 6–18 years, through reflection. It will seek to examine themes of gendered curriculum, teacher behavior, and the role of the guidance counselor, school leadership, parents, and peers in ensuring education for ALL. Kingston was listed as the parish where the largest number of respondents attended formal school, this number being 30 percent. St. Catherine, St. Andrew, St, James and Clarendon, rounded out the top five. Fifty-one percent of respondents are between the ages of 30–39, 28 percent between 18–29, 15 percent between 40–49, and the remaining 6 percent between 50–59. Sixty-seven percent of respondents had some form of university education/qualification, 17 percent had a college diploma and the remaining 16 percent had either a high school diploma or less. Fifty-one percent of respondents presently reside in Jamaica, 24 percent in Canada, 18 percent in the United States of America, and the remaining 6 percent in Europe (London and Spain).

When asked at what age they knew they were gay or different, 56 percent responded between the ages of 6–12 years, 27 percent between the ages of 13–15, 7 percent between 16—18, and the remaining 10 percent after age 19. Seventy-nine percent identified as gay, 16 percent as bisexual, 1 percent as questioning, and the remaining 4 percent as fluid. Sixty-one percent of the respondents subscribed to the arguments of nature/gene, as they believed they were born gay, 7 percent believed that being gay was a result of their environment, and the other 32 percent believed that being gay was a combination of both the nature and nurture arguments. A total of 90 percent of respondents knew they were gay or identified themselves as gay during primary school to high school. What does that mean for teaching? What does that mean for student engagement? What does that mean in a classroom that promotes culturally responsive teaching?

At age 11 I knew I was different. I knew I had to keep it quiet. My parents were homophobic and I understood things from an early age. I felt left out and miserable. There was no one to talk to and no one who understood me. Going to them would not work. (Teddy)

I am gay. It is kind of complicated but not complicated. I do acknowledge that I have a male anatomy but I live my life through a female experience. I am perfectly fine with the duality that I expressed. (Mike)

Forming and Maintaining Relationships in Formal Schooling

The majority of the respondents (76 percent) believed that their sexuality or perceived sexuality affected their relationships at school with their peers and teachers. It impacted what clubs they joined, it impacted what groups they were included in or allowed in and it impacted who became their friends. One of the focus group members explained that during his childhood he wanted to be with the girls because he couldn't connect with the boys. He always knew what he wanted to study. His teacher asked him, "wahkindabwoy are you?" At this time of uncertainty, many participants clearly did not know what to do or how to explain their feelings. Many were scared; they knew that what they felt was wrong by society's standards. They knew this from hearing the stories about other people and the names they were called. They knew this from the bitter and hated words that would be hurled at them and others who may have been effeminate. They knew something was "wrong" with them. How would they react? How should they react? Who could they tell? Who should they tell? Should they tell? These would be the questions of an invisible student, living in fear and suffering in silence.

Most gay students are either pushed or pulled into certain clubs and sorting areas/groups in school. Gay students find each other and form their own community of acceptance in school. They do this as a means of survival in high school. These young men were pushed to the edges. They were excluded in formal school. There are many layers that allow someone to feel excluded. There are many feelings that accompany such fear and confusion for a young child.

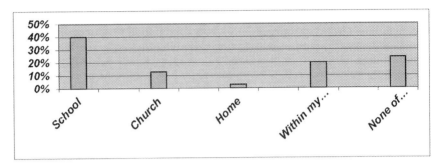

FIGURE 12.1. Places Where Students Felt Most Hated, Discriminated, or Excluded.

Safe Schools

When asked where they felt most hated, discriminated or excluded, 40 percent of respondents named school; another 20 percent said in their community; 11 percent identified church; 4 percent at home; and 25 percent reported that they did not feel discriminated or excluded in any of the listed spaces. What, then, are the implications for the impact on learning and development for the 40 percent? How do we ensure these students are engaged in the learning process? What steps can we take as educators to ensure a significant move from exclusion to inclusion? We will extend the conversations further in this chapter as we look at Education for All (EFA) as a framework for change during our conversation.

Table 12.1 summarizes the various negative experiences faced by homosexual students in schools as shared by participants. The most popular one was name-calling. Sixty-eight percent of respondents shared that they were called names, followed closely by verbal insults with 57 percent of respondents. Anti-gay remarks hurled at 56 percent and 45 percent confided that they were being bullied in one way or another. Twenty-two percent of respondents had objects thrown at them and 20 percent of respondents had their personal property damaged or destroyed. Thirteen percent of respondents reported being punched, hit, or kicked and 9 percent reported having been beaten. Another 9 percent listed others to include threats made on their lives. Four percent of respondents reported that they were spat upon and 3 percent of respondents reported being sexually assaulted. Twelve percent of respondents did not experience any of the above bad treatment. Lipkin (1999) states:

> Fear of exposure and alienation from community keeps young victims from seeking services and from reporting incidents to school personnel. Even adults who are attacked are known to remain silent to avoid being revealed or because they fear a hostile or indifferent police response. Indeed, most jurisdictions lack privacy protocols and general awareness of victims' concerns. (p. 147)

TABLE 12.1. Participant's Experiences at School

Experiences	Percentage	Number
Name-calling	68%	47
Verbal insults	57%	39
Anti-gay remarks	55%	38
Bullying	45%	31
Objects thrown	22%	15
Personal property damaged or destroyed	20%	14
Punched, hit, kicked	13%	9
Beaten	9%	6
Other	9%	6
Spat upon	4%	3
Sexually assaulted	3%	2
None of the above	12%	8

Most participants reported being called some of the most derogatory terms being used in Jamaica today. Sixty-nine percent of respondents were called sissy, 80 percent called gal, gal-boy or girl, 49 percent called batty-man, 37 percent faggot, 34 percent chi-chi, and 25 percent were called gay.

> *It was a constant feeling and dread of being harmed for me. You would always hear the whispers and the things that would be said about who you might be and what you might be. There are times I felt like someone would hurt me physically. I can remember when I was in grade 9 and there was no teacher in the class and the prefect came in and focused on me among all the other kids and slapped me in my face in front of everyone. He knew I was an easy target and wanted an excuse to hit me for the way I behaved. He was trying to keep me in check. I made a report and nothing came of it. I knew school was not a safe haven.* (Mike)

> *I was scared when coming from school many times having to walk past groups of boys who would bellow out remarks.* (Cameron)

> *I was called names. I remember when I was in 3rd form in a religious studies class and the teacher told the class to be careful of the boys who are quiet and don't talk much because they are usually gay. My PE teacher beat me once saying why was I good at the theoretical part of sports but could not play sports. I got teased a lot. However, I used to run very fast and he told me the reason why I ran so was because I ran like ten batty man.* (Obrien)

I was called several of the names listed and at the time I felt belittled, dirty, out of place in gender and society, and in-humane. (Teddy)

In Jamaican schools, homosexual students are targeted for bullying. As a matter of fact, effeminate boys are easy targets." Many people, in my company workshops, however, recall hearing the words 'faggot,' 'sissy,' 'fairy,' and 'queer' hurled like missiles at kids who seemed in any way different on the playground" (Fletcher, 2010, p. 10). Psychologist Claudine Hyatt, who heads the Department of Psychology, Counselling and Allied Services at Mico Care Centre, in Hunter (2012) remarked:

> I have anecdotal evidence of individuals coming in who have been bullied, they have been physically attacked, they have been verbally abused individuals, oftentimes these persons pursue or contemplate suicide as a means of resolving the unrest that they experience in their interpersonal relationship. As you can imagine, someone's sexuality is almost similar to their personality in that it is a part of their identity and so in Jamaica when we engage in homophobic bullying you are saying to the individual that they should repudiate who you are; they should get rid of that part of them," added Hyatt. (para 6–7)

Ms. Hyatt, in the same article, made the call for sensitization programmes to help our students to become more acceptable of peoples' decisions. She articulated the need for a curriculum that promotes respect for diversity and acceptance for differences. She suggested that tolerance should not just be promoted but taught to our students as a measure to reduce homophobic bullying. Homophobic bullying within the formal school system can result in a number of adverse experiences for the homosexual student. These include decline in grades, drop out, emotional isolation, sexual abuse, substance abuse, sexually transmitted diseases, low self-esteem, prostitution, physical and verbal abuse, homelessness and suicide.

PART III: STAKEHOLDERS' RESPONSIBILITY TO ENGAGE IN A COURAGEOUS CONVERSATION

As we move forward in this conversation, let us think of the ways that we will engage the following stakeholders in the conversation—educational policymakers, educational leaders (principals), community players, teacher preparation programmes, classroom teachers, guidance counselors, parents and students. All these stakeholders must be invited to this conversation. They should be encouraged to come to the conversation knowing and understanding their roles and the impact they have on the development of our students.

Education for all should be the framework by which we invite all stakeholders to take responsibility and engage in the conversation through policy and practice, leadership and advocacy, inclusion and access and teaching and engagement. Education for all is about access. These ideas of access and education for all go beyond the scope of basic classroom provisions, and extend to the community, our values and ethics as educational leaders and the level of responsibility we feel for social justice and issues of equality (Campbell, 2010, p. 197). School is about people: people who should be committed to change and advocacy and the effective inclusion of all students in our schools, regardless of race, class, gender, socio-economic status, abilities and sexual orientation. These people are important and essential to the conversation as their immediate actions can create the impetus for change.

Education for all should be seen as a basic human right. The task, therefore, is for stakeholders at all levels of the educational hierarchy to ensure that we bring tangible solutions to the conversation to foster development of a more inclusive school culture and climate and provide the evidence of change that is needed. The United Nations agreement outline, in the Rights of the Child, spells out certain basic human rights that every child under the age of 18 should be given. The right to survival, the right to develop to the fullest, to be protected from harmful influences, abuse, and exploitation and to participate fully in family, cultural and social forms part of these rights. Are our homosexual students in school truly protected and given the opportunity to develop to their fullest without fear of harm? Bernard (2001) states:

> *Each child counts.* The Convention on the Rights of the Child (CRC) affirms the right of *all* children to relevant and good quality education. It confirms the belief of many cultures that there is a social contract and moral commitment on the part of states to ensure the equity and well-being of all citizens. It brings the moral weight of an international instrument to propel a major shift in perspective for states and donors as they implement action to achieve Education for All (EFA). The CRC reconfirms the EFA imperative of an "expanded vision." (p. 2)

It is time all stakeholders, led by educational leaders, think about their part of the conversation and then respond during and after the conversation. The conversation is not one of what do we do with our gay students, but one of how do we include and protect the rights of all students, acknowledging that gay students do exist within our schools. They are not as invisible as we assumed, since their visibility has led them to be ridiculed, hurt, excluded and abused in many circumstances. As educational leaders, and creators and maintainers of the formal educational space, we have to begin with the very school culture and climate. Campbell (2010) states:

> School culture is what we make it, and the kind of culture that a school will have depends highly on the stakeholders involved. A great school culture can foster effectiveness, productivity, collegiality, collaboration, communication, problem-solving practices, promote innovation and school improvement, build commitment and motivation, and it can rejuvenate the vitality of the staff, students and community. In the same breath, a toxic culture can rip a school apart and leave people wondering what went wrong. (p. 139)

It is hoped that a conversation of this nature will lead to change within the education system. It will lead to educational leaders, teachers and all stakeholders within formal schooling to truly understand the urgency of inclusion and advocacy for all students, and understanding the educational and psychological impact that has for years burdened a percentage of our school population and provided access, both in policy and practice, for these students to enjoy their educational experience. Campbell (2010) writes:

> This change must be seen at all levels of the educational provision hierarchy and involving all stakeholders and of course especially the students themselves who identify as LGBT. True, we all come into the profession with our own views on the issue. It is imperative that no matter how we feel about the inclusiveness of everyone that we foster a positive environment that seek to understand and encourage children to be themselves. Teenage years are some of the most difficult years as it is. Having the stigma as a pariah sanctioned by the very system and individuals whose jobs are to protect our children goes against everything they should stand for. (p. 138)

What therefore are some practical guidelines and starting points of action for stakeholders to ensure education for all (EFA):

1. Educational policies on sexual orientation should be developed. There are already basic policies of discrimination within our educational system. These should be enhanced and ensure that the wording is clear on the protection of all students, clearly stating sexual orientation as a category;
2. Curriculum- and school-based educational literature should be developed from research that will inform and educate teachers and guidance counselors. We cannot allow our educational system to base their information on media sensationalization and propaganda. Educators are leaders and change agents and this should begin with curriculum development grounded in research;
3. Specialized training for school counselors on right practices in dealing with students who have self-identified as homosexuals and promoting schools as safe spaces through their practice and the ability to provide or direct students to resources that promote healthy living for homosexuals;
4. Teacher education programs at the college and university levels should develop more courses on diversity, inclusion, and advocacy;
5. Training for school leaders in inclusive education, diversity leadership and advocacy. Ensuring that school leaders understand importance of human rights, legal and ethical practices and their own responsibility and accountability in light of the principles of EFA;
6. The ministry of education should seek to promote inclusion and to value diversity through educational campaigns that include all stakeholders. The ministry of education must lead the charge in partnership with other stakeholders in educating the public on right practices in diversity;
7. The formation of partnerships with community players and advocacy groups to engage in the conversation and assist in informing policies and right practices;
8. School must lead the charge in educating parents on students who have self-identified as homosexuals. There is also the need to educate all par-

ents on basic human rights principles and this can be done through Parent Teachers Associations (PTA);
9. Educating all our students to respect all their fellow students. This can be done through aggressive campaigns around exclusion and bullying.

CONCLUSION

The time has come for all of us as stakeholders to engage in the conversation. While we refuse to engage in a conversation, and acknowledge the existence and vulnerability of our invisible population, those students remain excluded, abused, bullied and marginalized within a system that promises to create educational opportunity for all. Dialogue will impact change and signal an authentic approach to inclusive leadership and practices: "For school communities to promote critical consciousness and inclusive communities generally, they need to nurture dialogue" (Ryan, 2009, p. 119).

We cannot sit back and be complacent when a percentage of our students is being ignored and neglected. We cannot be satisfied that society's view of homosexuals will also be transferred within the walls of our school. Schools are incubators of change, educational leaders are change agents and advocates and the school will lead the wider community through to understand the need for visibility through systematic educational change, beginning with courageous conversations.

REFERENCES

Bernard, A. K. (2000). *Education for All 2000 Assessment. Thematic studies: Education for all and children who are excluded.* UNESCO. Paris, France. Retrieved from http://unesdoc.unesco.org/images/0012/001233/123330e.pdf

Boxill, I., Martin, J., Russell, R., Waller, L., Meikle, T., & Micthell, R. (2011). *National survey of attitude and perceptions of Jamaicans towards same sex relationships.* Retrieved from http://ufdc.ufl.edu/AA00003178/00001

Campbell, A. (2010) *Responding to diversity though education and policy.* Course material—EDLM1001. University of the West Indies Open Campus. UWIOC.

Campos, D. (2005) *Understanding Gay and Lesbian youth: Lesson for straight school teachers, counselors and administrators.* Lanham, MD: Rowman and Litterfield.

Chi-chi man. (2001). *Kingston.* Retrieved from https://www.youtube.com/watch?v=_3OD3n4-Cvo

Diversity in Public High Schools. (n.d.). *A look at the experience of Gay and Lesbian students.* Retrieved from http://www.mtholyoke.edu/~rlsmith/gayandlesbianadolescents.html

Fletcher, S. A. (2010). *The dance of difference book 1, the new frontier of sexual orientation, learning to value our common humanity.* Bethesda, MD: Pearson Publishing.

Hunter, N. (2012, July, 1). School bullies target effeminate boys. *The Gleaner.* Retrieved from http://jamaica-gleaner.com/gleaner/20120701/news/news2.html

Hussy-Whyte, D. (2012, May, 20). I tried my best to be manly, gay man says. *Jamaican Observer.* Retrieved from http://www.jamaicaobserver.com/news/I-tried-my-best-to-be-manly-gay-man-says_11504331

Lipkin, A. (1999). *Understanding homosexuality, changing schools*. Boulder, CO: Westview Press.
Padgett, T. (2006, April 12). The most homophobic place on earth? *Time World*. Retrieved from http://www.time.com/time/world/article/0,8599,1182991,00.html
Ryan, J. (2006). *Inclusive leadership*. Hoboken, NJ: Jossey-Bass.

CHAPTER 13

LISTENING TO THE VOICES OF CHILDREN WITH LEARNING DISABILITIES (LD) AND OR ATTENTION DEFICIT HYPERACTIVITY DISORDER (ADHD) ON THEIR EXPERIENCES OF TRANSITIONING TO HIGH SCHOOL

Dawn-Marie Keaveny

Research on issues that affect children has highlighted the need to listen to children's perspectives on issues that affect them (Morrow & Richards, 1996). This author conducted a small ethnographic research involving six students aged thirteen to fifteen, who were identified as having a learning disability (LD) and/or attention-deficit hyperactivity disorder (ADHD). LD is considered to be a language-based, neurological disorder that affects the way an individual perceives, processes, stores, retrieves and produces information (Scanlon, 2013). The Amer-

Caribbean Discourse in Inclusive Education:
Historical and Contemporary Issues, pages 225–243.
Copyright © 2017 by Information Age Publishing
All rights of reproduction in any form reserved.

ican Individuals with Disabilities Education Act (IDEA) defines LD as "a disorder in one or more of the basic psychological processes involved in understanding and using language ... which may manifest itself in an imperfect ability to listen, think, speak, read, write, spell, or do mathematical calculations ..." (Federal definition 1975, cited in Hallahan, Kauffman, & Pullen, 2009, p. 187). Jamaica uses the definition provided by IDEA to define LD. There are different types of LD; the most common are dyslexia (problems with reading), dyscalculia (problems with mathematics), and dysgraphia (problems with writing). The prevalence rate for LD in Jamaica is 7 percent of all school-age students (Dixon & Matalon, 2009).

ADHD is described as a disorder characterized by symptoms of inattention, hyperactivity and impulsiveness. The prevalence rate for ADHD in Jamaica among primary school children is 3 percent, but an alarming 19.6 percent demonstrated high levels of inattention, and hyperactivity (Pottinger, 2010). There is a high co-occurrence rate for LD and ADHD, since between 31–45 percent of students with ADHD also have LD (DuPaul, Gormley, & Laracy, 2013). Among the students who participated in the research 50 percent had LD only (dyslexia, dyscalculia & non-verbal learning disability), 33 percent had both LD and ADHD, and 17 percent had ADHD only.

The students attended four different traditional high schools in Jamaica. Since 2000, several secondary schools were upgraded and are now termed high schools. The term traditional high school is used to distinguish the former high schools from the newly upgraded high schools (Evans, 2001, p. 12). The students' schools all had religious affiliations, and were located in urban areas of Kingston. The oldest school was established in the early 1700s and the newest in the late 1960s. The schools included two all-girls schools, one all-boy school, and one co-educational school. Traditional high schools were selected because as Hyacinth Evans (2001) research confirms, traditional high schools are more likely to have better facilities, better resources and more highly qualified teachers. Additionally, Evans notes that they also produce better academic outcomes.

Although children's voices are increasingly being accepted as valid sources of information, the voices of children with disabilities remain conspicuously silent. The aim of the research was to gain insight into the school experiences of these students to better understand the challenges they may have in transitioning to high school. The questions guiding the research were: how is transitioning to high school perceived by students with LD and or ADHD? What support do high schools offer these students? What supports do these students perceive as helpful? What is the role of social capital, social networks and sense of belonging on students' transition experiences? And what are the implications for the future?

This chapter presents the students' voices from the research and highlights four factors that emerged as having an impact on the students' experiences of high school: pedagogy, ableism, the hidden curriculum and social networks.

METHODOLOGY

Sonali Shah, a disabled researcher, has done research that focuses on giving voice to persons with disabilities; she argues that there is value in accepting young people's views in understanding issues that affect their lives (Shah, 2006). This qualitative research focused on understanding students' perspectives of high school. The participants included four girls and two boys, and were selected based on their being identified with having LD and or ADHD. They were accessed through their schools and their parents. All the participants came from middle- and upper-middle-class backgrounds and lived with both parents. The participants sat the GSAT examination in grade six and were placed by the Ministry of Education in high schools. Only one participant was placed in his first choice school; however, all the students had transferred from their school of placement to the schools they presently attend.

Interviews were used to give students the opportunity to be heard. Three separate face-to-face interviews, of one hour each, were conducted over a four-month period, along with a telephone and group interview. The data collected from these interviews were analyzed using thematic analysis. There is no clear definition for thematic analysis, but it involves searching across a data set to find repeated patterns of meaning (Braun & Clarke, 2006), and is a widely-used qualitative analytic method (Boyatzie, 1998, cited by Braun & Clarke, 2006). Thematic analysis is commonly used to understand transcribed conversations collected from ethnographic interviews (Aronson, 1994) and is often associated with grounded theory, discourse analysis and narrative analysis. Braun and Clarke (2006) argue that thematic analysis is a method in its own right, as it is an effective method for identifying, analyzing and reporting patterns (themes) within data.

The children's conversations were audio recorded, transcribed and analyzed. A system of color coding was used to locate points of reference and compare responses. Important words, repeated words, commonalities and differences were coded as markers of possible significance. The color-coded selections were inductively and deductively analyzed to identify specific themes in the text. Themes are "topics that occur and re-occur" (Ryan & Bernard, 2003) in the data. Nine specific themes were identified: teachers, teaching and learning, perceptions of self, perceptions of school, friendships, belonging, supports, note-taking and homework. These themes were re-examined, and four general themes emerged: pedagogy, ableism, the hidden curriculum, and social networks. For example, the specific themes of friendships, belonging, perception of self, and note taking all related to the general theme of social networks.

Some specific themes were linked to more than one general theme. For example, teaching and learning related to pedagogy when teaching methodology was considered, but certain unspoken expectations and assumptions also made it suitable for placement under the hidden curriculum. This showed there was an interrelationship between the themes.

This author deduced that the theories of social capital (Bourdieu, 1986; Coleman, 1998; Putnam, 2000) and sense of belonging (Ma, 2003, and Beck & Mally, 1998) made them applicable as theoretical themes or anchors that could be useful in explaining the students' experiences of high school. Social capital is described by Pierre Bourdieu as the sum of capital an individual has, or has access to, through their membership in social networks (Bourdieu, 1986). Students who have well-functioning social networks (friendships) are likely to have large sources of social capital, and this is likely to have an impact on their experiences of school. Having a sense of belonging is a fundamental need (Maslow, 1962). In the school environment, a sense of belonging refers to students feeling that they are important and respected members of their school (Booker, 2004).

The hidden curriculum, ableist assumptions, social networks and pedagogy can have an impact on students' sense of belonging, and ultimately their perceptions of school. Based on the information collected from the students it would appear that having access to social capital and having a sense of belonging can help students in navigating their high school experiences. It would also appear that both these can support a smoother transition experience.

PEDAGOGY

Pedagogy can be considered to be the art and science of teaching. The art refers to the creative aspects of *how* teachers teach, and the science refers to the research and the theoretical framework that supports *what* teachers teach. Based on the themes that emerged from the students' stories, it appears that the pedagogical practices of many teachers were highly teacher-centred and focused on presenting the academic curriculum through traditional methods.

The students expressed strong feelings about what and how they were being taught and were critical of their teachers. "Learning is boring because of the way things are taught—mostly through reading and writing—it's the same every day" (Megan).

The students felt what they learned was often irrelevant to their life experiences. They wanted learning to be interesting, and they wanted to be active participants. They struggled to stay engaged in class because of the teachers' methodology. Amelia felt that "some subjects seem pointless, not really relevant." And Lee argued that "people say learning is a fun experience, but school is a boring thing; it doesn't really make sense."

The children's stories suggest the following pedagogical sub-themes significantly influence how they experience school: (1) traditional teaching; (2) teaching methodology and technology; (3) how teachers' pedagogy has an impact on children's sense of belonging; and (4) pedagogical practices that children perceive as oppressive.

Traditional Pedagogy

The students found the traditional lecture method used by many teachers to be boring. Julianne explained "When the teacher is just talking and you are just listening you get bored and you tend to sleep." It is possible that many teachers continue to use the lecture method in their classrooms because it provides structure, and allows easy dissemination of information. This method however, encourages passive learning, and is associated with poor retention (Long, 2012). It can also be an ineffective method to use with students who have language-based disorders and attention difficulties.

Listening to lectures, identifying the important points, and recording the information in a legible form assumes a certain level of language competence. This places students with language-based disorders, such as LD, at a disadvantage. Julianne explains how taking notes while trying to listen to a lecture can be confusing, "I cannot take notes in class … I can't catch the notes fast enough … when I am focusing on listening, when I am writing I tend to slow down, and I don't really understand."

In order to engage students in learning activities, teachers need to be creative, present pedagogy that is interesting and fosters creative thinking, and help students to see the relevance in what they are learning. The students' stories seem to indicate that this is not how they experience school. Lee's comments reflect his frustration: "I don't really like school because it's pretty boring—just writing on the board, having to take notes and doing tests … and some subjects are irrelevant … teach things that you are going to actually need."

Pedagogy and the Age of Technology

> They could use electronic means, they prefer markers and whiteboards but a power point would be better because we could go back and check the notes. This is good for students who can't write fast and they could email notes and you could get it at home. (Lee)

Today's generation of students is increasingly technology-savvy, and classrooms without access to popular technology are likely to increase the gap between what happens inside school, and what happens in students' experiences outside it. Research heavily supports the benefits of using technology in the classroom. Main and O'Rourke (2011) have argued that "using technology in the classroom in measured and thoughtful ways is likely to provide a stimulating environment for today's students" (p. 45). Downes (2002) supports this position and states that "educators need to recognize the discontinuity that exists between the learning affordances of the computer and the traditional pedagogies of classrooms" (pp. 31–32) and find ways to engage students in learning through more effective use of computers in the classroom. Likewise, Johnson and Gooliaff (2013) suggest that teachers should provide more opportunities for children to utilize their technological skills and engage in authentic learning, as this is likely to be more effective than a lecture or a teacher-driven approach (p. 5).

The students in this research were often not engaged in learning when teachers used traditional methods such as lectures and the chalk and board to present information. When students are not engaged with learning tasks they are likely to perform poorly and are unlikely to make the classroom gains expected of them (Main & O'Rourke, 2011, p. 43). As children become increasingly more computer savvy, they develop skills, dispositions and ways of learning that are likely to widen the gap between learning with technology and learning at school (Downes 2002, p. 32).

Teachers, Pedagogy, and Belonging

The students mostly shared negative feelings about their teachers, and those who had the strongest negative impressions of teachers also seemed to have greater challenges in school, and a stronger ambiguity about their sense of belonging. Lee observed that,

> "I don't really like school, the teachers don't really help you so you just have to take a lot more effort and it's hard because you try extremely hard, but it doesn't help because you are still not doing as well as the teacher wants." The practices of some teachers have a negative impact on their relationship with students, making students feel a sense of alienation. Giselle noted that "the maths teacher gets angry, so I am afraid to ask questions and some teachers ... the way they speak to you makes you feel uneasy."

Teachers have a responsibility to create classroom relationships that serve students' interests and should provide emotionally safe spaces for students to learn. Ben, who transferred to a different school during the research period, shared his experience at his new school "Where I am now, the teachers are more enthusiastic and will go out of their way to help you, they are eager to help and so you will ask without fear." This suggests, teachers at Ben's new school are perceived to be more interested in students and this increases students' motivation to learn.

Students feel motivated to learn in an environment in which they feel a sense of belonging. Ma (2003) argues that students' sense of belonging to school has social consequences (p. 340), while Edwards and Mullis (2001) contend that belonging affects academic success because when students feel they belong, they are more likely to perform proficiently, competently and responsibly (p. 197). The students in this research presented a picture of some teachers as harsh, unapproachable and uninterested. These perceptions are likely to affect teacher/student relationships, the sense of belonging, and motivation for learning. The following extracts suggest that some teachers' actions in the classroom serve to confuse rather than support students, and this may cause students to question whether they belong in the class.

I don't like any of the teachers. They give detentions and they give homework. The teachers don't know how to do their job properly because they are supposed to answer the questions, that's what they are supposed to do and they don't help anybody learn. (Lee)

There was no enthusiasm coming from the teacher. Teaching seemed like it was a bother, like they didn't want to teach us. It never seemed as if they wanted the best for us. (Ben, referring to his previous school)

Ma (2003) stated that "students perceive teachers who are attentive, respectful and helpful as caring and concerned about their social and academic wellbeing, which gives students a sense of belonging and fosters their academic engagement" (p. 341). Children are likely to fail in school when they feel alienated and isolated from others and from the educational process (Beck & Malley, 1998). In spite of the distant relationships the students had with many of their teachers, most of the students in this research felt a sense of belonging to their school. It is likely that the children's sense of belonging was protected by the quality of their social relationships and the family ties they had at school. This was an interesting insight since most of the literature on belonging focuses on the teacher's role in establishing the student's sense of belonging. The perspectives shared by the students indicate that friendships and family ties also appear to be significant factors in establishing feelings of belonging and may be particularly important when the teacher-student relationship is weak. Giselle stated: "I like my school. All my family went there. If I went to another school I would feel like a traitor." Megan's comment also supports the argument that family helps in supporting a sense of belonging "I feel more comfortable in the environment—I think it's just the right school for me and my sisters go there."

The students' social networks played a significant role in their experiences of school. It was through peers and social connections that the students received support for their academic and social life. When students have weak social networks, and experience poor student-teacher relationships, they seem to experience strong anti-school sentiments. Lee expresses his anger with school: "I go to school because I am forced to, I don't go by choice, the teachers are dunces, they cannot teach up to an acceptable standard, and I didn't care about belonging …" However when students feel connected to school, either through friendships, family ties or close teacher relationships, their perceptions of school are more positive as seen in Julianne's comment: "I feel accepted at school like people understand me. I would say the whole school is my friend. I feel more comfortable socially." Family ties and friendships seem to create a strong bond between the students and their school and act as a buffer to the challenges the students experience in the classroom.

Pedagogy and Note Taking

A large area of concern for the students was the volume of note-taking demanded in their schools. The focus on taking large amounts of notes, often dictated, fits with a teacher-centred pedagogy and a view that children are passive consumers rather than active, capable, thinking human beings (Gale & Densmore, 2000).

The academic curriculum encourages a teacher-centred pedagogy and focuses on delivering certain content and then testing to see whether it had been retained (Smith, 2012). This type of methodology embraces a pen and paper type of learning, and for students who have challenges with writing this is likely to place them at a disadvantage. None of the students in this research had note-takers and so they had to write their own notes. Accommodation was not made for their challenges with note–taking, and this often resulted in inadequate or poorly taken notes.

The students had mixed feelings about note taking. They could see the benefits of having notes, but had different perspectives on how notes should be given (written on the board, hand-outs, emailed or taped). The students' comments reflect the lack of accommodation they receive, and also indicated that they may lack strategic note-taking skills which are essential if they are to be efficient note takers.

Boyle (2011) argues that, for the average middle-schooler, note-taking during lectures can be a demanding process (p. 52). Effective note taking requires students to be able to listen attentively to the lecture, select the salient points, use appropriate abbreviations, rephrase information succinctly and record relevant information in an organized manner that can later be read for review or study purposes (Boyle, 2011). This can be a daunting task for students identified with ADHD as they are likely to have attention problems and may have difficulty dividing their attention between listening and writing. Students identified as having LD may have challenges with understanding, remembering, or processing what they hear, or they may be unable to spell words correctly or write legibly.

Giselle expresses her challenges in this area and her preference for teachers to write notes on the board, rather than dictate them, as this acts as a support for note-taking and provides a visual aid to her learning.

> I would prefer if they wrote notes on the board. I like that so I can get all the notes, spell the words right and I don't miss anything. If I had a choice, I'd type notes instead of writing. I don't like to take notes there is a lot of spelling and your hands hurt. (Giselle)

The participants suggested teachers could be more accommodating by providing easier access to notes, possibly through providing hand-outs or emailing the notes: "I prefer hand-outs so I don't have to write it" (Amelia). "I don't like writing. I'd prefer to record the notes. It's unnecessary [writing notes] and teachers give a lot of notes" (Lee). Ben did not mind taking notes because he felt they helped him to remember information. He explained, "I really don't like hand-outs. I use different colored pens, it keeps the notes neat, and while I'm writing I say it in my mind so it helps to stick even more."

ABLEISM

Ableism is a concept that views individuals within a framework of normalcy. Smith, Foley, and Chaney (2008) argue that ableism is a form of discrimination against individuals with disabilities and believes disability represents abnormality or a deficit rather than a dimension of difference (p. 304). Ableism expects individuals with disabilities to do things in the way "normal" people do.

Ableist views can influence how schools operate and how teachers teach, placing individuals with disabilities at a disadvantage. When teachers expect all students to learn the same things, in the same way, and at the same rate, they are practicing ableism. For example, participants shared their experiences with ableist assumptions when teachers failed to acknowledge their learning differences: Amelia explains that "the teacher assumes everyone understands and she moves ahead. Teachers lack sensitivity to the fact that many students with LD and ADHD require more time to think, and remember information. Giselle noted that "when I ask the teachers, they say, we did that in class, you should remember, but I don't."

Teachers practice ableist pedagogy when they pursue a one-size-fits-all approach to teaching, and are indifferent to student diversity. Lee's comment demonstrates how teachers fail to accommodate students with learning challenges:

> They do not respond to children differently who have LD and this is bad because you can't teach someone who like learns by listening, the same way like a student who can just write down notes and read it to themselves; and students who can't focus well will probably need something to help them focus on the topic. (Lee)

Giselle, who has ADHD, felt teachers did not seem to know how to help her in class: "I don't focus well and my mom writes a letter every time I get a new teacher, but they don't do anything about it, like giving me extra time."

Teachers perform within an ablest philosophy when they impose requirements that demand students with disabilities behave and learn in the same ways that nondisabled students do. This places disabled children at a distinct disadvantage (Hehir, 2002):

> Sometimes my teacher does not accept that I don't understand and she punishes me, like demand I write the same homework over, or get lunch detention. This means the bell rings for lunch but I have to stay back, then the lines are longer, and there is less food and what is left is more expensive food. Sometimes I don't eat and I feel sick, and I get tired and can't focus. I would prefer the teacher would explain to me what I don't understand instead of punishing me. (Amelia)

Teachers who have ableist assumptions may be unaware of the impact their practices have on students with disabilities, and this can prevent them from recognizing, for example, that not allowing a student with dyslexia to use a computer is likely to greatly diminish the student's ability to produce acceptable written work (Hehir, 2007, p. 17). Hehir further explains that an unwillingness to be flexible in how students access and or present information can lead to children with LD experiencing lowered educational attainment. The students in this research spoke about their difficulty with taking dictated notes such as: speed of writing, spelling difficulties and problems with focusing. Although this has resulted in gaps in their notes, and in some cases notes that were unintelligible, teachers failed to make accommodation within their practices for these students.

Failing to grasp information quickly, and writing lengthy responses, presented challenges for some students. These academic challenges were not accommodated, as students are expected to fit in with "normal" expectations. Teachers who practice ableist beliefs are likely to contribute to students feeling badly about themselves, resulting in these students experiencing lowered self-confidence and lowered self-efficacy. Lee is forced to write notes in spite of the challenges this poses for him, ultimately affecting his ability to take proper notes and to study from his notes. Lee noted that "My writing is difficult to read. My writing is not as bad as before, but it's still pretty difficult to read, I'm not good at spelling and sometimes I get distracted and I find it difficult to read notes I have taken."

Other participants shared experiences that demonstrate ableist practices within the classroom. These practices reflect teachers' expectations that may be unfair to students with disabilities. Julianne explained that "if the teacher could actually slow down or actually stop sometimes and give me the paper so I could get the notes to write; they could continue to read from the paper while I am writing, or just put the notes up on a website and then I could go there and get them." Amelia's anxiety about her performance is reflected in her comments: "I always feel like I am way behind in class so I feel annoyed and I get really stressed … it takes longer for me to understand, the teachers just go on … and the teachers get annoyed or bothered when you don't understand. I pretty much lie and say I understand it because I can tell they are getting annoyed."

Ableist beliefs can be concealed in the curriculum and promote exclusionary practices because ableism focuses on the "ideal" student. In the ablest curriculum, students are expected to read grade-level texts, and use language and skills with the same dexterousness as everyone else. These practices are likely to be more exclusive than inclusive because students are likely to have difficulty accessing information that is presented in ways that disregard their disability.

Although students differ in terms of their needs, interests, abilities and learning styles ableist beliefs may cause teachers to disregard these differences, and treat all students in the same way. Teachers may even perceive this as being fair. However, students perceived fairness differently. Fairness was described by these students as: "ensuring that you understand one way or another" (Julianne); "they don't ignore you" (Giselle); and "looking at different perspectives" (Lee).

Teachers who hold ableist beliefs inadvertently sort students into different niches. They are likely to channel students who are perceived to be of lesser ability towards subject options believed to be less mentally challenging. These actions limit students' opportunities and can truncate their life trajectory.

Ableism often results in little or no accommodation and support for students with disabilities, contributing to lower academic achievement for these students. This may result in teachers relating students' poor performance to their disability, rather than to lack of accommodations. Ableist beliefs cause teachers to see students with disabilities as less capable than their non-disabled peers. Lower levels of expectation result in many individuals with disabilities experiencing lower levels of education attainment (Hehir, 2002).

THE HIDDEN CURRICULUM

The hidden curriculum is defined as "the unintended knowledge, values and beliefs that are part of the learning process in schools" (Horn, 2003, p. 298). The hidden curriculum transmits the unofficial messages about school and helps to support the academic and social agendas of schools (Ahwee et al., 2004, p. 26). It is through the implied messages in the hidden curriculum that students come to understand issues of power, identity and efficacy (Horn, 2003).

Children learn from what they see, hear and experience, and come to understand who has power and who does not. They learn about identity—who people say they are and who they believe they are; they come to an awareness of where they belong; and they learn about efficacy; who achieves goals that are valued and what needs to be done to achieve these goals (Horn, 2003, p. 299). These lessons are not directly taught, but students pick them up through their interactions with teachers, administration and other students.

The messages of intellectual competence sent through the hidden curriculum, can cause students to believe they are not smart enough because they don't do things as quickly as other students, such as taking longer to understand concepts or to write notes. This perception is seen in Amelia's comments: "I don't like grammar and essays. I can't remember the rules and I can't make sense of it. Sometimes it's hard for me to remember things, and it takes me a longer time to think about things. I don't feel I am as smart as the others."

The hidden curriculum also cues students on the dynamics of expected classroom behaviors and consequences, as reflected in Megan's comments: "they [teachers] think I am very silent and they are usually nicer with the silent people because we don't give them trouble"; and Giselle's—"if you keep quiet it is not embarrassment, if you talk you can get embarrassed so I don't talk in class."

In the hidden curriculum, students are held to unspoken codes of behaviors. "The do's and don'ts are not spelled out, but everyone somehow knows them" (Myles & Simpson, 2001, p. 280). Intuition is integral to understanding the hidden curriculum (Redish, 2010) and helps students to be sensitive to the dynamics within their classrooms. Amelia has learned to be cautious in asking questions, "I don't actually ask a lot of questions because I don't feel I am as smart as the others, and maybe the answer is there but I really don't see it, so I feel afraid to ask in case I look silly in front of my classmates."

The hidden curriculum can impress on teachers the importance of focusing on coverage of the academic curriculum. The implication is that certain content must be covered within a certain time, regardless of students' needs. This can result in some students feeling their teachers do not care about helping them to understand, or do not have the time to give them extra attention. Giselle expressed her frustration: "I take notes, but it's not effective and when I miss a paragraph the teacher won't repeat … he says, get it from your friends, and this makes me feel angry because the teacher won't give me the notes for me to learn. I have gaps in my notes and he says move on, I'll get it to you later, but he never does."

The hidden curriculum can send the message that students who do well academically are more popular in school. Giselle explained: "If I get fifty-nine, that wouldn't be great to the students; but I think it's good enough because you didn't fail. Grades are more important than personality and the students only work with students who have good grades."

The hidden curriculum can also be reflected in the physical spaces of the school and demonstrates that exclusion occurs on many levels: socially, academically and geographically. Non-classroom physical settings such as the canteen areas, bathrooms and walkways have hidden curricula, and children learn who has dominance and power and who to avoid, who is accepted and who is rejected (Ahwee et al., 2004, p. 28). Giselle explained that "the cool people stay in particular areas and they throw stuff at you if you go in that area. You know where I have lunch? I sit near the back gate, and no one troubles me."

SOCIAL NETWORKS

Social networks in schools can be considered to be the groups of friendships students create and maintain for various purposes. Weller (2007) argues that social networks can provide social, emotional and cognitive supports for students (p. 340). Social networks and the social supports they can provide emerged as a significant factor in the students' experiences of high school. Their social networks functioned as a protective factor and acted as buffers for students as they navigate high school, helping students to be more resilient. Jindal-Snape and Miller (2008) define resilience as "a dynamic process encompassing positive adaptation within the context of significant adversity" (p. 218).

> High school is harder but fun, the best part is making friends. My friends read the hand-outs to me so I can understand it and help me, like lend me notes, test me with questions and stuff, they show me what to do; they notice if I am sad. (Julianne)

Social networks provide social supports for the students and helped them to build their self-esteem by accepting them and including them in the group. La-Baber (2008) argues social supports enhance self-esteem and helps students who may be at risk for school failure to adapt to the requirements of school.

Social networks provide social supports, information, and a place for students to belong. Belonging is the perception that one is "accepted, respected, included and supported" in the group (Ma, 2003, p. 340). The concepts of social networks, and belonging emerged as significant features in helping the students fit in, and cope with the academic and social challenges of high school. Julianne, Amelia and Giselle describe their social networks as providing a safe place where they felt accepted and supported.

> My friends never tease me, they make school fun; they are always there. I am really shy and my friends helped me to make friends in high school. They want me to be happy. (Julianne)

> I was not sure how people would react to me, but now I have made some friends and it doesn't matter anymore. They make me feel comfortable about myself. They accept me. I feel a part of the group. (Amelia)

> When I was in prep school I would get teased about having ADHD and it made me feel bad, but in high school it's easier because people don't care, and my friends don't tease. (Giselle)

Individuals with LD are more likely to develop negative self-perception than their peers without LD (LaBarber, 2008) because of the challenges they face academically and socially. For these reasons, having positive social networks are particularly important for these students if they are to be resilient in facing the challenges associated with high school.

Resilience is determined by how an individual perceives their risk factors and their protective factors (Bailey & Baines, 2012). Risk can be defined as internal or external factors that present challenges to a child, and the degree of challenge is determined by both the level of risk presented and the level of resilience the child has. Risk factors and protective factors have both internal and external features (Jindal-Snape & Miller, 2008). Examples of internal risk factors could be having a learning disability and low self-esteem; and external protective factors can include having strong social support systems such as supportive family and peers.

Blackman (2010) argues children learn school and classroom cultures through interaction with peers; teachers should therefore use peer relationships to encourage positive behaviors. Giselle describes how her friends help her navigate high school: "They help me to study, they explain things to me and they explain how things work. They helped me adjust to high school by being friendly, by telling me what's going to happen and warning me."

The students' social networks acted as a significant protective external factor in helping them adjust to high school. It is through friends that most students were able to access content information needed either by copying from their friends' notes, or having their friends explain concepts they did not grasp in class. Friends also supported them in studying and preparing for tests and encouraged them to get help from teachers when possible. Amelia shared "I am not quite social but my friends help me, encourage me to do things and talk to people I would not usually talk to. My friends make going to high school better socially and educationally."

Peer relationships are a vital part of the adolescent support system (Stanton-Salazar & Spina, 2005) influencing concepts of self-image and identity, as well as fostering feelings of connectedness and belonging, and ultimately enhancing academic achievement. Through their social networks, students are informed about rules, academic assignments, social activities and possible dangers such as school bullies.

The students' social networks provide multiple forms of social support and act as sounding boards for ideas, feelings and problems (Stanton-Salazar & Spina, 2005). The following comments demonstrate the many supports that students' social networks provide. Megan receives academic support, "sometimes the teachers go too fast and you don't get all of it down by the end of the class so I have to go to my friends and borrow their books." Ben gets information about social activities: "The students had friends outside of school and so there was always some social event happening and you'd know about it."

Students who find school especially challenging are likely to seek emotional support from their social networks. These networks of friends, affect students' school experiences by providing critical information and support as "friendships are a significant source of social support (Akos, 2002, p. 340). Giselle explained the importance of having friends: "Friends help make high school better, they make it fun and endurable ... and they warn me about bullies." With many schools facing the dangers of bullying, social networks can be an important source of support for vulnerable students.

The students' stories suggest that their social networks were life-lines in their transition experiences as the supports they receive from these networks, help tremendously in enabling them to handle the challenges, of transitioning to high school. Ganeson and Ehrich (2009) support this perception arguing that friendships are important for survival in high school (p. 68).

RECOMMENDATIONS

The students attended different high schools but shared similar concerns and experiences. This suggests certain practices that promote inequality and the marginalization of some students may be generalized across the secondary system. The following recommendations are suggested in response to the research findings. They are categorized under headings social policy, professional practice and pedagogical applications.

Social Policy

1. Increase public education on issues of disability;
2. Implement a national transition plan that hold schools accountable for the successful transitioning of students from primary to secondary school. The purpose is to ensure that students have the academic and social skills for successful transition to the secondary level; and
3. More special educators are needed in the general education classroom. These teachers would provide academic support to students with disabilities and professional support to class teachers.

Professional Practice

1. Teacher's colleges need to prepare every teacher for the diversity of today's classroom;
2. All teachers at the secondary level should be highly qualified in their area of expertise as well as have teacher training;
3. Schools need to provide accommodations for students with disabilities that allow access to equality of opportunities;
4. Schools need to value student's social capital, and create school environments that are accepting of all students; and
5. Principals need to lead by example, hold up a vision of the school as an inclusive community, encourage a sense of belonging, and hold teachers and students to high expectations.

Pedagogical Applications

1. Secondary schools should provide first-year students with a foundation course that helps students adjust to the expectations of high school. Skills necessary for success should be targeted such as skills in organization, scheduling, studying, research and note taking;
2. Teachers should encourage the development of positive social networks among students to build social capital within the classroom;
3. Teachers need to create communities of learners by fostering acceptance, respect and belonging in the classroom;
4. Teachers need to make learning more relevant to today's learners and incorporate technology in the classroom; and
5. Teachers need to be adept at differentiating instruction so they can effectively meet the needs and challenges of all learners in the classroom.

CONCLUSION

Transitioning to high school was generally perceived as a positive experience. However, some challenges were experienced that could be attributed to teachers' pedagogical practices, ableist beliefs, and the hidden curriculum. The students were resilient in the face of these challenges because of the strong social networks they had established that provided support and critical information for them.

There is much that can be done at the secondary level to improve the school experiences of students in the general education classrooms who have disabilities. The responsibility lies heavily with schools to create more welcoming and supportive learning environments so that all students can experience schools as places where they feel they belong and can succeed.

REFERENCES

Ahwee, S., Chiappone, L., Cuevas, P., Galloway, F., Hart, J., Lones, J., Medina, A., Menende, R., Pilonieta, P., Proveno, E., Shook, A., Stephens, P., Syrquin, A., & Tate, B. (2004). The hidden and null curriculum: An experiment in collective educational biography. *Educational Studies, 35*(1), 25–43. Retrieved November 13, 2013, from http://web.ebscohost.com/ehost/pdfviewer/pdfviewer?sid=759620a5-397e-46bd-96df-2684b2b4c4d5%40sessionmgr114&vid=6&hid=123

Akos, P. (2002). Student perception of transition from elementary to middle school. *Professional School Counseling, 5*(5), 339–45. Retrieved June 23, 2013, from http://search.proquest.com.eresources.shef.ac.uk/docview/213261989/fulltextPDF?accountid=13828

Aronson, J. (1994). A pragmatic view of thematic analysis. *The Qualitative Report, 2*(1), 1–3. Retrieved November 7, 2013, from http://www.nova.edu/ssss/QR/BackIssues/QR2-1/aronson.html

Bailey, S., & Baines, B. (2012).The impact of risk and resiliency factors on the adjustment of children after the transition from primary to secondary school. *Education & Child Psychology, 29*(1), 47–64. Retrieved June 18, 2013, from http://web.ebscohost.com/ehost/pdfviewer/pdfviewer?sid=c2467715-3ef8-4601-bb3-c2949f09b990%sessionmgr12&vid=10&hid=24

Beck, M., & Malley, J. (1998). A pedagogy of belonging. *Reclaiming Children and Youth, 7*(3), 133–137. Retrieved July 15, 2013, from http://www.cyc-net.org/cyc-online/cycol-0303-belonging.html

Blackman, S. (2010). Who I work with is important: Dyslexic students' narratives about benefits of grouping for inclusion in Caribbean classrooms. *Support for Learning, 25*(1), 4–10. doi:10.1111/j.1467-9604.2009.01432.x Retrieved November 9, 2013, from http://search.ebscohost.com/login.aspx?direct=true&db=afh&AN=47829190&site=ehost-live

Booker, K. (2004). Exploring school belonging and academic achievement in African American adolescent. *Curriculum and Teaching Dialogue, 6*(2), 131–43.Retrieved August 20, 2013, from http://search.ebscohost.com/login.aspx?direct=true&db=afh&AN=17274395&site=ehost-live

Bourdieu, P. (1986). The forms of capital. In J. Richardson (Ed.), *Handbook of Theory and Research for the Sociology of Education* (pp. 241–58). New York: Greenwood.

Boyle, J. (2011). Thinking strategically to record notes in content class. *American Secondary Education, 40(1)*, 51–66. Retrieved November 13, 2013, from http://search.ebscohost.com/login.aspx?direct=true&db=afh&AN=69712623&site=ehost-live

Braun, V., & Clarke, V. (2006). Using thematic analysis in psychology. *Qualitative Research, 3(2)*, 77–101. doi:10.1191/1478088706qp063oa. Retrieved March 2014 from http://eprints.uwe.ac.uk/11735/1/thematic_analysis_revisited_-_final.doc

Coleman, J. (1988). Social capital in the creation of human capital. *American Journal of Sociology, 94*, S95-S120. Retrieved September 2013 from http://www.jstor.org/stable/2780243

Dixon, M., & Matalon, B. (2009). *Exceptional children in the classroom.* Mona, Jamaica: University of the West Indies Mona Chalkboard Press.

Downes, T. (2002). Blending play, practice and performance: Children's use of the computer at home. *Journal of Educational Enquiry, 3*(2), 21–34. doi:10.1.1.473.2580&rep=rep&1type=pdf. Retrieved March 31, 2014, from http://www.ojs.unisa.edu.au/index.php/EDEQ/article/view/539/409

DuPaul, G., Gormley, M., & Laracy, S. (2013). Comorbidity of LD and ADHD: Implications of DSM-5 for assessment and treatment. *Journal of Learning Disabilities, 46*(1), 43–51. doi:10.1177/0022219412464351. Retrieved August 2013 from http://ldx.sagepub.com.eresources.shef.ac.uk/content/46/1/43.full.pdf+html

Edwards, D., & Mullis, F. (2001). Creating a sense of belonging to build safe schools. *Journal of Individual Psychology, 57*(2), 196. Retrieved August 21, 2013, from http://search.ebscohost.com/login.aspx?direct=true&db=afh&AN=9049827&site=ehost-live

Evans, H. (2001). *Inside Jamaican schools.* Kingston, Jamaica: University of the West Indies Press.

Gale, T., & Densmore, K. (2000). *Just schooling explorations in the cultural politics of teaching.* Philadelphia, PA: Open University Press.

Ganeson, K., & Ehrich, L. (2009). Transition into high school: A phenomenological study. *Educational Philosophy and Theory, 41(1)*, 60–78. doi: 10.1111/j.1469-5812.2008.00476.x. Retrieved June 18, 2013, from http://web.ebscohost.com/ehost/pdfviewer/pdfviewer?sid=c2463715-3ef8-4601-bb63-c2949f09b990%40sessionmgr12&vid=13&hid=24

Hallahan, D., Kauffman, J., & Pullen, P. (2009). *Exceptional learners: An introduction to special education.* Boston, MA: Pearson Ally & Bacon.

Hehir, T. (2002). Eliminating ableism in education. *Harvard Educational Review, 72*(1), 1–32. Retrieved September 5, 2013, from http://www.search.proquest.com.eresources.shef.ac.uk/docview/212279806/abstract?accountid=13828

Hehir, T. (2007). Confronting ableism. *Educational Leadership, 64*(5), 8–14. Retrieved February3, 2014, from http://web.a.ebscohost.com/ehost/pdfviewer/pdfviewer?sid=6665b51a-41c9-4347-81e6-4013fc2d3b82%40sessionmgr4005&vid=5&hid=4207

Horn, R. (2003). Developing a critical awareness of the hidden curriculum through media literacy. *Clearing House, 76*(6), 298–300. Retrieved November 13, 2013, from http://search.ebscohost.com/login.aspx?direct=true&db=afh&AN=11853188&site=ehost-live

Jindal-Snape, D., & Miller, D. (2008). A challenge of living? Understanding the psychosocial processes of the child during primary-secondary transition through resilience and self-esteem theories. *Educational Psychology Review, 20*(3), 217–36. doi: 10.1007/s10648-008-9074-7. Retrieved July 30, 2013, from http://search.ebscohost.com/login.aspx?direct=true&db=afh&AN=33332494&site=ehost-live

Johnson, C., & Gooliaff, S. (2013). Teaching to strengths: Engaging young boys in learning. *Reclaiming Children & Youth, 21*(4), 27–31. Retrieved November 4, 2013 from http://search.ebscohost.com/login.aspx?direct=true&db=tfh&AN=88303221&site=ehost-live

LaBaber, R. (2008). Perceived social support and self-esteem in adolescents with learning disabilities at a private school. *Learning Disabilities: A Contemporary Journal, 6*(1), 33–44. Retrieved August 17, 2013, from http://search.ebscohost.com/login.aspx?direct=true&db=afh&AN=29438637&site=ehost-live

Long, T. (2012). Overview of teaching strategies for cultural competence in nursing studies. *Journal of Cultural Diversity, 19(3),* 36–37. Retrieved November 12, 2013, from http://search.ebscohost.com/login.aspx?direct=true&db=afh&AN=79968255&site=ehost-live

Ma, X. (2003). Sense of belonging to school: Can schools make a difference? *Journal of Educational Research, 96*(6), 340–349. doi: 10.1080/00220670309596617. Retrieved August 20, 2013, from http://search.ebscohost.com/login.aspx?direct=true&db=afh&AN=10852912&site=ehost-live

Main, S., & O' Rourke, J. (2011). New directions for traditional lessons: Can handheld game consoles enhance mental mathematical skills? *Australian Journal of Teacher Education, 36*(2), 43–55. doi:10.1422/ajte.2011v36n2.4. Retrieved November 4, 2013, from http://files.eric.ed.gov/fulltext/EJ920022.pdf

Maslow, A. (1962). *Towards a psychology of being*. Princeton, NJ: D. Van Nostrand.

Morrow, V., & Richards, M. (1996). The ethics of social research with young people–An overview. *Children & Society, 10*, 90–105. Retrieved May 23, 2016, from https://www.researchgate.net/profile/Virginia_Morrow/publication/227727186_The_Ethics_of_Social_Research_with_Children_An_Overview1/links/54ddd4d90cf23bf20438ab29.pdf

Myles, B., & Simpson, R. (2001). Understanding the hidden curriculum: An essential social skill for children and youth with Asperger's syndrome. *Intervention in School & Clinic, 36*(5), 279–286. doi:10.1177/105345120103600504. Retrieved November 13, 2013, from http://search.ebscohost.com/login.aspx?direct=true&db=afh&AN=4390574&site=ehost-live

Pottinger, A. (2010). *Prevalence of attention deficit hyperactivity (ADHD) in students 4–15 years attending rural and urban schools in Jamaica.* A study commissioned by McCam Child Development and Resource Centre, April 2010. Retrieved March 2012 from http://mccamcentre.blogspot.com/2010/05/adhd-prevalence-study-in-jamaica.html

Putnam, R. (2000). *Bowling alone—The collapse and revival of American community.* New York: Simpson & Schuster Paperbacks.

Redish, E. (2010). Introducing students to the culture of physics: Explicating elements of the hidden curriculum. *AIP Conference Proceedings,1289*(1), 49–52. doi:10.1063/1.3515245. Retrieved January 27, 2014, from http://search.ebscohost.com/login.aspx?direct=true&db=afh&AN=54712091&site=ehost-live

Ryan, G., & Bernard, H. (2003). Techniques to identify themes. *Field Methods*, 15(1), 85–109. Retrieved March 2013 from http://crlte.engin.umich.edu/wp-content/uploads/sites/7/2013/06/Ryan-and-Bernard-Techniques-to-Identify-Themes.pdf

Scanlon, D. (2013). Specific learning disabilities and its newest definition: which is comprehensive? And which is insufficient? *Journal of Learning Disabilities*, 46(1), 26–33. Retrieved August 2016 from http://ldx.sagepub.comeresources.shef.ac.uk/content/46/1/26.full.pdf+html

Shah, S. (2006). Sharing the world: The researcher and the researched. *Qualitative Research*, 6(2), 207–220. doi: 10.1177/1468794106062710. Retrieved January 20, 2014, from http://qri.sagepub.com.eresources.shef.ac.uk/content/6/2/207.full.pdf+html

Smith, L., Foley, P., & Chaney, M. (2008). Addressing classism, ableism, and heterosexism in counselor education. *Journal of Counseling & Development, 86(3)*, 303–9. doi: 10.1002/J.1556-6678.2008.TB00513.x. Retrieved January 27, 2014, from http://search.ebscohost.com/login.aspx?direct=true&db=afh&AN=32732651&site=ehost-live

Smith, M. (2012). What is pedagogy? *The Encyclopaedia of Informal Education.* Retrieved November 11, 2013, from http://infed.org/mobi/what-is-pedagogy/

Stanton-Salazar, R., & Spina, S. (2005). Adolescent peer networks as a context for social and Emotional support. *Youth Society, 36*(4), 379–417. doi:10.1177/0044118X04267814. Retrieved August 17, 2013, from http://yas.sagepub.com.eresources.shef.ac.uk/content/36/4/379.full.pdf+html

Weller, S. (2007). Sticking with your mates? Children's friendship trajectories during the transition from primary to secondary school. *Children & Society, 21*, 339–51. doi: 10.1111/j.1099-0860.2006.00056.x. Retrieved July 9, 2013, from http://web.ebscohost.com/ehost/pdfviewer/pdfviewer?sid=0b682247-48ed-46d7-8b2d-56c090f19b72%40sessionmgr111&vid=16&hid=108

CHAPTER 14

SURVIVING THE SERENGETI

A Safe Corner Perspective

Kirk Felix, Margaret Bruce, Suzanne Charles,
Nickisha Borris-Lezama, and Myrtle Blackman

This chapter uses an arts-based fictional narrative inquiry approach within the qualitative tradition to share the story of stakeholders in one Caribbean special school. This approach was chosen since it draws the reader into the emotional world of the research topic, while at the same time promoting ethical reasons via the protection of confidentiality as described by Diversi (1998) and Barone (2000). The narrative presents the education system as the Serengeti, the school as the "Safe Corner," and characters as wildebeests in a "Safe Corner" of the Serengeti. The co-researchers present and perform a discussion that epitomizes how the representative learner and his mother/father figures navigate needs and contexts with only "seven minutes" to learn critical survival skills.

The findings reveal that a substantial number of students with special needs are unable to survive in the present education system. Several weaknesses affect any existing deliberate or organized plan hence; many drop out while others are forced out. Another finding is that of unfulfilled needs where poor organization of the education system led to untrained and unskilled personnel being placed in the classroom (this is, however, being addressed).

Educators also express frustrations over the inadequate support from off-site leaders whose limited engagements amount to a mismatch between policy development and policy enactment which barely enhances at-risk students' chances of survival or even boost teachers' morale.

Despite the many weaknesses in the system, strength nonetheless emerges as a speck of light in the distance that leads to the silver lining (resilience). Additionally, at-risk students are generally enthusiastic about their future and longing for guidance, they look to the adults to guide them through this journey in life.

THE CONTEXT

Wildebeest is Dutch for "wild beast" or "wild cattle" found within eastern and southern areas of Africa. New-born wildebeest calves weigh about twenty-one pounds/kilograms and scramble to their feet within seven minutes, being able to move with the herd in a matter of days. The free-spirited new-born wildebeest can represent different stakeholders at different levels in the education system: students, some, of whose only real sense of security is that they are part of the pack; teachers and special educators alike, running for survival in their efforts to provide a delivery of services within a safe, meaningful, learning context; and parents, often on the side-lines, helpless.

The education system in Trinidad and Tobago includes both public (government and government-assisted) and private schools. The education system is governed by the Ministry of Education and is comprised of five levels, namely, pre-primary, primary, secondary, post-secondary (Advanced Proficiency and Technical/Vocational) and tertiary levels. Special schools, private, as well as public school also form part of the primary education system. The public special schools, formerly "institutional schools" came under the purview of the Ministry of Education in 1980.

It was not until 1980 that a number of the institutions that basically provided care and skills training for persons with special educational needs were redesigned as special schools, and the Special Education Unit was established in 1981. Prior to this, it was the training that was provided through the University of Manitoba, that sparked the development of training courses in the field of Special Education through a partnership with the University of Sheffield, Trinidad and Tobago Unified Teachers Association (TTUTA) and The Association for Special Education of Trinidad and Tobago (TASETT), which brought about significant advancements and changes in the field of special education in Trinidad and Tobago. Over the years, there have been many initiatives in the education system to address the needs of those with special needs, from the Diagnostic Prescriptive Service to the present Student Support Services Division. While these services have managed to provide the required support for some students and teachers alike, they have all been inadequate.

More recently, in 2009, the Ministry of Education established an Inclusive Education Policy (Ministry of Education, 2009). This policy formed part of the

Government's wider initiative and "Vision 2020" action plan that was expected to be realized by the year 2015. The Vision 2020 policy has as its genesis the adherence to the United Nations Convention on education of which this country is a signatory. An example of one of the conventions subscribed to was the Dakar World Education Forum, in 2000).

The elements listed in the policy are the General Provision Underlying Principles, Provision for students with moderate to severe special needs and funding for students in Private Special Education Institutions. Some other elements are the provision of continuous professional development, information and research, funding inclusive education along with curriculum and assessment development. The final set of elements relate to the provision for school management; internal and external support services and parent partnership. Its vision for inclusive education is the gradual and seamless merging of special education services into mainstream education (Ministry of Education, 2008).

The special education personnel who work to provide support and intervention services, can also be likened to the wildebeest running in the Serengeti. They too face many challenges as they try to meet the needs of persons with special needs in the education system.

The life of the "wildebeest" in the Serengeti parallels that of the students in our education system. Within the first seven minutes of being born, the wildebeest has to develop the skills necessary for survival in the Serengeti. If these skills are well developed, the wildebeest successfully maneuvers through the Serengeti, and if not, then the outcome is obvious.

Many of the students are not successfully moving through the Serengeti of our education system. Perhaps it would be important to determine what success is, how it is measured in the context of the school system, and what is required to experience this success. A child enters the education system at 2½–3yrs in pre-school or kindergarten. These institutions were not previously regulated by Ministry of Education in terms of the methods used and content taught. At age 5, students move to primary school and are promoted from class to class based on end of term tests. At Standard 5, the final stage of the primary level, students write a placement exam to move them to secondary school. If the students pass the exams at each stage of the process, they are considered successful. The measurement for success remains unchanged, that is, passing written standardized tests.

The large majority of students with special needs do not survive the run in this Serengeti. Several of them do not make it, and their survival is left to chance, since there is no deliberate or organized plan to get them through the Serengeti. Many drop out, are forced out, or their parent/caregiver is told quite frankly that "this is not the place for your child. Why don't you take him/her out of school and let them go and learn a skill or a trade?" During these years, there were those who never even entered the plains of the Serengeti. They were kept at home or placed in institutions.

Although Special Education in Trinidad and Tobago has its genesis in the 1940s, the concept of students having Special Education Needs was a foreign one to most teachers. I recall my own experience on entering the teaching profession at the primary school level, and encountering a student who would spend the entire morning attempting to get his name and the date on the page. When he was finally finished, the handwriting was so large it covered the entire page and was very untidy. He was scolded for this untidy presentation and made to do it over. Privileges were withdrawn for untidy work and work not completed. I remember the tears that would well up in my eyes as I sat through teacher training classes. This came three years too late for this child, and many others, who had special educational needs. Their needs were not met due to the poor organization of an education system that would place untrained and unskilled personnel in the classroom. Where are these children today? What was their run in the Serengeti like? Did they survive?

The co-researchers use Bronfenbrenner's Ecological System Theory to provide a framework and analyze the narrative in navigating an apparent ambivalent system. The narrative represents the challenges faced and strategies utilized by stakeholders represented. The results reveal the need for the system to be more supportive to stakeholders if the rhetoric of inclusion is to become an effective experience and facilitate more survivors in our Serengeti.

METHODOLOGY

In this study the researchers employed a qualitative narrative approach based upon a fictional, and arts–based, research method. This proved to be a more suitable method for arriving at a complex, detailed understanding of the lived experiences of a small number of stakeholders selected from purposeful sampling (Creswell, 2013). These stakeholders include the researchers who also engaged the participants with their own stories, hence emerging from a collaborative milieu is a more accurate data collection instrument due to the use of face to face interviews and conversation (Riessman, 2008).

The narrative approach enabled the researchers to use the oral history of the participants, their personal reflections of events, along with the attending cause and effects, as stated by Plummer (1983), cited in Creswell, 2013. Czarniawska (2004) further described this approach as "a specific type of qualitative design in which narrative is understood as spoken or written text giving an account of event/actions, chronologically connected." Throughout the study participants shared their past and present experiences as well as their future expectations (Clandinin & Connelly, 2000).

Wyatt (2007) drew attention to the question of value and validity for the utilization of a fictional and arts-based approach to research. He argues that there are philosophical and theoretical arguments for using fiction as a tool in research. Fiction-based strategies can be used to craft research narratives so as to increase the capacity to convey, evoke, provoke and persuade (Knowles & Cole, 2008). Hence the reason for the co-authors used this approach.

A thematic analysis of the survey data collected was done using transcribed responses from participants (notes in story form). This type of analysis enabled the researchers to arrive at themes after identifying codes and finally the reporting of the findings. Throughout the study all ethical concerns were noted, hence, participants were informed about the nature and purpose of the research and their right of termination at any time. The protection of personal identity was observed via the use of pseudonyms.

The Safe Corner

The Wharton-Patrick School, formerly the School for the Mentally Handicapped of St Ann's Hospital was founded by Dr. Nesta Patrick, M.O.M, with some early support from volunteer Ms. Mildred Wharton. The school was officially established in 1958. In May 1979, the Ministry of Education identified it as one of a number of schools where special educational service was being provided. It was subsequently designated as a special school under the Special Education Unit of the Ministry of Education. The School was relocated from within the hospital to 2A Sydenham Avenue, St Ann's, in 1990.

Dr. Patrick is credited with giving birth to the school and was also the first Principal of the Wharton-Patrick School. Her emphasis was on the need for teacher education, and she also encouraged volunteerism in order to gain additional support for students. Another principal was Ms. Merle Gay, whose contribution ensured stability along with relocating the school out of the hospital.

Dr. Dennis Conrad was the school's third principal, from 1990–1997. His vision took the form of advocacy, lobbying for remodeling the building plan, expanding resources, and efforts to reshape the role of the school within an advisory/resource model for those schools that needed help. He was also instrumental in facilitating an arrangement between the Trinidad and Tobago Unified Teachers Association (TTUTA), The Association for Special Education of Trinidad and Tobago (TASETT), and the University of Sheffield to provide teacher education in special education. Dr. Launcelot Brown in 1997 served as acting principal for one year, at which time he oversaw the construction of the new facility. In August 2008, Ms. Margaret Bruce was appointed principal, and continues to serve in that capacity. Her contribution to the establishment involves encouraging collaboration with other agencies for the benefit of staff, students, parents and the community. These agencies are both nationally and internationally based, for example: the University of the Southern Caribbean (USC), College(s) of Science and Applied Arts of Trinidad and Tobago (COSTAATT), the University of the West Indies (UWI), the University of Trinidad and Tobago (UTT), and Consortium of Disability Organizations (CODO). The two international agencies are the State University of New York at Potsdam and VSA Arts. These agencies are engaged in field experience, clinical rotation and practicum. The school also benefits from the skills set of these groups.

The main task of the school is to effectively respond to or meet the needs of its students, which include emotional/behavioral and associated difficulties. Care is taken to ensure that the environment is child-centered, and free of physical and emotional threats, while providing the opportunities for growth and development of their fullest potential. Another task is to foster a responsive learning environment where a continuum of services is derived. These services are tailored to meet the functional, academic, social, personalized, and affective requirement of the children. These positions are clearly articulated in the vision and mission statements of the school.

The educational programme is tailored to engage the student population. Students can be grouped in one of three categories. These are those with learning and behavior disabilities; emotional disturbance and mild cognitive disabilities. Then there are some students with multiple disabilities. Finally, others have physical and health impairments. As a result, the students experience many challenges which negatively affect academic achievement, classroom behavior and peer relations.

Characters

There are six characters in this narrative. These comprise "Mystery," who is the narrator of this story. There is also Malonie, the Principal, who has served thirty-three years in the teaching service, eight of which were in regular primary school, and twenty-five in special schools. There is Maria, an experienced special education teacher who now serves as a Diagnostic Specialist. Then there are four practicing special education teachers: Charlene the Senior Special Education Teacher who worked in a regular setting for five years and has been at the school since then. Franklyn a former volunteer, turned teacher, currently completing his Masters in Inclusive and Special Education; Pam who is also completing her Masters in Inclusive and Special Education; and Myrna who recently completed her first degree in education-special education. There is also Muhammed, a parent, whose child (David) is a former student, and David, the student, who is currently enrolled at the school. Statements from David are also included.

THE SERENGETI

> I wish you were dry leaves so I can burn you, I hate you," are David's words to his teacher with outstretched arms and pointed fingers as he enters the classroom. Why is David so angry? What is the teacher's response to David's outburst? What support systems are there in place within the school and the wider education system for David? Will he survive?"

The following is a voice from the trenches, a teacher, as she recalls her experience on the first and other days, at a special school in the Caribbean.

I am Myrna, straight out of The University of Trinidad and Tobago, just having completed my Bachelor of Education with a specialization in Special Education with no prior teaching experience, well, except for my twelve weeks of practicum, during my four-year teacher education training, I entered the Safe Corner of the Serengeti.

I felt that here is exactly where I wanted to be,—seven minutes—and this wildebeest is ready to face whatever challenges are up ahead. Just then, my hand was snatched, squeezed, jerked and then the shout came, "Percy, let go! Sit and behave!" I was awakened out of my moment. I proceeded with caution through the open glass door and down the hall that led to the principal's office, where I introduced myself and stated my purpose for being at the river bank. After being introduced by the second in command of the pack, I was taken on a tour of the Serengeti. I thought to myself, small classrooms meant small population, wow! The days, weeks, months rolled by as my feet grew stronger and my eyes were opened to the challenges faced on an ALMOST daily basis. "I have abilities within my disabilities," were the cries that bellowed from within the students as they confronted their varying challenges on their journey through the Safe Corner of the Serengeti.

Suddenly, a stampede of feet was heard in the distance and right away thoughts had to spring into action. As quick as a flash of light, they were upon me. I regressed then attacked in what seemed as the same time and bam! He was on his back. I felt the air leaving me then returning as I tried to free myself. Surprisingly, the Safe Corner became quiet as the leader of the pack pleaded for my release and all but a few came to my rescue and I was etched out of a situation that could have been worst.

To the wildebeest, the Serengeti can be a haven, but it can also be hell. To co-exist with others from within and without your tribe, one must be equipped with the correct skills. The juxtaposition of varying survival models is essential. You have to make it in quick time, despite all the odds.

One survival strategy—is to constantly remind oneself to stay focused on the positives. The negatives like teasing, bullying, theft, disrespect must never outweigh the positives like kindness, compassion, caring, and a feeling being a valued member of the community ... that of belongness, that "I belong here."

Myrna, surmises:

There must be a way to overcome and be victorious. The lions, the tigers and other wild beasts must not get to me before I reach the river. Looking to my left there was everyone engulfed in their own survival; my right was no different but ahead was the silver lining on the horizon of the other side of the river. Myrna in recounting an experience, notes on one particular day amongst the stampede, ... a chair was airborne, followed by words and screams that told me I should look for cover. I focused on the thought of "resilience" ... as a speck of light in the distance that led to the silver lining. It occurred to me that I need to survive, the Serengeti is home. ONE NEEDS TO SURVIVE. (Myrna).

A second teacher, Pam, acknowledging limited experience in special education, moves center stage. She is in the final phase of her Masters in Special and

Inclusive Education, and had earlier completed her Bachelor in Education at the University of Trinidad and Trinidad.

> Having some experience as a volunteer in the Serengeti before, I had an initial feeling of tranquility, hopefulness and excitement to be a part of such a familiar territory … seemingly with all supports and systems in place to nurture the young. A reality check is however waiting. In less than seven minutes after officially re-entering the Serengeti, soon realized that it is a jungle where only the strong-willed can survive. The peaceful and all inviting image that I perceived from the outside looking in is quickly marred by threats to safety and successful learning outcomes from every angle.

Young wildebeests, enthusiastic about their future and longing for guidance, are looking to the adults to guide them through this journey in life. They can sense the struggles and dangers around them but are too inexperienced and helpless to fix it. In their first days and months for some they seem to escape dangers as they are sheltered by overprotective parents who form bonds with other nurturing adults. Parental protection soon fades away and the wildebeests are left to seek the protection and comfort of the other adults—the teachers.

> Teachers try their utmost to guide them/students through these difficult terrains but are exhausted from the challenges and threats they too face. How does one protect and guide the young and in the process keep oneself safe whilst maneuvering the difficult terrains? Calls for help seem to fade in the distance, as no one in the colony seems to hear.

However, the daily journey towards crossing the river (the education system to adulthood) is the goal, and for the wildebeest who survives, it is only at the other side of the bank he is recognized. Sadly, for some of the wildebeest who have been lost in the riptide, their struggles, their stories are never told.

Pam shares her frustrations about the fact that little or no supports or adjustments are made to proactively assist those students at risk and to enhance their chances of survival.

It appears to me, that the off-site leaders of the colony continue to sit on the mountain tops with an entertaining view. This, despite being aware of the daily struggles and losses. In the Safe Corner of the Serengeti both the young wildebeest and on-site leaders are asked to survive by instinct and "share luck" [Pam].

Franklyn

The challenges faced by these educators involved with the Serengeti, and particularly the Safe Corner, are voluminous.

> These include a lack of resources. Even a suitable physical space to operate from remains a challenge. These stakeholders attend to the task utilizing the limited resources as they also maneuver through this Serengeti. Despite its many dangers

and present challenges, the Serengeti speaks to opportunities to defy the odds and maneuver the system. These allow students to escape the claws of "the victim syndrome."

Students suffering from this syndrome usually complain about the bad experiences they encounter. They believe that they have little or no control over the negative factors they encountered. As a result, their behavior can be described as self-defeating.

Muhammed

He is a parent of a former student who has graduated from the Serengeti.

I felt a sense of hopelessness to the point where my son was just at home. His two previous schools were not prepared to work with him any longer, or is it more appropriate to say that they lacked the required skills and resources.

My son (David) exhibited disruptive behaviors, accompanied with acts of violence toward students and staff. Getting him into the Serengeti, however, was not based on professional advice, but by chance. It was a neighbor who saw my son simply being at home, and that very neighbor had just started a special education training programme, or something like that. That neighbor communicated with me that she knew someone and a place to go to get help for my son. So she sent me. That's how I went, had it not been for this observant and thoughtful neighbor I am scared to hazard a guess of what would have happened to my son without such timely intervention.

My son has survived and grown. Many do not ... depending on the communities they live in. Further, there is no clear referral process pointing you to a particular place. So your child remains without help or support.

Muhammed continues—after a long silence:

I must say when I got him into school there, I met the most committed persons who worked with my son. They were seeking out at-risk students who were in need of special education intervention. My son survived like a "Survivor" character in the Serengeti to the point that he made it through high school and today he is a Coast Guardsman. While he still has his challenges, he is able to cope to a great extent. I can never forget the school.

This parent, Muhammed, recently returned to express his appreciation for the great work that was done with his son.

David's Lamentations

Then there is David.

> I didn't sleep last night. Whenever I close my eyes I see him. He comes and talks with me I know the man who killed him. I saw his hand. It had a "kinda" tattoo. I know him. He was my friend, he use to give me stuff. I will not tell the police because then I will be dead. Yes, he would come and kill me too. [David Notes]

David appeared to channel his frustrations and fears against authority. He protests to a teacher with statements that include: "I wish you were dry leaves so I can burn you, I hate you" or "I hate my life! I wish I was dead!" [David Notes]. Or in referring to a "mother figure" sought retribution with:

> She gives me an empty lunch bag with no breakfast and lunch today. "Look at this! This is what she gave me! Later on, I will give her trouble. I will make her wake up and smell the coffee."

Maria—Diagnostic Specialist

Maria is a former special educator, now Diagnostic Specialist with Student Support Services Trinidad and Tobago. This is a division of the education system responsible for providing support services for students with special education needs. She summarized the challenges as being (1) about quality versus quantity; (2) the need for support staff, for policy that includes accountability and supervision; (3) communication to and education of parents; (4) effective recruitment of personnel and /or (5) effective teacher education

Quality vs quantity. Maria said that it took her team a year to complete psycho-educational assessments for 101 students. She contends that while assessment is important, it cannot be the sole determiner of support services provision: "Our services must go beyond numbers."

Student aides. Maria contends that one of the challenges faced in providing student aides as support staff lie with allocation based on the number of students in a given facility and not the severity of disability:

> I think however, we should be more qualitative than quantitative. The parents out there, if they want the student with a special need to be in the mainstream, they must have an Aide. So the student or teacher aide has become as a requirement, like the schoolbag, the crutch. There are not enough student aides available. Some parents now believe that if they don't come with the aide, nothing happens. The parents do not understand that it is a process."

Lack of expertise. Another area of concern for Maria is that many teachers do not understand the role of practice and rehearsals needed for students with disabilities to master a concept.

> I try to explain to my colleagues the regular child only needs to get ten rehearsals because they have been rehearsing all the time. They have had many interactions, so they are getting it. Our special needs children need four hundred rehearsals for that one concept.

Lack of policies. Maria acknowledged that services are not equitable nationwide.

> A small district like St. Patrick has 49 primary schools, and you know they can safely say that they have entered all their schools because they have about almost 100 student aides in their district. Even if they are running up and down the Serengeti, there is stability because the team has basically remained the same, with established processes, procedures and policies, which is what our overall system lacks.

Maria pauses reflectively and continues.

> Look at me, I started at capital city, and when I wanted to continue I went to a sub-rural district and then to a rural district. But those people in these two educational districts were fortunate to begin when Student Support Services was established in 2004 and are still there today. So they have that continuity and will be able to put things into place. You see the challenges and the loopholes and the near-death situations they got it and they survived it and they ran with it. And right now, the very things that they have done, that they would like to share, those who don't know, who make up the core of the Student Support Services Division, don't want to accept that.

Maria confirmed that the services offered depend on the persons involved and their vision.

> Right now, we have some unification in terms of forms and processes. At least it has intensified over this year, I must say, but every district is different. We talk about equity and equality, how equitable is it for each student, how feasible? They are going to survive, but is everyone going to survive as a blanket statement in one way? Or is it an individualize surviving? I think those are the questions that have been asked and need to be answered to improve the services provided throughout the system.

Effective communication. Maria argues that this is critical for parents:

> I remember with my last time here, I had two parents sit in the class and we formalized communication for parents. It was hard but we got parents to accept and understood. I could have been absent and the class would have continued effectively ... So it comes down to the same thing as support. The support that was available within, we now try to get it from outside the Safe Corner.

Accountability and supervision. Maria insisted that every child in a Special School whether in public or private school must have an IEP, even without a formal assessment. The objectives for the child must be clearly stated:

> From this, you may be able to say this is what we can provide; this is what is needed so this is what we are making a request for. So therefore you also have a paper trail there. So let's just say we have a child there and we need an assessment and you said you made the request on this date. If this assessment comes, these are my observa-

tions. From my observations I want to recommend this but I need this assessment so that these recommendations would be valid.

Recruitment/selection process. Maria observed:

> The eagle is high up and very selective of its prey, the cheetah is also selective, the alligator is very selective, the lion is selective, so what lesson are we getting there and it's the same Serengeti. The process by which we recruit persons to provide this service has to be different. The selection is what is going to, in the wider context, have continuity and strength to continue to embody the vision, embody the adaptation and the change. The pre-school where I send my children, that person who is the administrator, every worker who has come must embody what is that vision and focus and mission of the school or else you have to go. This is a strength.

The Principal

Malonie, the principal of the Safety Corner, recollects her impressions of and experiences with David:

> Prior to being admitted to Wharton Patrick School, David was out of school. He had changed three schools in less than 2 years. He was referred through Student Support Services Division; however, his mother had heard about the school from a teacher. She had initiated the move. His adjustments to the school can be described as tumultuous. His early days were punctuated with violent outbursts, sometimes as many as four per day.

> During the last term of the school year David was elected to represent the school on the school-based management team. In his acceptance speech to the student body he said, "Thank you for choosing me to represent you. I will meet up with you and get your ideas to take back to the principal. You will tell me what you want for the school; what you don't like and what must be changed." He was cheered by the group. He then took a deep breath, bowed and smiled radiantly. In this scenario, David's participation in school life is interactional and conformational. Interactional by his words, "I will take your information." And conformational by his words, "thank you for choosing me."

Malonie continues:

> Out on a field trip, David came to complain. He said "I know as the student representative I must not be saying this. But, sorry, you see that rat get him away from me before I exterminate him and let him burn in hell." Here, David showed maturity. He asked for help and he acknowledged his anger. He knows now what he says will be met with disapproval but he takes the decision to say it anyway. He knows that his message will be heard and dealt with. David has been afforded the opportunity to go on a field trip although voicing his displeasure with situation.

David came from the regular primary school to a special school. A move that many considered to be an "anti-inclusive" environment. In fact, ideally, it should have been the other way around. Has this move benefited David? Is this in his very best interest? Is he getting the necessary support that would allow him to successfully maneuver through the Safety Corner and Serengeti?

At Wharton-Patrick School, it is understood that educators are critical to the teaching and learning process for students. The main role of the school is to effectively address the needs of its students. This characterizes the role of educators as professional problem-solvers, committed to the task of improving their daily practices, as well as students' outcome (Clauset, Lick, & Murphy, 2008). Hence, "the concept of inclusive practice implies that all learners are welcome at their school as they are seen as the responsibility of all educators" McLeskey and Waldron (2011). They further noted that, in the general education classrooms where students with disabilities are valued and are active participants and are provided with the necessary supports, students will be (the) furnished with an opportunity to succeed.

The more traditional approach of segregated and mainstreamed schooling was not seamless and therefore subtly fostered discrimination. Social justice was not a guiding factor, and as such, the notion of education as a human right was underrepresented. In the earlier phases of special education provision, people with disabilities, particularly intellectual or emotionally challenged, initially were deemed uneducable. According to Gordon, Feldman, Tanttillo, and Perronel (2004) the history of special education evidenced persons with disabilities experiencing significantly higher levels of violations of basic human rights. Because the general society viewed them as a threat, as contaminated, many of these individuals were murdered or used for various types of entertainment.

Students at Wharton Patrick are admitted as walk-in clients, on recommendation from the courts, or referral by medical practitioners. Some are also school-age individuals who are residents of the St Ann's Psychiatric Hospital, and others are referred by the Student Support Services Division of Ministry of Education. A small number of our students have been formally diagnosed by assessment agencies. Consequently, the staff relies on anecdotal information from former schools and parents. This information is not always reliable and, therefore, needs to be verified by staff via student observation and further interviews. Even so, the focus remains on the child's interest and abilities to foster inclusion in the wider society which is consistent with the school's pledge. This remains one of the school's strengths.

The incorporation of the use of social stories and biblio-therapy, along with other media, provide(s) a forum for exploring self and others with respect to competencies such as empathy, teamwork, resilience and respect. Students are encouraged to take turns conducting assembly, accept feedback on their performance, engage in physical play with each other and to participate in organized games in order to reduce discrimination and to enhance the prospect of inclusion. Students are also actively engaged in discussions, role play and other reproduction of material (engaged). The students' voices are not repressed. In fact, they are cognizant that they can broadcast on topics of concern once it is void of discrimination or if the time is inappropriate for such engagement.

At Wharton Patrick School, operations are influenced to a certain extent by Bronfenbrenner's Ecological Systems Theory: the theory believes that an individual's development is affected by his or her environment. At Wharton Patrick School, partnerships are formed with parents, members of the community, health services, faith-based organizations, corporate Trinidad and Tobago, non-governmental organizations and other stakeholders by involving them in a number of our school programmes. Our parent partnership is one such example. Parents have in the past and continue to partner with us in a number of ways. Parents have volunteered in the classrooms as aides. They have been a part of our Agriculture Science programme by teaching lessons and demonstrating how to plant certain crops. Parents have even contributed to meeting the emotional, social and physical needs of other students in the school. Another example is our corporate partnership with BP who sponsored the equipment and furniture for our audio visual room, and Digicel, which is currently sponsoring two programmes at the school: an Aquaponics programme, which involves the rearing of tilapia fish and the growing of crops, and a therapy-based intervention programme, which provides training for staff and therapy for students. These partnerships are invaluable to the growth and development of students as well as staff.

O'Connor and McCartney (2007) identify and explain the utility of the Bronfenbrenner model of development, and identify the crucial role that genetics and the environment plays in the development of an individual. A range of factors is identified, such as the influences of school, family, peers and even the neighborhood which can be considered immediate contact O'Connor and McCartney (2007). Other recent influences are television, the Internet and other forms of media, according to Comstock and Scharrer (2006). To facilitate a more positive influence, Wharton-Patrick School encourages interested Non-Government Organizations (NGOs), Faith Based Organizations and other community-based institutions to be stakeholders. This approach fosters school improvement.

CONCLUSION

The Serengeti provides the opportunity for development at a rapid pace. Depending on how the experience is viewed, one can emerge scarred or resilient. At Wharton-Patrick School we strive to support the individual as he journeys—the student, the parent, the teacher, or any other individual who forms a part of the community. We value an environment that fosters a sense of belonging for students and all stakeholders, although it is not always a smooth road: however, "a teacher for every child—and every child a teacher" remains our goal (McLeskey & Waldron, 2011). These philosophies are similar to the scenario where even the lion created a sanctuary for the at-risk wildebeest until its return to its natural community. The institution also seeks to be unrelenting as it engages best-practices rooted in sound research theories to alleviate the challenges faced by its stakeholders and to utilize appropriate strategies to ensure that the rhetoric of inclusion becomes an effective experience. These practices can facilitate new survivors in our Serengeti, thereby increasing from seven minutes to learn to cultivate a culture of life-time learning.

REFERENCES

Barone, T. E. (2000). A*esthetics, politics and educational inquiry: Essays and examples.* New York, NY: Peter Lang.

Clandinin, D. J., & Connelly, F. M. (2000). *Narrative inquire: Experience and story in qualitative research.* San Francisco, CA: Jossey-Bass.

Clauset, K. H., Lick, D. W., & Murphy, C.U. (2008). *Schoolwide action research for professional learning communities: Improving student learning through the whole-faculty study group approach.* Thousand Oaks, CA: Corwin Press.

Comstock G., & Scharrer E. (2006). *Media and pop culture.* In W. Damon, R. M. Lerner (Eds.-in-Chief), K. A. Renninger, & I. Sigel (vol. Eds.), *Handbook of child psychology* (vol. 4, 6th ed., pp. 817–863). New York, NY: Wiley.

Creswell, J. W. (2013). *Qualitative inquire & research design: Choosing among five approach (3rd ed.).* Los Angeles, CA: SAGE.

Czarniawska, B. (2004). *Narratives in social sciences research.* London: Sage.

Diversi, M. (1998). *Glimpses of street life: Representing lived experiences through short stories. Qualitative Inquire, 4(2),* 132–147.

Gordon, P., Feldman, D., Tantillo, J., & Perrone, K. (2004). Attitudes regarding interpersonal relationships with people with mental illness and mental retardation. *Journal of Rehabilitation, 70,* 50–56.

Knowles, J. G., & Cole, A. L. (2008). *Handbook of the arts in qualitative research: perspectives methodologies, examples and issues.* Thousand Oaks, CA: Sage Publications.

McLeskey, J., & Waldron, N. L. (2011). *Educational programs for elementary students with learning disabilities: Can they be both effective and inclusive? Learning Disabilities Research & Practice, 26(1),* 48–57.

Ministry of Education, Trinidad and Tobago. (2009). *Inclusive education policy. Appendix 1. Special education policy review: All children can learn*! Draft Special Education Policy: Ministry of Education, Republic of Trinidad and Tobago.

Ministry of Education. (2008). *Forty-eight session of international conference on education (ICE): National report on the development of education in Trinidad and Tobago. Ministry of Education,* Republic of Trinidad and Tobago.

O'Connor, E., & McCartney, K. (2007). Examining teacher-child relationships and achievement as part of the ecological model of development. *American Educational Research Journal, 44(2),* 340–369. Retrieved from http://dx.doi.org/10.3102/0002831207302172

Plummer, K. (1983). *Documents of life: An introduction to the problems and literature of a humanistic method.* London: George Allen & Unwin.

Riessman, C. K. (2008). *Narrative methods for human sciences.* Los Angeles, CA: Sage.

Wyatt, J. (2007). *Research, narrative, and fiction: Conference story. The Qualitative Report, 12(2),* 318–331. Retrieved June 16, 2016, from http://www.nova.edu/ssss/QR/QR12-2/wyatt.pdf

CHAPTER 15

MOBILIZING CRITICAL PEDAGOGY TO TEACH QUEERLY

Keitha-Gail Martin-Kerr

Student:	Good morning teacher, did you hear what happen to Ms. Ruby's son last night?
Teacher:	Anything that happened to Ms. Ruby's son, he deserved it! God made man to look like man and act like man. God did not make man to look like woman and act like woman.
Student:	Teacher, you should hear how he was bawling when the police were putting him in the car.
Teacher:	Serve him right! Now take out your mathematics book and turn to page 91.

The issues that face Jamaican youth who transgress the sexual norms of heterosexuality cannot be ignored. Jamaica inherited the *Offences Against the Person Act* (1864), section 76, which criminalizes homosexual behaviors. The law states, "whoever shall be convicted of the abominable crime of buggery, committed either with mankind or with any animal, shall be liable to be imprisoned and kept to hard labor for a term not exceeding ten years." The law of buggery is unique to males; however, it also has ripple effects on women-who-love-women, as they are discriminated against in society.

Jamaica, a former British colony, inherited the *Offences Against the Person Act* from its colonizer. Britain has since revoked the *Offences Against the Person Act*; however, Jamaica decided to keep it. If a person is found guilty of being involved in homosexual relationships, that person can be imprisoned for up to ten years. This law has been part of the Jamaican value system upon which the nation was built. Section 76 of the *Offences Against the Person Act* is one of the many reasons for Jamaica to be referred to as the most homophobic country in the world (Padgett, 2006). Jamaican homosexual, lesbian, and transgender youth face issues of discrimination in schools and also in the society at large. Each year the media reports violent incidents of stoning, beating, and murder against youth who transgress the heterosexual norms. Due to the *Offences Against the Person Act* and for a myriad of other reasons, the inclusivity for gay, lesbian, and transgendered students remains elusive in the Jamaican education system.

I am Jamaican. I did most of my schooling in Jamaica from 1981 to 2001: elementary, secondary, and undergraduate education. During this 20-year period, I encountered only heterosexual families in the curriculum. Same-sex families were not discussed in schools. In this chapter, I argue giving students the opportunity to learn about people who are similar to them as well as those who are different from them. The classroom environment and the school curriculum may serve as both a mirror and window for students (Galda, 1998). Students may look in the classroom environment and the curriculum and see their values represented. Students may learn from the curriculum about other people and their values. The classroom environment and the curriculum may be used to diversify teaching and learning (Fox & Short, 2003).

As educators, it is our pedagogical responsibility to provide students with the education that will allow them to honor diversity (Kumashiro, 2002). It is important to educate students to value differences, and not to view differences as deficits; this can be done through critical pedagogy (Kincheloe, 2008). Mobilizing critical pedagogy in the classroom will help raise students' consciousness about oppressive systems and structures that are in place (Kumashiro, 2002). Critical pedagogy will teach students that these oppressive systems and structures need to be interrogated (Kincheloe, 2008). Implementing critical pedagogy, students learn to question how knowledge is produced, who benefits from particular knowledge, and who is marginalized because of certain types of knowledge.

The objective for this chapter is to present theories and practices that have been used to build and support inclusivity of queer[1] students and their families in schools. Queer, for many, has a derogatory meaning. However, I use the word queer as a form of activism to empower all people who push against gender bi-

---

[1] Queer is a liberating term used to resist heteronormativity and the traditional derogatory definition of queer people (Kumashiro, 2002).

nary[2] and heteronormativity[3] (Kumashiro, 2002). First, I discuss the need for critical pedagogy: the type of teaching that allows students to question knowledge and how knowledge is produced. Following, I explain how the enactment of critical pedagogy may support an inclusive school system. Next, I explain four theories and practices of anti-oppressive pedagogy that have been researched and implemented in relation to queer education (Kumashiro, 2002). Lastly, I explain five suggested propositions to teach queerly (Sears, 1999). The ideas presented in this chapter are suggestions that may facilitate the structures to build and support inclusivity in schools for students and families who are gay, lesbian, and transgendered.

CRITICAL PEDAGOGY

"Critical teachers listen for marginalized voices and learn about their struggles with their environments" (Kincheloe, 2008, pp. 32–33).

This statement begs the questions: Whose voices are marginalized in society? How can students be educated to understand the lived experiences of marginalized people? And, how can teachers and students participate in critical understanding of society in order to make the necessary changes? These questions are relevant and timely in the Jamaican education context in order to lessen and eventually eradicate the acts of violence met out to non-gender conforming and non-heterosexual individuals. When 16 alleged homosexual prisoners are massacred with no major outcry from society (*New York Times*[4], 1997), critical pedagogy is needed. When a university student, identified as homosexual, is chased by a mob, runs to security guards and the security guards hand him over to the mob (*Jamaica Star*, 2006), critical pedagogy is needed. When a cross-dresser youth is killed in Montego Bay with no one claiming to witness the crime (*Jamaica Gleaner*, 2013), critical pedagogy is needed. These are documented cases of violence that have befallen youth who transgress heteronormativity and gender binary in Jamaica. Inclusivity of students and families who transgress the heteronormativity and gender binary remains an illusion in the education system. Critical pedagogy may support an inclusive education for all students and families. Critical pedagogy may help to stop the violence against non-heterosexuals and non-gender-conforming people in the Jamaican society.

Critical pedagogy refers to a teaching philosophy grounded in the social and educational vision of justice and equality (Kincheloe, 2008). Critical pedagogues

---

[2] Gender binary is the social construction of male and female dichotomy (Davies, 2003).
[3] Heteronormativity "refers to the institutionalization of heterosexuality and heterosexual valued in a society imbuing them with high degree of moral rectitude and as corollary rejecting divergent outlooks" (Cowell & Saunders, 2011, p. 317).
[4] *The New York Times* was used to reference this article because the Jamaican Gleaner was not accessible online during the time of this incident.

work to expose and to contest oppressive forms of power. Many critical pedagogues focus on specific aspects of critical pedagogy such as anti-capitalism (Darder, 2002), culturally relevant pedagogy (Ladson-Billings, 1995), anti-oppressive pedagogy (Freire, 1993), eco-justice (Bowers, 2001), Red Pedagogy (Grande, 2004) and feminist pedagogy (Lather, 1991)—to name just a few.

The context in which education takes place is important to critical pedagogy. For example, anti-capitalist pedagogy is needed in societies that are crippled by an economy driven by a capitalist mentality. Antiracist pedagogy is essential for societies where whites have the power and the privilege, and people of color are deemed powerless and less privileged. Kincheloe (2008) describes how the context helps critical pedagogues gain an understanding of the complexities of the sociopolitical issues and power dynamics that influence and affect marginalized individuals. Since homosexuality is illegal in Jamaica, critical pedagogy is needed to question and raise consciousness about the criminalization of people because of their sexual orientation.

For critical educators, "students do not need to be tamed, controlled and/or rescued; they need to be respected, viewed as experts in their interest areas, and inspired with the impassioned spirit to use education to do good things in the world" (Kincheloe, 2008, p. 8). This belief in students is similar to what Freire (1993) describes as his alternative to banking education: problem-posing education. Here students have a voice, they are able to think analytically and to engage in the process of inquiry, based on issues of importance to their lives. Students' lives become the basis of the curriculum; this keeps students engaged in school because they are learning about their lived stories, of which they are the experts, or the lived experiences of marginalized groups in society.

For example, students and teacher can engage in higher order thinking, talking and writing about discrimination and violence faced by non-heterosexual and non-gender-conforming individuals. Teachers can use newspaper articles such as 16 alleged homosexual prisoners killed in Kingston (*New York Times*, 1997) and cross-dresser killed in Montego Bay (*Jamaica Gleaner*, 2013) to engage students in these critical conversations. A teacher can involve students in this conversation by reading a newspaper article or showing a video clip or commentary on one of these issues. The teacher can place signs in the classroom: agree, partially agree, or disagree. Students may walk to the sign that identifies their position on the issue. Students may have a conversation with others who agree with them or have a cross conversation with another group. Students may be placed in smaller groups to design presentation to express their views on these critical issues. Engaging in higher order thinking, talking, and writing about text serve to accelerate students' literacy growth (Peterson & Taylor, 2012).

It is possible to engage students in a critical inquiry about aspects of the culture that are oppressive. Critical pedagogy (Kincheloe, 2008) and problem-posing education (Freire, 1993) view teachers as facilitators in the learning process, where both teachers and students are being liberated. The teacher and students are jointly responsible for the process in which they all grow as learners. For Kincheloe, this means critical educators "push humans to new levels of social and cognitive achievement previously deemed impossible" (Kincheloe, 2008, p. 4). Critical educators value students' histories and see students' cognitive abilities as limitless, yet limited by the political arena of the education system. All students, especially queer students, would benefit from being taught by critical pedagogues.

CRITICAL PEDAGOGY IN JAMAICAN SCHOOLS

Schools are supposed to carry on the tradition of a society; however, if that society's tradition is harmful to some groups of people, should schools continue that tradition? Teachers who value the success of all students may want to interrogate the law—the tradition—that states homosexuality is a criminal act. A critical interrogation of this law and the abusive manner in which same-sex families are treated is needed in order to demystify the homonegativity that prevails in the Jamaican society.

The need for critical pedagogy in the Jamaican school system rests in anti-oppressive teaching as it relates to gays, lesbians, and transgendered people. In reference to Paulo Freire's position on critical pedagogy, Kincheloe stated, "Liberation and critical hope cannot be attained ... until students and teachers address the nature of naïve consciousness and the manœuvres involved in moving from naïve to critical consciousness" (Kincheloe, 2008. p. 72). If teachers and students in Jamaica participate in critically examining the issues that gays, lesbians, and transgendered folks face, there is a possibility that their levels of consciousness will be raised, and they will become more aware of this as a societal issue, not just a gay, lesbian, and transgendered issue. For example, teacher and students may listen to a recorded interview of a non-heterosexual or non-gender conforming individual to hear the individual's daily-lived experiences. Teacher and students may engage in a productive conversation that raises critical consciousness about issues faced by non-conforming individuals in the society.

To enact a critical pedagogy means to understand the political nature of the education system. Teaching and learning are not neutral (Kincheloe, 2008). "When education pretends to be politically neutral ...it supports the dominant, existing power structure" (Kincheloe, 2008, p. 11). Even though Kincheloe is referring to capitalism, his argument can be extended to any society that needs to understand the dominant ideologies that force that society to uphold its hegemony by privileging one group and marginalizing another. The political nature of heteronormativity needs to be understood by teachers and students for the education system to be changed. The dominance of heteronormative ideology that circulates is not neutral or natural. Heteronormative is learned through a process of socialization.

The power that heteronormativity has in society leaves same-sex-oriented individuals and same-sex families powerless. The imbalance of power between the two types of relationships and families causes a dichotomy. Society has learned to see this dichotomy as a choice between good and evil. Heteronormativity has the power; therefore, it is good. Same-sex oriented individuals and families have no power; therefore, they are evil. Having an understanding of this will allow students to critically question the heteronormative status quo and the blatant discrimination against gays, lesbians, and transgendered people in Jamaica. One way a teacher may facilitate this conversation is to explain to students that many people are refused health care because of their sexual orientation (White & Carr, 2005). Teachers and students may discuss this as a moral and social justice issue.

Many educators wish to be described as critical pedagogues, and many would take on that identity. However, Kincheloe reminds us that advocates of critical pedagogy cannot call for justice in one domain and remain oppressors in another. Jamaican teachers who consider themselves progressive, liberationist, and revolutionary pedagogues have to take a close look at their stances toward same-sex relationships before they can think or continue thinking of themselves as critical pedagogues. Critical pedagogues take the opportunity to engage students in intellectually stimulating conversations around heteronormativity and homonegativity. These conversations may be heated and filled with productive tensions.

Once I heard a Jamaican minister preach that the local church is the hope of the nation. I would say critical pedagogy is the hope of the local schools in Jamaica. The only hope of the nation is to educate students through the process of critical pedagogy to question the discrimination and killing of gays, lesbians, and transgendered folks. As I conclude this section, I leave you to ponder these questions: Are Jamaican teachers ready to listen to students who are attracted to someone of the same-sex? Are Jamaican teachers willing to work toward a vision of the not yet, as it relates to homosexuals, lesbians, and transgendered students? What would it mean for Jamaican students and teachers to have conversations on issues relating to heteronormativity?

In the following section, I briefly describe four theories and practices that have been researched and used to build structures that support anti-oppressive pedagogy. These theories and practices are transferable to any education system that wants to embrace students and families who have been traditionally marginalized in society, specifically queer students and their families.

QUEERING EDUCATION THROUGH ANTI-OPPRESSIVE PEDAGOGY

Queering education[5] is one way to build a sustainable structure that will allow teachers and students to do education differently. To think queerly is to think differently; to think in order to transgress the heteronormative discourse. Teachers and students may make use of opportunities to think and talk openly about homosexuals, lesbians, and transgendered youth and their families in schools. This type

---

[5] Queering education is teaching and learning that questions the dominant practices in relation to gender, sexuality, race and class in society.

of thinking and teaching will help to build support and facilitate inclusivity in the Jamaican school system.

In his book, *Troubling Education: Queer Activism and Anti-Oppressive Pedagogy*, Kevin Kumashiro outlines four theories and practices of anti-oppressive pedagogy that he thinks, "offers ways of thinking and talking about education, oppression, identity, and change for working against traditional ways of thinking and acting, teaching and learning" (2002, p. 9). The four approaches of anti-oppressive pedagogy are: 1) education for the Other; 2) education about the Other; 3) education that is critical of privileging and Othering; and 4) education that changes students and society. These four ways have been studied and practiced.

Kumashiro discusses the strengths and weaknesses of each theory and practice. Any one of these theories and practices can be implemented to build an anti-oppressive education. I believe that these theories and practices may serve to build support structures for a queer pedagogy in Jamaican schools. In the following section, I give a brief overview of each theory and practice that Kumashiro discusses, and share how it may help to provide a structure of inclusivity for queer students and their families in the Jamaican education system.

Education for the Other

The first approach used to support anti-oppressive education is education **for** the Other. Scholars who study and use this approach focus on "improving the experiences of students who are Othered or in some way oppressed in and by mainstream society" (Kumashiro, 2002, p. 33). These scholars look at external and internal ways in which the Other is treated poorly in schools. External harm may include being bullied by peers or school staff. Or, it may include a lack of action on administrators and staff to support students who are marginalized by society and the school system. Internal harm may include psychological harm done to students who are Othered.

Scholars who research and practice this approach believe in two systematic structures that can bring about change. These are 1): schools need to be a place for all students; and 2) schools need to provide a separate space where students who are Othered can go for support, resources, and advocacy. Based on this approach, in the Jamaica school system queer students may be supported by: 1) being respected and honoured by peers, teachers, and administrators by not being bullied and having a voice in the school; and 2) being given a separate room in the school building where they can go for support, resources, and advocacy. These two approaches will help to support queer students in the Jamaican schools and make the education system more inclusive.

Education About the Other

The second approach for anti-oppressive education is education *about* the Other. Scholars who studied and used this approach believe that the school's curriculum should help all students learn about the Other (Sears, 1987). These scholars believe that teaching and learning about the Other is essential to confronting oppression in schools. Teachers need to refrain from teaching oppressive knowledge. Teaching what society defines as "normal" is one example of oppressive knowledge. When students learn what society defines as "normal," everything else will be placed in an abnormal category. Another example of oppressive knowledge is partial knowledge about the Other that leads to stereotypes and myths. Scholars who research and practice this approach believe that schools can bring about change by: 1) expanding the curriculum to include specific units on the Other; and 2) integrating lessons and topics about the Other into the curriculum throughout the school year.

Using this approach in the Jamaican school system would involve integrating units of studies in the curriculum about homosexuals, lesbians, and transgendered youth and their families throughout the school year. These units of study could be integrated in the social studies curriculum or in the literacy or language arts curriculum. For example, in the third grade unit of study on the "Jamaica Government and How It Works," teachers may include ways of governing and laws that Jamaica inherited from the British one such law is *Offences Against the Person Act*. Another example from the third grade unit of study is "Rights, Freedom and Responsibilities of Jamaicans": throughout this unit the teacher can explain the rights of heterosexual, the illegal act of homosexuality and the discrimination against women-who-love-women. There is a need for curriculum used in Jamaican classrooms to be more inclusive of non-heterosexual and non-gender-conforming people.

Education That is Critical of Privileging and Othering

The third approach used to facilitate anti-oppressive education is education that is critical of privileging and Othering. Scholars who are drawn to this approach believe that examining the oppression in schools is not enough. Oppression needs to be investigated on a societal level (Butler, 1990).Schools are part of society. Schools reflect the ideologies of the privileged group and the marginalized group that is in society. The marginalized group for this chapter refers to students who come from same-sex families or students who are attracted to someone of the same-sex or students who transgress the gender binary.

Kumashiro states that "Understanding the oppression of queer students requires moving beyond an emphasis on homophobia and individual fear, to consider heterosexism ("heteronormativity") and how the social demands of being "normal" are what help to produce queer-based oppression" (Kumashiro, 2002. p. 45). Proponents of this approach think that to bring about change, teachers and students need to teach and learn from a critical perspective as it relates to oppressive structures and ideologies. Teachers and students need to examine oppression and come up with strategies to do away with it. Critical pedagogy may be used to bring about change in the Jamaican school system to question oppressive systems and come up with strategies to do away with these systems.

Using this approach, teachers and students would ask critical questions and raise awareness as it relates to heteronormativity and homonegativity in Jamaican society. Examining the oppression on a societal level may be done as early as third grade. In the social studies third-grade curriculum, unit five is social issues. Homophobia, discrimination and violence are social issues that need to be examined on a societal level, not only at the classroom level. The teacher may facilitate this conversation by asking students to generate a list of social issues that affects them or their neighbors. The teacher could ask open-ended questions to elicit responses from students. For example: 1) Why is crime a social issue? 2) Are there some groups of people who are targeted more than others, why are these groups of people targeted? 3) How do these crimes affect our society on a national and international level? This is one way in which teachers and students may examine oppression on a societal level.

Education That Changes Students and Society

The fourth approach for building and maintaining an anti-oppressive education is education that changes students and society (Quinn & Meiners, 2009). Scholars who support this approach believe that "oppression is produced by discourse, and in particular, is produced when certain discourses (especially ways of thinking that privilege certain identities and marginalize others) are cited over and over" (Kumashiro, 2002, p. 50). These scholars conceptualize oppression as the repetition of harmful citational practices (Kumashiro, 2002, p. 51). To bring about change, these scholars argue three points that need to be examined in the education system:

1. The problem of resistance needs to be interrogated. Kumashiro writes, "Perhaps we resist anti-oppressive practices because they trouble how we think and feel about not only the Other but also ourselves" (2002, p. 57). Anti-oppressive education may disrupt how people make sense of the world; people desire to be normal. They do not want to change the frame through which they traditionally view the world;
2. A partial curriculum is a danger to anti-oppressive education. Anti-oppressive education happens when critical questions are asked about the partial curriculum (Kumashiro, 2002, p. 62). Students need to read texts and "commonsense knowledge" critically. Commonsense knowledge refers to the dominant knowledge in a society; and
3. Learning and unlearning can place students and teachers in crisis. Teachers and students may choose to resist anti-oppressive pedagogy because this type of learning and unlearning can be uncomfortable.

In the Jamaican school system, teaching and learning that the way we do things are not only "partial, but also oppressive involves unlearning what we already learned" (Kumashiro, 2002, p. 63). This may place students and teachers who have been socialized in heteronormativity in a very uncomfortable position. The teachers and students would need to embrace the crisis that occurs from unlearning and learning, and understand that this crisis is an essential element of anti-oppressive education.

Kumashiro provided four theories and practices that have been studied and used to build support for anti-oppressive education: education for the Other; education about the Other; education that is critical of privileging the Other; and education that changes students and society. Any one of the four could be exercised in any school system to make it more inclusive. All four theories have strengths and weaknesses; however, employing one of these theories and practices would be a start in the Jamaican school system to be more inclusive of queer students and their families.

In the following section, I expand on the work of James Sears who identified five propositions for teaching queerly in schools. This section highlights knowledge that should be examined in order to teach queerly. I also describe some of the educational beliefs for teaching queerly. Teachers and administrators in the Jamaican school system may consider and examine some of these suggestions that support inclusivity for queer students and their families. Raising awareness and critically interrogating commonsense, societal knowledge is the starting point for building and supporting inclusivity.

TEACHING QUEERLY

Teaching queerly is teaching that challenges teachers and students to question dominant narratives. In part one of the edited book, *Queering Elementary Education: Advancing the Dialogue about Sexualities and Schooling*, Letts and Sears explain, "the task for the queer educator is creating classrooms that challenge categorical thinking, promote interpersonal intelligence, and foster critical consciousness" (1999, p. 1). This quote explains the purpose of queering education and the role of queer educators. It is important to explain that queer educators are not educators who are homosexuals, lesbians, transgendered, questioning, or intersexed individuals. Queer educators are teachers who believe in the philosophy of teaching to transgress heteronormativity. These educators enact a pedagogy that is anti-oppressive, especially for queer students and their families. Sears says; "Queer teachers are those who develop curricula and pedagogy that afford *every* child dignity rooted in self- worth and esteem for others" (Sears, 1999, p. 5). The task of queer education is not an ominous mission. It requires teachers to teach with respect and honor for all. It requires students to learn about and value all types of people as equals.

What does it mean to teach queerly? For Sears, teaching queerly is not teaching about sex. Teaching queerly is not teaching sex education. "It embodies educators who model honesty, civility, integrity, fairness, and respect" (1999, p. 4). As noted earlier, teaching queerly has nothing to do with teaching about intimacy. Teaching queerly has everything to do with equal rights and justice for all humans regardless of their sexual orientation. For teachers to teach queerly, Sears suggest five propositions that they may examine and consider: 1) diversity is a human hallmark; 2) (homo) sexualities are constructed essences; 3) homophobia and heterosexism are acquired; 4) childhood innocence is a fictive absolute; and 5) families are first. In the following section, I will go into details about each proposition that needs to be considered if teachers want to teach queerly.

THE FIVE PROPOSITIONS OF TEACHING QUEERLY

Diversity is a human hallmark. The first proposition is: diversity is a human hallmark. For Sears, educators know that humans are diverse beings. From complexion, to fingerprints, to blood type, to personalities, humans are diverse beings. However, in society, it seems as if diversity stops when it comes to gender and sexuality. Society does not want sexuality or sexual orientation to be diverse. Many students are taught, *if* they are taught, that gender and sexual identities come in a dichotomy: male/female (biological sex), man/woman (gender identity), heterosexual/homosexual (sexual orientation), masculine/feminine (gender roles), opposite/same (sexual behaviour), straight/gay (sexual identity). Sears decries, "when educators enter classrooms of differences, they bring with them these categorical blinders diminishing the richness of humanity" (1999, p. 5).

Jamaican teachers know diversity is a human hallmark. In the elementary curriculum, teachers teach about physical differences, for example people have different fingerprints and different physical features. Teachers also teach about differences in political beliefs, religion, and other ways of being different. Teachers can expand this to include diverse people and discuss homosexuals, lesbians, and transgendered youth in the society. This discussion could be part of the family unit in the early elementary curriculum. Teacher and students can engage in discussions about the different types of families that make up the Jamaican society.

Teaching queerly requires educators to move away from the dichotomous belief in gender and sexuality.

Teaching queerly requires teachers to see gender and sexuality as fluid. In the prologue of her book, *Shards of Glass: Children Reading and Writing Beyond Gendered Identities,* Davies writes that she hopes, "We might find ways of interacting with children and ways of speaking and writing that disrupted the apparent inevitability of the male-female binary" (2003, p. xi). Similar to Sears, Davies states, "I wanted to open up the possibility of multiple genders, of fluidity between categories, of movement in and out of a range of ways of being where we are not limited by binary categories of maleness and femaleness" (2003, p. xi). Teaching queerly means moving away from the categorical binaries of gender and sexuality.

Jamaican teachers can help students to realize that inherent in these binaries are prejudices and oppression for people who transgress heteronormativity. Teachers and students can engage in conversations that push against gender binary. For example, a teacher might facilitate a conversation and ask critical questions such as: suppose a person does not feel either male or female, what other options could people have? Why do people have to choose whether to be male or female? Who does this benefit when people decide that they are either male or female? Why is there a need for these two categories? Asking questions such as these will get students to dig deeply and explore the gender binary.

(Homo)sexualities are constructed essences. Understanding that (homo)sexualities are constructed essences is the second proposition for teaching queerly. When teachers understand that sexual identity is constructed within a cultural context they will be able to question the cultural factors that contribute to homophobia. Even though there is no scientific evidence to state the cause of homosexuality, Sears drew on a right-handed / left-handed analogy to explain the absurdity that homosexuals choose their "lifestyle." The question is did right-handed people choose to be right-handed? Did left-handed people choose to be left-handed? Sears cited research illustrative of his analogy; for example, identical twins have a one in two chance of both being gay if one is gay. Similarly, fraternal twins have a one in five chance, and adopted brothers have a one in ten chance. Sears' point is that if left-handed people did not choose to be left-handed, then homosexuals did not choose their "lifestyle." Understanding that people who use their left-hand did not decide to do so is similar to people who are homosexuals and lesbians who also did not choose their sexual orientation. Probably, having an understanding of this analogy may help teachers include non-heterosexual curriculum and textbooks in their classrooms.

Heterosexism is an acquired ideology. The third proposition needed to teach queerly is to recognize that homophobia and heterosexism are acquired ideologies that were introduced early in life. Homophobia is instilled early in a child's life. The superiority of heterosexuality is also indoctrinated early in a child's life. Students get these messages through curriculum materials and children's literature that honor the nuclear family. Sears argues that "elementary teachers unmindfully enforce "compulsory heterosexuality" through stories of nuclear animal families and questions about mommies and daddies" (1999, p. 11). Students also get these messages from religious conservatives and the media. Sexuality and gender are imparted through spoken and unspoken discourses from early childhood. After studying preschool children and gender Davies (2003) writes:

> Humanist discourse pervades school texts and talk. The preschool children's understanding of being male or female and of the possibilities of liberation from traditional binary understandings of these and other related terms was severely limited by the available discourses through which both they and their social worlds were constituted. These were not interpretations they had explicitly taught. Rather, they

were embedded in the ways of seeing, knowing, and being that were made available to them through text and talk (Davies, 2003, p. 11).

To disrupt sexuality and gender norms that we have been socialized in from an early stage, teachers need to teach differently. Teaching queerly requires that we "confront our prejudices inculcated through decades of heterosocialization" (Sears, 1999, p. 8). For teachers to teach queerly they need to be cognizant of the images and messages that they present to students and ensure that students are being exposed to heterosexual and non-heterosexual families. For example, when a teacher teaches that a woman should marry a man, students come to understand that marriage is made for heterosexuals.

Teachers who want to disrupt heteronormativity need to teach students to think critically about media images and messages and to question who is being recognized and who is being silenced in these media images and messages. Teaching students critical literacies is a transferable skill that students will bring with them to other institutions in which they interact, for example the church. Students' scrutiny will guide them to question what they are, and who this knowledge benefits and who it excludes. Having an understanding that homophobia and heterosexism are socially learned will help Jamaican teachers teach queerly.

Childhood innocence is a fictive construct. The fourth proposition to understand in order to teach queerly is that childhood innocence is a fictive construct made up by adults. Both Sears and Davies credited Philippe Aries for his groundbreaking work that shed light on the conception of childhood. Sears claims that "childhood innocence is a veneer that we as adults impress onto children, enabling us to deny desire comfortably and to silence sexuality" (1999, p. 9). Childhood innocence is an adult invention. Adults impose innocence on children for their own benefits. For example, adults claim that children are innocent, therefore children should not learn about same-sex families. Davies (2003) thinks that the notion of an innocent child is a construct of adults to rid children of their agency. To argue her point, Davies writes, "Children, like women and other marginalized groups, are constantly deprived of agency. Their subject status is never fully guaranteed. It is always partial and conditional. They can be positioned as beings without agency and autonomy at any moment, usually when they are read by adults as not knowing how they should behave" (2003, p. 9). Teaching queerly would require Jamaican teachers to see students as beings with agency. Students should have the agency to express their thoughts and feelings confidently. Students need to be seen without the adult-gaze. The adult-gaze turns students into fictitious innocent beings without any desire to know and without any agency to ask challenging questions. Teaching queerly would require Jamaican teachers to accept that students are fully human; they are agentic beings.

Heterosexual families are first. The fifth and last proposition that should be interrogated is the idea that heterosexual families are first and more important than homosexual and lesbian families. Sears writes, "The gravest threat that the recognition and acceptance of lesbian/gay families in elementary school pose is the removal of the family as instrument of heterosexual socialization" (1999, p. 10). When homosexual and lesbian families enter the discourse of school then students will question the traditional definition of family. Questioning the traditional definition of family means students will not be inculcated to believe that all families need a mother and father to be classified as a family unit. Critically thinking about the definition of a family will help students to respect and honor different configurations of families.

Teaching queerly requires teachers to help students understand that all families are first, and all families are important. Teachers and students can do this by challenging the heterosexual-family-first discourse that is prevalent in the Jamaican classrooms. For example, teachers may use children's books that reflect different types of families in their teaching. Children's books such as *The Family Book* by Todd Parr, *And Tango Makes Three* by Justin Richardson and Peter Parnell, and *In Our Mothers' House* by Patricia Polacco will challenge the dominant discourse that heterosexual families are the only type of family structure that should be valued.

Sears provides five propositions that should be considered in order to teach queerly. Teaching queerly requires teachers to understand that diversity is a human hallmark; (homo)sexualities are constructed essences; homophobia and heterosexism are socially constructed; childhood innocence is an adult construct, and all families should be first. Having an understanding of these propositions will help Jamaican teachers and school leaders build structures to support a queer pedagogy.

Conclusion

Mobilizing critical pedagogy and creating anti-oppressive pedagogical structures to teach queerly may seem idealistic in the Jamaican education system. Let's think what may happen if we do not begin to do this. Perhaps our youth who transgress gender binary and who digress from heteronormativity will continue to be criminalized, killed, and discriminated against. Using critical pedagogy to teach students to question dominant narratives that we take for granted can begin as early as students enter the school system. Students come to school with a natural sense of curiosity. Teachers can build on that level of inquiry and teach students to question knowledge, question things that we live with daily that harm some members of society and privilege others, question oppressive discourse, and question binary thinking.

Harking back to the conversation that happened at the beginning of this chapter, we could re-imagine a different conversation if Jamaican teachers and students use critical pedagogy to raise consciousness for all.

> Student: Good morning teacher, did you hear what happened to Ms. Ruby's son last night, what are your thoughts on the whole issue?

Teacher: What happened to Ms. Ruby's son was heart-wrenching. The situation can be argued from several different angles. Some people think that he deserved what happened to him because we have laws and what he did is against the country's laws. Other people would argue that all people should be free to love the person they want to be with. Laws should not force people to choose who to love. It seems as if you have been thinking about this a lot. Do you think we should engage the whole class in this conversation?

Student: That would be really beneficial for me and I think for other students. It is a tough topic. I really don't know where I stand. I need to think and talk it through with other people.

Inclusivity of homosexual, lesbian, and transgendered students and their families remains elusive in Jamaican classrooms. In this chapter, I discussed three pedagogical structures that may be put in place to facilitate a more inclusive educational environment. These three pedagogical structures are critical pedagogy, queering education through anti-oppressive pedagogy, and teaching queerly. I also provided practical examples that teachers may use to teach queerly. It is my hope that the Jamaican education system will move toward teaching queerly—teaching differently—in order to question the dominant practices in society.

REFERENCES

Bowers, C. A. (2001). *Educating for eco-justice and community*. Athens: University of Georgia Press.
Butler, J. (1990). *Gender trouble: Feminism and the subversion of identity*. New York: Routledge.
Cowell, N. M., & Saunders, T. S. (2011). Exploring heteronormativity in the public discourse of Jamaican legislators. *Sexuality & Culture, 15*(4), 315–331.
Davies, B. (2003). *Shards of glass: Children reading and writing beyond gendered identities*. Cresskill, NJ: Hampton Press.
Darder, A. (2002). *Reinventing Paulo Freire: A pedagogy of love*. Boulder, CO: Westview Press.
Freire, P. (1993). *Pedagogy of the oppressed* (20th anniversary ed.). New York: Continuum.
Fox, D., & Short, K. (Eds.). (2003). *Stories matter: The complexity of cultural authenticity in children's literature*. Urbana, IL: National Council of Teachers of English.
Galda, L. (1998). Mirrors and windows: Reading as transformation. In T. E. Raphael & K. H. Au (Eds.), *Literature-based instruction: Reshaping the curriculum* (pp. 1–12). Norwood, MA: Christopher Gordon.
Grande, S. (2004). *Red pedagogy: Native American social and political thought*. Lanham, MD: Rowman & Littlefield Publishers.
Jamaica Gleaner. (2013). *J-FLAG condemns mob killing of alleged Mobay cross-dresser.* Retrieved October 13, 2015, from Jamaica Gleaner: http://jamaica-gleaner.com/power/46697.
Jamaica Star. (2006). *UWI mob beats man*. Retrieved October 13, 2015, from Jamaica Star: http://jamaica-star.com/thestar/20060405/news/news1.html.

Kumashiro, K. K. (2002). *Troubling education: Queer activism and anti-oppressive pedagogy*. Psychology Press.
Kincheloe, J. L. (2008). *Critical pedagogy primer*. New York: P. Lang.
Ladson-Billings, G. (1995). But that's just good teaching! The case for culturally relevant pedagogy. *Theory into practice, 34*(3), 159–165.
Lather, P. (1991).*Getting smart: Feminist research and pedagogy with/in the postmodern*. New York: Routledge.
Letts, W. J., & Sears, J. T. (Eds.) (1999). *Queering elementary education: Advancing the dialogue* about *sexualities and schooling*. Lanham, MD: Rowman & Littlefield.
Ministry of Justice-Government of Jamaica, *Offences against the Person Act.* (1864). Retrieved August 1, 2015. http://www.moj.gov.jm/sites/default/files/laws/Offences Against the Person Act_0.pdf
New York Times (1997). *Jamaica tries to quiet two prisons after riot.* Retrieved October 13, 2015, from New York Times: http://www.nytimes.com/1997/08/25/world/jamaica-tries-to-quiet-2-prisons-after-riots.html
Padgett, T. (2006, April 12). The most homophobic place on Earth? *Time*. Retrieved from http://www.time.com/time/world/article/ 0,8599,1182991,00.html.
Peterson, D. S., & Taylor, B. M. (2012). Using higher order questioning to accelerate students' growth in reading. *The Reading Teacher, 65*(5), 295–304.
Quinn, T., & Meiners, E. R. (2009). *Flaunt it!: Queers organizing for public education and justice*. New York: Peter Lang.
Sears, J. T. (1987). Peering into the well of loneliness: The responsibility of educators to gay and lesbian youth. In A. Molner (Ed.), *Social issues and education: Challenge and responsibility.* (pp.146–164). Alexandria, VA: Assn for Supervision & Curriculum
Sears, J. T. (1999). Teaching queerly: Some elementary propositions. In Letts, W. J., & Sears, J. T. (Eds.), *Queering elementary education: Advancing the dialogue* about *sexualities and schooling*. (pp. 3–15) Lanham, MD: Rowman & Littlefield.
White, R. C., & Carr, R. (2005). Homosexuality and HIV/AIDS stigma in Jamaica. *Culture, Health & Sexuality, 7*(4), 347–359.

CHAPTER 16

BARBADIAN TEACHERS' PERSPECTIVES OF SCHOOL CULTURE

Support and Inclusion of Students With Disabilities

Stacey Blackman

This chapter documents the narratives of a selected group of Barbadian educators in inclusive and special education settings to understand how the cultural milieu of these settings facilitates or hinders the participation of students with disabilities. It is widely accepted that participation extends beyond academics and includes a sense of belonging, homophily and social capital all encapsulated within the socio-cultural context of school settings. Polat (2011); Riddell (2007); Barton and Armstrong (2001) argue that in order for students with disabilities to feel a sense of citizenship and participation in schools they must be supported by schools, teachers and students. Schools must embrace and establish cultures that adopt a posture of participation rather than segregation and isolation. School culture speaks to the beliefs, attitudes and values held by individuals at a deep level intermingled with surface-level attributes, i.e. behaviors that influence the diffusion of curriculum and assessment Lawson (1997). It is very difficult for students with disabilities to "choose" their own cultural climates and this influences how they participate socially and academically in their school settings.

At the international level, the participation of students with disabilities in regular education has been shown to accrue social and emotional benefits like the development of friendships and relationships with peers without disabilities (Male, 2007) and reduce feelings of social isolation (Frostad & Pijl, 2007). Social participation is the presence of positive social contact/interaction, acceptance, social relationships/friendships, and perception of acceptance by other peers (Koster, Pijl, Nakken, & Van Houten, 2010). One quantitative study by Wendelborg and Tøssebro (2011) in Norway with 262 children between the ages of 11 and 13 found that the type of disability and degree of impairment did not directly affect social participation. Rather, interaction via classroom participation had the most significant positive effect on social participation, while time spent in special education or with an assistant had a smaller negative effect on social participation. This finding is supported in other studies by Koster, Pijl, Nakken, & Van Houten (2010); Pijl, Frostad, & Mjaavatn (2010); Koster, Timmerman, Nakken, Pijl, & van Houten (2009) the Social Participation Questionnaire (SPQ). However, a recent quantitative study in the United States of America by Feldman, Carter, Asmus, and Brock (2016) with 108 high school students with severe disabilities found that students were not present for a substantial portion of the teaching time and were subject to reduced contact with their peers with disabilities. According to the findings of this research, students with severe impairments missed valuable opportunities to participate socially and build friendships with other non-disabled peers. They report that the overall pattern of proximity to peers never exceeded 50 percent of the time that these kids spent in the classroom with non-disabled peers. Other findings suggested that the nature of the impairment also determined the presence and proximity to peers without disabilities in regular education settings.

Participation is also fostered by teacher support, which is more commonly perceived as the need for resources, administrative support, peripatetic assistance, or co- and collaborative teaching; however, the need for teachers to work together cannot be overestimated (Giangreaco, Carter, Doyle, & Suter, 2010). How well teachers collaborate is based on teacher beliefs, the nature of relationships between teachers, attitudes, knowledge and skills. These can determine the kinds of support given to students and the quality of educational opportunity, service provided and success of inclusion (Villa, Thousand, Nevin, & Malgeri, 1996). A qualitative study by Boyle, Topping, Jindal-Snape and Norwich (2012) documented the narratives of 43 teachers in three schools in Scotland. Teacher-to-teacher support was imperative for staff working in inclusive settings, especially where a perceived lack of staff support from management existed at the school. Teachers thought it was important to work together as a team to design lessons that complemented one another within and across subject departments and monitor the progress of students.

In addition to support from teachers and paraprofessionals, it is also important to recognize that peers of students with disabilities also play an integral role in facilitating the successful academic and social inclusion of students with disabilities. Much of this research finds credence in approaches that emphasize collaborative and cooperative learning. But, more recently, Carter et al. (2016) has attempted to establish peer support as part of a continuum of evidence-based practices for special education. These researchers studied the efficacy of peer support arrangements for high school students with severe disabilities utilizing a randomized controlled experimental design. Special education teachers and paraprofessionals trained 106 peers to provide individualized support and corrective feedback, model age, and appropriate social and communication behaviors for their counterparts with severe impairments. Observers were also assigned to peer dyads to monitor levels of interaction between peers with and without disabilities and measure the fidelity of implementation of peer support strategies as opposed to adult mediated support. Carter et al. (2016) reported that students who took part in the peer support programme experienced increased interactions with other typically developing peers, academic and social participation and had a greater number of friendships than peers who were in adult delivered support. Moreover, this research also suggested that friendships lasted after the intervention concluded and thus suggests that peers can be an invaluable alternative to adult support for students with special needs in inclusive settings. Similar research is needed at the primary and kindergarten levels to see if these results can be generalized to these settings as well.

The importance of building school cultures that support the participation of all students is grounded at the international level by the inclusion agenda. According to Rioux (2007), in 1993 the United Nations (UN) General Assembly adopted the Standard Rules on the Equalization of Opportunities for Persons with Disabilities (UN General Assembly & High Commissioner for Human Rights, 1993) established and promoted a rights-based education agenda with an emphasis on democracy, participation and equality for all children and especially those with disabilities. To accomplish this, the rules stipulated flexibility in: educational planning, curriculum development, school organization, structural or systemic strategies, widely communicated policy, curriculum, materials, ongoing teacher training, and support for teachers (Rioux 2007, p. 113). It is therefore imperative that schools address cultures, implicit and explicit policies, and practices that are exclusionary that impedes the participation of children but especially those with disabilities in their school settings.

USING A SOCIOLOGICAL LENS TO UNDERSTAND PARTICIPATION

At the international level, both functionalists and social constructivists' theories (Riddell, 2007) have been used to explain the social treatment of persons with disabilities. These theories can also be applied to understand why some children, especially those with disabilities experience low levels of participation at school.

According to functionalism, in particular Emile Durkheim, a healthy school like society achieves a state of social cohesion when it integrates as many persons as possible. At the same time, persons who are not assimilated into society experience disassociation or exclusion (Levitass, 1998; Ravaud & Stiker, 2001). Ravaud and Stiker note that, "the way in which a society situates and treats [persons with disabilities] is not independent of the way in which it constructs social bonds or dissolves them" (Ravaud & Stiker, 2001, p. 490).

Since schools are a microcosm of the wider society, it is important to examine how processes of inclusion and exclusion are reproduced via the school's cultural practices and policies. For example, it might be the practice of a school to determine the placement of children with special needs based on psycho-educational assessments that includes some, and inadvertently excludes, others. Moreover, placement of children with disabilities includes a range of provision for example, regular education, special schools, special education units and annexes. Some writers, for example Barton and Armstrong (2001), contend that the continued existence of special schools, units and annexes represent a form of segregation that is at variance with the fundamental philosophy of inclusion and as such represent a barrier to the social participation of students with disabilities.

Riddell (2007) stridently makes the point that these approaches to educational provision are exclusionary. She notes that "this can be an invisible form of segregation, since the child's name may appear on the mainstream roll, whilst spending virtually all of his or her time in a separate location removed from the wider school community" (p. 35).

By contrast, social-constructivist approaches identified by Goffman (1968) challenged functionalism's mechanistic views of inclusion and disability, and instead argued for more emic approaches to study the influence of disability. According to this school of thought, it is more important to understand how individuals make sense of their world and negotiate their social identity in light of unwelcomed practices like categorization that encourages negative perceptions and labeling in special education. Goffman (1968) saw this approach as a feasible way to study educational and social inequality through the introduction of agentic factors and cultural elements. This theory invites studies that adopt a qualitative approach to understand how students with disabilities, teachers and principals interpret their socio-cultural contexts and its level of inclusion based on cultural, social and pedagogical dimensions.

THE BARBADIAN CONTEXT

In Barbados, the education system is tiered, and comprises pre-primary, primary, special, and tertiary education. The pre-primary to secondary levels of schooling cater to children from ages 3 to 16 years, after which young adults have the option of either pursuing post-secondary employment or accessing tertiary level education. According to the most recent Ministry of Education Statistics on Education in Barbados at a Glance report (2013–2014), special education serves some 599 students with a variety of needs, including those with: visual and hearing impairments, autism spectrum disorders, Down's Syndrome, cognitive challenges, and attention deficit disorders. These students receive their education in special schools, dedicated units attached to mainstream schools, inclusion units, and remedial programmes. This report also states that there are four public primary, three special and four private schools that deliver instruction to students with special education needs in Barbados.

The journey towards inclusive education in Barbados, like many Caribbean islands, was influenced by international conventions and conferences for example, the World Conference on Education for All, in Jomtien Thailand 1990, and the Universal Declaration of Human Rights. In response to this, Barbados developed the White Paper on Education for All, which has as its motto "Each one matters," and noted its commitment to inclusion. In spite of Barbados' acknowledgment and adoption of such, categorization still plays a key role in placement decisions of students with disabilities. For example, students with intellectual and physical impairments, students who experience "challenges" with their learning, students at risk, and those with specific learning disabilities, are listed among those placed in the least restrictive environment, whereas children classified as having mild to moderate mental challenges received their education in special education units located in regular education schools and classrooms. There is also the admission that children with the most severe impairments for example, those with locomotor and nervous system disorders, emotional and behavioral disorders and profound mental and physical disabilities are excluded from mainstream settings (Barbados Country Paper 2007, p. 2).

Within the Barbadian context, it is unclear how these classification systems are organized, by whom, and how the various levels of severity of impairments are defined. In England and the United States of America, for example the term "learning disability" is not mutually understood. According to the British Institute for Learning Disabilities, the term is reserved for those with different levels of need, i.e. mild, moderate, severe and profound impairments. For example, persons with profound impairments are regarded as having an intelligence quotient of below 20, and therefore severely limited in understanding. They might also have additional impairments in vision, hearing and movement; while those with mild needs are more independent and, can converse. The term "learning disability" is used to refer to specific disorders, for example dyslexia, dyscalculia, and dyspraxia. It is reasonable to suggest that Barbadian definitions of mild, moderate and severe impairments may reflect those definitions akin or aligned to the British system outlined above.

According to the now-dated Barbados Country Paper for 2007, in order to operationalise inclusion, a dual track approach was adopted that comprised both full and pull-out programmes to serve students with disabilities. Pull out programmes assisted students with learning difficulties and they spent part of the school day in a resource room where teachers utilized remediation approaches based on small group instruction. Teachers received assistance from learning support coordinators tasked with helping students in resource and general education classrooms. In the full inclusion model, students received all of their instruction in the regular education classroom on a full-time basis and participated with either adaptations or modifications to the curriculum.

Within the Caribbean, few studies have examined the participation of children with disabilities and how school culture and support for learning influences the inclusion of these students in regular education settings. This chapter reports the findings from a larger inquiry on the teaching and learning environments of selected special and inclusive education settings in Barbados. The project was conceptualized and funded by UNICEF in collaboration with the Ministry of Education in Barbados and UWI Consulting, a subsidiary of the University of the West Indies with responsibility for promoting regional research through interagency collaborations. Researchers from the School of Education at the University of the West Indies, Cave Hill Campus, collected and analyzed the data for the project and presented a report in 2011 based on the findings of the research. The goals of this larger project were to document education policy, quality assurance measures, curriculum, psychological and environmental factors that influenced teaching and learning in and across selected special education settings.

UNICEF used purposive sampling to select the schools for study based on parent consultation, the presence of students with disabilities at the school/s identified and concerns about the academic and social participation of children with disabilities at the selected schools. The objectives of the evaluation were:

1. To document quality education for children with special education needs;
2. To inform the provision of a seamless programme of special education services, transition and education options for children with special education needs; and
3. To inform the creation of socially just, equitable education policies that foster the inclusion of children with special educational needs through optimizing their educational and career experiences.

This research on school culture, social participation of students and support for student learning attempts to add to the extant literature at the international level by asking the following research questions: 1) How do Barbadian teachers describe the culture of their schools? 2) What are the teachers" perspectives of the social participation of students with special education needs at their schools? And 3) How do teachers support the learning of their students?

METHODOLOGY

Participants

The sample comprised two schools, School A, a rural primary school with a unit for students with special education needs, and School B an inclusive school. Within the Barbadian context, a unit can be a single building detached from the main buildings, located on the compound of a regular education school and managed by a coordinator. It can also be a classroom or set of classrooms designated to deliver remedial and special education programmes. In School A, two classrooms were sub-divided and shared by teachers to accommodate students with disabilities. One classroom shared by Class A1 and A2 comprised 15 students with various impairments. Class A1 comprised of a group of five students with a range of disabilities including: autism, Down's syndrome, behavioral disorder, learning disability, and cerebral palsy, while class A2, comprised one child with a physical impairment and nine other children with a range of developmental delays. The second classroom shared by Class A3 and A4 was comprised of kids who received mostly remedial instruction. These students were re-integrated into the general education classroom with peers once their academic skills and knowledge were proficient.

Teachers at School A ranged in age as well as levels of experience teaching; there was a senior teacher who served as the special education coordinator, together with four teachers in the special unit. The ages of teachers at this school ranged from 21–55 years old, and teaching experience ranged from 6–35 years in the service. One teacher in the unit possessed a certificate in special needs education, together with a BA,' three teachers held BAs,' and one teacher was qualified at the Associate Degree level in the area of psychology.

School B was an urban inclusive primary school that maintained a resource classroom staffed by two teachers. The layout of the resource room accommodated four groupings of students, and teachers used a combination of whole-class teaching, group-work and individual seatwork to teach students. Teachers ranged in age from 35–50 years old, both teachers' highest level of qualification was at the Masters level, one teacher specialized in special education and the other in literacy studies. Teaching experience ranged from 6–11 years.

Procedures

The researcher informed teachers about the broad goals of the study, its objectives and expectations regarding their participation. Schools assigned a teacher to act as a contact person to facilitate the distribution and collection of questionnaires. Questionnaires did not require teachers to provide any identifying information. This was followed by in-depth interviews conducted at the schools, usually at a time convenient to teachers, either in a group or in pairs for between 1–2 hours over a two-day period in a private room.

Teachers signed informed consent forms as an indication of their willingness to participate in the study. Informed consent forms briefed teachers about the aims of the research, explained the benefits and risks to their participation, and indicated how the findings from the study will be utilized. The researcher indicated to teachers that participation in the study was voluntary and that they could exit without any adverse implications for non-participation. The study was also approved by the University's Institutional Review Board and all artifacts including the inform consent form, recruitment information and data collection instruments were vetted.

Measures

The researcher gathered teachers' perceptions using a structured in-depth interview guide and an open-ended questionnaire adapted from Booth, Ainscow, Black-Hawkins, Vaughan, and Shaw's (2002) *Index for Inclusion*. The two instruments were triangulated so that the same data were collected using multiple methods and to corroborate participants' reflections. The questions taken from the *Index for Inclusion* were organized into five sections that examined: 1) the teachers' opinions of the school's location; 2) the physical environment and how well it accommodated students with special education needs; 3) the nature of relationships between staff and students; 4) the factors that hindered inclusion of students; and 5) the classroom environment. For the purposes of this research, however, questions in sections 2–5 were used to enquire into teachers' perspectives of the overall cultural milieu of the school.

Questions on the nature of the relationship between teachers, principals, students and parents included: How would you describe the nature of the relationship between staff in the special unit/classroom? How would you describe the nature of relationship between staff and parents of students with special needs? How would you describe the nature of the relationship between yourself and your students? How would you describe the nature of the relationship between students with special needs students and other children at the school? How well are initiatives supported by the principal and senior management at the school?

Questions on the culture of the school included: How would you describe the school's culture? How are students integrated into the wider activities of the school? What challenges do you see (teachers or other students at the school) that hinders the inclusion and participation of students with special needs in the school's activities? Questions on classroom environment included: What kind of classroom environment do you try to create for your students and how do you go about ensuring that it is accomplished?

DESIGN

This study is qualitative and utilized and in-depth interview strategy to elicit the teachers' perspectives about the culture of their schools and its influence on the participation of children with disabilities. In this way, teachers were able to reflect on and talk about their own cognitions about what made schools inclusive or what inhibited the process of inclusion and suggest how they supported students with disabilities within mainstream settings.

DATA ANALYSIS

The study utilized data distillation procedures recommended by Miles and Huberman (1994). These researchers describe a five-step systematic approach to analysis that includes the development of descriptive and inferential codes, memoing, partitioning of data into meta-matrices to facilitate within and cross-case analysis, and finally the creation of themes.

The researcher applied descriptive codes to units of text for example phrases, sentences, words or paragraphs. After repeated readings of interview transcripts, and open-ended questionnaires, the researcher used open-ended coding as a first level of analysis. This process produced around 60 codes guided by the research questions. An example is provided using the research question: how would you describe the nature of the relationship between staff? The participant indicated "In one word, a 'unit.' We *work very well together*. We look out and *care for another.*" The researcher applied the labels "work well" and "care" as shown in the example.

The next level of analysis distilled descriptive codes into larger categories called inferential codes. An example of an inferential category was "tokenistic" this adjective captured the following descriptive codes: "convenience," "inclusion in social and extracurricular activities," "have to defend presence," "need for involvement," "need for advocacy," and "lack of teaching exchange." This process produced eight broad classifications across the data.

Memoing captured the researcher's thoughts about patterns that emerged in the data and possible connections to theories. One pattern linked codes about school culture, teacher attitudes and teachers' perceived treatment of students with disabilities.

The researcher opted to use an Excel spreadsheet to organize and display data by school and across research questions in the study to assist with within and between schools analysis. The final stage of the data analysis process produced themes derived from a close review of inferential codes to grounded patterns and meanings in the research literature. The researcher asked teachers to check the veracity of interview transcripts as a form of member checking (Mertens & McLaughlin, 2004) to ensure the trustworthiness of data collected.

BUILDING INCLUSIVE COMMUNITIES

One important task for all schools is to build communities that are inclusive, and that enable all students to participate equally in the life of the school. Central to achieving this is understanding how the culture of a school includes or excludes students, in particular, those with disabilities. The first research question asked, How do Barbadian teachers in special education describe the culture of their schools? This study revealed that school culture, i.e. the nature of relationships, attitudes and behaviors, exerted a powerful influence on the way participation was construed by teachers. Teachers' narratives revealed that they were tensions inherent in the opinions and attitudes of various stakeholders within school settings. The theme "Building a sense of community—the need to re-imagine school culture" captured teachers' feelings that school cultures were not entirely inclusive and needed to undergo significant changes. At the heart of this tension was a belief that general educators remained separated from their counterparts in the special units and took little interest in what occurred in these contexts; this in turn, also limited the participation and inclusion of students in the units.

The Need to Re-Imagine School Culture

Teachers in the study at both Schools A and B described the culture of their schools as tokenistic. They suggest that, while there was a physical presence of students with disabilities on the compound of schools, any meaningful interaction between students with special needs, special unit teachers and their general education peers failed to materialize on a day-to-day basis. The limited opportunities taken by teachers in the general education settings to have contact with and be involved in activities, teaching exchanges and practices in the special education settings were expressions of this tokenism. At School A, teachers reported that:

Jenny is a Class 1 teacher, who taught in the special education unit at School A for four years, she noted that,

> I have been at this unit for four years and I can count on one hand how many teachers have actually graced the unit door ... some teachers have never ever been to the unit ...I don't know how many used to visit the class in terms of actually just coming to talk to the teachers in the unit. I can count how many persons would do that in a whole school year, some teachers have never ever been to the unit before in my four years (Jenny/Female School A).

Jenny also indicated that 'Let's say we are acknowledged for the mere fact that we are here and there is no mistaking that we are here. But we in the unit as teachers, we have to defend that cause' (Jenny/ Female School A). However, not all teachers shared Jenny's views about the culture of School A, some teachers felt that there was some level of support for the inclusion of students with special education needs, even if that support was not shared by all staff members, a typical response from this group of teachers was that: 'Seems generally supportive, but some teachers appear ignorant of special education and how to treat children who require such (Michelle/Female/School A).

Jase is a male teacher who joined the special unit after teaching in the general education setting, and noted:

> Some are and some aren't. They are several teachers that are supportive. I can give an example of a pull-out programme. I teach football for the main school, as the teacher of that class I would have come into the unit, that has been done several years before and also some teachers show particular interests in the unit they would come and check the unit. So they are some who are visibly and notably interested and concerned with the unit (Jase/Male/School A).

An important observation made by one teacher was the perception of the unit as a space that was in but not really a part of the school; perhaps an extension of the tokenism that demanded a strong response from teachers i.e. to defend and advocate for the unit. Moreover, building general education teachers' knowledge of and interest in special education remained central to fostering inclusion, contact and engagement with the activities of the special unit at School A.

At School B, one teacher's description suggested that the schools' culture was not supportive of inclusion:

> The school's culture is not supportive of students with special needs in my opinion. Otherwise the management would have insisted on training for the mainstream teachers when the unit came on board 8 years ago (Tina/Female/School B).

When one examines the narratives of teachers at Schools A and B, it is clear that teachers recognize the importance of teacher training and preparation for inclusion. Tina's comments suggest that principal leadership is an important component for inclusion to be a reality within school settings.

An equally important aspect of school culture is the nature of the relationships between various stakeholders in regular education settings that simultaneously host spaces, i.e. units and resource rooms for the inclusion of students with special needs. There was consensus among the five teachers at School A that teachers maintained a collaborative and cohesive relationship. The most frequently used adjective was "caring" and Anna (who worked with children with severe disabilities) provided an example of what teachers said. She stated, In one word, a "unit." We work very well together. We look out and care for another (Jase/Male/School A).

At School B, only one teacher commented on the nature of relationships between staff at the inclusive school just noting that "It is a relationship." It is difficult to infer exactly what the comment means, but the tone of skepticism the teacher adopted to communicate these words implied that there was a need for improvement in order to reshape the culture of the school.

It is important to note that at School A, the teacher described the interpersonal relationships between teachers in the unit rather than the relationship between teachers in the special unit and the general education setting which was noted earlier by some teachers as less than collegial. While at School B, the relationships between teachers in the general education setting and the inclusion unit mirrored those between teachers at School A in the special education unit and the mainstream school.

Teachers at Schools A and B described student-teacher relationships within the units as pastoral in nature. There was a consensus among teachers that these were supportive and augured well for the students. A typical comment noted among the group was,

> I'd say that we have a very good teacher-student relationship, but in that I do not tolerate nonsense from my children. I am not making excuses for children even if they are special needs. I think the basic thing called manners is still applicable to any individual and I have proven it by seeing for the last four years working in this unit and there are children who have passed through my hands and I always mention my two twins, (Student A) and (Student B), special needs (inaudible). I would get them

a job any day, they may not be academically inclined, but they know "Good Morning" and are respectful, but once a child know that and stays where they're supposed to in terms of respect I have no problem ... (Jenny/School A).

Pastoral care engendered high expectations and the maintaining of similar standards of conduct as expected of children in general education for students with special needs. Jenny's comments emphasizes that within her classroom there is an ethic of "everybody," where all children are held accountable for their behavior and impoliteness is not attributed to the nature of the child's impairment or disability.

A corollary to building inclusive cultures is the need for all students to experience a sense of belonging within their school settings. Belonging means achieving a sense of balance between the academic and social needs of the student and valuing them as citizens at school. Research Question 2 asked: What are teachers' perspectives of the participation of students with special education needs at their respective schools? Findings revealed that students with disabilities were only included socially in the life of their respective schools. In fact, teachers' [special education] comments suggest that the attitudes of general education teachers and students were, once again, powerful determinants of how well students with disabilities were included. The theme "social inclusion as participation" highlights the contradiction inherent in valuing students with disabilities on one hand for the contributions they make to the social standing of their schools in sports while not acknowledging them as citizens within their own school settings.

Social Inclusion as Participation

Teachers at both School A and B noted that students participated in a variety of sporting and extracurricular activities that helped to anchor them socially in the lives of their school community. A typical response was that,

> They are integrated in several ways: via sports. For example, several of the athletes in the unit are athletes for the main school .... This is done in athletics, football and cricket. In terms of cultural activities, we have students who will be part of the choir, part of the school band. Also we have students in the unit who are prefects in the main school. I think those are the three main areas. (Jase/Male/School A).

And:

> They are accommodated for games, arts and crafts, social studies and health science, and religious education. They also take part in sports days, prayers, and are all graduated together (Teacher 1/School B).

But other comments revealed that social participation was not always a smooth transition, especially with regards to homophily, one teacher at School A noted that,

> In terms when they are on the playground ... when the children in the mainstream have to relate to those you know their behaviour may seem odd and weird so on the playing field you do see the distinction there.
> Q: Do they disrespect children?
> Teacher 5: Yes, yes. (Jessi/Female/School A)

And:

> But then you might have another child ... she will get all of the attention needed, it depends when they are confused not understanding they do not respond appropriately. So you might have a sympathetic set of children you might have out of ignorance some cruel children (Jessi/Female/School A)

Clearly at the level of peer inclusion, the child's personality and the nature of the child's disability influenced social interaction, and whether or not they experienced pro versus anti-social and stereotypical behaviors. While extra-curricular activities do offer an opportunity to increase the contact between peers with and without disabilities it did not necessarily translate into increased acceptance of children with disabilities. The teachers' comments are a clear indication that children with disabilities must be taught to mitigate their behaviors if they are to successfully negotiate friendships with regular education students.

Several other challenges hampered the wider inclusion of students with disabilities within their respective settings, including the attitudes of some teachers which limited the academic inclusion of students, such as noted by Tina at School B, she noted that, 'Teachers cannot prevent students with special needs from being integrated, though they may limit participation in the academic pursuits of the students in their classes' (Tina/School B).

Jessi described teachers' low behavioral expectations and its negative influence on students with special needs. She notes that:

> like some teachers have this attitude and the children actually picked up on it so it's not, and you can see it also in terms of how they respond to certain special needs children in prayers if the child behave a certain way, they would say "Oh, he's from special needs" they talk to, they wouldn't correct the child so there's that attitude..." (Jessi /Female/ School A)

Jase believed that the stigmatization of children with special needs at School A explained the attitudes of some teachers, 'Stigmatization: some teachers label the students and write them off. Some teachers are negative towards the students. The students are sometimes given labels and are too easily written off' (Jase/Male/School A).

Teachers' low expectations and stigmatization of students with disabilities are some of the concerns which teachers in the special unit at School A believed would hamper the inclusion of students with impairments. Karen's comments revealed that children with special needs are intuitive and interpret their teachers' words and behaviors. This suggests a need for teachers to be more circumspect concerning the messages that they communicate verbally and non-verbally. This is even more important as it relates to the maintenance of similar expectations and standards of conduct for all students.

Supporting Student Learning—Autonomous Units?

This chapter would not be complete without an examination of how schools could best support the learning of all students. Support for learning goes beyond a cursory acknowledgment of pedagogy to also consider how special education settings can constitute a form of exclusion with its emphasis on separate placement for instruction and planning for students with special needs.

With regard to pedagogical support, teachers at School A and B employed a variety of strategies in order to support the learning of students. Teachers spoke about maintaining a high level of engagement from their students and they achieved this in a variety of ways, for example by fostering a sense of belonging, making their classes fun and making students comfortable. While this is commendable, it nevertheless served to reinforce the notion that segregated classrooms are the best placement options for students with special educational needs rather than spaces for support and remediation given to assist with re-inclusion into regular education classrooms.

Jessi's comments provide a typical example of how teachers tried to make classrooms open, comfortable, interesting places that catered to the personality of their students:

> Jessi: One in which every child is comfortable coming there, if the child is not comfortable coming to school obviously they will not be able to learn anything, so one in which they feel comfortable. One in which they can feel relaxed to answer or ask any questions within reason and within correct behaviour, appropriate behaviour, responses in which they can ask any question. I try to make it as interesting as possible, try to use as much colours, I try to get into their personalities, whatever would bring out their personality, concepts and how you could use that to bring out a concept or whatever the case may be. Since we have so many limitations, we just look to the positive and build on it as much as possible.
>
> Q: And how do you try to accomplish that in your classroom, like, physically what do you do?
>
> Jessi: I have a lot of charts up, I use a lot of colours when I'm trying to reinforce concepts, get the children to refer back to them, use things that they would have created so that it would be part of their input and not just teacher made all of these and teacher made all of that. Also on the board I use a lot of colour too, suppose we had the whole thing of sports you know, purple, orange, yellow, you know the children are in different houses so I use that to help the children

Based on the comments above, one can infer that this teacher believes in the ethic of everybody and in valuing the contributions of all her students by integrating aspects of their work during periods of instruction. In addition to this, Jessi's comments also reveal that she is acutely aware of the learning style of her students and tries to accommodate their interest and personality during teaching and learning. Other teachers at the school also indicated how they tried to support the learning of their students for example Jase talks about making the classroom a fun place and being approachable for his students, 'I try to create an open fun setting in the classroom. Students can usually approach me on any topic, they can ask questions and I usually try to crack a joke' (Jase/Male/School A).

In addition to what teachers reported about their pedagogical practices, it is also important to understand how the units functioned in relation to the rest of the school and what it indicated about the wider culture of these settings. Teachers generally functioned in an autonomous fashion with few opportunities to engage in collaboration with general education teachers. Some collaboration existed between teachers in the unit and one specialist teacher at School B that produced an integrated, horizontally articulated curriculum that supported student learning. Maude noted:

> Q: So is there going to be any collaboration between you and the Class 1 teacher on this issue?
>
> Maude: These same children also go to the reading teacher. So what we do is that we plan with her as well ... I know that when we met and planned I know that we looked at what word families would be done over the next four to six weeks. So there's liaising with the reading teacher so that all around they're getting reinforcement for whatever concept we're studying (Maude/Female/School B).

A common planning time facilitated many benefits like monitoring growth and reinforcement of concepts across more than one curriculum area. However, this collaborative approach with general education teachers was absent. Maude stated:

> To my knowledge I would say that there's a disconnect between what the Unit does and what the classroom does. Because in the classroom, they're probably doing Class 1 work, whereas in the Unit having done the pre-test we started where we saw the weaknesses (Maude/Female/School B)

At School A, although the school adopted a common theme for instructional planning, the unit still worked independently to plan appropriate instruction that catered to the "ability" of their students. The teacher in charge of the unit at School A indicated how planning was accomplished, she noted:

> Q: how does planning an appropriate programme of studies for the child happen, what role do you have in that?
>
> Mrs. Hart: as members of the main school we are all teachers at All Saints but the unit is a special section because of the ability of these children., but we all meet among ourselves in the general school and we form a topic each year we choose a different topic.
>
> Q: OK, so let us say that happens there is a third coming together of the unit, where the unit decides on a particular theme?

Mrs. Hart: Yes, when we come now to meet with ourselves, we may not use the wording that the school has, we use our wordings, we break them down to the children's ability that is why we have you see there, Barbados the Island I Love.

Interviewer: But does the unit choose one single theme?

Mrs. Hart: One thing is chosen, but in the unit you can have well the two below usually go with the same thing and these two groups up here might have a variation

Q: So once the theme has been decided on what's the next step in instructional planning?

Mrs. Hart: The next step in instructional planning would be ... unit teachers and we decide what we're going to do. We plan for tours according to, you know, to help the children to see the topic and understand it. Tours are planned according to the thing and we do activities from those tours, we base our language our math everything hinged on those topics.... (Mrs Hart/Female/School A).

Inferences from teachers' comments at School A and B suggest that units represent unique segregated spaces because of the nature of the children's impairments and challenges that students experience with learning. The units are places exclusively for remediation, but their approaches to curriculum, assessment and pedagogy produce a discrepancy between these spaces and the regular education classrooms. Moreover, this segregation engenders a wider culture of academic exclusion at both schools that threatens to undermine the true spirit of participation and belonging associated with inclusion.

DISCUSSION

This research documents the narratives of a select group of special education teachers in Barbados about the culture of their schools, the social participation of students and support of their students' learning. Findings indicated that the culture is tokenistic and at variance with the ideal of inclusion in the two schools in the study. The themes *"the need to re-imagine school culture"* and *"social participation as inclusion"* reveal the influence that interpersonal relationships and attitudes have on the cultural milieu of the two schools in the study. Teachers in both the special and inclusion units reported a lack of contact with and rotation of teaching assignments with regular education teachers and poor teacher attitudes towards children with disabilities. These findings seem to suggest that students and teachers in the units experienced social disassociation and occupied the fringes of their school settings (Ravaud & Stiker, 2001). Teachers believed that their general education peers lacked knowledge of and interest in the students that the units served and this accounted for their students' marginalized status (Ravaud & Stiker, 2001). Moreover, teachers indicated that principal leadership and teacher training could address general education teachers' poor attitudes (Ainscow, Dyson, Goldrick, & West, 2012; Conrad & Brown 2012; McLesky & Waldron, 2015) and ultimately change the culture of schools.

The next research question on teachers' perspectives of the social participation of students revealed that students with special needs were only socially integrated into the lives of their schools, and really did not enjoy a sense of citizenship within either mainstream or inclusive settings. Teachers indicated that the negative stereotypical view of children's behavior can be linked to the way peers without disabilities perceived the child's personality and the nature of the child's disability. Sociometric studies support the finding that it is difficult for these students to integrate and share close alliances with their peers without disabilities. These studies suggested that behavioral issues, lower peer status and poorer academic performance were deterrents to propinquity and homophily (Bossaert, de Boer, Frostad, & Pijl, 2015; Fredrickson & Furnham, 2004; Nabuzoka & Smith, 1993; Roberts & Zubrick, 1992). Another reasonable explanation is that the placement of students with impairments in segregated classrooms for a substantial period of time not only reduced their proximity to their peers, but also had a direct influence on their status as citizens within the regular education setting. As noted by Munn, Lloyd and Cullen (2000), "whilst the aim is to reintegrate children placed in special units back into the mainstream, this goal is scarcely ever achieved as the child increasingly drifts away from their peer group" (Munn, Lloyd, & Cullen, 2000, p. 35). The unintended consequences of this being that these kids experience a type of alienation and exclusion from their peers although situated within the regular education setting.

Finally, the last research question asked, How do teachers, support the learning of their students? The theme *"Supporting student learning—autonomous units"* captured the approaches to pedagogy and the challenges teachers in special and inclusion units experienced in these settings. A number of pedagogical approaches promoted student engagement, made learning fun and fostered a sense of belonging and interest among students in the units. While this is commendable, the teachers' comments revealed wider challenges with collaboration, curriculum articulation and planning at the whole school level. Teachers relied on teacher made assessments and their perceptions of students' cognitive abilities to adapt instruction for students with impairments. This invariably conflicted with the articulation of knowledge and skills covered in the unit and the regular education classroom. According to Barton and Armstrong (2001) and Riddell (2007), notions of difference perpetuate a belief that segregated spaces (like units) exists to cater to the weaknesses of students who undertake an individualized course of study apart from that of children in regular education classroom. While it is not the intention of this researcher to question the efficacy of catering to the individual needs of students, it is necessary to question the continued reliance and proliferation of special, inclusive units and annexes to support the learning of students with special needs in Barbados in this way.

According to Slee (2007), the challenge for schools, principals and teachers is to provide an environment where all students can be successful. In order for this to be a reality it means that schools in Barbados must work to reduce exclusion in all forms, be it socially constructed, in school policies, pedagogical practices, the curriculum, assessment or the placement of students in these settings. As noted by Riddell (2007) the notion of the annex and unit as an acceptable approach to education provision that simultaneously promotes a new form of exclusion and segregation of children with disabilities seems indefensible to maintain.

INCLUDING ALL STUDENTS THE WAY FORWARD

The above research sheds light on the problem of what education provision should look like for students with disabilities, and how schools can best serve these students. The answer to this question lies partially in accepting that there is a need for a continuum of placement options for students with disabilities, that is, special and inclusion units, pull-out and remedial programmes and resource rooms within the regular education settings. However, these settings must be fully integrated into the life of the whole school rather than left to exist on their own. This means that principals must see it as their duty to re-acculturate teachers and students to accept diversity and difference in and between students who sit in these settings. This would require that:

- Teachers in regular education must be trained in inclusive practices through ongoing in-service professional development activities that emphasise an ethic of everybody, co-agency and trust (Hart, Dixon, Drummond, & McIntyre, 2004);
- A whole school approach to curriculum planning, assessment based on the principles of Universal design for learning be utilized to support the learning of all students (Friesen, 2016);
- Peers without disabilities would need to be trained to support students with disabilities in regular education settings (Carter et al., 2015); and
- Co-teaching and collaborative approaches to teaching would facilitate common planning time and teaching between teachers in special education and their general education counterparts (Lyons, Thompson & Timmons, 2016).

REFERENCES

Ainscow, M., Dyson, A., Goldrick, S., & West. M. (2012). Making schools effective for all: rethinking the task. *School Leadership and Management*, *3*, 197–213.

Barbados Country Paper. (2007). *Caribbean symposium in inclusive education*. Kingston, JA: UNESCO, International Bureau of Education. Retrieved from http://www.ibe.unesco.org/fileadmin/user_upload/Inclusive_Education/Reports/kingston_07/barbados_inclusion_07.pdf

Barton, L., & Armstrong, F. (2001). Disability education and inclusion: Cross cultural issues and dilemmas. In G. L. Albrecht, K. D. Seelman, & M. Bury, *Handbook of disability studies* (pp. 693–710). Thousand Oaks, CA: SAGE.

Booth, T., Ainscow, M., Black-Hawkins, K., Vaughan, M., & Shaw, L. (2002). *Index for inclusion: Developing learning and participation in schools*. Bristol, London: Centre for Studies on Inclusive Education.

Bossaert, G., de Boer, A., Frostad, P., Pijl, S. J., & Petry, K. (2015). Social participation of students with special educational needs in different educational systems. *Irish Educational Studies*, *34*(1), 43–54.http://dx.doi.org/10.1080/03323315.2015.1010703

Boyle, C., Topping, K., Jindal-Snape, D., & Norwich, B. (2012). The importance of peer-support for teaching staff when including children with special educational needs. *School Psychology International*, *33*(2), 167–84. *http://dx.doi.org/10.1177/0143034311415783*

Carter, E. W., Asmus, J., Moss, C. K., Biggs, E. E., Bolt, D. M., Born, T. L., Brock, M. E., Cattey, G. N., Chen, R., Cooney, M., Fesperman, E., Hochman, J. M., Huber, H. B., Lequia, J. L., Lyons, G., Moyseenko, K. A., Riesch, L. M., Shalev, R. A., Vincent, L. B., & Weir, K. (2016). Randomized evaluation of peer support arrangements to support the inclusion of high school students with severe disabilities. *Exceptional Children*, *82*(2), 209–233. doi: 10.1177/0014402915598780.

Conrad, D. A., & Brown, L. (2012). Fostering inclusive education:principals' perspectives in Trinidad and Tobago. *International Journal of Inclusive Education*, *15*(9), 1017–29.

Feldman, R., Carter, E. W., Asmus, J., & Brock, M. E. (2016). Presence, proximity, and peer interactions of adolescents with severe disabilities in general education classrooms. *Exceptional Children*, *82*(2), 192–208. doi: 10.1177/0014402915585481

Frederickson, N. L., & Furnham, A.F. (2004). Peer assessed behavioural characteristics and sociometric rejection: Differences between pupils who have moderate learning difficulties and their mainstream peers. *British Journal of Education Psychology*, *74*, 391–410.

Friesen, S. (2016). Assessment for learning in a math classroom. In S. Scott, D. E. Scott, & C. Weber (Eds.), *Leadership of assessment, inclusion, and learning* (pp. 141–170). Cham, ZG: Springer International Publishing.

Frostad, P., & Pijl, S. J. (2007). Does being friendly help in making friends? The relation between the social position and social skills of pupils with special needs in mainstream education. *European Journal of Special Needs Education*, *22*, 15–30. doi:10.1080/08856250601082224

Goffman, E. (1961). *Asylums: Essays on the social situation of mental patients and other inmates*. New York, NY: Double Day Anchor.

Giangreco, M. F., Carter, E. W., Doyle, M. B., & Suter, J.C. (2010). Supporting students with disabilities in inclusive classrooms: personnel and peers. In R. Rose (Ed.) *Confronting obstacles to inclusion: International responses to developing inclusive education* (pp. 257–264). Milton Park, LN: Routledge

Hart, S., Dixon, A., Drummond, M. J., & McIntyre, D. (2004). *Learning without limits*. Maidenhead, ENG : Open University Press.

Koster, M., Pijl, S. J., Nakken, H., & Van Houten, E. (2010). Social participation of students with special needs in regular primary education in the Netherlands. *International Journal of Disability, Development and Education*, *57*(1), 59–75. doi:10.1080/10349120903537905

Koster, M., Timmerman, M. E., Nakken, H., Pijl, S. J., & van Houten, E. J. (2009). Evaluating social participation of pupils with special needs in regular primary schools: Examination of a teacher questionnaire 1238. *European Journal of Psychological Assessment*, *25*(4), 213–222. doi: 10.1027/1015-5759.25.4.213

Pijl, S. J., Frostad, P., & Mjaavatn, P. E. (2010). Segregation in the classroom: What does it take to be accepted as a friend? *Social Psychology of Education, 14*, 41–55. http://dx.doi.org/10.1007/s11218-010-9135-x

Lawton, D. (1997) *Values and education: a curriculum for the 21st century. Values and the Curriculum Conference*. University of London Institute of Education, 10–11 April.

Levitas, R. (1998). *The inclusive society? Social exclusion and new labour laws*. Basingstoke: McMillan.

Lyons, W. E., Thompson, S. A., & Timmons, V. (2016). 'We are inclusive. We are a team. Let's just do it': Commitment, collective, efficacy, and agency in four inclusive schools. *International Journal of Inclusive Education, 20*(80), 889–907.

Male, D. (2007). The friendships and peer relationships of children and young people who experience difficulties in learning. In L. Florian, *Sage handbook of special education* (pp. 460–474). Thousand Oaks, CA: SAGE.

McLesky, J., & Waldron, N.L. (2015). Effective leadership makes schools truly inclusive. *Phi Delta Kappan, 96*(5), 68–73. http://dx.doi.org/10.1177/0031721715569474

Mertens, D. M., & McLaughlin, J.A. (2004). *Research and evaluation methods in special education*. Thousand Oaks, California: Corwin Press.

Miles, R. P., & Huberman, A. (1994). *Qualitative data analysis* (2nd ed.). Beverly Hills, CA: Sage.

Ministry of Education. (2013–2014). *Statistics on education in Barbados at a glance*. Bridgetown, BAR: Ministry of Education, Science, Technology and Innovation.

Munn, P., Lloyd, G., & Cullen, M. A. (2000). *Exclusion from school and alternatives*. London: Paul Chapman Publishing.

Nabuzoka, D. & Smith, P.K. (1993). Sociometric status and social behaviour of children with and without learning difficulties. *Journal of Child Psychology and Psychiatry, 34*, 1435–1448. http://dx.doi.org/10.1111/j.1469-7610.1993.tb02101.x

Polat, F. (2011). Inclusion in education: A step toward social justice. *International Journal of Educational Development, 31(1)*, 50–58. http://dx.doi.org/10.1016/j.ijedudev.2010.06.009

Ravaud, J., Stiker, H. J. (2001). Inclusion/Exclusion: An analysis of historical and cultural meanings. In G. L. Albrecht, K. D. Seelman, & M. Bury (Eds.), *Handbook of disability studies* (pp. 490–514). London, UK: SAGE.

Riddell, S. (2007). A sociology of special education. In L. Florian (Ed.), *The Sage handbook of special education* (pp. 34–45). London, UK: SAGE.

Rioux, M. (2007). Disability rights in education. In L. Florian (Ed.), *The Sage handbook of special education* (pp. 107–116). London, UK: SAGE.

United Nations General Assembly & High Commissioner for Human Rights. (1993). *Standard rules on the equalisation of opportunities for persons with disabilities*. 48th session, 85th mtg., resolution 48/96. UN Document A/RES/48/96

Villa, R. A., Thousand, J. S. & Nevin, A. (2004). Instilling collaboration for inclusive schooling as a way of doing business in public schools. *Remedial and Special Education, 17*(3), 169–181. http://dx.doi.org/10.1177/074193259601700306

Villa, R. A., Thousand, J. S., Nevin, A. I., & Malgeri, C. (1996). Instilling collaboration for inclusive schooling as a way of doing business in public schools. *Remedial and Special Education, 17*(3), 169–181.

Wendelborg, C., & Tøssebro, J. (2011). Educational arrangements and social participation with peers amongst children with disabilities in regular schools. *International Journal of Inclusive Education, 15(5)*, 497–512.

BIOGRAPHIES

EDITORS

Stacey Blackman is a lecturer in Special Education at the University of the West Indies Cave Hill campus. She completed her first and second degrees at the University of the West Indies, and her PhD at Cambridge University (UK) as a Cambridge Commonwealth and Chevening Scholar. She was also a past Deputy Dean of the Faculty of Humanities and Education at the University of the West Indies, Cave Hill. She is a Fellow of the Cambridge Commonwealth Trust and member of many professional organizations such as the American Education Research Association (AERA), The Council for Exceptional Children (CEC) and the British Psychological Association. Her research addresses a broad range of topics and activities on teachers' pedagogical practices, inclusion, pupil perspectives and wider issues related to persons with disabilities in the Caribbean region.

Dennis A. Conrad Before completing his Ph.D. in Policy Studies and Educational Leadership- at Virginia Tech, Professor Conrad completed studies at Mausica Teachers College, Sheffield University and the University of London. He taught in regular and special schools; and was an alternate school principal. Dennis has received several awards including the President's Award for Excellence in Research and Scholarship related to Cultural Pluralism. He has been a board member of the EERA and Chair of AERA's- Caribbean and African Studies in Education SIG. He is also the Chair of the Department of Inclusive and Special Education at SUNY-Potsdam.

CONTRIBUTORS

Myrtle Blackman B.Ed, is presently living her dream by teaching at the Wharton-Patrick School where she was placed after completing her Bachelors in Education Degree. Her passion for caring, sharing, nurturing and housing student with challenges where and when necessary leads to her research interest factors stimulate resilience among at-risk to experience greater levels of individual success. Her research interest is in the area of absenteeism and its negative impact students.

Nickisha Borris-Lezama B.Ed. in Special Needs Education from the University of Trinidad and Tobago is a level two teacher at Wharton-Patrick School that caters to meet the needs of students with emotional, behavioral and educational difficulties. Nickisha is committed to the nurturing of disadvantaged children so when not in the classroom she can be found with these kids outdoor hiking and enjoying nature. She is currently completing her Masters of Education in Inclusive and Special Education at the University of West Indies and has a special interest in research in the area of supports and career planning for students with Emotional and Behavioural Disorders.

Cheryl M. Bowrin, B.A. (Hons.), M.Ed, is a Senior Instructor (Curriculum Studies, Teaching of Primary Social Studies, Action Research and Educational Foundations) at the University of Trinidad and Tobago. She has taught at all levels of the education system of Trinidad and Tobago for the past 28 years, and also delivered courses to the Bachelor of Education students at the School of Education, UWI (St Augustine, and Open Campus) and in St Vincent. At present, she is completing a Ph.D in Education with focus on the issue of Teacher Professionalism in Trinidad and Tobago with Walden University

Laurette Bristol is currently the President of the Catholic College of Mandeville, Jamaica. She is also an Adjunct member of the Research Institute for Professional Practice, Learning and Education (RIPPLE) and a member of the Pedagogy, Education and Praxis (PEP), **C**aribbean Ed**u**cators **R**esearch Initiati**ve** (CURVE) and the CURVE-Y-FRiENDS (C-Y-F) research and peer mentoring networks. Her research interests explore the intersection between historical traditions and practices in educational sites. She has a growing international research profile in the areas of school leadership, mentoring, practice theory, in-service teacher education and professional learning. She believes that educational practices are located in history and sites and that if educators are to intervene in practice they must first apprehend the intersubjective relationship between practice traditions, context, understandings and actions.

Margaret Bruce M.Ed, Special and Inclusive Education from the University of Sheffield is the principal of Wharton-Patrick School. She has collected children's journals, drawings and more recently children's unique sayings and stories by looking at and listening to them. Margaret uses this collection to teach both children and teachers how to dream, reach and experience success. Her research work focused on using story grammar to improve comprehension skills in children with intellectual disabilities, and using stories to teach social and behavioral skills to children with behavioral issues. She is a co-author of the article *Special Schools and the Search for Social Justice in Trinidad and Tobago : Perspectives from Two Marginalized Context in Caribbean Curriculum Volume 17, 2010, 59– 84.*

Andrew B. Campbell (DR. ABC) is a graduate of the Ontario Institute for Studies in Education (OISE) at the University of Toronto, with a PhD. in Educational Leadership, Diversity & Policy. He holds a teacher's diploma in Primary Education from Mico University College, B.A. in General Studies and Counselling Psychology from Jamaica Theological Seminary and a Masters of Education in School Administration from the University of the West Indies. For the past twenty years, he has worked in various areas of education and at all levels in Jamaica, The Bahamas, and Canada. Dr. Campbell teaches courses in Educational Leadership, Early Childhood Education, and Diversity Studies for the University of the West Indies Open Campus (UWIOC), Seneca College (Canada) and Durham College (Canada). Dr. Campbell has written courses in diversity for the University of the West Indies and is presently conducting research that focuses of homosexuality in Jamaica, advocacy and culturally relevant pedagogy.

Suzanne Charles Cert. Special Education, is the Senior Special Education Teacher at Wharton-Patrick School for children with emotional and behavioral disorders. She has eighteen years experience in this field. Her passion fuels research interest in the use of academic intervention as a strategy to allow students to experience success and to improve self-esteem. The Certificate in Education (Special Education) is from the University of Sheffield. She form part of a team as co-author to the article *Special Schools and the Search for Social Justice in Trinidad and Tobago : Perspectives from Two Marginalized Context in The Caribbean Curriculum Volume 17, 2010, 59—84.*

Elna Carrington-Blaides is the Coordinator of the M.Ed. Programme in Inclusive and Special Education at the School of Education, the University of the West Indies, St. Augustine Campus. She completed her Master's degree at the City University of New York, USA and she studied for a Ph.D. in Special Education at Southern University, Louisiana, USA. She has over 30 years' experience teaching/lecturing at all levels of the education system in Trinidad and Tobago and the United States of America. She is responsible for the development programmes in Inclusive and Special Education in Trinidad and Tobago. First, the Bachelor's programme at the University of Trinidad and Tobago was developed and implemented and more recently the Master's programme at the University of the West Indies. Her research interests include reading in inclusive classrooms, behavior disorders in children and youth, special education policy in the Caribbean and international special education policy.

Jerome De Lisle, B.Sc (Hons), Dip Ed. Ph.D. is currently Senior Lecturer in Educational Administration at the School of Education, the University of the West Indies, St. Augustine. From 1998 to 2005 he was Lecturer in Measurement and Evaluation at the Centre for Medical Sciences Education, Faculty of Medical Sciences. His main research interests are in the areas of educational assessment, programme evaluation, and system reform. He has published widely in several regional and international peer-refereed publications and regularly presents at the American Educational Research Association (AERA) and the American Evaluation Association (AEA).

Kirk Felix, B.Ed, is currently a teacher at the Wharton-Patrick School which caters to students with behavioral and learning disabilities. He is a strong advocate of voluntary service and is of the conviction that Citizens should dedicate time and effort to provide beneficiaries with the opportunity and skills to become productive members of the national community. His work as a co-author along with other colleagues is publish entitled *Special Schools and the Search for Social Justice in Trinidad and Tobago : Perspectives from Two Marginalized Context in Caribbean Curriculum Volume 17, 2010, 59—84.* Kirk is completing a Master of Education in Special and Inclusive Education at The University of the West Indies. His research interest is in the area of transitional planning for at-risk students and adults with special needs. Kirk Felix remains a passionate and dedicated educator

Kimberly Glasgow-Charles is a PhD candidate at the School of Education, UWI, St. Augustine. She has been a primary school for the past 16 years. Kimberly is also a sessional early childhood lecturer at the University of the West Indies, St. Augustine and the College of Science Technology and Applied Arts of Trinidad and Tobago (COSTAATT). She is a member of the Education Discussion Group (Trinidad) and Association for Childhood Education International. Her research interests include early childhood development, care and education, early childhood inclusive education; leadership in early childhood; children's voices; curriculum development and implementation; and teacher professional development.

Iris Hewitt-Bradshaw has been an educator for 35 years and has taught at the secondary school level and at Teachers College. She is currently a Senior Instructor in Language and Linguistics at the University of Trinidad and Tobago where she also mentors prospective teachers on practicum field teaching and supervises undergraduate and post-graduate research. She possesses a Ph.D. and a Master of Philosophy in Language Education and a Bachelor of Arts degree in Language and Linguistics. Dr. Hewitt-Bradshaw regularly presents at regional and international conferences and facilitates school workshops in language and literacy. Her research interests include issues in language education in multi-lingual contexts and developing literacy competence across school disciplines.

Grace-Anne Jackman is a lecturer in Educational Testing, Measurement and Evaluation in the School of Education, University of the West Indies, Cave Hill, Barbados. She holds a PhD in Research and Evaluation Methodology from the University of Florida. Her current research interests are in the areas of Item Response Theory, Differential Item Functioning, Formative Assessment and Creativity Research.

Dawn-Marie Keaveny is a lecturer at the Mico University College in Kingston, Jamaica. She has been a special educator for over thirty years and has worked with children who have been identified with learning disabilities, attention deficit hyperactivity disorder, autism, intellectual disability and deafness. She holds a Doctorate in Education from the University of Sheffield, England, with her focus being on the inclusion experiences of children with LD and ADHD in the general education classroom. Dr Keaveny has given workshops to teachers in general and special education schools and has presented on how to identify and teach the child with special needs in the general education classroom, how to design engaging learning centers and how to write effective IEPs. Dr Keaveny is married and has five children.

Nadia Laptiste-Francis, B.Ed (Hons). M.Ed., is a Ph.D. candidate with specialization in Inclusive Education at The University of the West Indies, St. Augustine Campus. She is the recipient of a Postgraduate scholarship from the Government of the Republic of Trinidad and Tobago. She obtained her undergraduate degree from the University of Trinidad and Tobago in 2010 and her postgraduate degree from The University of the West Indies, St. Augustine in 2014. Ms Laptiste-Francis has experience teaching at-risk youths in state institutions in Trinidad. Her research interests include inclusive education, educational assessment and educational policy.

Ian Alwyn Marshall is an educator with fifteen (15) years teaching experience at the secondary level and seven (7) years teaching experience at the tertiary level. He is currently attached to the University of the West Indies, as a Lecturer in Educational Leadership. He completed all of his studies at The University of the West Indies, Cave Hill and has a BA (Hons) in Political Science and History, a Diploma in Education, a Post-Graduate Certificate in University Teaching and Learning, a Master's in Educational Administration and Management, and a Doctor of Philosophy in Education. He is a teacher trainer and the University Coordinator for the Diploma in Education (primary) programme. He is also an Educational Consultant and travels throughout the Eastern Caribbean, training current and prospective educational leaders in leadership best practices. His research interests include principal and teacher leadership, effective schools, parental involvement and student academic achievement.

Keitha-Gail Martin-Kerr is a teaching specialist at the University of Minnesota in the Department of Curriculum and Instruction. She teaches graduate students literacy content and pedagogy courses. She has been in education for 21 years. She has taught at the elementary level in Jamaica, Turks and Caicos, and New York City before moving to Minnesota to be in higher education full-time. Her research interest is in the area of understanding the lived experiences of women-who-love-women in the Caribbean and the implications for teaching, learning, and curriculum development at the elementary level. She has presented at several conferences both nationally and internationally. She currently serves in professional organizations such as the Literacy Research Association and The American Education Research Association. She has written several articles and encyclopedia entries related to instruction in the elementary grades.

Sandra Richards Mayo, PhD, is Associate Professor in Educational Leadership and Director of the Doctoral Program in Educational Leadership at Azusa Pacific University. Her research examines racial disparities in education from a historical perspective, identifying larger patterns of social exclusion that are perpetuated in deficit attitudes and practices. Drawing on critical social theory and a framework of historical reconciliation, her writing seeks to reshape dominant cultural narratives that contribute to harmful understandings of race and racial difference. Her work appears in the *Journal of Higher Education, Caribbean Quarterly*, and *The International Christian Community for Teacher Education Journal*. She is also a contributor to *Black Protest Thought and* Education (W.H. Watkins, Editor) and *The Dictionary of Caribbean and Afro-Latin American Biography* (F.W. Wright and H.L. Gates, Jr. Editors)

Dyanis A. D. Popova is an assistant professor of Curriculum and Instruction at the University of South Dakota. She is a graduate of Virginia Tech, with an academic focus in Multicultural Education and the Teaching of English as a Second Language. She also holds a graduate certificate in Race and Social Policy. Dr. Popova's research interests include indigenous and endarkened methodologies, critical autoethnography, ESL curricula reform, critical pedagogy, Caribbean studies in education, and the intersections of privilege, power, and social justice. Her professional memberships include the American Educational Research Association (AERA), the National Association for Multicultural Education (NAME), and Teachers of English to Speakers of Other Languages (TESOL).

Sabrina McMillan Solomon, B.Ed. (Hons.), M.Ed. is currently a PhD candidate at the School of Education, University of the West Indies, St. Augustine. She has worked in the education system as an elementary school teacher for eighteen years. She is a national scholar. She is the holder of a B.Ed. (Mathematics) with First Class Honours and M.Ed. (Reading) with Distinction from the University of the West Indies. She also has training and experience in the use of grounded theory as a methodology and hierarchical linear modeling as a statistical technique for hierarchical data. Her research interests are in the areas of numeracy, literacy and achievement with a special focus upon inequality.

James E.J. Young is a third-year doctoral candidate in Educational Testing, Measurement and Evaluation at the University of the West Indies, Cave Hill, Barbados. His background at the Bachelor and Master degree levels is Science Education and Educational Testing, Measurement and Evaluation, respectively. His main research interests are formative assessment, creativity in education and scientific inquiry methods.

Printed in the United States
By Bookmasters